Memory Management and Multitasking Beyond 640K

Memory Management and Multitasking Beyond 640K

Lenny Bailes
John Mueller

Foreword by John C. Dvorak

Windcrest®/McGraw-Hill

CREDITS

WordPerfect®	WordPerfect Corporation®
OS/2®	IBM Corporation

And special thanks to:
AddStor, Inc.
Central Point Software
Roger Cross, Hyperware

FIRST EDITION
FIRST PRINTING

Library of Congress Cataloging-in-Publication Data

Bailes, Lenny.
   Memory management and multitasking beyond 640K / by Lenny Bailes
and John Mueller.
       p.   cm.
   Includes index.
   ISBN 0-8306-3476-2 (hardback)   ISBN 0-8306-3456-8 (pbk.)
   1. Memory management (Computer science) 2. Multitasking (Computer
science) I. Mueller, John, 1958-   II. Title.
QA76.9.M45B35 1992
004.5'3—dc20   92-6395
                                           CIP

TAB Books offers software for sale. For information and a catalog, please contact TAB Software Department, Blue Ridge Summit, PA 17294-0850.

Acquisitions Editor: Brad Schepp
Book Editor: David M. McCandless
Director of Production: Katherine G. Brown
Series Design: Jaclyn J. Boone
Cover Design: Sandra Blair Design and
                Brent Blair Photography, Harrisburg, PA   WT1

Contents

Chapter 10. Using DESQview 313

Foreword

For years, people have tried to wring productivity out of PCs with batch files, TSR-utilities and task-switching software. Each new release of popular productivity software eats up more memory than the last. The 640K limit of DOS has become a frustrating barrier for all users.

All the networked companies (including almost every business listed in the Fortune 1000) must conduct a daily struggle to make huge word processing and spreadsheet applications coexist with network software inside of 640K.

The key is memory management. Unfortunately, it's the least understood aspect of PC operation. Nowadays 386 and 486 (and even 286) machines are routinely sold with four to eight megabytes of memory. Still, most users don't know what to do with that memory. Worse, owners of 640K and 1M PCs face a jungle of competing expansion options. They, too, would like to take advantage of DOS-extended programs, networking environments, and 32-bit applications specially written for the 386.

This book, *Multitasking & Memory Management Beyond 640K*, explains the hidden processing power of the 80286 and 80386 cpu chips. Readers learn why DOS can use only 1M of memory and how PC software manufacturers (and how you) can circumvent that limitation.

Bailes and Mueller present a wide range of hardware and software information that is usually concealed from PC end users. Readers will learn how to easily navigate the "advanced CMOS setup options" and begin to understand "Shadow-RAM" and "wait states"—AND how to turn them on and off. "Multitasking & Memory Management" teaches users how to maximize conventional memory by loading TSR's, network and device drivers above 640K. A special section evaluates the most popular memory management packages and explains how to use the "loadhigh" utilities included with each.

The third part of the book is devoted to whipping into shape multitasking environments like DESQview, Microsoft Windows and OS/2. PC users are sick of staring at screens that say "please wait" while a spreadsheet recalculates, or a long Postscript file is swallowed by the printer. They would rather multi-task. Users know that Microsoft Windows and DESQview are supposed to offer solutions, but they don't know how to make multitasking work.

Two chapters of *Multitasking & Memory Management* show these people how to get their money's worth. The book offers practical tips to make everyday applications work in a multitasking environment. Readers will learn how to customize DESQview and Windows to increase productivity. Practical-minded users will simply learn how to run more applications and get them running faster. More sophisticated readers will finally have a reference that teaches them the difference between LIM 3.2, EEMS, software-compatible EMS 4.0, hardware-compatible EMS 4.0, and XMS.

Multitasking & Memory Management deals with the day-to-day problems of running productivity software. Multiple tips and screenshots teach users to optimize performance of spreadsheets, word processors and desktop publishing applications in networked, multitasking environments.

Here are the kinds of questions this book answers:

- Should I upgrade my current system hardware to handle Windows and other new applications? What should I buy? How do I install it?
- How can I use Microsoft's MS-DOS 5 or Digital's DR DOS6 to improve my total of conventional memory.
- How can I use the software I've already got to improve performance with my everyday applications? (WordPerfect, Lotus 1-2-3, DBASE III/IV, etc.)
- Why do I need multitasking or task switching? How will it improve my productivity with the computer?
- What's the difference between expanded and extended memory? When do I need one, and when do I need the other?
- Do I need a third party memory manager? What's the advantage of a product like Quarterdeck's QEMM386 over the features included with MS-DOS 5?
- How can I speed up the performance of Microsoft Windows? How can I get more memory for DOS applications under Windows?
- How does Quarterdeck's DESQview work? Is it as good as Windows?
- Can I multitask programs over a network? How do I set up a network and still have memory left over to run my applications.
- What can I do when my software crashes, and I keep getting strange error messages from DOS or Windows?

These are the kinds of questions that readers are asking. This book provides the answers.

Personally I hope that someday in a more perfect future a book like this isn't needed and that all these dilemmas will be automatically solved by quality software. That day is distant. You need this book.

John C. Dvorak
Berkeley, CA
March 1992

Acknowledgments

This is for all of the people who egged this book on from a daydream to a finished work: my family—Murray, Kenny, and Mitchell Bailes—and my "second family" in San Francisco—Karl, Jan, Betty, Bill, and Dale Henderscheid.

With thanks to Nick Anis, my co-author John Mueller, and editor Brad Schepp, who put up with my "expansive visions" and humored me whenever possible.

Thanks also to Dan Sallit at Quarterdeck, Mike Spielo at Helix Software, and the technical crews at Qualitas and All Computer Company for their invaluable technical assistance, and to Paula Toth, John King, Mary Eisenhart, Paul Hoffman, Fred Davis, and Sylvia Paull for "nerdish spiritual advice in the MS-DOS desert."

Special thanks to Uncle Ralph's Computers and Pan Pacific Computer Company for their hardware support, and to Dale Henderscheid, who took the photographs in the book.

Lenny Bailes
San Francisco
March 1992

Introduction

You might be wondering why an entire book should be devoted to the subject of PC memory management. After all, some people would say that you should spend your time and money on a reference book for a "real" application like WordPerfect or Excel. But is that all there really is to getting the most out of your application?

Self-help texts on individual software applications are useful. Many users complain about the poor quality of the documentation provided with software. As a result, books with lots of pictures, written in simple English, or books containing the technical information the manual left out are both in demand by users. However, knowing everything there is to know about a single program still isn't enough.

The purpose of this book is to help you get your applications working as a team. PC programs don't run in a vacuum. Applications are dependent on the DOS operating system, which in turn is dependent upon the installed hardware. A powerful environment like Microsoft Windows doesn't do much good if it won't run properly on your computer. Spreadsheets or CAD drawing programs aren't much fun if they execute at a tortoise-like pace.

Your hardware and its system configuration control baseline system performance, affecting the speed of all the applications that run on your machine. If you learn to understand the environment where applications live and work, you'll get more mileage out of your software. Memory management is a key element in this scenario. As you read this book, you'll learn that system and memory configuration can dramatically affect the flexibility and speed of applications.

The object of *Multitasking and Memory Management* is to teach you to configure your computer for maximum performance. Instead of watching "Please Wait" messages on the screen, you'll learn how to continue working during a complicated print job or spreadsheet recalculation. You'll also get some problem solving strategies to overcome common computer frustrations. Why does the computer lock up when you install new programs? Why do programs that used to work suddenly stop working?

Multitasking is a natural operating mode for most interesting human endeavors. Creative minds don't shut down while they run through sequential tasks. A creative mind looks ahead, looks back, and looks sideways in its journey from point A to point B. You might have several inner dialogs going on simultaneously. Using modern software, your computer can use the same techniques to manage more than one task at the same time. As in the human mind, each application should be allowed to proceed without shutting down the others.

Whether the computer serves us as a mind extension or simply as a desk extension, then its natural operating mode is multitasking. What would you say if you saw someone take a pen out of a desk drawer, write a few lines, put the pen back in the drawer, open another drawer, take out a calculator, punch in some numbers, put the calculator in the drawer again, open a calendar, put the calendar away, take the pen back out of the drawer, and so on? Most people just don't operate that way. We leave our tools out on the desk, picking them up as we need them. We look at the calendar, use the telephone, and write with the pen simultaneously.

Likewise, the computer should allow us to keep our tools on the desk. I use my computer for word processing and can call a bulletin board at the same time. I can check my email or download shareware utility programs while I compose a document. As I accumulate information, I might use a second word processor as a container for text that I cut and paste from several sources. I typically shift my attention between several different chores. As I rotate between tasks, I plan my day—catching up with projects that need to be completed and occasionally starting new ones. Just as I keep my physical tools out on my desk, a computer that provides a multitasking environment allows me to keep my software tools available for use.

This book is for you if you own a powerful multitasking environment like Microsoft Windows or DESQview. This book is also for you if your computer is on a network and you need to wring out more memory for applications. As a user, your concern is that the hardware and software cooperate most efficiently. The information you need to accomplish this is not usually included in the manual that comes with individual applications. When reading this book, you'll see how to use print spoolers and disk caches, set up multitasking environments, and build a suite of productivity applications that support one another.

Unlike the physical desktop or the human mind, computers do not come prepared to provide a multitasking environment. You will face certain problems in getting two applications that are used to owning the entire machine to work together. This book will help you to the resolve minor but irritating quirks that crop up in a complex PC computing environment. It provides problem solving strategies—how to track down conflicts in software and hardware to eliminate bugs.

Chapter 1 presents an introduction to PC hardware. You'll gain familiarity with the features and limitations of the 8088/286/386/486 Intel family of processors. This will provide you with the basic vocabulary and background to understand the internal parts and configuration of your PC. You'll see how the PC setup program works to control hardware performance and learn some tricks usually hidden within the motherboard documentation.

Chapter 2 shows you how to take stock of your system. Do you have enough memory? Is the CPU powerful enough to run your applications? Inventory and diagnostic software can help you to make a list of the important pieces of your system. Once you know what parts your system contains, you can determine if they will do the job you need them to do.

Chapter 3 shows you how DOS uses the first megabyte of memory. For example, where does DOS really put your program? Once you understand how DOS uses memory, you will be able to see places where you can improve memory usage and therefore performance. An introduction to hexadecimal notation helps you to see the structure and usage of the memory area from 640K to 1M. This chapter also examines some of the basic memory management utilities: print spoolers, disk caches and RAM disks. You'll see how to use these tools to improve your PC's performance.

Chapter 4 defines and discusses memory beyond the first megabyte. You'll see how each Intel processor uses the memory "above 640K." Because DOS cannot access this memory directly, we must use additional software tools to access it. In this chapter, we survey three of the more common ways to use this memory: expanded memory (using an expanded memory manager like Quarterdeck's QEMM), DOS extenders (like the Rational Systems DOS extender used to enhance Lotus 1-2-3 v3 and above), and Microsoft's extended memory specification (XMS—used with Windows). The information provided in this chapter will let you take stock of your PC's memory environment. This chapter also explores task switching and multitasking: How are these two procedures different, and how do they make DOS more convenient?

Chapter 5 surveys the hardware requirements for different PC productivity situations. Alternate upgrade options are examined for all PC types. The chapter provides a purchasing guide and detailed instructions on the ins and outs of memory hardware.

Chapter 6 provides strategies for improving performance by minimizing the overhead of your current applications. For example, you can preserve memory by loading your word processor without including the spelling checker. To help make this procedure as easy as possible, we offer tips for optimizing individual programs. We also examine the usefulness of TSR utilities and task switching.

Chapter 7 shows you how to perform basic memory management with the utilities bundled in Microsoft's DOS 5. You'll see how to use DOS Shell as a task switcher and how to load programs and device drivers into upper memory.

Chapter 8 covers memory management with Digital Research's DR DOS 6 and shows you more advanced memory management with third-party packages. We provide tutorials on popular memory management packages. This chapter will also help you to decide whether you need a third-party memory manager to supplement the features included in DOS.

Chapter 9 is dedicated to Microsoft Windows. We explain how to configure memory management software for Windows 3.xx exploring the difference in the Windows' multiple operating modes. You'll see how Windows operates on 286 vs. 386/486 systems. We give you a quick tour of Windows' multitasking capabilities and provide strategies for coordinating Windows and DOS applications to build a productivity environment.

Chapter 10 looks at Quarterdeck's DESQview, a viable multitasking alternative to Windows. This chapter shows you how DESQview can coordinate your applications and give you more flexibility in your PC work habits.

Chapter 11 spells out the basics on configuring IBM's OS/2 2.0, an alternative operating system that also runs MS-DOS and Microsoft Windows applications. You'll see the advantages and disadvantages of the three OS/2 installation procedures and learn how to customize the OS/2 CONFIG.SYS.

The appendices provide troubleshooting tips for third-party memory management in networked environments. Also included is an introduction to the shareware utilities diskette bundled with this book, a list of vendor addresses, and a list of free bulleting board systems that carry technical conferences on Windows and DESQview, as well as additional shareware utilities.

Good reference material
to supplement this book

As you begin to explore this book, you might find it useful to have some additional reference material on hand to supplement the concepts we explore:

- Somewhere around your PC there should be a user's manual, possibly a small paperbound booklet. The user's manual provides information about the motherboard in your machine, the kind of memory chips used in your system, and (for 286/386/486 machines) how to use the setup program.

- Find the DOS reference manual for the version of DOS installed on your PC. (You may substitute a third-party reference guide.) The DOS reference will allow you to see command options for some of the programs we'll use, including DEBUG.

As you progress through this book, you will discover many tuning secrets to improve your software's performance. We hope that studying the science of memory management will open some new doors for you in the world of personal computing.

What you need to know about memory management

Hardware issues

The procedures for adding more memory to a PC vary with the processor type:

- 80386/486 machines are easiest to upgrade. In many cases, you can add memory directly to the motherboard.
- 8088/80286 machines can use added memory, but the installation procedure is usually more difficult than newer machines. Often you will need to purchase a memory board to hold the memory.
- 8088/80286 machines can be upgraded to 386 machines using a combination add-on cards and plug-in modules. While this is useful in some work environments, it's often more cost-effective simply to buy a new 80386 machine.

Software issues

On 80286/80386/80486 machines,

- New versions of DOS from Microsoft and Digital Research, Inc. now have built-in memory management options. You may load DOS (and some of your programs) outside the traditional 640K conventional memory area.
- Utilities, network software, and other device drivers may now be installed above 640K. This can increase the memory available for other applications.

For all PC types,

- Third party memory managers can increase your conventional memory with old and new DOS versions from 3.xx on up.
- You can reconfigure your everyday programs to use less memory.
- You can use existing memory to improve program performance
- You can improve your productivity by running more than one program at the same time.

Final note: Abbreviations

No matter what computer book you happen to look at, you'll usually see the words *kilobyte* and *megabyte* abbreviated in different ways. For example, if you wanted to say "512 kilobytes," you could say 512 kilobytes, 512K, 512 K,

512KB, 512 KB, 512Kb, or 512 Kb (and perhaps even something else!). The term "megabyte" suffers the same problem many times, also being able to be abbreviated in a wide variety of ways. Because of this wide and sometimes confusing variety of usage, a book should refer to a term consistently in order to help the reader make sense of the text.

Over time, it seems that the letter K flush with the number has become the accepted usage in the computer industry for the term "kilobyte," even if it originally didn't start out that way. Thus, if you look at the previous example, this book chooses 512K to represent "512 kilobytes." And in order to stay consistent, "megabytes" also will be represented by the letter M flush with the number (e.g., 512M).

1

Meet the hardware

What makes the PC different from other computers on the market? The PC has an interesting history different than many machines on the market today.

What are the differences between 8088/80286/80386/80486 machines? All run MS-DOS software, but additional computing modes are available on the more powerful 80286/386/486 Intel processors.

What are the basic parts in a PC? How do they work? CPU/ROM/BIOS/RAM/ PERIPHERALS/BUS (8-bit/16-bit/32-bit/ISA/MCA/EISA)

Memory basics: RAM comes in different sizes, speeds, and packaging. How do you know which is best for your machine?

Performance issues: What do you need to know to setup and fine tune your hardware for best performance?

Some history

The IBM PC was born into the world in August, 1981. At the time, the state of the art in microcomputers was a popular operating system called CP/M. (You might have a hard time finding someone who still remembers that these initials were an acronym for "Control Program for Microcomputers".)

The PC entered the marketplace in competition with machines from companies like Osborne, Epson, and KayPro. The competing CP/M computers used a central processing chip called the Z80 (a microprocessor based on the Intel 8080 introduced in 1975). In 1981, CP/M software and the Z80 were riding a crest of user popularity. Adam Osborne had even invented a Z80 plug-in card that ran WordStar on the Apple II. (Normally, Apple II software was programmed for a different microprocessor called the 6502. The 6502 chip was produced by Motorola, Intel's chief competitor in the microprocessor field.)

IBM decided to use the Intel 8088 (introduced in 1980) instead of the Z80 for its PC. This processor offered the definite speed advantage of 16-bit processing and a larger instruction set than the Z80. While the Intel 8086 (introduced in 1978) would have provided a 16-bit bus in place of the 8088's 8-bit bus, the 8088 offered the opportunity to reduce manufacturing costs, an important consideration when trying to introduce a new machine architecture on the market.

The first PC from IBM was a definite departure from the standard of the time. In addition to using the 8088 processor, it used a new operating system as well. The PC was equipped with 16K of user memory. Using a proposed expansion board, you could boost this to an amazing 320K of RAM; but the CP/M machines and the Apple II, already shipped with a whopping 64K in the box. Within a few months, IBM increased the standard on-board user memory to 64K to compete with the CP/M machines. (This meant that you no longer had to buy chips to upgrade the machine for standard applications.)

By today's standards, 64K seems like a pitifully small amount of memory. In 1981 it was enough to handle any program likely to appear on the market. (Some of the popular 8080 and Z80 computers used only 48K. This was sufficient to run CP/M word processors, databases, and programming languages.)

To accompany the new 16-bit processor, IBM commissioned a 16-bit operating system. The legend has it that IBM first approached Digital Research, Inc., the producers of 8-bit CP/M. The authors of CP/M were reluctant to explore new territory with a 16-bit operating system, so IBM took the job to Bill Gates of Microsoft instead. (Digital later acknowledged that the PC was a good investment and came out with a 16-bit version called CP/M 86 for the PC. By then it was too late, DOS was a firmly established operating system.) Gates was famous at the time for having written the world's first microcomputer BASIC interpreter.

Bill Gates didn't have a 16-bit operating system for IBM in his pocket, but he knew of some people across town who did! The Seattle Computer Products Company had been working for months on something called SCP-DOS (Seattle Computer Company Disk Operating System). Gates made arrangements to purchase the operating system from Seattle Computer Products. He fine-tuned and repackaged it into Microsoft DOS for IBM.

IBM released the PC XT in 1983. This machine was a faster, streamlined version of the PC. The XT allowed 640K to be included on the motherboard.

In August, 1984 IBM released the PC AT. This was the first machine to make use of Intel's newer 80286 processor. The PC AT could run DOS compatible programs at three to six times the speed of the XT. The 80286 chip also had the ability to address more than 1 MB of RAM, but DOS, alas, could not make use of this. Initially, the only difference between the XT and the AT was the AT's considerably faster performance.

In 1985, IBM began to face competition in the PC marketplace, first from compatible manufacturers and then from clones. The compatibles and clones appropriated the open IBM architecture to build faster, more efficient machines than IBM's XT and AT. The IBM compatibles were the Leading Edge, Epson Equity, Kaypro PC, Victor PC and others. In many cases these compatible machines would not run programs that would run under the PC or XT. The reason was simple, the ROM BIOS used in the PC was copyrighted by IBM. As a result, the other vendors had to use ROM BIOS chips that attempted to copy what the IBM ROM did without actually copying the code. In addition, even though these compatible machines used the same bus as the PC, they often used non-standard configurations of components. For example, the Kaypro machines combined motherboard and floppy disk controller on one card, and placed display adapter and serial/parallel ports on another card. This didn't mean that you couldn't put standard cards into the machines, but it did mean that you might have a harder time doing so.

COMPAQ Corporation ushered in the generation of clones that succeeded the compatibles. The clones were machines that had both hardware and software compatibility with IBM's PCs. They used the same arrangement of motherboard and expansion card components as did the PC. In addition, the BIOS chips in these machines more closely mimicked the actions of the IBM BIOS.

In 1986, the first PC using Intel's 80386 chip was released not by IBM but again by COMPAQ Corporation. IBM introduced its own line of "PS/2" machines in 1987, including one that used the 80386 processor (PS/2 Model 70).

The IBM PS/2s (except for the Models 20 and 30), included a new proprietary bus architecture called Microchannel Architecture or MCA. MCA was designed to improve performance speed and flexibility. IBM hoped to win customers back to its machines by revamping the basic structure of the data bus to increase speed and efficiency. To the present date, that effort has been only partially successful. Peripheral cards from the traditional clones were incompatible with the new MCA architecture, although all of the machines ran MS-DOS and used the same software. (Users with a substantial investment in peripheral equipment for the older PCs were—and are still—reluctant to simply discard their investment for IBM's new system architecture.) The traditional architecture used in the original PCs and their clones is referred to as ISA (Industry Standard Architecture). Clone makers have continued to successfully produce 286, 386, and now 486 machines using the standard bus architecture of the first generation of IBM PCs.

To further complicate things, in 1988 a consortium led by COMPAQ, Intel, AST, and other leading "cloners" developed a third bus standard to compete with IBM's MCA. The result of COMPAQ's alliance was a bus system called EISA (Extended Industry Standard Architecture). The EISA bus included the speed and flexibility of IBM's PS/2 machines, but retained compatibility with the earlier ISA architecture. Users could take their video cards and disk controllers from older machines and use them in the EISA models, or upgrade to special 32-bit EISA peripherals.

Currently, the traditional/ISA motherboards still dominate the marketplace. Fortunately, all of the competing bus systems have been designed to run the same software. For the purposes of this book, the differences between the different bus architectures are minor. (We'll let you know about any special exceptions which arise from dealing with MCA and EISA machines as we cover each topic.)

Today's PC marketplace

The original design of the IBM XT and AT has been widely copied and standardized by so many individual manufacturers, that "IBM compatibility" for these machines is no longer really an issue. The PCs we use today make use of a varied assortment of hardware and software. Almost all machines that run MS-DOS will run all MS-DOS software. In the last several years, the clone makers have consistently outpaced IBM's own technical development. One PC improvement instituted by clone makers was the use of Intel processors running at higher clock speeds than IBM's models. 16 MHz and 20 MHz versions of the 80286, superseded IBM's 8 MHz AT.[1]

Microprocessor basics

The microprocessor or central processing unit (CPU) is the part of the computer that actually does all the work. It reads information delivered along the computer bus and performs the requested instructions. Some of these instructions are arithmetic in nature. You can tell the microprocessor to add two numbers together,

---

[1]The clock speed of the CPU (measured in Megahertz) determines the speed at which instructions can be processed and sent back to the data bus.

for example. Other instructions are logical in nature—for instance, when you have the computer compare two items. You can also tell the computer to move things around in memory or to talk with peripheral devices.

The IBM PC, PC AT, 80386, 80486 and IBM PS/2 machines all make use of the Intel family of central processing units (CPUs). In this book, we will be concerned with the various CPU types as they affect the PC's ability to use memory.

Intel CPU types

The term *XT* (Extended Technology) is widely used to refer to computers that use the 8088 CPU. *AT* (Advanced Technology) refers to computers that use the 80286. To make things confusing, IBM also sold an "XT 286" at one time. Currently, we have 80386 and 80486 to contend with as well. For simplicity, this book refers to computers by processor type. An 8088 machine means an IBM PC, XT or clone using the 8088 processor. A 286 machine means a computer that uses the 80286 processor. 386SX and 386DX are used for machines that use the 80386 processors, and 486SX/486DX for machines that use an 80486 processor. (We describe the differences between the SX and DX versions of the chips a little later on.)

Intel processor operating modes

The Intel family of processors uses three distinct operating modes. They all share the ability to use the mode designed for the 8088.

Real Mode   The 8088 or "real mode" is used by the MS-DOS operating system. DOS, in real mode, addresses a total memory space of 1M. (384K of this space is traditionally "reserved" for peripherals. 640K remains for user programs. In Chapter 4, we'll see how some of the 384K "reserved" space can be used to run device drivers and utilities.) Figure 1-1 shows the memory structure of the first megabyte for an 8088 computer.

A small number of early PC clones ran real mode/MS-DOS software with the 8086 chip, an older Intel CPU. The 8086 differed from the 8088 only in its ability

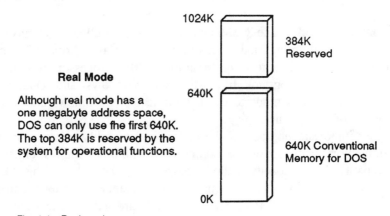

Real Mode

Although real mode has a one megabyte address space, DOS can only use the first 640K. The top 384K is reserved by the system for operational functions.

1024K

384K Reserved

640K

640K Conventional Memory for DOS

0K

Fig. 1-1   Real mode. © 1989, ALL Computers, Inc.

to export data. The 8086 could export data in 16-bit words (it used a 16-bit bus). The 8088 chip reads 16-bit words using an 8-bit bus, which means that it takes approximately twice as many clock cycles for an 8088 to do its work. (The 8088 was limited by Intel to 8-bit data export for compatibility with earlier systems running 8-bit CP/M software. Because of this, many people refer to systems using the 8088 as 8-bit, rather than 16-bit systems.)

The 8086 and 8088 processors can never see more than 1M at a time. We'll see, however, that they can be tricked into swapping part of that megabyte into an unaddressed RAM storage area. This swapping trick is called expanded memory. We'll learn how expanded memory works in Chapter 4.

The 80286   The 80286 is a true 16-bit processor. It exports instructions to a 16-bit data bus. Consequently, when the 80286 runs MS-DOS in real mode, performance is three times as efficient as with an 8088 operating at the same clock speed. Additionally, most 286 machines operate at twice to five times the clock speeds of 8088s, for a total speed increase of 600 to 1500 percent.

Protected Mode   The second operating mode for the Intel processors is called *protected mode*. Protected mode processing is built into all 80286, 80386, and 80486 chips, and is not available in the 8088 or 8086. Protected mode processing lets the CPU address more than 1M of physical memory space and also allows "advanced operating systems" (read OS/2) to safeguard data integrity against individual program conflicts. Under protected mode, the memory above 1M is assigned a contiguous address space and referred to as "Extended Memory." Operating systems like OS/2 may access up to 16M of extended memory on the 80286, or 4 gigabytes on the 80386 and 80486.

The 80386   The 80386DX is a 32-bit processor that uses a 32-bit bus. The 80386SX is a 32-bit processor that is limited to a 16-bit bus. The 80386 has the built-in capacity to execute real mode instructions three times as fast as an 80286 running at the same clock speed. The DX and SX versions of the 80386 are identical except for their data-bus capacity. Both versions include the same programmed instruction set. Intel's 80486 processor, shown in Fig. 1-2, uses the same instruction set.

Virtual 8086 Mode   The 80386 and all higher intel CPUs may make use of the third Intel programming mode. This mode, known as "Virtual 8086 mode" allows the processor to imitate several real mode 8086 processors running at the same time. Control programs like Microsoft Windows and Quarterdeck's DESQview may use this mode to open multiple 640K windows and run them independently of one another.

Another important upgrade in the 80386 is the ability to swap individual chunks of memory anywhere on the motherboard with other chunks, either above or below 640K. This capacity, called "paged memory" allows the 80386 to deliver its onboard RAM to applications as either expanded or extended memory.

Figure 1-3 shows a COMPAQ 80386 motherboard with an EISA bus.

Fig. 1-2 Intel 80486 microprocessor. Reprinted by permission of Intel Corporation.

Peripheral device basics

There are a lot of peripheral devices in your computer. Anything outside of memory or the microprocessor itself is considered a peripheral. There are two classes of these devices; the first is the expansion board. We'll cover these in detail in the following chapters. The second class of peripheral device are chips or circuits required to make the computer work. For example, the timer circuit that allows you to create sounds using the PC's speaker also provides timing for the rest of the system. In most cases, you won't need to worry about this second class of peripheral device. The few occasions that you do are mentioned in this chapter.

Bus basics

The computer bus is the electronic network that conducts information from peripheral cards (also known as expansion boards), disk drives, and other peripheral devices to the CPU and back. Slots on the motherboard allow the various peripherals (video adaptor, disk controller, input/output card) to connect on the bus. Sometimes the computer bus is referred to by its capacity to transfer data.

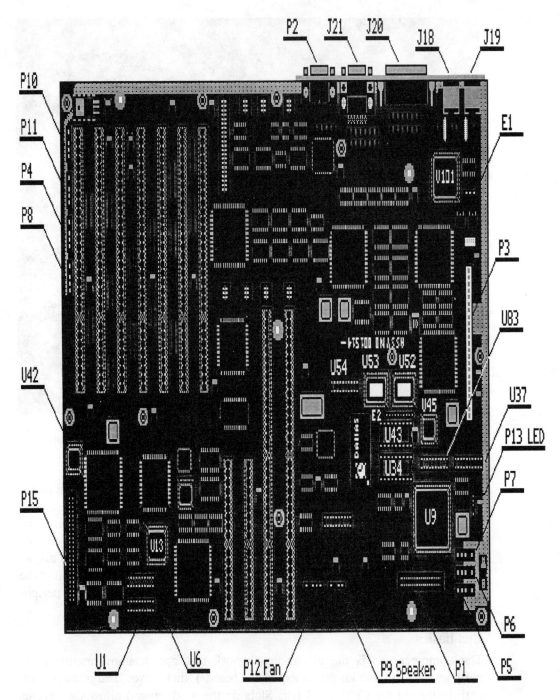

P2   J21   J20   J18   J19

P10

P11

P4

P8

E1

P3

U83

U42

U37

P13 LED

P7

P15

U45

E2

U43

U34

U9

U54   U53   U52

U13

U1   U6   P12 Fan   P9 Speaker   P1   P5   P6

COMPAQ SYSTEMPRO System I/O Bus Board   (Assy No. 001514)

Fig. 1-3   COMPAQ EISA 386 motherboard.

The original IBM PC and subsequent 8088 clones used an 8-bit data bus. The IBM PC AT and the 80286 clones use a 16-bit bus. 80386 and 80486 machines have a 32-bit bus capacity, though they often use the same peripheral cards that work on the 8 and 16-bit buses. (A special, cheaper version of the 80386 chip called the 80386SX is designed to provide 386 processing power on motherboards limited to the 16-bit bus.)

The printer, modem, disk drives, etc. are connected to the PC's bus by cards mounted in slots on the motherboard. The number of slots on individual PCs varies depending on the motherboard design and processor type. 8088 motherboards usually have six slots for cards while 286/386/486 systems typically provide eight. When you examine your motherboard, you might find that some of the slots have different sizes. (For 8088 systems, the slots are all the same size.)

Bus Capacity   Peripheral cards for PCs come in 8-bit, 16-bit and 32-bit versions. Most standard 286 and 386 motherboards have four 16-bit slots and two 8-bit slots. Some 386 motherboards may have an additional 32-bit slot. This slot on a 386 is usually intended for a memory expansion card. EISA motherboards have slots that perform a dual function. EISA slots can accept ordinary 8-bit and 16-bit cards, but may also be used for special 32-bit EISA peripherals. Figure 1-3 shows the slots on a typical 80486 EISA motherboard.

Types of expansion boards

Many different types of boards plug into the expansion slots in your computer, with each type of board serving a different function. The following paragraphs describe some of the more common types and uses.

Some systems might have additional memory installed by way of a memory card plugged into a slot on the bus. If the memory card is configured as extended, the PC will add the total on the card to the total on the motherboard. If the card on the bus is configured as expanded memory, the expanded memory will not be included in the power-on memory total. (See Chapter 4 for more details.)

The memory installed on the motherboard and on bus expansion cards is the RAM intended for use with programs or as data storage area. There might also be some other bits and pieces of memory on your PC used for internal operating system functions.

The video display adaptor is the card that takes information from computer memory and displays it on your monitor. To perform this task more quickly, the display adapter contains from 64K to 1M of video display memory. RAM mounted on the video card is not used directly by DOS. The video card's RAM stores text and graphics pages for screen display. These pages are fed to DOS through a reserved video area within the first megabyte of user RAM. (See Chapter 3.)

Your disk controller card is an interface between the motherboard and your hard/floppy disk. In most cases it contains a ROM BIOS that defines how the card interacts with the disk drive and the computer system. The disk controller card may contain onboard RAM used to speed up disk read and write operations (See the section on disk caching in Chapter 2.)

Memory basics

As you can see from the history outlined in the first section, processor speed, instruction size, and memory addressing capability were the three things that set the original IBM PC apart from the competition. In many respects this is still true today. RAM size is still one of the determining factors in deciding how usable your machine will be. The following paragraphs answer the question how you configure your machine to use RAM.

RAM vs. ROM

Some of the memory used by the PC is temporary; this type of memory is RAM. Software applications read information from disk into storage chips on the machine. When a new application is started, the information stored on the chips gets overwritten by new data. RAM is the "user memory" on a PC. It reads programs from diskette and allows you to create data files (documents, spreadsheets, pictures, etc.). The 64K advertised on 1981's microcomputers refers to Random Access Memory.

The PC does also have a small amount of permanent memory called ROM (read-only memory). Some necessary instructions for the CPU are "burned into" (the technical term for writing to read-only memory) the ROM. These instructions include routines for starting your computer and for accessing some of the peripheral devices. This information never goes away, even when you turn off the power. In addition to the ROM chips on your motherboard, some peripheral devices have ROM chips. For example, the display adapter has its own ROM. The ROM BIOS (Basic Input-Output System) is the chip set that tells the PC how to start up, read the disk drives, and load the DOS operating system into RAM.

Bits and bytes

Computers store information in binary format. A bit is either on or off, just like a light switch; and 1's and 0's are used to indicate that a particular electronic pathway is open or closed. Any number we use in our traditional decimal system of counting can be represented in binary notation by a series of 1's and 0's. Instead of representing numbers as powers of ten (1's, 10's, 100's, etc.), the binary numbering system represents values as powers of 2, (1's, 2's, 4's and so on). For example, the number 8 in decimal is written as 1000 in binary.

Because the computer uses numbers to represent everything, we must have a technique for translating between the characters we use and the numbers the computer uses. One standard method for doing this is ASCII (American Standard

Code for Information Interchange). Standard ASCII uses a 7-bit code to represent a character, which gives us 2^7 or 128 different combinations. The standard code uses the eighth bit for error checking. IBM decided to use the eighth bit as part of the character. If each character is represented by an 8-bit string, then 2^8 or 256 different combinations are possible. The extended ASCII character set uses the additional 128 characters to represent foreign characters and special drawing characters.

A group of eight bits is referred to as a byte. Each byte is used to store one character or letter in the computer's memory. Numbers normally require two or more bytes. The byte is the basic unit for counting memory. We measure memory in bytes, thousands of bytes and millions of bytes. One kilobyte (abbreviated 1K) is equivalent to 1024 bytes. One Megabyte (abbreviated 1M) is equivalent to 1024K or 1,048,576 bytes. The reason these "thousands" are counted in 1024 units is because the computer uses a binary system architecture. We are measuring powers of 2 instead of powers of 10. The 8088 has 20 address lines with which to access memory. That means we have 2^{20} memory locations or a 1,048,576 (1M) address space.

About hexadecimal notation

One of the more important techniques you'll learn from this book is how to gain extra memory for your programs after you load DOS. You'll also learn how to stop mysterious crashes from occurring while several programs work at once. To do these things, you'll need a basic familiarity with hexadecimal notation. DOS uses hexadecimal notation to communicate with the PC's hardware, and most memory management tools use hexadecimal numbers to tell DOS how to juggle program address space.

Two methods are commonly used to count memory. Hexadecimal notation (base 16) is used by many programmers because the processor itself counts in this manner. In addition, many programs—including the DOS MEM program—use hexadecimal notation to show where various programs are loaded in memory and how much space they take. Decimal notation (base 10) is used by many programs to count memory in terms that humans can more easily understand. In most cases, the CMOS setup program in ROM will use decimal notation to make it easier to configure your machine. 400 bytes hexadecimal (often represented as simply h) equals 1024 bytes decimal, which equals 1K.

Hexadecimal notation is simply a way of writing numerical address locations in base-16 instead of the traditional decimal form. The letters A through F are used to represent decimal numbers 10 through 15. Thus F000h = 61,440 decimal (0 in the 1's place, 0 in the 16's place, 0 in the 256's place, 15 in the 4096's place—$4096 \times 15 = 61,440$).

As stated earlier, an 8088 processor uses 16-bit registers. Using our hexadecimal addressing scheme, we would seemingly be limited to 64K of total RAM.

However, a complete PC address consists of a 4-digit (16 bit) segment address and a 4-digit (16 bit) offset address to create a total of 20-bits or access to 1,048,576 (1M) of memory. Think of a segment as a portion of memory 64K long. An offset is a particular location within that portion of memory. Because the 8088 can actually address 20-bits, the segment address is presumed to be staggered 4 bits (1 hex column) to the left. Say that we wanted to look at segment A000h and the 0100h byte within that segment. The actual 20-bit address would appear as follows:

```
Segment           A 0 0 0 (0)
Offset              0 1 0  0
_____
20-bit Address    A 0 1 0  0
```

The PC uses a segmented memory scheme, unlike the Apple II, which uses a flat addressing scheme. Programmers commonly show the segment and offset of an address by separating them with a colon as follows: A000:0100. This is equivalent to the hexadecimal number A0100 or 655,616 in decimal. For the purposes of this book we will be dealing with "round" address segments whose offsets are zero whenever possible.

In the next chapter, we begin our description of how DOS actually allocates and manages memory. It will be useful to familiarize ourselves with some basic hexadecimal equivalences. Table 1-1 shows some of the more common hexadecimal equivalences and where they reside in memory. The zeros within parentheses

Table 1-1   Standard memory locations.

Decimal notation	Hexadecimal Notation
Default memory sizes	
1024 bytes (= 1K)	0040(0) h
65,536 bytes (= 64K)	1000(0) h
Conventional memory area	
0K - 128K	0000(0) - 2000(0) h
128K - 256K	2000(0) - 4000(0) h
256K - 384K	4000(0) - 6000(0) h
384K - 512K	6000(0) - 8000(0) h
512K - 640K	8000(0) - A000(0) h
Upper memory area	
640K - 704K	A000(0) - B000(0) h
704K - 768K	B000(0) - C000(0) h
768K - 832K	C000(0) - D000(0) h
832K - 896K	D000(0) - E000(0) h
896K - 960K	E000(0) - F000(0) h
960K - 1M	F000(0) - 10000(0) h

in the table are usually omitted when programmers deal with round address segments. The address segments are assumed to be shifted one place to the left. Notice that the 1M address area of the 8088 is divided into two areas. We will explore these areas in the following chapters. Suffice it to say that the area below A0000h is user memory and the area above to 100000h is for device ROMs (like the display adapter ROM), adapter memory, and certain types of device drivers.

Memory management basics

Programs can run on the same physical hardware in a variety of different ways. For example, some programs allow you to load them as either TSRs (terminate and stay resident) or as non-resident programs. Loading more than a few of these programs as TSRs will impact the amount of memory available to other applications. Loading these utilities non-resident prohibits them from being accessed while other programs are running. In many cases, providing more memory for your applications to use can improve their performance. For example, a word processor could load more of the document you're editing into RAM instead of reading it from the hard drive. This also means that a search and replace or a spell check will take less time. Memory management is the process of determining how you want to use the memory in your machine. Using memory in one way can increase the flexibility of your machine, while using it in another might improve performance. The following performance factors are dependent on proper memory management:

- Speed—The time it takes for programs to come up on the screen, the time it takes to recalculate a spreadsheet, and the time it takes to save a file to disk or print it.

- Power of your applications—The size of the data files the application can work with, and the number of command options available in the program. For example, spreadsheets normally load an entire document into memory. As a result, the largest worksheet you can create is directly proportional to the amount of memory available. (More memory allows you to run larger, more powerful applications).

- User flexibility—Proper memory management allows you to do DOS file maintenance while other applications remain active. You may find it useful to view two applications on the screen at the same time. Task switching is the technique of "freezing" one application without closing it, when you switch to another. Even better, you might want two applications to keep working at the same time (say, a communications program and a word processor). This is multitasking. IBM PCs were not originally designed to task switch or to multitask; these privileges were traditionally reserved for users of mainframe and minicomputers. As we progress in this book, you'll see that there's no reason why a PC can't multitask like its bigger (and more expensive) brothers.

CMOS options and wait states

A large part of memory management is understanding type, speed, and size of memory you have installed in your machine. In all cases you must tell the motherboard how much memory it contains. (Some of the newer motherboards do this automatically for you.) In addition, you might need to tell the motherboard what type of RAM packaging is used, since some motherboards accept more than one type (either DIPs or SIMMs, for example). Figure 1-4 shows a SIMM.

Fig. 1-4   1M SIMM modules. Photo courtesy of Micron Technology, Inc., Boise, Idaho.

Notice the big difference in packaging methods and you'll quickly understand why it is so important to know what type your computer uses. In fact, depending on the motherboard, you may have wide range of configuration options to consider. The information you supply tells the motherboard how to configure itself and ultimately affects how much memory you'll actually see. More importantly, it will affect how your applications perform.

You have two common ways to configure your computer. An 8086/8088 computer uses DIP switches to tell the computer how much memory is available. As a result of this limited configuration method, the 8088 lacks some of the sophisticated options of newer 286/386/486 machines. For example, the 8088 must keep track of the current time and date with an external clock chip. In some cases it can only recognize 1.2M and 1.44M floppy drives when special information is built into the floppy controller. Most 8088-based motherboards recognize and format a hard disk through add-on ROM mounted on the controller card. In some cases the machine lacks even this capability, requiring you to use an external program.

On the other hand, 80286/80386/80486 computers use a special program stored in ROM to set this configuration information using electronic switches in a special chip known as CMOS (Complimentary Metal-Oxide Semiconductor) memory. Being more complex than the 8088, these machines must keep track of a series of operating parameters. In many cases, support for the clock, hard drive, and advanced system diagnostics are built right into the motherboard. When you turn your computer off, a battery keeps power supplied to the CMOS memory so that it remembers the computer configuration when you turn the computer back on. Most importantly, using CMOS also provides the added flexibility of being able to configure RAM in more ways than fixed switches will allow (we will explore this issue later).

Information is entered into the CMOS through a setup program. On older systems the setup program must be accessed through DOS from a floppy diskette. Newer systems have the setup program built into the ROM BIOS. The CMOS setup controls several memory variables that affect system speed and reliability:

- wait states.
- bus speed.
- instruction shadowing (Shadow RAM).

Wait States and Memory Speed   The memory chips on the motherboard go through a periodic electronic cycle that refreshes information. In addition, they must recover from each access by the CPU or other peripheral device. With the advent of high speed processors, the CPU might process information faster than the memory chips can recover. To keep the system happy, artificial pauses called *wait states* are added to the processor instruction cycle. Every time the processor completes an instruction cycle, it waits one clock cycle before it starts to process the next one. The faster the memory chips, the fewer wait states are required.

The actual method for calculating the number of wait states your machine will have is quite complex. However, you can calculate an estimate using the following equation:

$$\frac{1}{Memory\ Clock\ Speed}$$

For example, the original IBM PC had a clock speed of 4.77 MHz. This meant that the time interval between clock cycles was 1/4,770,000 or 209 ns (nano-second). If you used 250 ns memory, then you would have to add 1 wait state to allow recovery after an access by the CPU. Of course, these machines commonly used 200 ns memory, so there was no need to add a wait state. Look what happens when we increase the clock speed to 20 MHz. Using our equation from before we see that we now need 50 ns memory. Because most memory is not that fast, we must add a wait state.

Of course, manufacturers can get around the problem of using high speed memory by using clever memory configuration techniques. What if we place the memory in two banks and access is strictly regulated? If the processor accesses bank A and then bank B, and we use 80 ns memory, then bank A will have sufficient time to recover before the next access. As a result, no wait state is required. This is called *bank switched memory*. A lot of other memory configuration techniques are equally effective. As you can see, a good knowledge of what is going on in your machine is required to configure your machine properly. Some of the more common machines use the following wait state configurations:

- The original IBM PC had 0 built-in wait states, using memory chips rated at 150−200 ns.

- 10 MHz 8088 and 80286 motherboards typically use 1 wait state operating with memory chips rated at 120 ns. They used 0 wait states with memory chips rated at 100 ns.

- 12 MHz/16 MHz/20 MHz 80286 motherboards can typically be configured to run with 0, 1 or 2 wait states. As previously stated, this all depends on the speed and configuration of the memory you use. The 0-wait state configuration yields faster performance. A non-interleaved 12 MHz machine using memory chips rated at 80 ns can run with 0 wait states. On the other hand, a non-interleaved 20 MHz machine using 120 ns memory requires 2 wait states. The wait state option for the computer may be set by a hardware jumper on the motherboard, or it may be changed through the setup program.

- 16 MHz to 50 MHz 386/486 motherboards often have separate wait state configurations for different functions. The internal chip set may operate at 3−4 wait states while the bus and RAM chips use 0 to 1 wait state. The wait state defaults may be permanently hardwired or changeable through the setup program. 0 wait state 16 MHz to 25 MHz motherboards usually require 80 ns memory chips used in a bank switched or interleaved configuration. Motherboards running at 33 MHz or higher frequencies require 60 to 70 ns RAM.

Bus Speed As stated previously, the computation of exactly how many wait states your machine might have is a very complex undertaking. What would happen if part of the memory in your machine ran at one speed, and part at another? How would you know what speed of memory to use? Many AT configuration programs allow you to select the bus speed of your computer. This is the clock that is sent to the bus in place of the CPU clock. The reason for this second clock is quite simple: many expansion boards are incapable of operating at the high speed of the CPU clock. In fact, a lot of expansion boards are limited to 8 MHz. Even if your memory board is capable of a higher speed clock, you must set the bus to the lowest speed required by any of the cards you wish to put in your machine. For example, if you had three expansion boards in your machine and the first was capable of 10 MHz, the second 12 MHz, and the third 8 MHz, you would have to select the 8 MHz bus speed to accommodate the third board.

How does the bus speed setting affect memory speed? First, it affects the speed of the memory you put on the expansion board. Using our calculation from before, 1 / 8,000,000 equals 125 ns. You would need to get 120 ns or better memory for the expansion board to work properly. Second, it affects the number of wait states incurred when you access the expansion board (not the motherboard) memory. For example, if you were using a 20 MHz motherboard, then 2 wait states would be incurred whenever you used expansion board memory, while you might not incur any at all when using motherboard memory. This is the reason that many motherboard manufacturers are providing more room on the motherboard for memory rather than using expansion boards.

Instruction Shadowing (Shadow RAM) The memory chips used for Random Access Memory (user program memory) are generally much faster than the corresponding chips used for Read Only Memory (permanent, fixed instructions). Because of this, clone makers invented a feature called ROM shadowing. Most new 286/386/486 machines now have a user option to "copy" the ROM instructions into an area of volatile user RAM. When the ROM BIOS has been "shadowed" in this way, video display and input/output instructions are speeded up.

ROM shadowing copies the fixed ROM at address F000-FFFF into "extra" onboard RAM. (Video ROM at address C000 is also commonly shadowed). The RAM in the shadow cache takes the place of the fixed ROM chips. When DOS tries to access the BIOS in the "F" block, a pointer now refers to the Shadow RAM cache, instead.

When you buy a machine with 1M of RAM onboard, the typical configuration is 640K used for conventional memory and 384K set aside for use as shadow RAM. 384K is actually more memory than you need for the shadow cache. The memory blocks that are commonly shadowed contain only 64K to 256K of ROM instructions. Some systems will let you remap part of the shadow RAM cache to an address space above 1M. When the cache is remapped, it adds to the total of extended memory on your system.

Running the setup program

On newer machines, you'll see a note about Setup displayed on the screen immediately after the power-on self check. Usually, if you press a designated key (i.e., the Delete key, F1, or Ctrl-Esc), the computer enters the setup program. Inside of Setup, you'll see a list of configuration parameters on the screen. The setup menu varies, depending on which manufacturer supplied your computer's BIOS. If you can't find a prompt on your machine to run a built-in setup program, Setup may be supplied separately on a floppy disk, or located in a subdirectory of your hard disk. For older machines, you enter the setup program by running it from the DOS command line. (The original IBM PC AT came with a setup boot disk, to be used instead of DOS.)

You might see menu choices in the setup program for "easy setup" or "advanced setup," or you might be able to page through a series of screens that display all of the available options. Figure 1-5 shows a typical setup menu for the "easy setup" provided by many vendors.

EXTENDED CMOS SETUP PROGRAM Ver - 1.50 ,(C)1988, American Megatrends Inc.

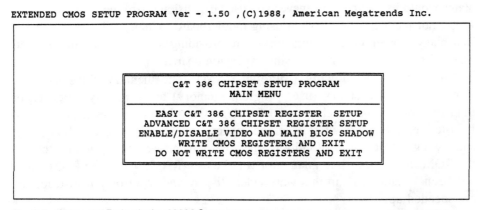

Fig. 1-5 Chips and Technologies 80386 Setup menu. Chips and Technologies, Ltd.

Before you change anything in the setup program, write down the current settings on a piece of paper. The choices you make might directly alter performance at a hardware level. If your computer comes with a set of instructions on the setup program, read the instructions before you make any changes! Some of the options (like setting the date and time) are easy to correct. If you change the settings for your hard disk type or any of the chip timing parameters, you might find that the computer will no longer start up.[2]

---

[2]In the event this happens to you, most setup programs will allow you to reset the standard defaults. Read your manual for details.

You may experiment with the option for "wait states" if you find it in the "easy" or "basic" setup. Generally the choice will be between 0 or 1. If your machine has been set to "1 wait state," changing the setting to 0 may increase performance speed. Of course, you need to determine if it is possible to safely speed up your machine using the equation we discussed previously. Never push your memory beyond its rated capacity since this could result in loss of data, machine failures, or other unforeseen consequences.

The "advanced" wait state options for the computer's bus are generally set correctly by the manufacturer. You may increase performance speed by altering the "clock" or "bus speed" wait states, but this might also make the computer perform erratically. Extreme caution should be exercised before changing any options listed in a setup program's "advanced" section. Always determine the correct bus speed setting by determining the rated clock speed of the cards in your machine. If your CPU (system) clock is 24 MHz, and the rated speed of your cards is 8 MHz, then you need to divide the CPU clock by 3 to get the proper bus speed. Figure 1-6 shows the complexity of a typical extended CMOS configuration screen. Notice the wait state configuration option.

```
EXTENDED CMOS SETUP PROGRAM Ver - 1.50 ,(C)1988, American Megatrends Inc.
                       Memory Configuration
      Bank       Enable/Disable      DRAM Type        Waitstate
      ----       --------------      ---------        ---------
      0          ENABLED             256K             0 WAIT STATE
      1          ENABLED             256K             0 WAIT STATE
      2          DISABLED                             0 WAIT STATE
      3          DISABLED                             0 WAIT STATE

                          Clock Source
      Processor Clock       Bus Clock         DMA Clock       ┌────────────────────────┐
      ---------------       ---------         ---------       │ ZERO WAIT STATE        │
      PROCESSOR OSCILLATOR  PROC CLOCK/3      SCLK/2          │ ONE WAIT STATE         │
                                                             ├────────────────────────┤
              Shadow Ram\Memory Interleave                    │ MOVE BAR-<PgUp/PgDn>   │
      BIOS Shadow       Video Shadow          Memory          │ CHANGE WINDOWS ↑↓→     │
      F0000H,64K    C0000H,16K  C4000H,16K    Interleave      │ EXIT-<ESC>             │
      -----------   ----------  ----------    ----------      └────────────────────────┘
      ENABLED       DISABLED    DISABLED      ENABLED
```

Fig. 1-6 Chips and Technologies Extended CMOS Setup—Wait state configuration. Chips and Technologies, Ltd.

How to enable/disable shadow RAM

If your 286/386/486 allows manual control of shadow RAM, you may turn it off and on with the setup program. Machines that use the older AMI BIOS, show menus for "easy setup," "advanced setup," and/or "enable shadow RAM." Select the "shadow RAM" or "easy setup" choice. The next menu (Fig. 1-7) displays separate options for BIOS shadowing and VIDEO shadowing. You may toggle these settings on or off and exit the setup program. (On machines with a Phoenix, Award, or DTK BIOS you may see a single screen that offers the option "Remap Shadow RAM to Extended Memory.")

```
┌──────────────────────────────────┐   ┌────────────────────────────────────┐
│   SETUP SHADOW RAM FOR 212        │   │ Go to Prev/Next Register  -↑↓       │
│                                   │   │ Go to   Prev/Next Entry   - →       │
│ MAIN  BIOS SHADOW AT F0000H,64K ->1│  │         Scroll Bit value - PgUp/PgDn│
│ VIDEO BIOS SHADOW AT C0000H,16K ->0│  │     Return to MAIN MENU - <ESC>     │
│ VIDEO BIOS SHADOW AT C4000H,16K ->0│  └────────────────────────────────────┘
└──────────────────────────────────┘
                                        ┌────────────────────────────────────┐
                                        │ VIDEO BIOS SHADOW AT C4000H,16K     │
                                        │                                     │
                                        │  1=SHADOW ENABLE                    │
                                        │  0=SHADOW DISABLE                   │
                                        └────────────────────────────────────┘
```

Fig. 1-7   Chips and Technologies Extended CMOS Setup—Shadow RAM configuration. Chips and Technologies, Ltd.

Some motherboards let you physically remap the shadow RAM memory to an address above 1M, while others don't. Why should you want to do this? Because disabling the shadow RAM effectively adds 384K of extended memory to your system. If you decide to go for the extended memory, you lose the slightly faster BIOS and video performance. (We'll see in Chapter 6, that some memory managers let you "recreate" the shadow option using expanded memory, instead of the system's onboard cache.) When you choose to disable shadow RAM, you are in effect saying that it's ok for your computer to operate more slowly so that you can receive the extra extended memory.

On some machines you might have to go into the "advanced setup" menu to find the "remap shadow RAM" option.[3] Figure 1-8 shows a typical extended CMOS setup screen.

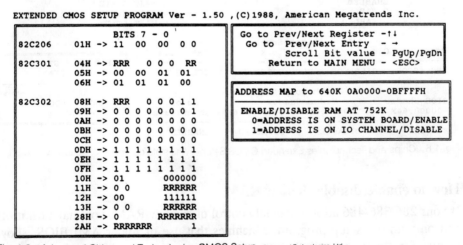

```
┌──────────────────────────────┐   ┌────────────────────────────────────┐
│            BITS 7 - 0         │   │ Go to Prev/Next Register  -↑↓       │
│82C206  01H -> 11  00  00  0 0 │   │ Go to   Prev/Next Entry   - →       │
│                               │   │         Scroll Bit value - PgUp/PgDn│
│82C301  04H -> RRR   0  0  RR  │   │     Return to MAIN MENU - <ESC>     │
│        05H -> 00  00  01  01  │   └────────────────────────────────────┘
│        06H -> 01  01  01  00  │
│                               │   ┌────────────────────────────────────┐
│82C302  08H -> RRR   0  0 0 1 1│   │ ADDRESS MAP to 640K 0A0000-0BFFFFH  │
│        09H -> 0 0 0 0 0 0 0 1 │   │                                     │
│        0AH -> 0 0 0 0 0 0 0 0 │   │ ENABLE/DISABLE RAM AT 752K          │
│        0BH -> 0 0 0 0 0 0 0 0 │   │   0=ADDRESS IS ON SYSTEM BOARD/ENABLE│
│        0CH -> 0 0 0 0 0 0 0 0 │   │   1=ADDRESS IS ON IO CHANNEL/DISABLE │
│        0DH -> 1 1 1 1 1 1 1 1 │   └────────────────────────────────────┘
│        0EH -> 1 1 1 1 1 1 1 1 │
│        0FH -> 1 1 1 1 1 1 1 1 │
│        10H -> 01      000000  │
│        11H -> 0 0     RRRRR   │
│        12H -> 00      111111  │
│        13H -> 0 0     RRRRR   │
│        28H -> 0       RRRRRR  │
│        2AH -> RRRRRRR       1 │
└──────────────────────────────┘
```

Fig. 1-8   Advanced Chips and Technologies CMOS Setup. Chips and Technologies, Ltd.

---

[3] Systems that use the Chips and Technology chipset have the "remap" option hidden within a series of 1's and 0's in the advanced setup. The option may not work if more than 1M is installed on the motherboard.

Remember, be careful inside of the "advanced setup." Record all of the settings with a pencil and paper before you make any changes. Some machine-BIOS combinations don't allow manual control of shadow RAM. If you can't find the option in your setup program, you might have to live with the factory settings.

After you exit the setup program, the system may require you to run the simple setup program again. In most cases you will see an error message stating that the memory size found does not match the configuration size. You will usually see a message telling you how to get back into the setup program. The diagnostics will show an additional 384K of extended memory when you get into the setup program. Quit and reboot the machine to make the change permanent. If you don't get the error message, you will normally see the additional 384K of memory when you reboot the machine.

Shadow RAM vs. extended memory

When you buy a 286/386/486 machine that has more than 1M of RAM onboard, the memory from the second megabyte on up is extended memory. You'll see this memory counted when you turn on the computer. Some systems lump the conventional and the extended memory together and others count them separately.

You can check for the presence of extended memory after the machine boots up. Newer versions of DOS use a command called MEM. With older DOS versions, you need to use a third party utility. There are plenty of free and shareware memory checkers available on Public Bulletin Boards. If you own a memory manager like QEMM or 386Max, memory checking utilities are included.

For instance, if the computer counts up to 4096K, you might find that total extended memory is reported as 3072K. 640K of the first megabyte has been allocated as conventional memory and 384K as shadow RAM.

Conclusion

This chapter has provided you with information essential to understanding memory management on your computer system. We have presented some of the more important aspects of the hardware and shown you how they relate to the overall picture. In addition, you have learned about some of the pitfalls of trying to tune your computer to its highest level of performance. The next chapter shows you how to "take stock of your PC," and see what's "under the hood."

2
CHAPTER

Taking stock of your system

Taking stock of your PC's components will help you to make choices about hardware and software options. For example, will your machine allow you to add that second serial port? How should you configure your software to make maximum use of available hardware?

You can use diagnostic tools to help you take inventory of your system. Diagnostic tools for your PC can be found within programs you might already own or from free bulletin board systems. Commercial vendors are a source for sophisticated inventory packages.

Getting started

To take full advantage of what your PC can do, you need to know about what's inside of the box: installed memory, video card, hard disk, and peripherals. Familiarity with the hardware environment will help you plan your software environment. A working knowledge of your PC will also be useful when you need to make upgrade decisions.

Basic hardware information

Whenever you plan something, it's important to ask the right questions. Of course, you could start looking at your PC as a hodgepodge of unrelated parts. However, a better way to do things is to start with the basics and look at your hardware in an organized way. Familiarity with the hardware environment will help you to plan your software environment! Here are some questions about your PC that you'll want to know the answers to:

- What kind of processor does the PC use? Back in Chapter 1, we examined some of the reasons that the processor type is so important.

- How much memory does the motherboard provide room for? If you have an older machine, you might want to know if the motherboard can hold a full 640K. On newer machines, you'll want to know whether to buy an add-on memory card or whether you can simply plug more RAM chips into the motherboard.

- Does the machine use EMS 4.0 Expanded Memory? Some hardware vendors claim compatibility with EMS 4.0 memory but fail to deliver it in important aspects. (See p. 92−93 for the full story on this.) You'll want to know how much expanded memory your machine can actually provide for applications.

- If the machine is an 80286/386/486, how much extended memory is installed? By installing the proper memory management software, you can convert that extended memory to XMS (extended memory specification) or EMS (expanded memory specification) memory to use with your applications.

- How much storage space is available on the hard disk? Not only do you need this for program and data storage, but some programs use the paging feature of the 80386 to swap portions of RAM to the hard drive when not in use. This effectively gives you more RAM than you have available in the machine. Microsoft Windows running in enhanced mode uses this technique.

- What kind of video display adaptor is installed? There are places in upper memory that you can use as part of conventional memory. One of these areas is in the video memory area. CGA and monochrome display adapters contain less video RAM (i.e., use less upper memory address space) than either EGA or VGA adaptors.

- How many serial and parallel ports are installed? You need to know not only how *many* are installed but *how* they are installed. In some cases, you will need to know what interrupts and I/O (input/output) address space these ports use to avoid conflicts. For example, you should avoid assigning interrupt 2 on an AT or higher-powered machine when using Windows.

- What other peripherals are in the machine? Just like the parallel and serial ports, it's important to know how your other peripheral devices are configured as well.

Advanced hardware information

The questions in the previous section are only a starting point. In most cases, knowing this information will get you close to an optimal configuration. However, you probably want to obtain the *best performance possible* from your machine to fully realize the potential of the applications you use. As you fine tune the system, some of these questions open the door to more technical considerations:

- What type and speed are the memory chips in the system? See Chapter 1 for an explanation of why this is such an important consideration.

- Can an expanded memory driver be used to multitask? Many of the early expanded memory drivers were so poorly designed that they barely worked, much less enabled you to multitask applications.

- What kind of controller does the hard disk use? Some controllers transfer data faster than others. A typical MFM controller transfers data at 5 Mbits/ second, while some ESDI drives transfer data at speeds approaching 20 Mbits/second. Is there a hardware cache? Disk intensive programs like database management systems and word processors rely on fast, efficient access to the information stored on disk. In many cases, you will notice a greater performance boost by concentrating resources on disk I/O rather than other areas. One technique for doing this is to store data in fast RAM rather than reading it from disk all the time.

- How much display memory is installed on the video card? Graphics-oriented programs often need the memory on a video card to perform their very best. For example, while the user is looking at one display, the program could be drawing the next display in video memory. The users will see an apparent instantaneous screen change when they request the next one from the application. What screen resolutions can it display? While higher resolutions and increased colors can greatly improve the appearance of a display, they can also impact the performance of the application.

Operating system information

Some people think that increasing the efficiency of the hardware they use is the end of the performance question. Nothing could be further from the truth. Whether the machine is "fast enough" might depend on the programs you use. A machine that is adequate for word processing can put you through a terrible ordeal when you use it for desktop publishing. The machine's operating system also plays a part in computing efficiency. Your applications call upon the operating system to perform many tasks during the course of a computing session. For example, much of the contact you have with peripherals like the printer, display, and hard drive go through the operating system. As a result, increasing the efficiency of the operating system will affect the performance of all applications that run on your machine. Here are some operating system questions that may affect your future computing potential:

- What version of DOS/other operating system does the machine use? Different versions of DOS have different capabilities. Efficient use of these capabilities often translate into increased productivity.

- How much conventional memory remains after the machine boots up? For most of the history of DOS, as the version number increased, conventional memory available to applications decreased. This changed with DOS 5.0. Not only do you get enhanced operating system capabilities, but increased space for programs as well.

- How much expanded memory is available after bootup? Many programs use this type of memory to relocate data or program code. Often, the more you have available to applications that use it, the better the application performance.

- How much extended/XMS memory is available after bootup? Many operating system environments for 80286 and above machines use this type of memory. For example, Microsoft Windows uses XMS memory. The more memory you have available, the greater the number of tasks you can run.

- Can the system load drivers and TSRs between addresses 640K and 1M? (This is a very important consideration for computers in light of today's "RAM Cram." Some 8088 and 80286 machines use EMS memory or special chip sets to emulate the 80386's ability to remap memory.) Loading TSRs and device drivers high will provide more conventional memory for applications.

Taking stock—
Inventory techniques and how to use them

There are many tools and techniques you can use to create an inventory of your machine. For example, you can perform a visual inspection to determine display adapter types, number of serial ports, and the locations of jumpers. A software inspection might reveal the amount and type of memory on your machine. The following paragraphs help you understand the ways that you can inventory your computer.

Performing a visual inspection

One obvious way to start your PC inventory is with a physical inspection of the machine. A glance at the front panel tells you if the computer has a turbo switch or reset button. (Some vendors place one or both of these switches in the rear of the machine.) Studying the back of the machine might reveal the installed peripherals. If you haven't already done so, you might want to identify and label each I/O port.

A visual inspection might also involve taking the top off your machine and visually inspecting each peripheral card and the motherboard inside. You should note the positions of jumpers on each card and verify their importance using the documentation provided with your machine. Many people also record such items as the serial numbers and revision levels of the peripheral cards and any BIOS chips. This can be of assistance when you need help diagnosing a problem later.

Performing a free software inspection

Some of the software you already own might provide additional information about your PC's configuration. For example, it is not always convenient to count the amount of memory located on your motherboard. In addition, some people do not want to open their computer. Using software, it's possible to learn a great deal about the machine without opening the box. The following are some common software sources for information:

- The PC's power on self-test/setup/internal diagnostics
- Utilities included with DOS
- Utilities hidden in popular application software
- Shareware and Public Domain system utilities
- Commercial system checking utilities

Self-test/Setup/Diagnostics We saw in Chapter 1 that every PC counts installed memory at boot time. The power-on memory count displays the totals of conventional memory, shadow RAM, and extended memory on the system. Some machines display the totals separately, and some lump all of this memory together. Expanded memory is not counted by the system until the expanded memory manager is loaded in CONFIG.SYS.

If you watch carefully, you'll see some other information flash by on the screen before DOS begins to load. The system will display the manufacturer, date, and/or version number of the BIOS. Information about the video BIOS may also appear. Some BIOS manufacturers include a summary of installed memory, types and number of ports, video display type, and hard drive size and type in the start-up screen. Some displays include the port addresses for any ports installed on the machine. If you want to examine this information more closely, try starting the machine at its slowest speed. That way you can read the system information as it goes by. Past a certain point in the boot process, you can also pause the display with the Ctrl-S key on a standard keyboard, or Pause key on an extended keyboard. Figure 2-1 shows the system configuration information for an AMI BIOS. Each BIOS manufacturer uses a slightly different display, so your display might not match the one shown exactly. The important thing to remember is that all BIOS vendors do provide a display similar to this one.

```
System Configuration (C) Copyright 1985-1989, American Megatrends Inc,.

Main Processor      : 80386         Base Memory Size   : 640 KB
Numeric Processor   : None          Ext. Memory Size   : 1024 KB
Floppy Drive A:     : 1.2 MB, 5¼"   Hard Disk C: Type  : 47
Floppy Drive B:     : 1.44 MB, 3½"  Hard Disk D: Type  : None
Display Type        : Monochrome    Serial Port(s)     : 3E8
ROM-BIOS Date       : 09/15/89      Parallel Port(s)   : 3BC

Bank 0/1 DRAM Type  : 256K DRAM     Bank 0/1 DRAM W/S  : 0 W/S
Bank 2/3 DRAM Type  : Disabled      Bank 2/3 DRAM W/S  : 0 W/S
Memory Interleave   : Enabled       Processor Clock    : CLK2IN
Shadow C0000H,16K   : Disabled      Bus Clock          : CLK2IN/3
Shadow C4000H,16K   : Disabled      DMA Clock          : SCLK/2
Shadow F0000H,64K   : Enabled
```

Fig. 2-1 AMI System configuration information. AMI.

On 286/386/486 machines, more information can be found within the setup program. You should find instructions on how to run the setup program in your computer's user manual. There might also be a message about Setup displayed on screen before DOS loads. Commonly, the setup program is called up by pressing a hot key combination. For example, many AMI BIOS chips use the Del key, while Award and Phoenix use the Ctrl-Alt-Esc key combination. In most systems this control key combination is disabled once DOS begins to load, so you must press it immediately after the boot sequence begins. Older systems might run Setup from a separate system diskette. (This is also standard on IBM PS/2 models and some EISA motherboards.) The setup screen shows information on installed memory, memory wait states, video display type, and disk drives: the drive types and capacities. Figure 2-2 shows a typical setup screen for an AMI BIOS. Your setup screen should look similar, even though screens vary from vendor to vendor.

```
┌─────────────────────────────────────────────────────────────────────────┐
│        CMOS SETUP (C) Copyright 1985-1989, American Megatrends Inc,.      │
├──────────────────────────────────────┬──────────────────────────────────┤
│ Date (mn/date/year): Tue, Aug 20 1991 │ Base memory size  : 640 KB       │
│ Time (hour/min/sec): 16 : 21 : 22     │ Ext. memory size  : 1024 KB      │
│ Floppy drive A:    : 1.2  MB, 5¼"     │ Numeric processor : Not Installed │
│ Floppy drive B:    : 1.44 MB, 3½"     ├──────────────────────────────────┤
│                                       │ Cyln Head WPcom LZone Sec  Size   │
│ Hard disk C: type  : 47 = USER TYPE   │ 845   7    0    845   35  101 MB  │
│ Hard disk D: type  : Not Installed    │                                   │
│ Primary display    : Monochrome       ├────┬───┬───┬───┬───┬───┬───┬────┤
│ Keyboard           : Installed        │    │Sun│Mon│Tue│Wed│Thu│Fri│Sat │
│                                       ├────┼───┼───┼───┼───┼───┼───┼────┤
│ Scratch RAM option : 1                │    │28 │29 │30 │31 │ 1 │ 2 │  3 │
│                                       │    ├───┼───┼───┼───┼───┼───┼────┤
│                                       │    │ 4 │ 5 │ 6 │ 7 │ 8 │ 9 │ 10 │
│                                       │    ├───┼───┼───┼───┼───┼───┼────┤
│                                       │    │11 │12 │13 │14 │15 │16 │ 17 │
├───────────────────────────────────────    ├───┼───┼───┼───┼───┼───┼────┤
│ Month : Jan, Feb,.....Dec             │    │18 │19 │20 │21 │22 │23 │ 24 │
│ Date  : 01, 02, 03,...31              │    ├───┼───┼───┼───┼───┼───┼────┤
│ Year  : 1901, 1902,...2099            │    │25 │26 │27 │28 │29 │30 │ 31 │
├───────────────────────────────────────────┼───┼───┼───┼───┼───┼───┼────┤
│ ESC = Exit, ↓ → ↑ = Select, PgUp/PgDn = Modify │ 1 │ 2 │ 3 │ 4 │ 5 │ 6 │  7 │
└─────────────────────────────────────────────┴───┴───┴───┴───┴───┴───┴────┘
```

Fig. 2-2   AMI Basic Setup program.

Unfortunately, 8088 machines generally don't have built-in setup programs. Instead, 8088's are configured by dip switch and jumper settings on the motherboard. If you have an 8088 machine, you might still be able to avoid opening the machine and searching for the switch settings. A check out utility run from DOS might give you the information you need. (See the next section.)

Utilities Hidden in Applications   Some people believe that they have to buy an expensive product like CheckIt to inventory their system. Fortunately, you might already have access to a good system inventory program without being aware of it! WordPerfect 5.x, PCTools, The Norton Utilities, and Lotus 1-2-3 all include system inventory programs. In many cases, you can use these utilities to create a complete listing of your hardware configuration and installed memory. Of course, some utilities provide less information than others. For example, the utility supplied with PC Tools is a lot more comprehensive than the program supplied with Lotus 1-2-3.

Some of these utilities also allow you to make a printout of your system configuration. Unless you want to run the utility every time you need to reconfigure your system, it is best to get your system's configuration down on paper. That way you can refer to your printed list when you install or upgrade an application the next time. For example, Fig. 2-3 shows a printout created by WPInfo, a utility supplied with WordPerfect.

Note   If an information utility has no built-in print feature, you can dump the information to a printer with the PrintScreen key, or redirect screen information to a disk file. The DOS redirection switch (>) is used to intercept screen output and save it to disk. For example,

```
WPINFO > INFO.LST
```

```
                WordPerfect Information
Machine Type . . . . . . . . . . .  PC-AT or equivalent
BIOS Make . . . . . . . . . . .     UNKNOWN
BIOS Date . . . . . . . . . .       01/24/91
Processor Type . . . . . . . . .    Intel 80386
Math Coprocessor . . . . . . . .    Present
RAM Memory . . . . . . . . . . .    640K total RAM, 493K available
Expanded Memory . . . . . . . .     None
Keyboard Supported . . . . . . .    Enhanced
Display Type . . . . . . . . . .    VGA
Display Size . . . . . . . . . .    80 columns, 25 rows
File Handles Available to WP . .    20
I/O Ports . . . . . . . . . . .     2 parallel, 3 serial
DOS Version . . . . . . . . . .     3.30
Number of DOS Buffers . . . . .     30
Drive Types . . . . . . . . . .     2 Diskette: A,B
                                    6 Fixed: C,E,F,G,H,I
                                    1 RAM: D
                                    (No Network drives found)
WPCORP Software . . . . . . . .     None
```

Fig. 2-3   WPInfo Utility display.

will redirect output from the inventory utility supplied with WordPerfect to a disk file called INFO.LST. (If you do this, you'll be running the program blind, so you may want to take a trial run and memorize the commands to display the next information page and exit. When the redirected program is terminated, the normal screen display will be restored.)

Microsoft's utility shows information on CPU type, installed peripherals, physical memory, and memory usage. MSD allows you to search anywhere in the first megabyte of memory for a specified ASCII string. MSD's other very useful feature is its display of system interrupt usage. System interrupts are used by all of your installed peripherals. Each peripheral reserves one or more interrupt request lines (IRQs) for internal use. If two peripherals try to grab the same interrupt, conflicts might result. When you add a serial port, mouse, modem, scanner, or network card, you want to avoid duplicating IRQ usage. MSD can show you which interrupts on your system remain unused. This information can be useful to help you properly set up new add-on cards or troubleshoot problems (See Chapter 12). Figure 2-4 shows a typical MSD display.

Notice that this display shows the output for an AT because there are 16 interrupts; a PC display would only show 8 interrupts. Also notice that interrupt 2 is used by the second interrupt controller, so there are only 15 interrupts actually available.

Utilities Included with DOS CHKDSK provides information on system memory and hard disk usage. Unfortunately, it only displays the amount of conventional memory available, not extended or expanded memory. This utility is available with any version of DOS. MS DOS 5.0 adds the ability to display every file on your hard drive as CHKDSK checks them. If you redirect CHKDSK's output to the printer, you can also use this utility to create a listing of your hard drive's contents.

```
Microsoft Diagnostics 1.10.43
┌ IRQ Status ─────────────────────────────────────────────────────────────
   IRQ   Address    Description        Detected            Handled By
   ───   ───────    ───────────        ────────            ──────────
    0   13C1:1831   Timer Click        Yes                 GRAB.EXE
    1   13C1:18CD   Keyboard           Yes                 GRAB.EXE
    2   12B0:0057   Second 8259A       Yes                 DOS System Area
    3   12B0:006F   COM2: COM4:        COM2:               DOS System Area
    4   DBDF:1148   COM1: COM3:        COM1: COM3: Serial Mouse Unknown
    5   12B0:009F   LPT2:              Yes                 DOS System Area
    6   12B0:00B7   Floppy Disk        Yes                 DOS System Area
    7   0070:06F4   LPT1:              Yes                 DOS System Area
    8   12B0:0052   Real-Time Clock    No                  DOS System Area
    9   0BAB:01C4   Redirected IRQ2    Yes                 DOS System Area
   10   12B0:00CF   (Reserved)                             DOS System Area
   11   12B0:00E7   (Reserved)                             DOS System Area
   12   12B0:00FF   (Reserved)                             DOS System Area
   13   0BAA:01D4   Math Coprocessor   No                  DOS System Area
   14   12B0:0117   Fixed Disk         Yes                 DOS System Area
   15   12B0:012F   (Reserved)                             DOS System Area


Press any key to continue...
Hardware IRQ information
```

Fig. 2-4 Microsoft Diagnostics display.

Figure 2-5 shows a typical CHKDSK display.

```
C:\>CHKDSK

Volume JOHN'S DATA created 07-03-1991 3:54p
Volume Serial Number is 16E3-8948

210583552 bytes total disk space
  8470528 bytes in 3 hidden files
   737280 bytes in 173 directories
108785664 bytes in 3868 user files
     8192 bytes in bad sectors
 92581888 bytes available on disk

     4096 bytes in each allocation unit
    51412 total allocation units on disk
    22603 available allocation units on disk

   655360 total bytes memory
   505520 bytes free

C:\>
```

Fig. 2-5 DOS CHKDSK Command display.

DOS 4's MEM utility lists extended and expanded memory information.
DOS 5 greatly enhances the capability of this utility. While CHKDSK provides
only a modicum of information, MEM can provide extensive information about
how individual device drivers and TSRs use memory on your system. As a minimum, MEM can provide you with the amount of conventional, extended, EMS,
and XMS memory on your machine. Figure 2-6 displays the output of MEM
using the /CLASSIFY switch added in DOS 5. (See Chapter 6 for details on
working with MEM.)

```
PCKWIN            736    (  0.7K)       2E0
COMMAND          3392    (  3.3K)       D40
win386           6032    (  5.9K)      1790
MOUSE           11120    ( 10.9K)      2B70
DATAMON         16576    ( 16.2K)      40C0
SUPERPCK        66304    ( 64.8K)     10300
WIN               864    (  0.8K)       360
COMMAND          2832    (  2.8K)       B10
GRAB            23808    ( 23.3K)      5D00
FREE           505744    (493.9K)     7B790

Total  FREE :  505744    (493.9K)


Total bytes available to programs :                505744    (493.9K)
Largest executable program size :                  505520    (493.7K)

    1572864 bytes total EMS memory
     524288 bytes free EMS memory

    8716288 bytes total contiguous extended memory
          0 bytes available contiguous extended memory
    1048576 bytes available XMS memory
            MS-DOS resident in High Memory Area

C:\>
```

Fig. 2-6   DOS 5.0 MEM Command display.

Shareware and Public Domain Utilities   The best of these is Qualitas'
ASQ 1.3. This system checker offers a series of nested menus that guide you to a
variety of information about your computer.

Qualitas' ASQ is both an information utility and an on-line tutorial. It corre-
lates general information on memory management with specific information
about your system. Like MSD, it generates a list of basic system information. Figure 2-7 shows the ASQ main menu.

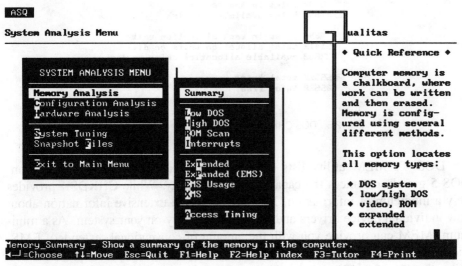

Fig. 2-7   Qualitas' ASQ display. Qualitas, Inc.

ASQ provides more specific information than MSD in the areas of disk drive types and memory usage. For disk drives, ASQ will display the size, number of heads and cylinders, number of sectors per track and BIOS drive type. The memory information is comprehensive. You might see the type and version of EMS and XMS memory managers, number of available pages, and assignment of EMS handles. ASQ also presents an interrupt table, and detailed listing of memory usage by address. You can see how each segment of memory is used, both above and below 640K. At any display, you may access a help menu to explain what the information means, or go into a tutorial lesson about that part of the information summary. Versions of ASQ later than 1.3 are proprietary and work only with Qualitas' commercial products. ASQ 1.3 is in the public domain. It works on any system and can be found on many public bulletin boards.

Other shareware and public domain utilities might display more specialized information. SYSID is a public domain program that lists over 15 pages of configuration information. PMAP and MAPMEM provide information on memory usage and addresses of installed programs, similar to DOS 5's MEM command. HDTEST is a shareware utility for testing and fine tuning hard disks. Figure 2-8 shows a typical HDTEST display. Notice that this utility also serves as a disk diagnosis and repair program.

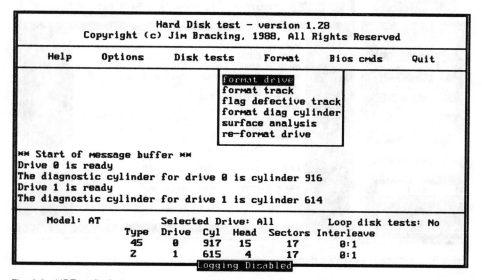

Fig. 2-8   HDTest display.

Performing a software inspection with commercial tools

Commercial inventory utilities might provide information in a more concise and readable form than DOS utilities or shareware (Quarterdeck's Manifest is particularly good in that area). Some commercial programs also include utility options to modify your system's performance.

Manifest Quarterdeck bundles this utility with its 286 and 386 memory management products. Manifest provides the same types of information as MSD or ASQ but in an easier to read, more accessible interface. Manifest also provides more detailed information on how the system interacts with Quarterdeck's memory managers and other programs in general. The pictorial charts make it easy to use as a guide to fine tuning your system's performance.

Manifest also provides a series of timing benchmarks for conventional and expanded memory. The benchmarks can be used to determine whether your system will handle high speed telecommunication and to evaluate the performance of your expanded memory hardware. Manifest can be used to study the effect of any DOS program on your system. It can be configured as a pop-up utility and called while another application is running. Manifest is particularly useful for fine tuning a system to yield the greatest amount of memory for applications in a multitasking environment. Figure 2-9 shows the Manifest main menu. Notice how Manifest's superior menuing and organization make it easy to survey your system at a glance.

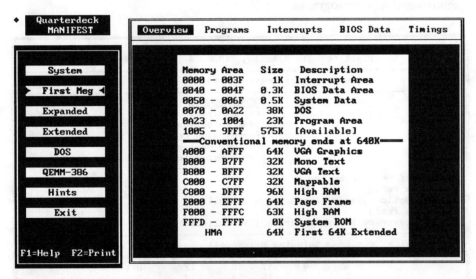

Fig. 2-9   Quarterdeck's Manifest display. Quarterdeck Office Systems.

System Sleuth Pro This package from Dariana Technologies combines information on Memory, Video, Disk, and Hardware usage with a suite of system diagnostics. The included utilities package provides a 386 expanded memory manager and a 286 expanded memory emulator. Sleuth provides a detailed analysis of system IRQ and port usage. It also allows the user to view the contents of all memory within the first megabyte using hexadecimal address location. Figure

2-10 shows a typical System Sleuth Pro display. Notice that this display highlights the IRQ availability screen, a handy feature when you're looking for places to put a new piece of hardware.

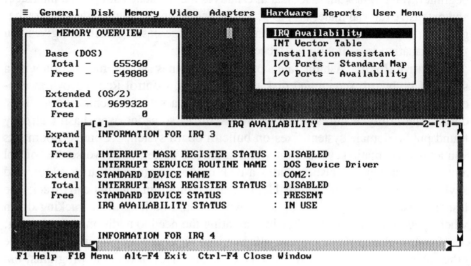

Fig. 2-10   Dariana's System Sleuth display.

System Sleuth Pro also provides detailed information on the contents of upper memory blocks (UMBs). This is the area between 640K and 1M (where DOS normally loads device drivers and ROM code resides). The UMBs are address areas left over after the (drivers load). For example, if you have a VGA display adapter, the last address segment used by the display adapter is C7FFh, and the next address segment used is E800h, then the area between C800h and E7FFh is a UMB. A memory manager like QEMM could use this area to load DOS programs instead of using conventional memory.

The memory manager section under memory information shows the EMS version and says whether your expanded memory card is EMS 4.0 hardware compatible. This is important because so many expanded memory boards claim EMS 4.0 compatibility when they really don't support it fully. Using an incompatible board often leads to problems getting software that supports EMS calls to work properly. One of the most common problems is that you can't get your software to multitask.

Sleuth also obviates the need to open up the case to check dip switch settings on 8088 machine. It shows the current switch settings on an easy to read display. This makes it much easier to check the settings when you need to troubleshoot a problem machine.

The set of system diagnostics provided by Sleuth are fairly extensive. They can be used to verify standard low-level motherboard and disk controller functions or to isolate faulty memory chips.

Documentation for System Sleuth Pro is fairly dry and technical. If you already have familiarity with the low-level workings of your PC, the program can serve as a valuable diagnostic aid. If you're approaching the inventory issue as a beginner, you might want to look at alternatives that present a simplified interface, and extensive tutorial material. ASQ, MSD, and Manifest all provide graphic diagrams of expanded memory usage on a page by page basis. Sleuth Pro gives you the information in a slightly less accessible table.

Control Room Ashton Tate's program combines system information with a series of keyboard, screen and disk utility options. Control Room provides general information about installed peripherals, and a set of benchmarks for hard disks. The utility features might prove useful to someone who hasn't already found public domain system fixes on bulletin board systems. Control Room lets you adjust typematic keyboard rate, and keystroke buffer, and reverse the control and caps lock keys. It also includes a disk cache, command history editor, and keyboard macro creation facility. Notice that the program automatically tracks the last time you monitored your system—which could be helpful in tracking down when specific events occurred or in evaluating the need to additional monitoring.

Control Room provides less information about memory than some of the other utilities. It lists assigned EMS handles, and sizes of resident programs, but not their addresses in RAM. No IRQ listing is provided, and no representation of mappable EMS pages and UMB use. These limitations might make it more difficult to use Control Room to fully inventory your system. They also limit Control Room's usefulness as a troubleshooting aid.

Control Room generates a system report/essay based on what it finds in the check-out phase. The section on hard drive performance is particularly extensive and informative. Control Room's system report can serve as a good novice-level introduction to the internal features of your computer. Its performance benchmarks attempt to rate the performance of your peripherals, memory, and motherboard in comparison with the prevailing hardware standards of the marketplace.

CheckIt This utility emphasizes hardware inventory and testing. It offers some of the features of System Sleuth combined with a more extensive set of system diagnostics. One of the most valuable features of CheckIt is its ability to test all of the RAM on the motherboard and expansion cards, and identify defective chips. It actually shows a picture depicting which chip on the board is defective. This makes replacing defective memory chips a snap. Of course, to make full use of this feature, you must provide CheckIt with the chip layout of your memory boards.

You can also fully test the I/O ports on your machine using CheckIt. You use a special adapter called a *loopback plug* to test not only the electronics for the port but the connector as well. This is useful in situations where the port electronics check out, but replacing the cable connected to the port does not seem to alleviate any hardware problems you might have. Unfortunately, you must purchase the loopback plugs separately or make them yourself. Table 2-1 provides a listing of the connections you will need to make to create your own loopback plugs.

Table 2-1   Loopback plug connections.

Connection 1	Connection 2	Signals
DB9F Serial Loopback		
2	3	Received Data (RD) to Transmitted Data (TD)
7	8	Request to Send (RTS) to Clear to Send (CTS)
6 and 1	4 and 9	Data Set Ready (DSR) and Carrier Detect (CD) to Data Terminal Ready (DTR) and Ring Indicator (RI)
DB25F Serial Loopback		
3	2	Received Data (RD) to Transmitted Data (TD)
4	5	Request to Send (RTS) to Clear to Send (CTS)
6 and 8	20 and 22	Data Set Ready (DSR) and Carrier Detect (CD) to Data Terminal Ready (DTR) and Ring Indicator (RI)
DB25M Parallel Loopback		
11	17	+Busy to Select Input
10	16	-Acknoledge to -Initialize Printer
12	14	+Paper Out to -Autofeed
13	1	+Select to -Strobe
2	15	+Data 0 to -Error

Any electronics store will stock the required parts, which consist of a plug, solder, wire, and a soldering iron. For serial ports, you will need either a DB9F or DB25F plug. For parallel ports, you will need a DB25M plug.

CheckIt also includes a built in virus scanner and a low-level hard disk formatter. It has a user-friendly interface. The results of automatic diagnostics are displayed in an easy-to-read, understandable format. The batch mode of operation allows you to test one or more components a set number of times. This is very useful for finding intermittent problems. Figure 2-11 shows the results of the system board test. Notice that little is left to the user's interpretation.

QAPlus/QAPlus-FE QAPlus is a system diagnostic utility similar to CheckIt in its options and features. QAPlus is a less intuitive tool than CheckIt for novice users, but it provides more in-depth diagnostic testing. This is particularly true in the keyboard, and parallel/serial port procedures. (QAPlus includes both parallel and serial loopback plugs that simulate peripherals attached to the port. You must purchase these plugs separately when using CheckIt.) Figure 2-12 provides an example of the user interface provided by QAPlus.

QAPlus-FE (Field Engineer) is a professional-level version of the package, designed for consultants and repairmen. Additional features of the FE module allow the user to test computers across networks or through a modem. Of all the

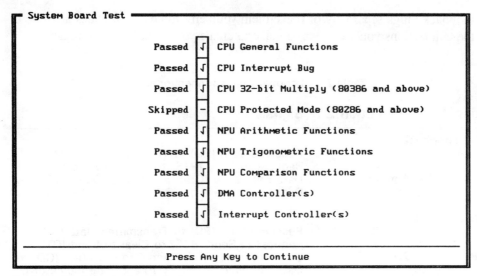

Fig. 2-11 Touchstone's CheckIt display. Touchstone Software.

Fig. 2-12 DiagSoft's QAPlus-FE(TM) Information screen. Produced by DiagSoft, Inc.

packages described here, QAPlus-FE provides the most thorough low-level diagnostics for motherboard and hardware peripherals.

Like CheckIt, QAPlus-FE provides a benchmarking module. QAPlus-FE's PowerMeter is also available as a standalone utility. PowerMeter provides an exhaustive series of CPU, memory, disk drive, and video performance tests.

Conclusion

This chapter has provided you with a list of the questions you should ask to fully inventory your system. There are three areas you need to look at: basic hardware, advanced hardware, and the operating system. This chapter also provides a list of tools commonly used to accomplish your system inventory. Your choice of tools should be determined by the depth of the analysis you want to conduct. The next chapter formally begins our explanation of memory management by examining how DOS uses the first megabyte of memory installed on your PC.

3
CHAPTER

How DOS
uses memory

DOS divides the first megabyte into 640K of conventional memory and a 384K reserved area.

Both the conventional and reserved memory areas are organized into 64K blocks because of the segmentation scheme used by the Intel processor family. The 64K blocks in the reserved memory area are called upper memory blocks (UMBs).

DOS uses the reserved memory area to control fixed hardware functions.

You can examine the contents of the reserved memory area to get information about the configuration of your system.

Some applications borrow memory to improve system performance. These include disk caches, print spoolers and RAM disks (which handle disk intensive functions).

In this chapter, you'll learn how DOS works with the PC hardware to allocate memory.

Viewing the four memory areas

It is essential for anyone wanting to control their PC environment to understand what the four memory areas are, how they affect the machine's capability, and what steps they can take to fully utilize them. This section describes the four memory areas, provides a little history on their development, and talks about some of the problems you will encounter in each area.

Conventional memory—The first 640K

When MS-DOS was first written, it was almost impossible for anyone to foresee the future needs of the personal computer market. MS-DOS 1.0 didn't even allow the user to modify the operating system environment to accommodate new hardware devices. As a result, many devices wouldn't work together. While MS-DOS 2.0 was written to accommodate some hardware expansion, no one could anticipate the requirements that today's machines would place on that potential. As a result, even though MS-DOS was ahead of its time when it was developed, many people find the environment constrained today.

Unlike CP/M, MS-DOS could recognize a full megabyte of address space. IBM's plan was to reserve the top 384K of that megabyte for proprietary ROM. This would leave 640K for user applications, ten times the memory available under CP/M. This was a phenomenal amount of memory when the PC was developed, but it no longer fulfills the needs of many programs.

The first program to challenge the memory boundaries of the original PC was Lotus 1-2-3. 1-2-3 was an innovative successor to VisiCalc. VisiCalc was the first spreadsheet, written originally for the Apple II. It allowed users to enter numeric data in tabular form, transforming the table through a series of "what if" numerical calculations. This spreadsheet concept became so popular that users demanded more and more power from Lotus on the PC.

As a result of these customer demands, Lotus introduced a 128K version of 1-2-3. This, in turn, required a memory expansion of the original 64K IBM PC. Because there was no more expansion potential on the PC motherboard, another way to add memory was found. Third-party vendors stepped in to provide memory upgrades in the form of expansion boards. AST Research and other vendors introduced a series of memory boards to plug into slots on the PC's bus. The original PCs were upgraded first to 256K, then to the full 640K limit anticipated by IBM.

When Lotus 1-2-3 became a big success, other vendors increased the size of their programs. Database and word processing programs added new features. Of course, this started the memory spiral we see today. As users became more adept at using the computer, they wanted their applications to do more. This, in turn, increased memory requirements.

When MS-DOS 1.0 arrived on the market, the user could only run one application at a time. To run another application, you had to unload the first from memory and then load the new one. By the time MS-DOS 2.0 arrived, IBM had asked Microsoft to build in a new capability that would allow the user to load more than one program in memory at once. PRINT.COM was the first "Terminate and Stay Resident" (TSR) program available; it allowed the user to print in the background. Whenever PRINT.COM sensed the processor was idle, it would use that time to send more material to the printer (if necessary). However, because this TSR capability of DOS was undocumented, it took some time for third-party vendors to make use of it.

Borland popularized TSRs with its Sidekick utility. Sidekick was installed and lay dormant until the user pressed a hot key. Then Sidekick would pop up over other applications, offering access to a calculator, desk calendar or notepad. Sidekick was the first popular TSR utility from a third-party vendor. Many more such utilities soon followed from other vendors. Each terminate and stay resident program would load in the system before regular applications like WordStar or 1-2-3. Each TSR consumed an additional portion of the available 640K.

What had been inconceivable in 1981 became a marketplace reality by 1985. 640K simply wasn't enough memory for all of the things users wanted to do with their PCs! The market created pressures that forced vendors to find ways around the 8088/8086 memory limitation. This chapter will show you how hardware and software manufacturers were able to break through the 640K DOS barrier.

PC programmers use memory in 64K pieces called *segments*. This is not surprising because 64K (2^{16} or 65,536 bytes) is the amount of memory that each 8088 segment register can point to.[1]

There are 16 segments in the 1M address range. Sixteen segments $\times$ 64K pointed to by each segment = 1024K (or 1M) total address range, the total memory that DOS and the 8088 CPU can address. As we've already learned, DOS uses the bottom ten 64K segments to run the operating system and your applications. This memory begins at address 0K and ordinarily terminates at 640K. The 0K $-$ 640K user area is referred to as conventional memory.[2]

Reserved memory (Upper memory blocks)

There are six 64K segments between 640K and 1M. Originally, this area was called "Reserved Memory" because IBM reserved it for add-on peripherals and BIOS extensions. In current jargon, you will see the 640K to 1M area referred to

---

[1]Simple PC programs with the .COM extension group all of their code into one 64K segment. Both data and code must fit into one 64K block. More sophisticated programs with the .EXE extension allow code to be stored in more than one segment. Data and code are placed in separate segments.

[2]Some students of PC history say that the traditional 640K limit on user memory was the result of an arbitrary whim. Rumor has it that Don Estridge, the head of the original IBM development team, wanted to allow users a full megabyte. Like Buddy Holly, Estridge was killed in a tragic plane crash. No one knows what would have happened if IBM had heeded his recommendations.

by a new name: "Upper Memory Blocks" or "UMB." Microsoft invented the term UMB when programmers learned how to circumvent IBM's original plan. Faced with a demand for more conventional memory, programmers from Quarterdeck Office Systems figured out how to use the "reserved" area as additional space for user programs. Microsoft eventually incorporated some of these techniques into the DOS operating system (starting with MS-DOS 5.0). For consistency, throughout this book we'll use Microsoft's terminology to name the 640K to 1M region.

The PC uses available memory from "bottom" to "top." When DOS is loaded, memory is filled from the "bottom" at 0K. 640K is the "top" of conventional memory. 1M is the "top" of all memory available to DOS and the 8088 processor (including the ROM BIOS). On 286/386/486 machines, extended memory begins at address 1M. Extended memory is beyond the control of DOS (more on this in the next section). Figure 3-1 provides a look at how the PC uses memory.

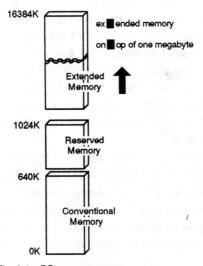

Fig. 3-1   PC memory usage. © 1989, ALL Computers, Inc.

In the original IBM scheme, the whole 640K to 1M area was reserved. Only a small portion of these six 64K blocks was actually used to execute ROM instructions. Hard disk controllers, EGA and VGA graphics cards used up some of the UMB address space, but large areas of the UMB remained unused—address space unclaimed by the BIOS or by add-on peripherals.

When consumers began to feel the 640K memory crunch, PC programmers began to get sneaky. First they invented expanded memory. Initial versions of expanded memory could only be used for data. Later versions allowed the programmer to swap program code in and out of the UMB as well. Programmers eventually discovered that DOS could use the UMB area to run programs and device drivers. (A detailed discussion of how "load high" utilities work is included in Chapter 6.)

The extended memory vs. expanded memory dilemma

A constant complaint from many computer users is that no one can satisfactorily differentiate between Extended and Expanded Memory. This is one whimsical reply from a BBS message:

> Extended memory has real, physical address space assigned to it, starting at 1M. The 80286 can see and hear Extended Memory in its higher mode of consciousness (Protected Mode). Poor old DOS is down in a lower, 8088 mode of consciousness (Real Mode). For DOS, Extended Memory is just a dream. With spirit guidance from enlightened programmers, the 80286 whispers to DOS in its dreams. DOS tosses in its sleep, awakening with the aftertaste of data storage space on its virtual tongue.

Conversely, a local computer humorist once described expanded memory as follows:

> The EMS manager tricks DOS by replacing the brick wall at 640K with a photograph of a brick wall. Then it snatches the photograph away when DOS isn't looking.

Of course, neither of these answers was exceptionally helpful, but they do serve to show the predicament of many users today. The following paragraphs should help you understand the differences between extended and expanded memory.

Extended memory

As mentioned in Chapter 1, the 8088 processor only operates in one mode, Real. The 80286 processor has an addition mode called Protected, and the 80386 processor provides a third mode called Virtual 86. Because DOS was created for the 8088 processor, it always performs its job within real mode. This means that it can only address the 1M of RAM that the 8088 can address. When DOS runs on a 286 or 386 machine, it works the same way. The more powerful processors still run DOS in the 8088's Real Mode. If additional memory is installed on the computer, DOS doesn't see it.

The 80286 and 80386 processors are not limited to 1M of directly addressable RAM. The memory used by protected and virtual 86 mode is extended memory. Both of these modes can directly address memory over 1M. The processor does not require any special hardware or software tricks to use this memory; it only needs an operating system or other software that operates in either protected or virtual 86 mode to use it.

Extended memory can be used for a disk cache, print spooler, or RAM disk. These utilities use extended memory for data storage under DOS, but DOS is completely unaware of the process! They work by switching to protected mode long enough to access extended memory and then switch back to real mode before returning control to DOS. This switching back and forth allows the utility to transfer data between extended memory that DOS *can't* see to conventional memory that DOS *can* see. Because DOS is not active when the transfer takes place, it is completely unaware that anything has happened.

In the PC computing environment, these principles are not limited to data. Operating environments like DESQview and Windows use the same techniques on 386/486 machines to allow you to switch between programs. They operate in extended memory using either protected or virtual 86 mode to access memory and provide the programs space to operate. On 8088 and 286 machines, DESQview uses expanded memory. When the program needs DOS, the operating environment software merely switches back to real mode long enough for DOS to take care of the need.

Expanded memory

Unlike extended memory, the processor cannot directly address expanded memory. It needs special hardware and/or software to make the memory available. Expanded memory does not rely any of the special modes available to 80286 and above machines. As a result, even 8088/8086 machines can use expanded memory.

The expanded memory manager (EMM) is a special device driver you load into memory by placing an entry in CONFIG.SYS. It creates a 64K page frame in the UMB. Many EMMs use the segment starting at D000, but this is not always true. In most cases the EMM splits the page frame into four 16K windows. Each window provides access to a piece of the expanded memory outside the processor's address area. The processor is not aware of where this memory resides but depends on the EMM to keep track of it. The EMM moves these windows around in the expanded memory area as needed by the application using it.

If you have an 8088 or other computer that uses an expanded memory card, you won't see the machine count this memory at bootup. Expanded memory has no DOS-assigned address space. (For details on expanded memory, see Chapter 4.)

Understanding the first megabyte

To build a solid understanding of how DOS uses memory, we turn first to the structure of the first megabyte. Some familiarity with hexadecimal notation will help you to get the maximum benefit from this discussion. (You might want to review the table at the end of Chapter 1.)

The first megabyte addressed by DOS is divided into sixteen 64K segments. The initial ten segments (numbered 0000h to 9000h in hexadecimal) make up conventional memory. (When you add the offsets to these segments, the actual range is 00000h to 9FFFFh.) The next six segments (A000h to F000h) are Upper Memory Blocks or "reserved memory." 0000h is referred to as the "bottom" of conventional memory, while A000h is the "top" of conventional memory. When you first turn the PC on, the system BIOS power on start-up test (POST) routine counts the memory and executes a series of diagnostic self-checks.

After the self-check, a routine called the *bootstrap loader* searches your disk drives for two system files. The first file contains extensions to the ROM BIOS routines and is usually called the DOS BIOS. These extensions became necessary as DOS and the applications running on PCs became more complex. Microsoft added them with MS-DOS 2.0. The second file contains the DOS interrupt routines. These are the routines that actually make up the DOS kernel. While the first file extends the ROM routines to handle the complexity of the hardware installed on your machine, the second file defines DOS itself. Under IBM PC-DOS, the system files are called IBMBIO.COM and IBMDOS.COM. In MS-DOS, they're called IO.SYS and MSDOS.SYS. (You can't see these files when you do a directory of your boot disk because the file attributes are set to hidden/read only.)

Once these two files are loaded, DOS can begin to configure your machine's memory. First, it sets up a small area at the bottom of memory called the Interrupt Vector Table. This table contains addresses to the instructions that DOS must follow each time an interrupt occurs. An interrupt for the computer is the same as an interruption for you. In essence, you get called away from whatever you're currently doing to perform some other task. DOS then creates an area for the DOS BIOS and data. Finally, DOS creates an area for its own interrupt routines.

Once these basic system elements are loaded, DOS can concentrate on the specific configuration for your machine. Device drivers, files and buffers statements in the CONFIG.SYS are loaded into memory next. Finally, COMMAND .COM, the DOS command processor is loaded. COMMAND.COM interprets every command you type at the prompt. It is responsible for loading any application you want to use and also contains some internal commands like DIR. If you search your disk, you will never find DIR.COM or DIR.EXE—this command is provided as part of the command processor. Once DOS loads COMMAND.COM (or any other command processor you specify in CONFIG.SYS), it searches the boot disk for an AUTOEXEC.BAT (automatic execution batch file), and processes any instructions found in it. This completes the boot process.

Generally, the DOS BIOS routines, data area, system files, device drivers, files, buffers, and command processor all fit into the first 64K address segment.[3] The remainder of conventional memory is available to run utilities and application software.

Normally, DOS sets the top of conventional memory at 640K, but you might have seen machines where the DOS CHKDSK program reports a little more than

---

[3]We'll see in Chapter 5 that newer versions of DOS allow device drivers and some of the operating system to be loaded above 640K instead of in the first address segment.

this. Early IBM PCs and the IBM PCjr could show 704K to 736K of conventional memory by adding a supplementary RAM card to the computer bus. This worked because the address segment immediately following the top of conventional memory is traditionally reserved for EGA or VGA video. If your system uses a CGA, MDA or Hercules monochrome card, the video segment at A000H is unused. Appropriate software can annex the "A000" block to conventional memory if RAM is provided on an external card.

Figure 3-2 shows how DOS uses the complete megabyte available for 8088 (Real Mode) computing. Table 3-1 provides a complete listing (map) of the addresses used for the first megabyte.

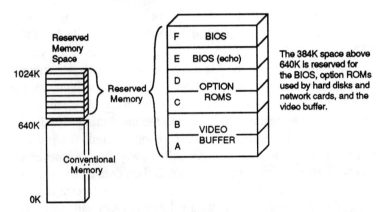

Fig. 3-2   How DOS uses the first megabyte. © 1989, ALL Computers, Inc.

Table 3-1   DOS 1M memory map.

Address	Function
00000 - 9FFFF	Conventional Memory. DOS (IO.SYS, MSDOS.SYS, and COMMAND.COM) loads at the bottom. The remainder of conventional memory is used to execute device drivers, utilities, and application programs.
00000 - 0003F	Hardware/Software* Interrupt Vectors
00000 - 00003	Divide-by-Zero
00004 - 00007	Single Step
00008 - 0000B	Non-Maskable Interrupt (NMI)
0000C - 0000F	Breakpoint
00010 - 00013	Overflow
00014 - 00017	BOUND Exceeded, Print Screen* (Int 5)
00018 - 0001B	Invalid Opcode, Reserved* (Int 6)
0001C - 0001F	Processor Extension Not Available, Reserved* (Int 7)

00020 - 00023	Double Fault, IRQ0 Timer Tick* (Int 8)
00024 - 00027	Segment Overrun, IRQ1 Keyboard* (Int 9)
00028 - 0002B	Invalid Task-State Segment, IRQ2 Cascade from Slave 8259A PIC* (Int Ah)
0002C - 0002F	Segment Not Present, IRQ3 Serial Communications COM2* (Int Bh)
00030 - 00033	Stack Segment Overrun, IRQ4 Serial Communications COM1* (Int Ch)
00034 - 00037	General Protection Fault, IRQ5 Fixed Disk--PC or Parallel Printer LPT2--AT* (Int Dh)
00038 - 0003B	Page Fault, IRQ6 Floppy Disk* (Int Eh)
0003C - 0003F	Reserved, IRQ7 Parallel Printer LPT1 (Int Fh)
00040 - 0007F	BIOS Interrupt Vectors
00040 - 00043	Numeric Co-Processor Error, Video Services* (Int 10h)
00044 - 00047	Equipment Check* (Int 11h)
00044 - 0007F	Reserved
00048 - 0004B	Conventional Memory Size* (Int 12h)
0004C - 0004F	Disk Driver* (Int 13h)
00050 - 00053	Communications Driver* (Int 14h)
00054 - 00057	Cassette Driver--PC, I/O System Extensions--AT* (Int 15h)
00058 - 0005B	Keyboard Driver* (Int 16h)
0005C - 0005F	Printer Driver* (Int 17h)
00060 - 00063	BASIC* (Int 18h)
00064 - 00067	ROM BIOS Bootstrap* (Int 19h)
00068 - 0006B	Time of Day* (Int 1Ah)
0006C - 0006F	Ctrl-Break* (Int 1Bh)
00070 - 00073	ROM BIOS Timer Tick* (Int 1Ch)
00074 - 00077	Video Parameter Table* (Int 1Dh)
00078 - 0007B	Floppy Disk Parameters* (Int 1Eh)
0007C - 0007F	ROM BIOS Font--Characters 80h to FFh* (Int 1Fh)
00080 - 000FF	DOS Interrupt Vectors
00080 - 00083	Terminate Process* (Int 20h)
00084 - 00087	Function Dispatcher* (Int 21h)
00088 - 0008B	Terminate Address* (Int 22h)
0008C - 0008F	Ctrl-C Handler Address* (Int 23h)
00090 - 00093	Critical Error Handler Address* (Int 24h)
00094 - 00097	Absolute Disk Read* (Int 25h)
00098 - 0009B	Absolute Disk Write* (Int 26h)

Table 3-1   Continued

0009C - 0009F	Terminate and Stay Resident* (Int 27h)
00100 - 003FF	Assignable Interrupt Vectors
00100 - 00103	Idle Interrupt* (Int 28h)
00104 - 00107	Reserved (Int 29h)
00108 - 0010B	Network Redirector* (Int 2Ah)
0010C - 0011B	Reserved (Int 2Bh - 2Eh)
0011C - 0011F	Multiplex Interrupt* (Int 2Fh)
00120 - 0015F	Reserved (Int 30h - 3Fh)
00400 - 004FF	ROM BIOS Data Area
00400 - 00416	Hardware Parameters
00417 - 0043D	Keyboard Buffer/Status Bytes
0043E - 00448	Disk Status Bytes
00449 - 00466	Video Display Data
00467 - 00470	Option ROM and Timer Data
00471 - 00487	Additional Status Bytes
00488 - 004FF	Reserved
00500 - 005FF	DOS Data Area
A0000 - BFFFF	Video Display Area
A0000 - BFFFF	EGA 128K/VGA--Reserved for the graphics display. EGA and VGA graphics use this address range to transfer data from host memory to the RAM on your video card. With CGA, MDA, and Hercules adapters, this area is unused. It may be assigned to expanded memory (See Chapter 3) or annexed to conventional memory. This is also true of EGA and VGA display adapters using text mode only.
A0000 - AFFFF	EGA 64K
B0000 - BFFFF	Reserved for text display. Depending on your graphics adapter type, 32K of this area is either unused, or used for RAM fonts or other video purposes.
B0000 - B0FFF	Monochrome 4K
B0000 - B7FFF	EGA Monochrome Emulation 32K
B8000 - BBFFF	CGA 16K
B8000 - BFFFF	EGA CGA Emulation 32K
C0000 - F3FFF	BIOS Extensions
C0000 - CFFFF	Reserved for Video ROM. EGA and VGA graphics cards contain onboard ROM instructions that are plugged into at least the first 32K of this segment (C0000h - C7FFFh). Disk controller and SCSI host adapter cards often contain ROM that is plugged into the second 32K (C8000h - CFFFFh).
D0000 - DFFFF	Reserved for network adapter cards, backup cartridges, and other

	peripherals. On the IBM PCjr, this space was used for software cartridges. On most systems, this 64K block of memory is generally empty. IBM PS/2 systems often use this space as an expanded memory page frame (See Chapter 4).
E0000 - EFFFF	PS/2 Extended BIOS Code. On most non-PS/2 systems this area is usually empty. This generally makes the "E block" a good candidate to hold an expanded memory page frame. On some systems, the E block is used as a special cache area called shadow RAM.
F0000 - FFFFF	Reserved for ROM BIOS. On IBM machines, the first 32K is taken up with ROM instructions for IBM BASIC. Machines that use clone BIOS sets from companies like Phoenix, AMI, Award, DTC, etc., do not contain the BASIC ROM. They may use some of this area for other purposes.
F4000 - FDFFF	System ROM/Stand-Alone BASIC
FE000 - FFFFF	ROM BIOS

---

* *These addresses are assigned by software only. Because they are not hardwired into the machine, these addresses could change at any time.*

Examining the contents of memory

This is a useful thing to learn how to do. If you plan to work with above-640K areas, you may need to troubleshoot hardware/software conflicts. For example, you might want to examine the contents of ROM to determine the manufacturer of your BIOS, video card, or disk controller. Or you might want to examine the contents of RAM to see where a program is resident in memory.

Using Microsoft Diagnostics

The Microsoft Diagnostics utility mentioned in Chapter 2 can examine the contents of memory. Select "Memory Browser" from the Main Menu. The next menu lets you choose an address range to search. If you type in an ASCII string, MSD searches for it throughout the designated address range. You can use this feature to track down BIOS signatures of your hardware or to see whether a device driver has been installed. Figure 3-3 shows MSD set to browse the first megabyte of memory for the text string "MOUSE". Figure 3-4 shows a list of memory addresses that contain the text string "MOUSE".

Using DEBUG

The DEBUG utility included with DOS allows you to examine the contents of any RAM or ROM area within the first megabyte. For example, suppose we want to determine the manufacturer and revision date of a VGA graphics card. From our

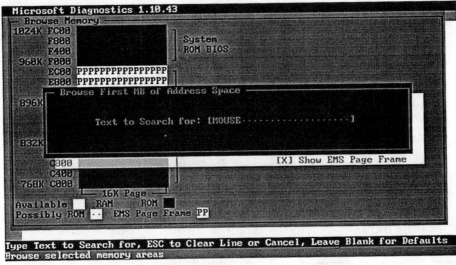

Fig. 3-3   Microsoft Diagnostic Memory Browser.

```
Microsoft Diagnostics 1.10.43
— Memory Browser — Searching Segment D000 for: "MOUSE"
  4000:02EA   Logitech PS2 Mouse
  4000:02FD   MS PS2 Style Mouse
  4000:0326   PS/2 Style Mouse
  4000:28B6   MOUSE
  4000:9CB6   ?,?,??,?
              000-C7FF,[386enh],SYSTEM.INIEmmExclude=C000-CBFF,[386enh],SYSTE
              M.INIEmmExclude=C000-EFFF,[386enh],SYSTEM.INIEmmExclude=?,[386e
              nh],SYSTEM.INIEmmPageFrame=?,[386enh],SYSTEM.INIMouse=?,[386enh
              ],SYSTEM.INIPrograms=com exe bat pif,[windows],W
  4000:9D5E   ?,[386enh],SYSTEM.INIMouse=?,[386enh],SYSTEM.INIPrograms=com ex
              e·bat pif,[windows],WIN.INIFILE:=,[ports],WIN.INIFILES=40, , CO
              NFIG.SYSBUFFERS=20, , CONFIG.SYSDEVICE=?, , CONFIG.SYSMOUSE, ,
              AUTOEXEC.BATSET TEMP=?, , AUTOEXEC.BATSET TMP=?, , AUT
  4000:A036   Mouse=?                                    [386enh]        SYST
              EM.INI
  4000:A1E2   MOUSE                                                      AUTO
              EXEC.BAT
  D000:4547   CMDLINE=e:\qemm\loadhi /r:1 c:\dos\micmouse.com
Press any key to continue.

Press ESC to cancel search
Browse selected memory areas
```

Fig. 3-4   Microsoft Diagnostic Memory Search display.

table in the first part of this chapter, we know that VGA video ROM is usually mapped to address area C000h–C7FFh. The following procedure takes you through the steps required to find this information.

1. At the DOS prompt type DEBUG and press Enter. Once DEBUG loads, you will get the "-" prompt.

2. At the "-" prompt, type D (for display) C000 : 0000. If there is a VGA

card installed in your computer, you will see something like the display in Fig. 3-5.

DEBUG shows the contents of memory in hexadecimal form on the right, and in ASCII on the left. The BIOS signature at address C000 reveals the manufacturer of the graphics card.

```
C:\>debug
-d c000:0000
C000:0000  55 AA 40 EB 5B 54 68 69-73 20 69 73 20 6E 6F 74    U.@.[This is not
C000:0010  20 61 20 70 72 6F 64 75-63 74 20 6F 66 20 49 42     a product of IB
C000:0020  4D 20 20 28 49 42 4D 20-69 73 20 61 20 74 72 61    M  (IBM is a tra
C000:0030  64 65 6D 61 72 6B 20 6F-66 20 49 6E 74 65 72 6E    demark of Intern
C000:0040  61 74 69 6F 6E 61 6C 20-42 75 73 69 6E 65 73 73    ational Business
C000:0050  20 4D 61 63 68 69 6E 65-73 20 43 6F 72 70 2E 29     Machines Corp.)
C000:0060  EB 59 20 2A 20 43 6F 70-79 72 69 67 68 74 28 63    .Y * Copyright(c
C000:0070  29 31 39 38 38 20 50 69-78 65 6C 20 45 6E 67 69    )1988 Pixel Engi
-d
C000:0080  6E 65 65 72 69 6E 67 2C-20 49 6E 63 2E 20 20 30    neering, Inc. 0
C000:0090  31 2F 31 36 2F 39 31 20-56 38 2E 35 45 58 01 00    1/16/91 V8.5EX..
C000:00A0  68 00 C0 00 00 00 00 00-00 00 00 00 00 00 00 BD    h..............
C000:00B0  00 00 C0 00 00 00 00 00-00 00 00 EB 3E 1A 00 D7    ............>...
C000:00C0  00 00 C0 00 00 00 00 00-00 00 00 00 00 00 00 00    ................
C000:00D0  00 00 00 00 00 00 00 10-01 08 00 00 00 00 01 00    ................
C000:00E0  02 02 01 00 04 04 01 00-05 02 05 00 06 01 06 05    ................
C000:00F0  06 00 08 01 08 00 07 02-07 06 07 BA C3 03 B0 01    ................
-
```

Fig. 3-5 Debug Memory Dump.

Strategies for better program performance

Now that you know the basics about DOS and the first megabyte, let's put that knowledge to work with some strategies for improving the performance of your application software.

If you work with large documents or database files, you might have noticed that your system's performance becomes sluggish: it might take an annoying amount of time to search and replace text, recalculate a spreadsheet, or save a file. When you work with large files, the application reads and writes information to disk more frequently—hence the slowdown in performance. High-powered DOS applications can actually manipulate data files larger than available conventional memory by swapping unused portions of the document to temporary files on the hard disk.

Printing large documents can also slow the system down. Some applications make you wait while the file is printed. Others allow you to continue working but slow down considerably while the document is being printed. The first group devotes the entire capacity of your computer to the problem of printing. This wastes your time and computer resources. The second group allows you to use the computer while it prints in the background but uses some of the computer's resources to do so, which is why the application seems to bog down. Disk caches and print spoolers are software tools designed to solve these problems. They can dramatically improve your system's performance while still providing the benefits of background processing.

A disk cache sets aside a portion of RAM to store information an application reads frequently from disk. The program is redirected to the RAM cache each time it tries to read the information from disk. In most cases, the disk cache will use either expanded or extended memory. However, some disk cache programs will also allow you to set aside conventional memory. In most cases, using conventional memory is self-defeating because it's a lack of memory that caused some of the slow down in the first place.

A good disk cache can make an old, slow hard disk perform like a fast new one. If your system has expanded or extended memory, you can create a 512K to 1M disk cache without sacrificing large amounts of conventional memory. Of course, the benefit you receive from the disk cache is dependent on the applications you use. If the application seldom requests the same information from disk, the amount of performance boost you'll receive from the disk cache is minimal.

A print spooler makes applications seem to print large documents almost instantaneously. Actually, the printer information is dumped to a RAM cache area in extended or expanded memory. (As with the disk cache, some print spoolers will use conventional memory, but this is usually self-defeating. In addition, some print spoolers will swap information to the hard drive. This results in slower spooling to the printer, but still allows you to work in the printing application instead of having to wait for the job to finish.) When the print spooler (a TSR) detects that the processor is idle, it uses that time to send information to the printer. The document continues to "spool" to the printer in the background as you run your other programs in the foreground. Many current word processors now have some limited spooling capacity built-in, allowing you to print in the background without loading a TSR.

A RAM disk is a "virtual" disk drive created in memory. Loading programs from a RAM disk is another way to make them run faster. When you copy files to a RAM disk or use it execute programs, the RAM disk behaves just like a real disk drive. The difference is that DOS can read data from a RAM disk almost instantaneously.

Disk caches

A disk cache selectively remembers information that your programs frequently request. The cache stores bits and pieces of information, unlike a RAM disk, which stores whole files. The usefulness of a disk cache varies according to the type of program and the size of the cache. Some programs tend to jump around, accessing lots of different pieces of information. Other programs use the same information over and over. The success of the disk cache depends on its ability to guess which information the program will want next, and keep that information ready.

Most disk caches also "pre-fetch" data from disk. If you optimize your hard drive on a fairly regular basis, the information for a particular program is stored in contiguous clusters (storage areas on disk). Theoretically, if the disk cache reads four or five contiguous clusters into memory instead of just the one requested, then the next piece of data should already be in the cache when the program requests it.

Disk cache efficiency can be measured by a factor called "hit rate." The cache program might keep an internal record of how many times the program asks for information vs. how many times the information was ready for the program in RAM. Naturally, the larger the size of the disk cache, the more information is likely to be available for a requesting program.

A 512K disk cache will improve DOS's efficiency at loading small programs and saving files. A 1M or 2M cache is extremely useful with complex applications that work with large data files. A desktop publishing or graphic drawing program will redraw the screen much more rapidly if it doesn't have to keep rereading the file after each change. If your database or spreadsheet programs don't automatically use extended or expanded memory, they, too, will benefit from a large disk cache.

Of course, seeing is believing. Figure 3-6 shows the performance of a hard drive without any disk cache installed.

```
            Multisoft's BenchPCK.    Version 1.20.
          Copyright 1988, 1991, Multisoft Corporation.
                Small (256 Kb) file size test

                                          512 records       64 records
                                          of 512 bytes.     of 4096 bytes.
                                          Avg of 1 pass.    Avg of 1 pass.
                                          Seconds           Seconds
Creating test file.                         9.56              2.31
Sequentially writing records to test file.  9.12              2.09
Sequentially reading records from test file. 9.17             2.14
Randomly writing records to test file.      7.47              1.92
Randomly reading records from test file.    7.41              1.87
Closing and deleting test file.             0.27              0.11
                                          ----------        ----------
Total                                       43.01             10.44
Combined Total                                       53.44


Test currently running on drive C.
Super PC-Kwik is not installed.
```

Fig. 3-6   Multisoft's Performance Benchmark—No disk cache. Multisoft Corporation.

Figure 3-7 shows the performance on the same hard drive with Multisoft's SuperPCKwik installed. Notice the vast improvement in the benchmark speed. The hard drive runs an impressive 6.36 times faster with the disk cache than without.

```
            Multisoft's BenchPCK.    Version 1.20.
        Copyright 1988, 1991, Multisoft Corporation.
            Small (256 Kb) file size test

                                        512 records        64 records
                                        of 512 bytes.      of 4096 bytes.
                                        Avg of 1 pass.     Avg of 1 pass.
                                        Seconds            Seconds
Creating test file.                        0.44               0.11
Sequentially writing records to test file. 0.55               0.05
Sequentially reading records from test file. 0.44             0.11
Randomly writing records to test file.     5.77               0.16
Randomly reading records from test file.   0.66               0.11
Closing and deleting test file.            0.00               0.00
                                        ----------         ----------
Total                                      7.85               0.55
Combined Total                                  8.40

Test currently running on drive C.
Super PC-Kwik is installed with a 2048K byte Extended memory cache buffer.
The following parameters are in effect: /B+,/D+,/H+,/O+,/Q-,/T+,/U+,/W+
```

Fig. 3-7   Multisoft's Performance Benchmark—Super PC-Kwik disk cache installed. Multisoft Corporation.

Figure 3-8 shows the results using Hyperware's Hyperdisk. This shows that not all disk cache programs are created equal. The Hyperdisk results are 2.68 times faster than using SuperPCKwick and 17.07 times faster than no disk cache at all.

```
            Multisoft's BenchPCK.    Version 1.20.
        Copyright 1988, 1991, Multisoft Corporation.
            Small (256 Kb) file size test

                                        512 records        64 records
                                        of 512 bytes.      of 4096 bytes.
                                        Avg of 1 pass.     Avg of 1 pass.
                                        Seconds            Seconds
Creating test file.                        0.49               0.05
Sequentially writing records to test file. 0.44               0.11
Sequentially reading records from test file. 0.38             0.11
Randomly writing records to test file.     0.66               0.11
Randomly reading records from test file.   0.66               0.11
Closing and deleting test file.            0.00               0.00
                                        ----------         ----------
Total                                      2.64               0.49
Combined Total                                  3.13

Test currently running on drive C.
Hyperdisk Cache installed with buffer of 2048K.
```

Fig. 3-8   Multisoft's Performance Benchmark—Hyperware's Hyperdisk disk cache installed. Multisoft Corporation.

Staged vs. write-through caching

All disk caches store information when an application attempts to read a disk drive. Some have the added capability to anticipate what the program will want to write to disk. "Staged-write" caches allow you to save documents instantaneously while you continue to enter keyboard input. The "saved" information is written to disk on delay. The cache holds the data in RAM until the system is idle. When the system is idle, then the saved information gets written to disk.

"Staged-write" caches involve a certain user risk. The information stored in the cache and the information on the disk drive are supposed to be identical. If the power goes out or you turn off your machine before the disk cache writes the information to disk, then that information is lost. In addition, the information that is stored on disk might become corrupted or unusable. For example, database records and CAD files are very susceptible to damage. (A staged write cache can usually be set up to force the write operation to conclude within a designated number of seconds).

Write-through caching is slower, but safer in many cases. The cache forces information to be saved to disk as soon as the program dumps it into the cache. The choice is up to you of course. A write-through cache will cost you some speed, but the staged-write cache may pose too great a threat to some types of data.

Disk-caching programs

Disk caches are versatile utilities that can be configured in conventional, extended, or expanded memory. The following paragraphs provide you with examples of some of the more popular programs on the market.

Smartdrive This is a utility bundled with Microsoft Windows, also available with MS-DOS 4.0 and 5.0. Smartdrive is a write-through cache that cannot be adjusted or removed from memory without rebooting your computer. Smartdrive is a fast performer on disk reads, and is designed to cooperate with Microsoft Windows. The current version of Smartdrive can only be used safely with hard disks limited to 80M (1024 cylinder) storage capacity. (Microsoft upgraded the newer version of Smartdrive bundled with Windows 3.1 to include write caching. This new version is considerably faster than the versions included with MS-DOS 5.0 and Windows 3.0.)

Hyperdisk Hyperdisk is a shareware program available on many public bulletin board systems. We have included it in the memory utilities diskette that accompanies this book. (A fuller featured version with printed manual is supplied when you register.) Hyperdisk allows the cache to be loaded from either the AUTOEXEC.BAT or CONFIG.SYS, and lets the user downsize it, or adjust it from the command line. Staged write or write-through options can be toggled with user hot keys. Hyperdisk is also written to be compatible with third-party disk partitioning schemes like Ontrack's Disk Manager and Storage Dimensions' Speedstor. Figure 3-9 shows Hyperdisk's startup display.

Super PC-Kwik This commercial cache program is sold as a stand-alone utility or as part of a package that includes a print spooler, RAM disk, and screen accelerator. The cache, print spooler and RAM disk can be set up to share mem-

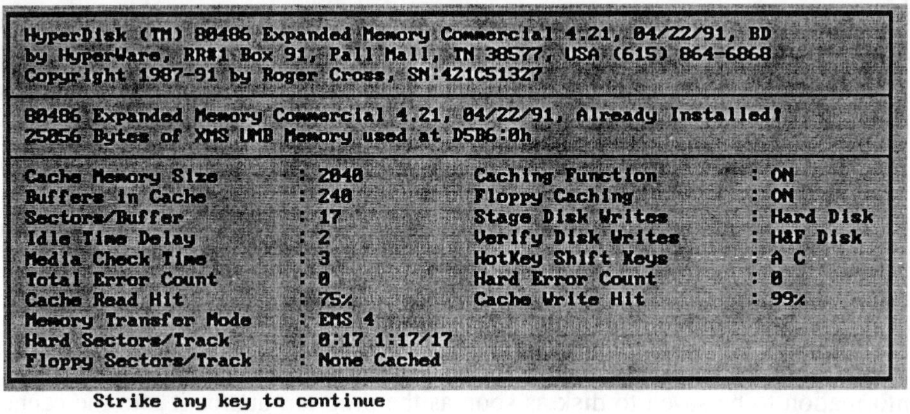

```
HyperDisk (TM) 80486 Expanded Memory Commercial 4.21, 04/22/91, BD
by HyperWare, RR#1 Box 91, Pall Mall, TN 38577, USA (615) 864-6868
Copyright 1987-91 by Roger Cross, SN:421CS1327

80486 Expanded Memory Commercial 4.21, 04/22/91, Already Installed!
25856 Bytes of XMS UMB Memory used at D5B6:0h

Cache Memory Size        : 2048        Caching Function      : ON
Buffers in Cache         : 240         Floppy Caching        : ON
Sectors/Buffer           : 17          Stage Disk Writes     : Hard Disk
Idle Time Delay          : 2           Verify Disk Writes    : H&F Disk
Media Check Time         : 3           HotKey Shift Keys     : A C
Total Error Count        : 0           Hard Error Count      : 0
Cache Read Hit           : 75%         Cache Write Hit       : 99%
Memory Transfer Mode     : EMS 4
Hard Sectors/Track       : 0:17 1:17/17
Floppy Sectors/Track     : None Cached

            Strike any key to continue
```

Fig. 3-9 Hyperdisk Startup screen.

ory dynamically with one another. The RAM disk or print spooler will borrow memory from the cache when extra memory is needed, and return the memory to the cache when idle. Like Hyperdisk, PC-Kwik has a number of fine tuning options. The cache may be turned on or off, toggled for PowerWrite or write-through caching, or you may adjust the allocated buffer size. An OEM version of Super PC-Kwik (just the disk cache) is now bundled with Digital Research's DR DOS 6.0. There is also a special version for Windows users that includes a Windows compatible performance monitor.

Multipurpose Packages PCtools, The Norton Utilities, and the Mace Utilities are multi-utility packages that include a disk cache as one user option. In general, these caches provide slightly less flexibility than dedicated packages, but many people use them and find them satisfactory.

Hardware caching

Some disk controller cards contain built-in RAM to allow for caching. This RAM does not subtract from your available pool of conventional and extended memory. Hardware caching can deliver faster performance than the software caches we examined earlier, but a hardware cache might not be able to work with more than one disk drive at a time. The software caches might cover all of your hard disks as well as floppy drives. (See appendix for a list of manufacturers of controller cards that include hardware caching.)

Using DOS buffers

The DOS BUFFERS command is a primitive type of cache built into the operating system. DOS uses the allocated RAM buffer space in the course of normal disk access. Each DOS buffer uses about 512 bytes of conventional memory. Depending on your PC configuration and DOS version, the default number of buffers can vary from 3 to 15. The number of buffers available to DOS can be specified with a line in CONFIG.SYS; BUFFERS = 20 is considered sufficient on most systems. If your system also uses a disk cache, you might want to decrease the number of buffers to eliminate redundancy. Consult the documentation of your disk cache software for a suggested minimum buffer setting.

Unfortunately, using too many DOS buffers can actually decrease system performance. Because DOS does not provide the complex cache search techniques used by disk caching programs, it might actually spend more time searching the cache for a piece of information than it would take to read the data from disk. You might want to experiment with the number of buffers you use, but in most cases you will not want above 50 with versions of DOS 4.0 and below, or 60 with versions of DOS 5.0 and above.

DOS 4.x and 5.0 will also let you place buffers above 640K with 386 machines or systems that use expanded memory. Some third-party memory managers allow you to do this with DOS 3.0 – 3.3. (More on this in Chapters 6 & 7.)

MS DOS 4.x and 5.0 include an added option with the BUFFERS statement. The "lookahead" feature allows your PC to read more than one sector from disk at a time. The importance of lookahead was discussed in the previous section. To set the number of buffers to 15 with a lookahead of 2 sectors, your CONFIG.SYS statement would read BUFFERS = 15 , 2.

Note   Some programs might have problems with the lookahead parameter. If you experience unusual results or see strange error messages on the screen, you might want to remove it from the buffers statement.

Print spoolers

Some applications have built-in print spooling. When you send a document to the printer, the application just blinks for a second and lets you to continue to work. Other applications put up a "Please Wait" message on the screen and force you to sit idle while you print. Third-party print spoolers take the load off your application. The print job is stored in a portion of RAM or as a temporary disk file. The spooler sends the job to the printer in periodic bursts.

When you use a dedicated print spooler, you can continue working in the program that originally contained the document, or you can quit that program and start a different one. This is an advantage over using the built-in print spooler of an application because you must wait for the document to finish printing before you can leave the application. A dedicated spooler continues to work in the "background" no matter what you do in the "foreground." Print spooling is our first primitive example of multitasking. It works on all PC types. When we say that print spooling runs in the "background," this means the spooler continues to send data to the printer independently of what you do at the keyboard, or of which program is running in the "foreground." The "foreground" application is the program that controls the screen and accepts keyboard input.

A good print spooler might also allow you to queue up a series of documents, stop printing one, and rush print another. Some spoolers are controlled by instructions issued from the DOS command line, while others let you pop up a control window over your current application.

Print spooler programs

Print spoolers are versatile utilities that can be configured in conventional, extended, or expanded memory. The following paragraphs provide you with examples of some of the more popular programs on the market.

DMP   This is a simple but useful shareware product that you'll find on the utilities diskette included with this book. DMP can set up print buffers in conventional, extended, or expanded memory. The spooler can intercept print requests to either parallel or serial ports, and also use hard disk space to store the spool data. DMP uses 16K of conventional memory and is compatible with both Windows and DESQview.

Printcache 2.2   This commercial program is the successor to LaserTorq. It works with Windows and DESQview and uses 5−9K of conventional memory. Printcache has the ability to "squeeze" graphics documents to allow full-page graphics to print at 300 dpi on HP's Laserjet II series, even when the printer contains only 512K of printer memory. Normally the HP printers must have 1M or more internally installed to allow printing of full-page graphics.

Super PC-Kwik   The Super PC-Kwik spooler is included as part of Multisoft's PowerPak, which includes the disk cache discussed previously and a RAM disk utility as well. This spooler works well under both Windows and DESQview. You may pop up the spooler's control panel over any text-based application, monitor a print job, cancel, or rearrange jobs in the printing queue. This spooler may use conventional, extended, or expanded memory. It will not swap files to disk, as DMP will, but it may borrow unused RAM from the PC-Kwik disk cache.

SuperPrint   This is a utility for printing with Windows 2.1 or Windows 3 applications. It replaces Windows' built-in Print Manager. SuperPrint allows Windows documents to print up to three times faster than normal, and includes a set of 22 scaleable typefaces, as well. SuperPrint works only with HP Laserjet printers.

Hardware print buffers

As with disk caching, you may also buy a dedicated hardware print buffer. A hardware print buffer can direct output from more than one computer and/or convert serial output to parallel output. (Parallel output is carried to the printer much more rapidly than serial output). See the appendix for a list of hardware print buffer products.

RAM disks

A third use for memory is to set up a portion of RAM to emulate a disk drive. This technique is useful for slow-moving applications that must constantly access program overlays on disk or that generate temporary files. (When a DOS program is too large to be completely contained in memory, it may be divided up into separate modules. DOS reads these overlay modules as new program functions are invoked by the user. Some programs create temporary files to store data that won't fit in memory or as a means of protecting data during file manipulations.) A RAM disk sets up an electronic storage area in memory which emulates an actual disk drive. RAM disks may be established in conventional, extended, or expanded memory. Their only drawback is that they consume a lot of memory, and they are temporary. When you turn off the computer, or should there be an unexpected power failure, all information stored on the RAM disk is lost. (Some hardware versions of RAM disks use a battery backup to retain the information you place on them when power is removed from the PC.)

RAM disks are created in DOS through device drivers loaded in the CON FIG.SYS and/or commands issued from the command line. More sophisticated software lets you dynamically adjust the size of the RAM disk without rebooting. In addition, some applications allow you to control the address in memory where the RAM disk installs. When a RAM disk runs in extended memory, it is useful to be able to control the installation address to avoid conflicts with other extended memory drivers.

Using your RAM disk

Once you've created your RAM disk, it will have its own drive letter under DOS. This will usually be one higher than your last hard drive. If you have two floppy drives and two hard disk partitions installed, your RAM disk will be designated drive E.

To copy your program files to the RAM disk, set up a batch file. For example, if you want to run WordStar from a RAM disk, you can create the following batch file:

```
CD \WS
COPY WS*.* E:
COPY *.PDF E:
E:
WS
```

To use some of WordStar's advanced, add-in functions, you need to copy other WordStar-related files to the RAM disk. If your RAM disk is large enough, you can simply make the batch file transfer everything in the WordStar directory.

You may also use a RAM disk as just a storage area for your data files. You might write the following batch file to copy a dBASE work file to the RAM disk and start the database program:

```
CD \DBIII\CLIENTS
COPY %1 E:
CD \DBIII
DBASE %1
COPY E:\%1 C:\DBIII\CLIENTS
```

The last line of the batch file ensures that your work file will be recopied to the hard disk when you exit dBASE—otherwise you might turn off the power or reboot the machine and lose it.

RAM disk programs

The following paragraphs describe some of the more popular RAM programs on the market.

VDISK/RAMdrive   PC-DOS and MS-DOS versions 3 and above include a simple RAM disk driver. The file is called VDISK.SYS in PC DOS and RAM DRIVE.SYS in MS DOS. The driver is placed in CONFIG.SYS along with designated disk size and optional loading in extended or expanded memory. You may also specify the number of files and directories that can be created in the RAM disk's root directory and the disk sector size. Default values are 64 directory entries and 512 byte sector size. An entry of DEVICE = RAMDISK.SYS 512 512 128 /E in your CONFIG.SYS file creates a RAM disk of 512K using 512 byte sectors with a maximum of 128 entries in the root directory. The /E parameter creates the RAM disk in extended memory.

Nifty James RAM Disk   This reliable shareware utility (included on the bundled utilities disk) establishes a RAM disk of any user-designated size in extended or expanded memory. It can coexist with temperamental applications like Windows.

Multisoft Powerpak   The RAM disk is one of the included utilities in Multisoft's PC-Kwik PowerPak. The Powerpak RAM disk can be configured in conventional, extended, or expanded memory. It coexists with the disk cache, sharing the memory allocated to the PC-Kwik disk cache. The RAM disk dynamically reallocates its memory usage when other applications want to use the disk cache or print spooler.

Disk compression utilities

Disk compression utilities, technically, are not memory management tools. Disk compression software is designed to conserve hard disk storage space rather than

RAM. Still, it might be useful to know that packages like STACKER and SUPERSTOR might effectively double the amount of storage space available on any hard disk. These utilities apply special algorithms to files on your hard disk, squeezing them into a compressed format. When you want to execute a program, read a document or copy a file, the file is automatically decompressed. This technique is similar to applying an archive utility like PKZIP or ARC to each file on the disk, except that compression and decompression are automatic and transparent to the user. An OEM version of SuperStor is currently bundled with DR-DOS, v.6. Figure 3-10 shows the SuperStor statistics screen. Notice that we are able to store 33M of data on a 21M hard drive.

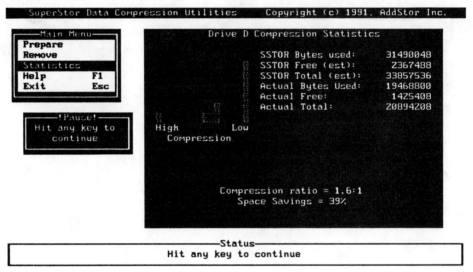

Fig. 3-10   SuperStor display.

Hardware RAM disks

This is also a special category of RAM disk that you can install on your machine. It usually consists of a card filled with conventional RAM or a new type of ROM called Flash ROM. The cards that use standard RAM include a battery to save the data after you remove power from the system. The Flash ROM cards use a special type of chip that you can write to like RAM but that retains its contents after you remove power like ROM. In both cases, the drive looks just like a standard drive, and in some cases you don't have to include any special drivers to use one. Unlike a standard RAM drive, you never need to include a RAM disk driver in your CONFIG.SYS when using a hardware RAM disk.

Conclusion

This chapter has given you a taste of the performance improvements you can have with clever use of memory. The utilities discussed here use extended or expanded memory to give your PC a real lift. The next chapter will provide an overview of how extended and expanded memory work and show you some other uses for memory "beyond 640K."

4
CHAPTER

Extended and expanded memory

Extended memory is RAM above 1M installed on 80286/80386/80486 machines.

Expanded memory is "extra" RAM added to any PC. It is swapped from an unaddressable area of memory into a fixed block of addresses within the reserved memory area (usually between segments C800h to EFFFh).

Expanded memory (EMS 4.0) allows DOS to multitask a series of applications. Some expanded memory managers (EMMs) claim v4.0 compatibility but do not fully implement it. The same can be said for some expanded memory boards.

DOS Extender technology allows applications to break the 640K barrier by using extended memory.

XMS (extended memory specification), Microsoft's new standard for managing extended memory, gives 80286/386/486 machines added functionality.

Methods of easing memory crunch

In the last chapter, we learned that it's possible to circumvent DOS's 640K memory limitation. In this chapter, we begin our examination of the techniques used to do it. Three different methods allow DOS applications to break the 640K barrier:

- Expanded memory
- DOS Extenders
- XMS (Microsoft's Extended Memory Specification)

Expanded memory

Expanded memory was the first technique used to circumvent the 640K limitation. The first version appeared in 1985, while the current version was finalized in 1986. You can use expanded memory on any PC type. All it does is funnel data from an unaddressable memory area into the first megabyte. Expanded memory allows DOS to multitask without ever addressing more than 1M at one time.

DOS extenders

DOS extenders were developed next (around 1988). DOS extenders are special drivers that load applications larger than 640K from DOS and subsequently run in protected mode. Whenever the application requires a DOS service, the extender transfers the required data to the conventional memory area and runs in real mode until the request is satisfied. It then switches back to protected mode to enable the application to address the larger memory space.

We saw in Chapter 1 that 80286 computers can address 16M of extended memory, while 80386/80486 computers can address 4G (gigabytes) of extended memory. Depending on the extender you use, you might or might not be able to use all this addressing capability. No matter which extender you use, DOS (running in real mode) sees only 1M. DOS extenders let programs like 1-2-3, release 3 and AutoCad run code in more than 640K. DOS extenders shift the 80286/386/486 processor back and forth between real mode and protected mode without interrupting the client application. DOS extender applications must be specially written to cooperate with DOS extender drivers.

Extended memory specification

Microsoft's extended memory specification (XMS) was developed in 1989–1990 in collaboration with Intel, AST Research, and Lotus Corp. XMS borrows techniques from the DOS Extenders to provide more generic extended memory management. In addition to Microsoft's well-known Windows 3, a number of other applications now take advantage of XMS memory to load all or part of themselves above 640K.

Until the release of Microsoft's Windows 3, extended memory had little generic value for most PC users. Disk caches, print spoolers and RAM disks made use of it as storage area. Some programs used DOS extenders to run code outside the 640K area. However, this didn't affect programs as a whole because DOS, the real mode operating system, could not use extended memory to run programs.

Differences in expanded memory

Expanded memory first appeared in 1985 as a means to bypass the DOS address limitations. This initial version allowed you to place data in the expanded memory area, but not code. In 1985, the buying public was putting considerable pressure on software manufacturers to find more memory for spreadsheet and database applications. This meant running code in the expanded memory area. Lotus 1-2-3 and dBASE III users were creating larger and larger data files. The applications handled large files by swapping information to the hard disk, a slow and unwieldy procedure. If the user paged down in a spreadsheet or address list, the application would pause to read the next page from disk.

To make things worse, other software manufacturers were adding to the memory crunch with terminate-and-stay-resident menu shells and file management utilities. Users could "pop up" these TSRs on the screen over other applications by pressing a hot key. But TSRs consumed another 64K to 128K of conventional memory, leaving even less for 1-2-3, dBASE III, or AutoCad.

640K was no longer sufficient to handle the PC work load. Although IBM intended the 640K-to-1M area be reserved for ROM instructions, nothing prevented programmers from using part of "reserved memory" to address RAM, instead. Under pressure from the marketplace for more memory, that's what they did.

The expanded memory dBASE 3.0

Lotus and Intel announced EMS 3.0 at the Spring COMDEX in 1985. This was a specification designed to head off the rapid demise of 8088/8086 machines. However, this specification was short lived because Microsoft almost immediately announced that it would support EMS in the fall of 1985. Microsoft further promised to enhance Windows to use the memory made available by EMS hardware and software.

The LIM 3.2 expanded memory specification

The LIM expanded memory standard, v3.2, was a joint effort of three companies, Lotus, Intel, and Microsoft. LIM 3.2 memory allowed 1-2-3, Symphony, dBASE III, and Framework to hold data files larger than the amount of space left over in the 640K area after DOS and the application were loaded. Before expanded memory was introduced, the only way to manipulate large spreadsheets was to swap portions to and from disk. Under LIM 3.2, memory cards containing from 64K to 8M of RAM could be added using expansion slots on the PC's bus. This RAM was unaddressable by DOS, only the EMM could address it and make it available to DOS. All PCs (including 8088 machines) could use LIM 3.2 memory to ferry information to applications from the expanded memory card.

LIM 3.2 memory transferred information to DOS through a 64K memory block called the EMS pageframe. The pageframe was placed in reserved memory between 640K and 1M. Normally, this pageframe appeared at segment D000h, but other pageframe segments could be used as well.

The LIM 3.2 EMM could tag and stash 16K chunks of data, shipping them to the "warehouse" of extra RAM on the expanded memory card. When an application claimed the data, the pageframe fetched it back, 16K at a time. Storing data in expanded memory was similar to storing it on a RAM disk; applications could retrieve the information without time consuming hard disk access. Figure 4-1 provides an illustration of how the LIM 3.2 EMM ferries data between expanded memory and DOS using the EMS pageframe.

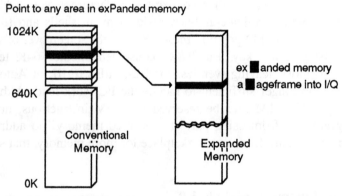

Fig. 4-1   How LIM 3.2 works. © 1989, ALL Computers, Inc.

The Enhanced Expanded Memory Specification (EEMS)

The LIM 3.2 standard (sometimes called Expanded Memory Specification, v3.2) was fine for storing spreadsheets, but PC users wanted even more power from their machines. They wanted memory to multitask DOS applications. Unfortunately, LIM 3.2 provided neither the hardware basis, nor the software interface to multitask applications. LIM 3.2 memory could not be used to actually run program code. This annoying limitation of LIM/EMS v3.2 was tied to the fact that DOS could not directly access the expanded memory hardware, only the EMM was allowed to do that. In addition, the memory mapping hardware limited where the pageframe could be placed and how big each page could be.

Sophisticated PC users wanted features more advanced than TSR utilities. Mainframe and minicomputers could provide "windowed" environments where two or more programs ran concurrently on separate parts of the screen. PC users wanted to do the same thing.

In 1986, AST Research Corporation, QUADRAM Corporation, and Ashton-Tate added some enhancements to the Lotus-Intel-Microsoft specification. Their improved standard (Enhanced Expanded Memory Specification) was a watershed breakthrough in the PC industry.

EEMS revised the hardware functions of memory cards to improve the software standard. With EEMS, areas larger than 64K could be used as a pageframe. The pageframe could be mapped below 640K as well as between 640K and 1M. This permitted entire programs to run in enhanced expanded memory.

When AST Research's EEMS cards were combined with Quarterdeck's DESQview, PCs had the ability to multitask a number of applications, exceeding 640K. A communication program could download files while a spreadsheet was recalculated. The user could type a document in a word processor and format a floppy diskette concurrently.

The LIM 4.0 expanded memory specification

Lotus, Intel and Microsoft eventually recognized the superiority of EEMS to LIM 3.2. In 1987 the L-I-M partners collaborated with AST Research, QUADRAM, and Ashton Tate to define a new, joint standard called EMS 4.0. EMS 4.0 superseded AST's EEMS by allowing the memory manager to control 32M of expanded memory instead of 8. It incorporated many—but not all—the features provided by EEMS. Improvements of EMS 4.0 over EMS 3.2 included:

- Ability to hold larger spreadsheets and databases in memory.
- Ability to address more than 64K at a time (although the pageframe is still 64K).
- Ability to map memory both above and below 640K.

How EMS 4.0 works

There are many differences between EMS 4.0 and its predecessors. Under EMS 4.0, allocated expanded memory may be mapped as conventional memory. The memory is usually divided up into 16K segments called "standard pages." However, a program may use pages other than the standard 16K size. These pages are referred to as "raw pages." Obviously, determining the number of pages of memory available is no longer a matter of simply knowing how many 16K segments are installed, so EMS 4.0 also provides methods of determining the number of raw and standard pages.

Instead of only providing access to expanded memory through the pageframe (as LIM 3.2 memory does), any number of standard or raw pages can be mapped between conventional memory and the RAM set aside for EMS. In addition, EMS 4.0 provides methods for moving memory regions between conventional and expanded memory. This makes it possible to execute multiple programs up to the full 640K address range. The EMS manager addresses both the conventional and expanded memory storage area. The EMS manager marks a chunk of EMS storage memory for each program and assigns it an "EMS handle" for DOS. Expanded memory works like a "lazy susan" tray. Each separate serving area of the tray contains a group of pages loaded with a different program. The memory manager decides which program DOS will address by mapping the appropriate "hors d'oeuvre" to an area below 640K.

Other, more subtle differences, include handle management. Under EMS 3.2 there was no standard technique for managing handles. EMS 4.0 provides the means to get, set, and search for handle names. This enables an application to not only determine what memory is in use, but who owns it.

Even with these changes, however, it would be impossible to run specific types of programs without another capability added to EMS 4.0. Some programs perform direct memory access (DMA) transfers. For example, many backup programs and some telecommunication programs do this. It would take too long to transfer information a byte at a time through the processor, so the program creates a direct link between one storage device and another. Unlike EMS 3.2, EMS 4.0 allows specific types of DMA transfers to occur. This is made possible through the use of alternate register sets, part of the hardware (or hardware emulation). Alternate register sets also allow a whole range of other unique and powerful software management routines, many of which are at the operating system level.

One of the most unique differences between the two versions is that EMS 4.0 provides the means to allow the contents of expanded memory to survive a warm boot. In fact, DESQview uses this capability to allow you to reboot a hung window without affecting any other windows. Of course, should the errant application affect the memory containing the EMM, your only recourse is the big red switch. Figure 4-2 depicts some of the differences between EMS 3.2 and EMS 4.0.

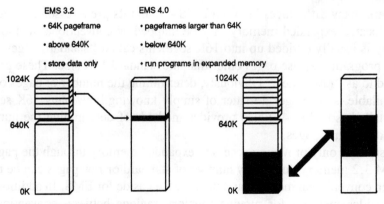

Fig. 4-2   EMS 3.2 vs EMS 4.0. © 1989, ALL Computers, Inc.

Note A number of 286 motherboards, and cheaper memory expansion cards are advertised as EMS 4.0 compatible. This advertising can be misleading: Sometimes the included software memory manager is EMS 4.0 compatible, but the hardware is not fully compatible. (See Chapter 5 for a detailed discussion of memory management hardware issues.)

Adding expanded memory to your system

You can add expanded memory to a PC in the following ways:

- Software emulation on 8088/286. Hard disk space or extended memory (on 286) can be used to simulate some expanded memory functions. EMS data storage space is available, but EMS emulation can't be used for multitasking or for loading drivers "high," above 640K. There are two good reasons for this. First, the emulation cannot create the register sets and other hardware features required for multitasking. Second, because the EMM is using disk storage to add the memory, switching between tasks would be too slow.

- Expanded memory card. An EMS 3.2 card can provide up to 8M of RAM for data storage. It does not provide any multitasking capability or the ability to run program code. An EMS 4.0 compliant board (one without hardware memory mapping) can provide up to 16M of RAM for data storage (32M on a 386/486 machine). In many cases, it cannot provide load high capability or support for multitasking. However, some EMS 4.0 compliant boards when used with some EMMs can be used to load programs high by disabling the use of expanded memory, entirely. The board's fixed 64K pageframe is used as an upper memory load-high area instead of an expanded memory swapping area. This is generally a poor alternative because users want both load high capability and expanded memory available on their systems, but it can be used in emergency situations. An EMS 4.0 compatible board (one with hardware memory mapping) can provide up to 16 or 32M for data storage. Drivers and TSRs can be loaded above 640K. If the board also provides alternate register sets, then it will support multitasking on all PC platforms. However, you still need appropriate software to take advantage of these features.

- Memory Management Unit (MMU). An MMU is a small plug-in chip module inserted into the CPU slot between a standard 80286 processor and the motherboard. An MMU converts all memory on the motherboard to mappable pages. This allows full EMS 4.0 compatibility on 80286 machines (data storage, load high capability and multitasking support.) An MMU provides more flexibility and better performance than an add-on EMS card. (See Chapter 5, page 125.)

- PS/2 286 MCA motherboard. IBM's microchannel 286 motherboards can provide all features of EMS 4.0 with appropriate software. Hardware limitations require that the first megabyte of memory on the motherboard be disabled to take advantage of expanded memory. Thus, a PS/2 with 4M of installed RAM will have only 3M available for applications when configured for expanded memory. (Of course, this assumes that any clone motherboard you use complies with all the applicable IBM specifications. Some manufacturers purchased a license to produce MCA motherboards. These boards might or might not be 100 percent compatible with the IBM versions.)

- 80286 motherboard (special chip set). 286 clone motherboards that use special chip sets might include limited built-in EMS 4.0 support. Sometimes these machines make use of shadow RAM for the load high function. Generally, they support EMS data storage, but not multitasking. (Full EMS support can be added with an MMU or external EMS card.)

- 386 Memory manager (Software). All 80386 motherboards have paged memory capacity built in as part of the processor. Extended memory on the motherboard may be converted to EMS 4.0 with appropriate software (MS-DOS 5, DR-DOS 6, or a third party 386 memory manager.) No additional hardware upgrade is required.

Task switching & multitasking— What's the difference?

If you own Microsoft's DOS 5 or Digital's DOS 6, you probably know that you can open more than one application at a time. However, only one application at a time can remain active. In other words, there is no background processing taking place (other than TSRs). The difference between a task switcher like DOSShell and a multitasker like DESQview or Windows is that a true multitasker allows other applications to execute tasks in the background. Background programs may be run "off-screen" or in small on-screen windows.

Using expanded memory with DESQview

If you run Quarterdeck's DESQview, under some configurations it might report 0K of expanded memory available for applications. Even if you have several megabytes of EMS installed on the system, DESQview can't use it for multitasking. As explained in the previous sections, the memory used to multitask must be fully EMS 4.0 compatible. Any other type of expanded memory will not provide the support required for memory mapping.

You can verify the amount of expanded memory available in DESQview by opening its memory status utility. (Type MS from the DESQview menu.) If you find some expanded memory available in the "total memory" window but 0K in the "Largest Available" window, then your expanded memory can't be used for multitasking. You have LIM 3.2 memory hardware, or "software emulation" of EMS 4.0. Figure 4-3 shows what the memory status window would look like if your expanded memory can't be used for multitasking.

1═Memory═Status	Total Memory	Total Available	Largest Available
Common Memory	30720	25994	25992
Conventional Memory	362K	355K	355K
Expanded Memory	8992K	8944K	0K

Fig. 4-3 DESQView's Memory Status display.

Quarterdeck's DESQview requires "hardware memory mapping," either EEMS or EMS 4.0, to multitask above 640K. EEMS and EMS 4.0 provide the capabilities required to map expanded memory within the conventional memory area. EEMS and EMS 4.0 require almost the same hardware to multitask (EMS 4.0 provides more alternate register sets and some additional operating system level capabilities). Any memory card that delivers EEMS should be able to deliver EMS 4.0 with an appropriate software driver.

Even though DESQview (and other multitaskers) can't multitask programs in LIM 3.2 memory, the memory can be put to some good use for task switching. Task switching, again, is the trick of "freeze drying" one program to make room for another. When you task switch between two applications, one of them goes to sleep while the other is in use.

Let's say, for example, that you have a 500K program running under DESQview and attempt to start another 500K program. With LIM 3.2 memory, DESQview packs up the first program and sends it to the EMS area for storage. 500K of conventional memory is freed for DOS to run the second program. The first program is frozen. DOS can't run them both because the first program wants to use 500K all at once. EMS 3.2 can only feed information to DOS 64K at a time. When you want to switch back to the first program, the second program is swapped to EMS. The first program is reactivated at the point where it was frozen.

If there is no expanded memory at all on your system, a task switcher can store programs as files on your hard disk. This is how the DOS shell task switcher works. When you switch back to the "stored" program, the task switcher swaps the currently active program to disk. The first program is poured back into conventional memory. With no expanded memory, this swapping process is laboriously slow; DOS must read and write all program information from the hard disk.

Using expanded memory with Windows

Unlike DESQview, Windows 3.0 requires EMS 4.0 compatible expanded memory, if you configure it for EMS usage at all. You cannot use EEMS or EMS 3.2 memory. In addition, Windows handles expanded memory differently than DESQview. Windows 3.0 will only use expanded memory in real mode. You must use extended memory with Windows if you run it in either standard or enhanced 386 mode. In Windows 3.1, real mode has been discontinued. You must use extended memory to gain more than 640K.

The second difference is the most important. When Windows 3.0 starts in real mode, it checks to see what type of memory your machine has available. If you have expanded memory available, Windows checks to see how much. It uses the small-frame EMS mode when you have little EMS memory available. This mode is most useful for running one large application. If your machine contains a lot of expanded memory, then Windows uses the large-frame EMS mode. This mode is most useful for running a few applications concurrently. Of course, each application receives less memory than in the small-frame EMS mode. You can force Windows 3.0 to use the small-frame EMS mode with a command line switch. In addition, other command line switches will determine how Windows distributes memory in the large-frame EMS mode.

There is an easy method for determining the mode, type, and amount of memory available in Windows. Select the About option of the Help menu in the Program Manager. Windows will display a dialog box similar to the one shown in Fig. 4-4 for small-frame mode, or Fig. 4-5 for large-frame mode. Notice that in small-frame mode that Windows reports 0K of the EMS memory is used as "Free Memory" (conventional memory). All the available expanded memory is used for just that purpose. Now look at the large-frame mode display. Windows reports that 219K of EMS memory is being used as Free Memory. By starting Windows 3.0 with the /L parameter, you can change the amounts of memory used in each area.

What kind of EMS do I have?

To find out what your system can do with its onboard memory, first install the memory manager supplied with your expansion card or motherboard. Next, run a memory analysis utility that can display information about mappable pages and EMS registers. (We reviewed some of these in Chapter 2.) ASQ, from Qualitas, Inc. is a free utility included with this book. Manifest, from Quarterdeck Office Systems, is included with their 286 and 386 memory management software.

The information you're looking for is the number of "mappable" EMS pages

Fig. 4-4   Window's About Dialog Box display—Small-frame EMS mode. Qualitas, Inc.

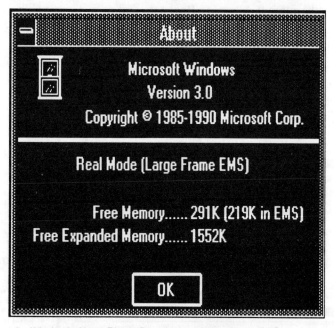

Fig. 4-5   Window's About Dialog Box display—Large-frame EMS mode. Qualitas, Inc.

below 640K and the number of available "alternate mapping registers." With Qualitas' ASQ, select the Analysis Menu, the Memory Analysis submenu, and

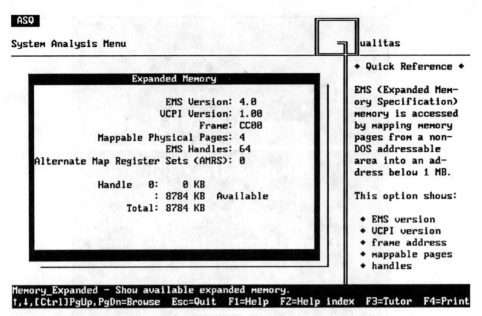

Fig. 4-6   Qualitas ASQ EMS 4.0 Incompatible display.

the Expanded (EMS) summary. In Fig. 4-6, we see that although 1024K of EMS is available, there are 0 Alternate Registers and only 4 mappable physical pages. This information tells us that even though the driver is labeled "EMS 4.0," the system will not be able to run programs in expanded memory. The available EMS can be accessed only through the 64K pageframe. Figure 4-7 shows a configuration that is fully EMS 4.0 compatible.

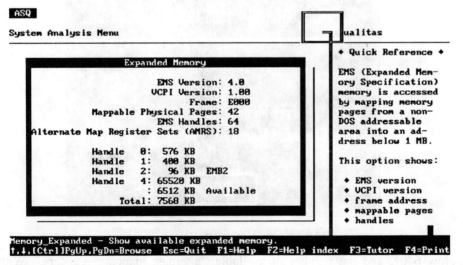

Fig. 4-7   Qualitas ASQ EMS 4.0 Compatible display.

DOS extenders

DOS extenders allow applications to break the 640K barrier by running in protected mode. DOS extenders come in two types: 16-bit extenders for the 80286/80386/80486, and 32-bit extenders for the 80386/80486. (Because 8088 machines don't address extended memory, they can't use DOS Extenders.) DOS Extended applications start up in real mode, but eventually use extended memory to run code in protected mode. The additional memory available allows DOS extended applications more power and flexibility than programs limited to 640K.

The DOS Extender serves as the protected mode loader for application software. The loader starts running in real mode, under DOS, and builds what are called descriptor tables for the application. After compiling a table of interrupts, the loader switches the computer into protected mode, spawning the application in extended memory. Whenever the application makes a DOS or BIOS request, the extender kernel intercepts it, acting as a replacement for Real mode interrupt services.

The two primary suppliers of DOS extenders are Rational Systems, Inc. and Phar Lap Software. Originally, Rational specialized in 16-bit/80286 loaders, while Phar Lap manufactured 32-bit/80386 loaders. AutoCAD v10, Lotus 1-2-3 r3, TOPS v3, Informix SQL, and Instant-C are all applications that use Rational's DOS/16M 80286 software. Interleaf Publisher, Mathematica, AutoCAD 386 (version 11), Paradox 386, and Foxbase+ 386 are applications that use Phar Lap's 80386/DOS extender.

16-bit vs. 32-bit

Naturally, applications written to address a 32-bit processor can execute code more rapidly. The 80386's 32-bit flat address space avoids the 80286's address segmentation. Instead of breaking the memory into segments, the 80386 can address it as one contiguous piece. Even though an 80286 can address 16M of memory, no individual code object can exceed 64K in size (64K is the amount of memory pointed to by one segment register). Because the 80386 doesn't have to use a segmented memory mode, code objects might be as large as 4 gigabytes.

Hardware paging and virtual memory

The 80386 also allows disk storage space to be used as virtual memory. The virtual memory space for code and data might be larger than the total physical RAM present on the machine. Virtual memory allows the operating system to swap portions of code to a disk swap file. The hard disk takes the place of physical memory chips. A program "pages" information from disk in 16K chunks. Demand paging is the feature that allows Microsoft Windows to display 8000K to 14,000K of available user memory, when only 4M of physical RAM is installed on the machine. (We'll learn more about Microsoft Windows memory management in Chapter 8.)

VCPI vs. DPMI

To give programs access to expanded memory multitasking and DOS extender technology at the same time, some traffic rules are necessary. An 80386 multitasks DOS applications in the Virtual 8086 mode. DOS extenders operate in protected mode. To avoid conflicts between programs using Virtual 8086 mode and programs running in protected mode, a standard was devised by Quarterdeck Office Systems, Rational Systems, Phar Lap and other companies. The Virtual Control Program Interface (VCPI) is the standard that allows DOS extended programs to coexist in an 80386 multitasking environment. Under VCPI, users of DESQview can run protected mode AutoCAD, 1-2-3, or Paradox side-by-side with other DOS applications.

Curiously, IBM and Microsoft did not choose to actively support VCPI. Perhaps in 1988 – 1989 their expectations were that OS/2 would soon replace DOS, so it wasn't worth the trouble. In 1990 Microsoft premiered its own independent, protected-mode standard called the DOS Protected-Mode Interface (DPMI). DPMI was developed specifically for Windows 3.x. Like VCPI, DPMI provides mode-switching and extended memory management to client programs, but DPMI works exclusively with Windows. Microsoft's DPMI standard for Windows 3.0 was incompatible with the VCPI DOS extender software available at the time on the marketplace. In most cases, users couldn't run 386 versions of Paradox, AutoCAD, etc., as DOS tasks under Windows. Quarterdeck's QEMM did make it possible to task switch to a VCPI program in Standard mode, but unfortunately you couldn't multitask these applications in Windows 3.0, even when using QEMM.

Microsoft eventually agreed to participate in a committee that included representatives from Quarterdeck, Intel, Lotus, Phar Lap, and Rational Systems. The committee's goal was to develop a more generic version of DPMI. The resultant standard—DPMI 1.0—is fully VCPI compatible. At the last minute, Microsoft incorporated this newer DPMI into Windows 3.1, making the program fully VCPI-compliant.

In July of 1991, Rational Systems introduced a series of 32-bit DOS extenders designed to be Windows 3.0 compatible under the older DPMI standard. It is hoped that, by the time you are reading this book, the conflict between DOS extender applications and Microsoft Windows will no longer exist.

Microsoft's extended memory specification

Microsoft's Extended Memory Specification (XMS) got its start from the discovery of a Quarterdeck programmer in 1986. At the time, Quarterdeck was looking for any means possible to reduce the conventional memory overhead of DESQview, their multitasking product.

We saw in Chapter 2 that the first megabyte of memory is broken down into sixteen 64K address segments. When the processor combines these segments with an offset, it obtains a 20-bit address. Each of these bits controls an address line gate circuit.

The A20 gate circuit (21st address line) is not present in the original PC. Therefore, when an address exceeds the amount addressable by 20 address lines, the address simply wraps to low memory. For example, if we have segment FFFFh and offset 0002h, then the resulting address is 100001h. The PC simply lops the 1 off the left and ends up with address 00001h.

What the Quarterdeck programmer discovered in 1986 was that turning the A20 gate of an 80286/80386/80486 chip on also turned off the wrap around. Because these chips do have a 21st address line (actually the 80286 has 24 and the 80386/80486 have 32), you can address the additional memory as if it were conventional memory. If a program was instructed to load code between 960K and 1024K, up to 64K of code could spill over into the first segment beyond 1024K. DOS could actually address code placed in the first segment of extended memory. Because the last segment of DOS memory is not normally contiguous with conventional memory, it can't be used by programs automatically. But the last segment of DOS memory can be specially programmed to hold up to 64K of a single device driver or application program.

This bug or feature of the 80286 and above architecture prompted Quarterdeck to develop its QEXT.SYS device driver to reduce the conventional memory overhead of DESQview. In 1987, Microsoft formalized the quirk by issuing its own driver, HIMEM.SYS, and by naming the first segment above 1M the High Memory Area (HMA). By publishing instructions on how to use the HMA, Microsoft allowed other third party vendors to reduce the conventional overhead of their programs. Xerox was one of the first to recognize the HMA with Ventura Publisher. Microsoft's popularization of the HMA with HIMEM.SYS was the beginning of their Extended Memory Specification.

In 1990, Microsoft revised its HIMEM.SYS driver with the release of Windows 3.0. The scope of XMS memory was increased to include all of extended memory. The new release of Windows could use all of extended memory to multitask Windows applications.[1] Disk caches, print spoolers and RAM disks could

---

[1] Actually, Windows 3.0 only runs properly with up to 12M of extended memory installed on the system. After that, it starts developing problems.

now access extended memory through Microsoft's device driver. Formerly, any driver using extended memory had to provide its own scheme for switching in and out of protected mode. Microsoft established new terminology for all memory above 640K:

UMB Upper Memory Blocks. This became the term for the memory area above the 640K boundary and below the one megabyte boundary.

HMA High Memory Area. This term refers to the 64K block of memory starting at the one megabyte boundary (1024K). This is the beginning of extended memory on 80286 and 80386 systems.

EMB Extended Memory Blocks. This term refers to the remaining extended memory (above the HMA) available to an XMS driver.

Loading programs "high": Using the UMB

For several years software developers had been eying the UMB region covetously. UMB lies within DOS's 1M address space. Already, expanded memory had been invented to make partial use of this area. How convenient it would be, if individual programs could also load code there. DOS's real memory limit should be 1M, not 640K! The problem is that all those troublesome ROM adaptors and BIOS instructions have to fit in there, too.

In 1986, a company called RYBS Electronics marketed a "Hicard" that allowed users to load device drivers into RAM between 640K and 1M. If a 64K area of the UMB could be used as an EMS pageframe, then why not map more of the UMB to expanded memory for device drivers and memory resident utilities? If device drivers and TSR programs could reside above 640K, then everyone would have more conventional memory left over for applications. In 1987, Qualitas, Inc., implemented a "load high" feature into their 386MAX control program for 80386 machines.

The technology of "loadhigh" software has been improving steadily. Quarterdeck was not far behind Qualitas in adding this capability to their QEMM memory manager. In 1988, ALL computers, Ltd., brought loadhigh capability to 286 machines with their ALL ChargeCard. Quarterdeck and Qualitas issued more generic 80286 and 8088 load high software in the following year. Loadhigh became an official operating system feature with Digital Research's DR DOS 5 in 1990. Finally, Microsoft incorporated it in MS-DOS 5.

Programmers have developed several techniques for mapping UMB addresses for use by DOS. Recall that most computers have no physical RAM installed from 640K to 1M. The address space is provided for DOS, but only ROM hardware actually uses it. Where does the RAM come from when programs are loaded high? One technique is to map pages from expanded memory into the UMB. This is the way DOS 5.x and most third-party memory managers solve the problem.

Thus, to load programs high, you need expanded memory in the system and an expanded memory manager in your CONFIG.SYS.

An alternate technique is to borrow the memory from Shadow RAM. Many motherboards are shipped with 1M: 640K of conventional memory and 384K of memory reserved for use as Shadow RAM. Some load high utilities can steal the Shadow RAM to allow programs to be loaded high. Memory managers that borrow shadow RAM usually require specific 80286 or 80386 chip sets to make this trick work.

Quarterdeck's latest products can make use of a third method to load high by borrowing extended memory in protected mode, instead of using expanded memory or shadow RAM. (This will be explored further in the chapter on memory managers.)

Conclusion

This chapter has shown you the difference between extended and expanded memory. In addition, it has provided detailed information on how some DOS programs and operating environments like Windows and DESQview can make use of both types of memory. Most importantly, the chapter has presented the information you need to fully understand how extended and expanded memory can enhance the capabilities of your machine.

Now that you have some understanding of how DOS is able to use memory above 640K, you will want to know how to actually add some memory to your system.

5
CHAPTER

Ins and outs of memory hardware

Choose your software first. You'll become aware of your hardware needs once you look at the requirements to run the software.

If your software won't run on an 8088, a new machine might be a better upgrade option than an accelerator card or motherboard swap.

80286 machines have multiple upgrade options. A memory upgrade solves short term problems, but a 386/486 upgrade might be a better long term investment.

Reasons to upgrade

Because you're reading this book, you undoubtedly feel some dissatisfaction with your current PC and hope to improve its power and performance. This chapter will guide you through the complex world of PC hardware add-ons. It's a truism that no matter what kind of PC you have now, some manufacturer out there hopes to sell you something to improve it. How can you decide exactly what to buy? One of the best yardsticks for measuring hardware requirements is your software. (Of course, one of the other yardsticks is the amount of money you have to invest in your system.)

General considerations

Before you buy new equipment, it makes sense to think about what you plan to do with the computer. Here are a few questions you can ask yourself:

- What kind of work has the computer been used for in the past? A lot of people never monitor their computer usage. Doing so can help you understand how much time you actually spend working on a particular type of task. This, in turn, can show you where to invest your upgrade dollars to receive the maximum benefit.

- What software do you already own? Sometimes a user might own a machine that provides marginal support for a particular application—such as running WordPerfect 5.1 or Ventura Publisher without expanded memory. Improving on that hardware can enhance the performance you receive from your current software. In addition, understanding the requirements of your current software can help you prepare for the requirements of software you intend to purchase in the future.

- How will the computer be used in the future? Because you are taking the time to evaluate your needs and upgrade your hardware, wouldn't it be better to add a little capacity for tomorrow's needs as well? Building some added capacity into your machine now means that you will not only need to upgrade less often, but that your machine will be able to handle any unforeseen needs as well.

- What kind of new work do you plan to do? Think about what you'll be doing a year from now. As your computer knowledge and skills increase, so do the demands that both you and your software place on the computer.

- What software will you need to buy? Always decide what software you want to purchase first, determine its requirements, and then purchase the hardware required to fulfill those needs.

Accounting and word processing considerations

Some people use their word processing systems for a lot more than writing letters or getting a company memo out. Some word processing programs today almost qualify as low-end desktop publishing systems. Many spreadsheets now include desktop publishing and multimedia features as well, allowing you to produce superior presentations and reports. Of course, none of these features come without cost. You might need to consider some of these questions related to specific word processing and accounting system tasks:

- Do you need a graphic interface? If you want to see what your document is going to look like before you print it, you'll need a word processing program that supports WYSIWYG ("What You See Is What You Get"). Often this means that you'll also need an advanced display adapter, an 80386 machine (to get decent performance), and plenty of expanded memory.

- Will you be producing charts and graphs? Spreadsheets and some accounting packages have always allowed you to display your data in the form of graphs and charts. In addition, a lot of word processors allow you to include graphs, charts, and other types of graphic information within your documents. All these types of tasks require not only a graphics interface, but the processing power provided by a fast machine with lots of RAM.

- Are you planning on creating newsletters and brochures? Surprisingly, many people do not need the advanced capabilities required to create massive books or eye catching presentations. They might only need to create a company newsletter or a quick brochure. In some cases, you might be able to get by with an older PC for these applications. Many low end packages run on PCs with a monochrome display and a mere 512K of RAM. Of course, as you add features, those requirements increase.

Database management considerations

Database management systems (DBMS) are unique in their ability to store vast amounts of information in a fast and easy to use format. Unlike spreadsheets and word processors, DBMS always involve heavy disk usage because they store most of their information on disk instead of in RAM. Because of this, the needs of a database manager differ from those of many programs in use today. The following list of questions will help you understand the unique requirements for tasks related to this product.

- Will you be working with flat or relational databases? The so-called "flat" database usually employs a single data file that stores information in a relatively inflexible format of columns (called fields) and rows. Due to the simplicity of this application, you can often get good performance from an 8088/8086 machine. Enhancements might include expanded memory used as a disk cache to speed database accesses. On the other hand, a relational database often employs more than one file (or table) joined together in complex relationships. The more closely the application follows the rules relating to relational databases, the more resources it uses. For example, a product like dBASE might use considerably less resources than an SQL product. In either event, you will want a fairly fast computer with a fast hard drive and a large disk cache to achieve maximum performance.

- Will you be desktop publishing database reports? Database managers often store a vast amount of information in diverse files. Printing this information using proportional fonts could vastly increase the time required for completion. Using a print spooler will free your computer up faster.

Graphics and desktop publishing considerations

Graphics programs like CorelDRAW and PC Paintbrush allow you to express an idea using pictures rather than words. Harvard Graphics and Freelance Plus allow you to express abstract numbers as more easily understood charts and graphs. Desktop publishing programs allow you to combine pictures, charts, and graphs with words to fully express the concepts you want the reader to understand. Of all the tasks explored so far, these are the most demanding. Graphics and desktop publishing documents tend to use large amounts of hard drive space for file storage. In addition, they make huge demands on your computer for math intensive operations like displaying a picture, graph, chart or document in graphic format on screen. The following questions will help you evaluate some of the strains that programs like these place on your system.

- Will you be working with graphic illustrations frequently, occasionally, or not at all? Because of the demands placed on your system by some programs, you must consider how often you will actually use them before you make the large investment. If you only intend to use these programs on an occasional basis, you might want to use a less powerful program rather than go to the expense required to fully utilize a power-hungry program. For example, the requirements to use a program like PC Paintbrush are a lot less than the requirements for CorelDRAW. However, CorelDRAW will give you vastly superior results.

- Will you need to produce large documents in a hurry, or will you be producing shorter documents for linotronic output? (A *linotronic printer* is a high resolution output device. Magazines and other businesses requiring high resolution output usually format a document for linotronic output at a service bureau, rather than use a local printer.) Deciding where your resources are best used is always a difficult task. If you must produce large documents that require a lot of disk access time, then your expanded memory resources might best be used as a disk cache. On the other hand, you might not want to take the time required to wait for such a document to print. In these cases, a large print spooler might be a better use for the limited memory resources of your machine. Some high resolution graphics are very math-intensive. Those destined for linotronic output are almost always this way. In these cases, it might be better to eliminate the print spooler altogether, reduce the size of the disk cache, and set aside more memory for the application. However, if you are producing short documents destined for linotronic output, you might be able to get by with less memory and a less powerful CPU because the final printing will be done on another system and speed might not be as critical an issue.

Telecommunication considerations

Telecommunication programs are often the least demanding on system resources. Unfortunately, they also make your system unavailable for long periods of time. Uploading or downloading a large file at 2400 baud could takes hours. Because of this, telecommunication programs are perfect candidates for background processing. You can easily do other work while the telecommunication program downloads a file in the background. The following questions help you understand the needs of a telecommunication program.

- Will you be using a MODEM or FAX board frequently, occasionally, or not at all? If you are only going to use these programs once in a while, it might not be worth the time and effort to multitask them. Moderate use warrants multitasking in most cases. Doing so will greatly increase your productivity. If your a heavy MODEM or FAX user, using an old PC exclusively for that use might be the best solution. Not only does this provide a means to utilize that old PC sitting in your closet, it means that your machine won't be tied up waiting for a FAX or other telecommunication task. Even the small speed differential you will notice when multitasking could make a difference if you use the MODEM or FAX frequently.

- Will you be transferring large documents or downloading databases from information services? The larger the document, the longer you will wait for it to download. Because you often have little or no control over the speed at which the remote station transmits information, multitasking may be the only way you can increase your productivity.

- Will you be using a high-speed modem (9600bps or faster)? Use of a high-speed modem for background file transfers may require somewhat more powerful memory hardware (see the section on alternate register sets for 8088/80286 expanded memory cards.)

Upgrade an 8088?

Some people are still happily productive using old software on 8088 machines. An 8088 can multitask a word processor, spreadsheet, or database with a telecommunications program when you add the appropriate amount of EEMS or EMS 4.0 memory and appropriate software. (Lotus 1-2-3 release 2, WordPerfect 4.2, and ProComm 2.42 are still fine programs that can cooperate for this purpose. Word-Perfect 4.2 and ProComm 2.42 can even be multitasked in 640K without expanded memory!)

Although old versions of software are not available in stores, many people still use them. You might frequently find older versions of programs heavily discounted at weekend swap meets. You don't always need the latest and greatest to get the job done. But one word of warning: don't plan on using old software unless you're already familiar with it. You should know that the software is reliable for the work you want to do. You won't get much technical support from manufacturers for old versions of their products.

In addition, some older software won't reliably work with newer versions of DOS. You might experience some problems with hardware as well. For example, some versions of older software might not work well with newer mouse drivers or hard drive compression schemes like Stacker. (Stacker, from Stac software, uses a coprocessor board to compress files, which increases the space available on your hard drive.) However, even with these limitations, an 8088 computer can still be a useful tool for someone on a budget. Ventura Publisher 2.0 and WordPerfect 5.1 perform adequately on an 8088 as stand-alone applications.

If your 8088 doesn't already have expanded memory, you should think twice about spending money for an upgrade card. Several years ago, it was fashionable to upgrade 8088 machines by replacing the motherboard or adding an accelerator card. In most cases, these upgrades changed the processor from an 8088/8086 to an 80286 or 80386. Unfortunately, 80286 computers have their own limitations with expanded memory. They can't emulate true EEMS or EMS 4.0 memory because they lack some of the capabilities of the 80386 processor. The 80386 accelerator cards for old PCs are generally not 100% compatible with a true 386 system. Part of this has to do with differences between an 8088/8086 ROM BIOS and the 32-bit ROM BIOS used for an 80386 system. In addition, there are other hardware differences like the size of the internal bus that create unexpected anomalies for software attempting to use the 80386 in anything other than real mode.

Another problem is inherent in upgrading an 8088 by swapping the motherboard or adding a 386 accelerator: your original 8088 peripherals might be overmatched. The hard disks found in 8088 systems generally have low storage capacity and slow performance. Furthermore, Hercules and CGA graphics cards don't do justice to modern graphics programs.

Initially, it might seem cheaper to transplant parts into an 8088 instead of buying a new computer. In the long run, this is less efficient and returns less value for your dollar. If you want to run 80286 and 80386 specific software, you're better off buying a new machine. Prices are going down every day. A new 386SX starter system will probably include VGA graphics and a fast hard disk for less than a quarter of the cost of the original PC. When you do buy a new machine, you'll have two computers. The 8088 computer is still intact. Your old machine might be useful to a friend as a word processing machine, to a child as a first computer, or to you as a communications machine. If you're an 8088 owner and have decided that you need an upgrade, we're recommending that you skip the 286 platform entirely. Think 386.

Upgrade an 80286?

The 80286 machine has been the workhorse of the PC community for the past five years. Within the last year or two, the price of 80386 and 80486 systems has dropped drastically. Software developers are currently focusing on 80386-specific, 32-bit programming for new applications. This makes the 80386 the recommended minimum platform for a new computer purchase.

Where does this leave all the 286 machines? Apart from the natural inclination to keep up with the latest and greatest software, there are three reasons why you might want to upgrade the memory or CPU of a 286:

- Speed. You want your applications to run faster.

- Network Compatibility. Your 286 is a client or server on a network. As a client, you don't have enough conventional memory to run some of your applications because of the network drivers you need to load in conventional memory (although newer versions of Netware allow you to load these drivers in either expanded or extended memory.) As a server, you receive a performance hit because of the inability of the 80286 to run in virtual 86 mode. Even in protected mode, the server software cannot use a flat address space with the 80286, slowing some operations to a crawl because of the memory segmentation scheme.

- Multitasking. You would like to take advantage of Windows or DESQview 386 to run several applications concurrently. While DESQview will multitask applications, it doesn't provide all the capabilities of DESQview 386.

Speed

Many text-based DOS applications run at about the same speed on a 12 MHz to 16 MHz 80286 compared with a 16 MHz 80386SX. In fact, some applications actually do better on the 80286! This is related to the way the programmers have compiled the application code and the inherent capabilities of the chip itself. Some compilers automatically optimize program code for faster performance with the 80286 instruction set. Applications compiled in this way might be more efficient on an 80286 than an 80386SX with similar clock speed.

The applications that really take advantage of the 80386 are the ones that perform memory intensive calculations: spreadsheets, CAD programs, and graphic-based applications. Some of these same applications perform better on an 80486 because of its built-in math co-processor and other features. Other factors also affect performance: the speed of your hard disk, the presence of hardware or software caching, and the speed of the video display. Sometimes a faster hard disk, a disk cache, or the addition of a math co-processor can make programs run faster than a CPU upgrade.

To sum it all up, if your main computing tasks are word processing and database maintenance with text-based programs, a hard disk upgrade might give you more mileage than a memory upgrade. Of course, a memory upgrade might be useful to run a disk cache or RAM disk, but getting a faster hard drive might be your best bet. Once you perform the hard drive upgrade, you might find that a CPU upgrade is unnecessary. If your main computing tasks are CAD, spreadsheet, or other math intensive programs, then a math co-processor might provide you with a real speed boost. Of course, the program must be written to take advantage of a math coprocessor when present. Most spreadsheet and CAD programs are.

Networking

The networking issue is the most obvious concern for users of 80286 machines in corporate environments. Networks like BANYAN, NOVELL, 3-COM, and LANTastic have a memory overhead ranging from 32K to 400K of conventional memory on a workstation. This can leave a client machine incapable of running heavy-weight productivity applications. Most networks can't do anything with the native extended memory on an 80286 motherboard.[1] You can use a combination of expanded memory and "load-high" utilities to place network drivers above 640K. This frees up precious conventional memory resources for use by applications.

Multitasking

Extended memory on an 80286 can be used to run 16-bit DOS extended programs (Lotus 1-2-3, release 3.x) or Microsoft Windows applications. An 80286 can't

---

[1] Recent developments in DOS-extender technology are changing this situation. And Novell's Netware now includes a built-in feature to load its network shell into extended memory.

multitask ordinary DOS applications unless it is equipped with hardware compatible expanded memory.

Performing the upgrade

Once you decide that your 80286 will no longer perform the tasks you need it to do, you have to decide to either replace or upgrade it. You might find it less expensive in the short term to upgrade the machine instead of replacing it outright. These are four ways to upgrade an 80286, to add more memory or multitasking capabilities:

- Add an EMS 4.0 expanded memory card to a slot on the bus. Install an EMM to make it available to your applications.
- Add more memory to the motherboard; then install a memory management unit to convert the memory to EMS 4.0.
- Replace the motherboard: substitute an 80386SX motherboard and retain the 286 case, power supply, and peripherals. (This option is impractical for owners of IBM PS/2 systems.)
- Add a 386SX plug-in module to your current motherboard. (This option is available for IBM PS/2 systems as well as ordinary clones.)

80286 obsolescence

An EMS add-on card or a plug-in memory management unit (see page 105 for details) can beef up an 80286 to make it "almost as good" as an 80386. But before you spend money on "beefing up" your 80286, consider your options carefully. In the 1990's, the fate of the 80286 might be similar to that of the IBM PCjr in the 1980's.[2]

80286 machines are limited by the CPU's lack of the "virtual 8086" processing mode. The internal architecture of most 80286 motherboards also limits their ability to map expanded memory within the reserved area (640K to 1M). A lot of time and money were spent during the '80s to overcome these limitations. Today, spending that money to upgrade an 80286 makes less sense. 80386SX machines commonly sell for only $200 to $300 more than comparable 80286 units with the same hard disk and video options. With an 80386SX, you may expect to run most PC software that will be written in the next two to three years.[3]

---

[2]One of the authors started his computing career with an IBM PCjr. For several years, he delighted in confounding the experts. He equipped his Junior with 736K of memory, three floppy disk drives, and two hard drives. But eventually the time came when it no longer made sense to spend another hundred dollars to add another Junior-compatible gimmick. It was much easier to accept the current standard and start over with a newer machine.

[3]Microsoft will be issuing a 32-bit operating system later this year tailored for the 80386-and-above platforms. At the time of this writing, motherboard manufacturers are beginning to offer "universal" upgrade options. The plan is to let you upgrade from an 80386SX to an 80386DX, 80486SX or DX, or even an 80586 computer simply by replacing a card containing the CPU.

For completeness' sake (and because the majority of computers in the hands of users were manufactured before 1992), we will explore upgrade options for all platforms in detail.

8088/80286/80386 accelerator cards

The first generation of upgrades offered for 8088/8086 machines were accelerator cards designed to fit in a PC bus-slot. Quadram, Orchid, Intel, and other companies offered boards to convert a slow 8088 machine to a faster 8088 or even to an 80286 or 80386. Because prices for new motherboards and starter systems are so low today, accelerator cards are no longer very practical. Intel's Inboard PC, perhaps the most widely used of these options, requires a special OEM version of Microsoft Windows. In addition, the Inboard PC is not completely compatible with some 80386-specific software. One of the biggest problems with using an accelerator card is that they are limited by the bus speed of the original computer and the quality of the original peripherals. Bus width also plays a major part in these limitations. For example, if you install an 80386 accelerator in the 8-bit slot of an 8088, then it will take at least four times as long to retrieve a word from memory as it would using a 32-bit bus of the same clock speed.

A newer generation of processor upgrades plug directly into the CPU slot. Plug-in CPUs are slightly more viable as an expansion option than accelerator cards. (See the section on 80386 plug-in modules, later in this chapter.)

8088/80286 expanded memory cards

Expanded memory cards are an option for 8088 and 80286 machines. Single applications like Lotus 1-2-3, release 2.x use expanded memory to work with data files larger than 640K. An EMS 4.0 compatible expanded memory card also allows Quarterdeck's DESQview to multitask above 1M on any PC platform. (An EMS card might not be the best solution for DESQview multitasking. See the description in the next section on "backfilling" and motherboard limitations.)

A good expanded memory card for an 80286 machine can also be configured as an extended memory card. In some cases, you can backfill motherboard memory, provide some EMS 4.0 memory, and use the rest as extended memory. The Intel Above Board + is an example of a software configured expanded memory board that offers these features. Additional extended memory on the 80286 can be used to multitask Microsoft Windows applications (but not DOS programs under Windows)[4]. MS-DOS 5 and DR DOS 5/6 can use the first 64K of extended memory (HMA) to load most of the operating system above 1M.

---

[4]You need to use Window's enhanced (80386) mode to provide true multitasking.

EMS hardware compatibility

Let's emphasize again: Multitasking with expanded memory requires specially wired hardware that can swap individual memory pages. This is why EMS 4.0 or EEMS compatible memory cards are required with ordinary 8088 or 80286 machines. Both EMS 4.0 and EEMS memory cards can do what 8088/80286 motherboards cannot do—map EMS pages into their onboard memory banks! This means that they can't multitask in EMS. Beware of manufacturers who offer "EMS 4.0 compatible motherboards." Unless the machine is an 80386, this generally means the motherboard can emulate some of the EMS 4.0 functions but won't let you multitask. (The AST line of 80286 machines is an exception to this rule. Like the AST memory cards, AST 80286 motherboards are equipped with special, EMS mappable, memory banks. These memory banks provide the registers required for true EMS 4.0 support.)

Expanded memory or extended memory cards are installed in the computer by insertion in an 8-bit or 16-bit slot on the motherboard. The CPU accesses the additional memory through the computer's bus. This means that the memory speed of an add-in card is limited to the speed of the bus. So memory added with an EMS card might be considerably slower than conventional memory. On 8088/80286 machines, the bus speed is usually limited to 8 MHz, even if the CPU runs at 16 MHz or 20 MHz. This means that it takes approximately two to three times as long to retrieve information from the bus as it does from main memory.

80286 motherboards of more recent design hold 2M to 16M of RAM without add-on cards. This RAM is generally available only as extended memory.[5] All RAM installed on the motherboard runs at the speed of the CPU rather than at the bus speed. Programs that use extended memory (like Windows) will run faster if the RAM is mounted directly on the motherboard.

Some 8088/80286 motherboards can hold only 640K to 1M of RAM. In fact, some might not even hold a full 640K of RAM. For example, the original PC could only hold 64K on the motherboard. For these systems, an add-on card is the only way to get more than 1M of memory. (You can also swap the motherboard, or buy a new computer. These are serious alternatives covered in the next section.)

Installing memory and backfilling

Installing and backfilling memory on an older machine might require some patience and experimentation on your part. Some PCs, like the original 64K PC require that you simply install the EMS board, configure it and the switches on the motherboard correctly, then install any required software. However, for some

---

[5]The manufacturer might provide software that emulates EMS in extended memory, but the EMS emulation is usually not truly compatible with all expanded memory functions. In most cases, the memory bank lacks the essential registers required for true EMS 4.0 support.

8088 and 80286 machines to multitask in expanded memory, part of the memory on the motherboard must be physically removed or disabled. This is especially true if the motherboard originally provides space for 640K or more of RAM. Mappable RAM on the EMS card replaces some of the non-mappable conventional memory on the motherboard. This borrowing of RAM from the EMS card is called *backfilling*. Some of the RAM on the EMS card is lent or "backfilled" to conventional memory. The "backfilled" memory situated on the EMS card replaces the chips removed from the motherboard.[6]

If no memory is backfilled from the EMS card, then one of two situations occur. If the motherboard supports bank switching, then you can still receive the full benefit of EMS 4.0 compatible memory. However, most older motherboards do not support bank switching. In these cases, the EMS 4.0 compatible memory works just like the older LIM 3.2 standard, you cannot use the expanded memory for multitasking on the 8088 or 80286 motherboard. There is a simple reason for this. The motherboard does not provide any means for mapping part of conventional memory into the expanded memory area. However, single applications like 1-2-3 can still use the expanded memory for file storage space because they aren't trying to run program code above 640K. What you can't do is run a program in expanded memory at the same time as an application in conventional memory. (See also "What kind of EMS do I have" in Chapter 3.)

Backfilling on an 8088   On 8088 machines, backfilling from a "true" EMS 4.0 card is very useful. Some 8088's can boot with 256K or less present on the motherboard. When using a 256K motherboard, the EMS card backfills 384K, bringing the conventional memory total to 640K. This permits DESQview to multitask a large conventional memory window with a series of expanded memory windows matching the size of the backfilled memory. The machine can open as many windows in expanded memory as the total RAM on the EMS card permits. (As you might guess, the maximum size of the expanded memory window is equal to the amount of backfilled RAM loaned to the motherboard for conventional memory.)

Backfilling on an 80286   The "classic" 80286 motherboards of the '80s would not boot with only 256K onboard. At least 512K had to be on the motherboard for the system to start. These 80286 systems permitted only 128K of conventional memory to be backfilled from the EMS card. Consequently, an 80286 with 512K of onboard conventional memory could multitask one large conventional memory window with a series of 128K expanded memory windows. Some 80286 machines were actually limited to smaller expanded memory windows than some of the 8088s. Figure 5-1 illustrates different expanded memory scenarios that you might expect to see.

---

[6]This complicated state of affairs is one of the reasons why consultants recommend upgrades to 80486 machines. With an 80486, all motherboard memory can be mapped. The expanded memory limitations of 80286 motherboards disappear.

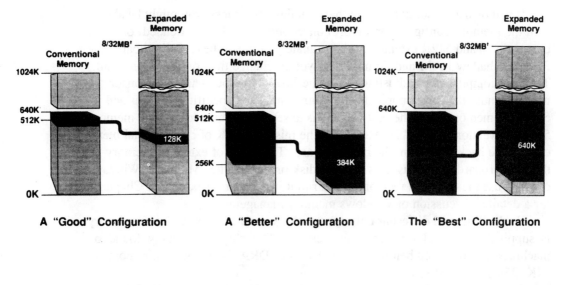

A "Good" Configuration	A "Better" Configuration	The "Best" Configuration

EEMS memory supplies 128 K of conventional memory—so, multiple programs up to 128K in size can run in expanded memory

EEMS memory supplies 384K of conventional memory—so multiple programs up to 384K in size can run in expanded memory

EEMS memory supplies *all* of conventional memory—so multiple programs up to 532K in size can run in expanded memory simultaneously.

These areas represent memory that's provided by your motherboard or by an add-on memory board. Since it's not provided by EMS4 or EEMS memory, it can't be mapped and can thus only be used by one program.

These areas represent high memory that's not available for running programs.

These areas represent a single block of EMS4 or EEMS memory that's being mapped into a like-sized block of conventional memory below 640K. Since different blocks of EMS4 or EEMS memory can be mapped simultaneously into the same block of conventional memory, different programs can be running concurrently in the same conventional memory—at least as far as your PC'S processor is concerned.

These areas represent blocks of EMS4 or EEMS memory that are available to run additional programs—or, for data storage, for use as a RAM disk, print spooler, or disk cache, or for swapping graphics screens.

Fig. 5-1　Quarterdeck Office Systems display. Quarterdeck Office Systems.

If you own an older 286 system that contains 1M or less, you might be able to split the memory configuration: 640K conventional and 384K extended, or 512K conventional and 512K extended. (Unfortunately, some of these motherboards use 384K as shadow RAM and do not allow you to change the configuration at all.) This is accomplished by adjusting the motherboard's jumper settings. (Consult the user's manual that was supplied with your system for specifics). If you add an expanded memory card, the best strategy is to set the machine to split the memory 512K conventional and 512K extended. The missing 128K of conventional memory will be backfilled from the memory card. The 512K of extended memory on the motherboard can be used as a RAM disk or disk cache. Microsoft Windows can also use the extended memory if you run it in Standard Mode. (See Chapter 9 for a detailed discussion of Windows memory management.)

Backfilling and different chip types As we saw in Chapter 1, PC memory is supplied in several different chip designs. The chips commonly found on machines manufactured before 1988 are banks of DRAMs. DRAM chips come in 64K, 256K, and 1M sizes.

A typical motherboard uses four rows of nine DRAM sockets. Each row on the motherboard is referred to as a "bank." Sometimes the sockets are wired in groups of two rows. This is especially true of motherboards that support bank switching or interleaving. In this case, two rows of 9 sockets constitute a bank. When you want to determine how to backfill your machine, you must consider the size of the chips in each bank. Figure 5-2 shows an 80286 motherboard configured with 512K on the motherboard in 2 rows of 256K DRAM chips.

Fig. 5-2   80286 motherboard.

The two empty banks to the left might hold either 2 rows by 9 of 64K DRAMS (128K) or another 2 rows by 9 of 256K DRAMS (512K). Your motherboard manual will tell you what size chips each bank might hold. In addition, it will tell you if you need to change the position of any jumpers to tell the motherboard what size chips are installed.

If you plan to install an EMS card to work with a motherboard like the one shown in Fig. 5-2, you would physically remove all DRAM in the two banks on the left, leaving 512K installed in the two banks on the right. As before, look in your motherboard manual to determine the minimum amount of memory that your motherboard will hold. In some cases you might be able to remove three banks, leaving 256K on the motherboard. If your EMS card uses the same size DRAM as your motherboard, then you might be able to transfer the displaced motherboard chips to banks on the EMS card.

Most motherboards manufactured in the last several years have slot-like memory banks that accept SIMMs (Single In-line Memory Module). 9 chips are soldered to each card. A SIMM may contain 256K, 1M, 2M, or 4M. SIPPS (Single In-line Pin Package) are a slightly less common variant. Some motherboards allow either DRAMs or SIPPs to be installed, with a jumper setting for each alternative. Some SIMMs are soldered onto the motherboard or expansion card at the factory, but most systems let you slide them in and out of a series of white plastic brackets. The SIPPs terminate in a series of 40 pins that must be lined up with circular holes in the sockets. Figure 5-3 shows both a 1M SIMM and a 1M SIPP. Notice the differences between the two methods of memory packaging. Figure 5-4 illustrates the technique used to insert a SIMM into a socket on a motherboard. Notice that SIMMs are a lot easier to install than the old DRAM chips were. In addition, inserting one SIMM is a lot faster than nine DRAMs.

Fig. 5-3   Memory packaging techniques.

Limitations of expanded memory

The mapping limitations of many 8088 and 80286 motherboards present an annoying obstacle to DOS multitasking. 384K is barely enough to run current versions of most software; 128K is even worse. Fortunately, users of CGA and Hercules graphics cards may increment the size of EMS windows, slightly.

Fig. 5-4 Installing SIMMs in a motherboard.

Annexing video memory to increase EMS window size

Recall from Chapter 3 that the 64K memory segment directly above 640K is reserved for EGA and VGA graphics. CGA and Hercules monochrome adaptors don't touch this memory. Because the A000 segment (640K to 704K) is directly contiguous with conventional memory, DOS can be instructed to include it. Annexing the A000 video segment changes the top of conventional memory from 640K to 704K. A shareware utility called EEMRAM (included on our shareware disk) can work with any hardware compatible EMS 4.0 board to annex an additional 64K to DOS. The EEMRAM package from Cove Software includes a diagnostic utility called EMSINFO. EMSINFO examines the system and presents a list of mappable 16K pages. If mappable RAM for these ranges is present on the EMS card, the maximum size of expanded memory windows is increased by 64K. This permits 448K EMS windows with a 256K 8088 motherboard, and 192K windows with a 512K 80286 motherboard.

The same size windows can be configured by remapping RAM on an EGA or VGA card. Quarterdeck supplies a utility called VIDRAM that accomplishes this along with DESQview. VIDRAM transfers control of the A000h block to DOS, mapping the 64K address space to chips on the video card. So long as VIDRAM is in effect, the user must refrain from running EGA or VGA graphics applications until VIDRAM is deactivated. CGA and Hercules graphics can still be used.

EMS card features

Once you decide to purchase an EMS card to enhance your system, it is very important to get one that adheres to specific standards. A well-designed expanded memory card will have the following features:

- Blocks of memory may be assigned for backfilled conventional memory, extended memory, or expanded memory. The card should allow you to use the memory in more than one and preferably all three areas.

- It should also allow you to portion the memory in 128K increments. Although the card might demand that physical chips be installed in 512K or 1M increments, you should be able to parcel out memory usage in 128K or smaller chunks.

- You should be able to configure the memory card for wait states ranging from 3 to 0. This will generally allow the card to accommodate both slow and fast systems.

- The card should also be configured for either 8-bit and 16-bit data transfer. Note that if the card is configured for 16-bit data transfer, you can't use it in an 8-bit slot. Figure 5-5 shows an 8-bit card that you can place in either an 8- or 16-bit slot. Figure 5-6 shows a 16-bit card that you must place in a 16-bit slot.

- The memory card should contain at least 8 alternate mapping registers. Alternate mapping registers allow the card to rapidly switch between different groups of mapped pages. The more alternate map registers, the better the card's multitasking performance.

Tips for installing memory modules

Installing and removing memory from your machine is a task that requires some attention to detail and a lot of patience. The following tips can help make this task a lot easier and less error prone.

- Always turn the power switch off so that the motherboard is disconnected from the power source. However, you should leave the machine plugged in to provide a ground source. Before touching the memory modules, ground yourself by touching some grounded metal. The top of the power supply is an excellent place because it contains a lot of unpainted metal. Static electricity can ruin sensitive memory chips. Even if you don't feel the shock accompanied by a discharge of static, your hands might contain enough of a charge to ruin the chips.

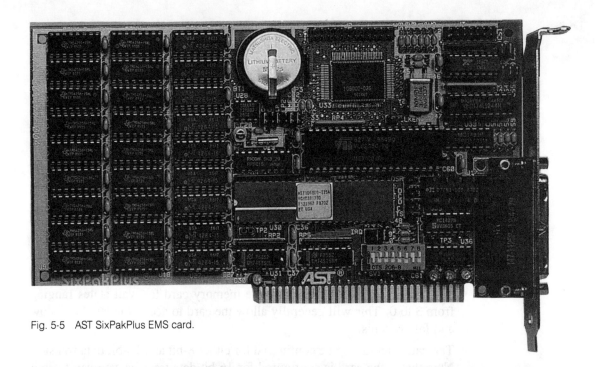

Fig. 5-5   AST SixPakPlus EMS card.

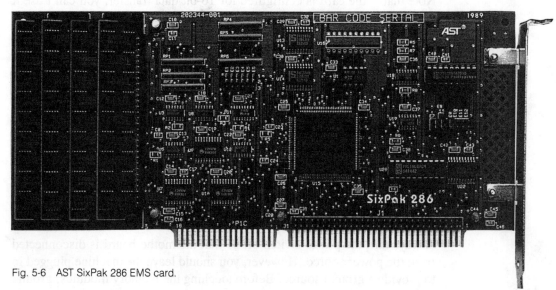

Fig. 5-6   AST SixPak 286 EMS card.

- Determine what banks on the motherboard or memory card will hold the new chips. (Check for a diagram in the manual if this isn't immediately clear just from looking at the board.) Be sure to check the manual for any changes you need to make in jumper configurations or dip switches. (Some expanded memory cards come with installation software that displays a visual map of dip switch settings on the screen once you've typed in the desired setup parameters. Others use a software setup to configure electronic dip switches.)

- If you're installing DRAM chips, check to see which way the other chips on the motherboard or card are facing. Failing that, look at the chip socket for an indentation on one end. There will be a triangular indentation or dot on the side of each chip to guide you. Match the indentation on the chip with the indentation on the socket. Place the chip in the socket and press down gently. Before applying pressure, check to see that all eight legs are properly inserted in the socket. If you encounter resistance, you may place the memory chip on its side on a flat surface and rock it gently to curve the legs slightly inward. When you're sure that all the legs are going into their sockets, exert an even pressure on the top of the chip until it slides into place.

- For SIPPs, identify the pin on the chip marked 0, and line it up with the hole marked 0 on the motherboard. Make sure that each of the forty pins is aligned correctly with its hole in the socket. It's very easy to break one pin off if you're careless. Figure 5-7 illustrates how to insert a SIPP into its socket.

Fig. 5-7   Installing a 40-pin SIPP module.

- SIMMs should be aligned over the mounting brackets at a 45 degree angle and then rotated to a vertical position before tamping them down. (See Fig. 5-3 on page 97.) Make absolutely certain that you either feel the module click in place or verify that the two holding pins on the socket go through the holes in each end of the SIMM.

- To install a memory card, mount the chips in the same way that you would on the motherboard. Check the manual for instructions about jumper and dip switch settings. Some memory cards include diagnostic software that allows you to type in the configuration. The software then displays a picture of the dip switch and jumper configuration. When the card has been set correctly, remove the metal guard from an appropriate slot on the motherboard. Align the memory card over the slot and press gently before you tamp it down. (Remember that a 16-bit card requires a 16-bit slot.) After the memory card has been inserted, reboot the machine and run the setup software supplied with the card. (You might need to refer to the manual again for instructions on configuring the memory manager.)

Memory cards in the current market

If you want to upgrade an old 8088 or 80286 for limited multitasking or other EMS use, you might do well to haunt weekend swap meets for older AST models. The AST Premium+ and Rampage cards generally don't work on machines with higher bus clock speeds than 10 MHz, but they can be found for less than $100. With 256K DRAM chips available as cheaply as they are today, $200 might buy you a 2M expansion. If you want to multitask, be leery of older cards from manufacturers like Intel, Quadram, and Everex.

If you're determined to add an EMS card to a newer 80286 or 80386 machine, look for one that can handle bus speeds of 12 MHz to 20 MHz. (20 MHz is generally the upper speed limit). Take into consideration the number of wait states, the memory configuration options, and the available alternate mapping registers.

Most of the expanded memory cards currently being sold have evolved past the level of the early AST and Intel boards. Many can hold 8M to 16M of RAM in SIMMs, rather than 2M of DRAM chips. Some memory cards also include input/output options like serial, parallel, and game ports.

Note Most memory cards support only one form of memory packaging. In those cases where the listings say that a card will support either one type of packaging or another, then you need to buy a card specifically for that type of packaging. For example, if a vendor supplies cards that will support either DRAMs or SIMMs, then you need to buy a card which specifically accepts DRAMs or SIMMs depending on your needs.

The most popular vendors of current fully compatible LIM 4.0 cards are as follows:

AST Research—Rampage Series/SixPak 286   The SixPak 286 holds up to 4M of RAM and supports bus speeds up to 20 MHz. It uses either 1M or 256K SIMMs and costs approximately $169 with 0K onboard. (See Fig. 5-6 on page 100.)

Use the Rampage PC for XT (8088) machines. It holds up to 2M of RAM. You can add a piggyback board with an additional 2M of RAM. The RAMpage PC uses either 1M or 256K SIMMs. It provides 2 mapping registers and costs approximately $395 with 256K onboard. (See Fig. 5-5 on page 100.)

The Rampage+ 286 holds up to 8M of RAM and supports bus speeds up to 20 MHz. It uses either 1M or 256K SIMMs and provides 32 mapping registers. It costs approximately $595 with 0K onboard.

Use the Rampage+/MC 286 EMS Board for IBM PS/2 30/50/60 Micro Channel machines. It holds up to 8M of RAM and uses either 1M or 256K SIMMs. The RAMpage+/MC 286 provides 32 Mapping Registers. It costs approximately $595 with 0K of RAM installed.

Micro Channel machines with 80386 and 80486 processors can use the Rampage+/MC 386 EMS board. It uses either 1M or 256K SIMMs and provides 80386 EMS Emulation. The RAMpage+/MC 386 costs approximately $449 with 0K of RAM installed.

Intel—Above Board Series   Use the Above Board+ for XT and AT machines. It holds 2M of RAM and uses 256K DRAM chips. You can purchase optional piggyback cards with 2M and 6M capacities. The Above Board+ costs approximately $595 with 512K.

The Above Board +8 is for XT, 80286 or IBM PS2 25/30 machines. It holds 8M and uses 1M DRAM chips. It costs approximately $895 with 2M installed. Figure 5-8 shows the Above Board +8.

Use the Above Board 2+ for IBM PS/2 50, 50Z, 55, 65 machines. It holds 8M of RAM and uses 1M SIMMs. This board provides the capability of incre-

Fig. 5-8   Intel Above Board Plus 8 comes with 2M and expands to 8M on board, 14M total with Piggy-back option. Reprinted by permission of Intel Corporation.

menting extended/expanded memory in 128K segments. It costs approximately $495 with 0K on board.

PS/2 Micro Channel machines with 80386 and 80486 processors may use the Above Board MC32. This board uses 1M SIMMs and costs approximately $595 with 0K RAM installed.

Because the Intel boards have no alternate mapping registers, they perform slower than other boards when used for expanded memory. They can still multitask programs in expanded memory but are not reliable for high speed (9600 bps) telecommunication. The earlier Above Board 286 requires a hardware upgrade in order to multitask programs in EMS.

CEI of America—RAMFlex/SUPERMicro series The RAMFlex is for AT machines. It holds 2–8M of RAM using 1M DRAM chips and provides 64 mapping registers. This board got rave reviews last year in INFOworld as the fastest performer of all. The RAMFlex costs approximately $495 with 0K of memory installed.

Use the RAMFlex+ for AT machines. It holds up to 32M installed in 2M increments. The RAMFlex+ uses either 1M or 4M SIMMs and provides 64 mapping registers. It costs approximately $695 with 0K on board.

IBM PS/2 50, 50Z, 60 require the SUPERMicro 4. This board holds up to 4M of RAM and uses 1M DRAM chips. It costs $495 with 0K of memory installed.

Everex Systems, Inc.—RAMBANK series for 80286 and above machines RAMBANK 3000 versions manufactured after December 1990 are fully EMS 4.0 compatible. The board holds up to 3M of RAM and uses 256K DRAM chips. It costs approximately $149 with 0K of RAM installed. Figure 5-9 shows the RAMBANK 3000.

The RAMBANK 8000 holds between 2 and 8M of RAM. It can be populated in 2M increments using 1M DRAM chips. The RAMBANK 8000 costs approximately $299 with 0K of RAM installed.

The RAMBANK 10000 holds 2–10M. It can be populated in 2M increments using 1M DRAM chips. The RAMBANK 10000 costs approximately $199 with 0K of RAM installed.

Note The Everex RAMBANK 10000 is not fully EMS 4.0 compatible. It will not multitask programs in expanded memory under DESQview. The RAMBANK 10000 and early versions of the RAMBANK 3000 may be upgraded with a hardware kit to full EMS 4.0 compatibility. Call Everex at (415) 498-4499 and ask for the chip upgrade kit, or write to

> Everex
> Customer Service
> 901 Page Ave.
> Fremont, CA 94538

Fig. 5-9   Everex RAMBANK 3000 EMS card. Everex Systems, Inc.

Teletek Enterprises—X series   Use the X-Bandit with XT or 286 machines. This board holds up to 2M of RAM. It uses 256K DRAM chips and provides 7 mapping registers. The X-Bandit costs approximately $340 with 512K installed.

Use the X-Tender 8 with 80286 and above machines. It holds up to 8M of RAM installed in 2M increments using 1M SIMMs. The X-Tender costs approximately $483 with 2M of memory installed.

Longshine Technology—Longshine 8661 series   These cards are clones of the AST boards. One of the authors tested an early version several years ago and found it to perform satisfactorily with DESQview as an EEMS board on systems running up to 12 MHz clock speed. The current versions are advertised as fully EMS 4.0 compatible on machines up to 20 MHz. They increment extended/ expanded memory in 128K segments and use 64 mapping registers.

The 8661N holds 8M of RAM using SIMMs. It costs approximately $97.

The 8661N2 holds 32M of RAM using SIMMs. It costs approximately $107.

Memory management units

Memory management units (MMUs) are a compromise expansion option for 80286 machines. They eliminate the backfilling dilemma of EMS cards by providing the hardware functions required to use extended memory as expanded memory. MMUs cost more than DOS add-ons but less than 80386SX plug-in modules or a new motherboard. If your 80286 motherboard can hold 2−8M of memory, the MMU converts all or part of this to expanded memory. In the '80s, the MMU was the ideal solution for the 80286 user who wanted to multitask. In today's market, an MMU is still an inexpensive alternative for 80286 machines on a network or for upgrading an IBM PS/2.

The MMU is a set of chips about the size of a credit card. It fits on the motherboard between the CPU socket and the 80286 processor. When the 80286 processor is placed in a socket on the MMU, the memory address lines are reconfigured. Recall that the difference between the way that 80286 and 80386 CPUs manage memory is twofold: the 80386 provides the ability to remap memory and has the added virtual 8086 processing mode. The MMU brings half of that capability to an 80286. With an MMU, the 80286 motherboard can map RAM into 16K pages. If your motherboard can hold 2 – 8M of extended memory, the MMU automatically converts that memory into EMS 4.0 compatible memory.[7] The MMU eliminates the need to backfill memory to the motherboard from an EMS card.

The MMU provides its own memory management software that cooperates completely with Quarterdeck's DESQview. You can open multiple windows in expanded memory, each up to 640K in size—there is no more 128K or 384K limitation. (Of course, DOS still takes some of the space, making the actual window size about 550K without additional drivers.) If the converted EMS is mapped from motherboard RAM, then programs in expanded memory run at the same speed as programs in conventional memory. An MMU can transform an 80286 system into a viable low-cost multitasking platform for character mode DOS applications. (Graphics applications still probably require an 80386 for optimal performance.) The MMU also allows you to partition the RAM above 1M. Some of it can be configured as expanded memory and some saved for use as extended memory. Partitioning the RAM permits Microsoft Windows in Standard Mode to coexist with expanded memory applications. You can even run Windows as an individual task under DESQview. Last, but not least, an MMU permits 80286 machines to load device drivers and TSRs above 640K in the UMB.

On the down side, the MMU lacks the speed of a 20 MHz 80386 CPU. It also lacks the virtual 8086 capability. DESQview is not dependent on virtual 8086 mode for multitasking, but without virtual 8086 there are fewer user options. Windows 3.0/3.1 uses the 80286's protected mode to run Windows applications, but without the virtual 8086 mode Windows can't multitask DOS applications. In addition, Windows can't use the page swapping capability of the 80386 to provide your applications with virtual memory. This means that the number of applications you can run is limited to the actual size of RAM in your machine.

The two principal manufacturers of MMUs are ALL Computers, Inc. of Toronto, Canada, and SOTA Technologies of California. The MMU technology

---

[7]If your 286 motherboard is limited to 1M, the MMU can work with memory on an add-on card. The memory on the card should be configured as extended memory instead of expanded. The MMU does the conversion to EMS 4.0 with its own software.

was invented by ALL Computers in 1988. The ChargeCard is listed by IBM as an officially recommended OEM enhancement for their PS/2 systems.

ALL Computers ChargeCard   The ALL ChargeCard works with machines running from 6 MHz to 25 MHz. It is bundled with an expanded memory manager and a set of utilities for mapping device drivers and TSR utilities into the UMB. The ChargeCard's memory utilities include a graphic display inventory program similar to Quarterdeck's Manifest.

The ChargeCard package also includes a special chip puller to allow you to remove the 80286 chip from your motherboard's socket and replace it with the ChargeCard. The 80286 chip must be socketed, rather than soldered. Figure 5-10 illustrates the procedure for performing this task.

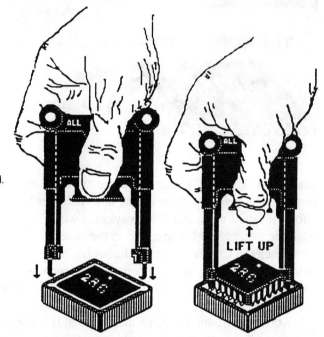

Fig. 5-10   ALL 286 ChargeCard.
© 1989, ALL Computers, Inc.

80286 motherboards have three basic socket types that hold the CPU chip: PGA (Pin Grid Array), PLCC (Plastic Leaded Chip Carrier, and LCC (Leadless Chip Carrier). The PLCC socket resembles a plastic tub surrounding the chip. The PGA socket is a platform with a series of holes that accept a pin-mounted CPU, (The PGA CPU is usually gray or in color). Figure 5-11 shows an 80286 using the PGA style packaging. Figure 5-12 shows an 80286 using the LCC style packaging, while Fig. 5-13 shows the PLCC style packaging.

The current version of the ChargeCard is designed to fit into a PLCC socket because this is the type most commonly used. For IBM PS/2 systems (which use the PGA socket) and other nonstandard systems, ALL provides a separate cable

The 80286 PGA Package

Fig. 5-11   PGA Type 80286 processor. © 1989, ALL Computers, Inc.

The 80286 LCC Package

Fig. 5-12   LCC Type 80286 processor. © 1989, ALL Computers, Inc.

The 80286 PLCC Package

Fig. 5-13   PLCC Type 80286 processor. © 1989, ALL Computers, Inc.

adaptor kit. The CPU socket on the motherboard might be located in an inconvenient position, next to a drive bay or in some other inaccessible area. The cable kit allows the card to be installed in systems with CPU sockets that are inaccessible once the motherboard is installed in the case.

When the ChargeCard is in the socket, it is transparent to the computer until you load the memory management device driver. At this point, the memory manager activates the ChargeCard, converting a designated amount of RAM into expanded memory.

SOTA Technologies Pop Card   The SOTA Pop Card from SOTA Technologies is similar to the ChargeCard. It is slightly less expensive, and ships with a slightly less convenient chip puller.

Replacing the motherboard

An 80286 system can be upgraded directly to an 80386 system by replacing the motherboard. This option might be only slightly more expensive than adding a memory management unit. You might need to buy new RAM chips if your old system was much slower or used a different type of RAM module. The general minimum requirement for memory speed on RAM chips is shown in Table 5-1.

Many motherboard vendors will perform a swap of the motherboard in your system for a small additional fee. In many cases, this means that you will be with-

Table 5-1 CPU speed vs chip speed.

CPU speed	Chip speed
10Mhz-12MHz	120 ns
12Mhz-20Mhz	100 ns
20Mhz-25Mhz	80 ns
33Mhz	60 ns

out your system for a few days. The following tips will help you avoid some of the most common problems of installing the new motherboard if you decide to do it yourself.

- Make a diagram of the cables inside the PC and label them with tape to identify their functions. Be particularly careful about the cables that plug into the motherboard from the power supply. (The black wires on the two plugs always face each other.) You probably won't have to remove the disk drives or power supply from the case.

- Always ground yourself before handling the motherboard. Static electricity can damage many of the motherboard components. Placing your hand on top of the power supply is one good way to eliminate any static.

- Make certain that you have enough stand-offs (the white plastic pieces that raise the motherboard above the bottom case) to insert in all the holes on the motherboard except for the two holes used to secure it. When you insert the motherboard into the case, check to see that the indents on the stand-offs go into the slots on the bottom of the case, rather than sitting on top of it. Observing these precautions will help you avoid cracking your new motherboard when you insert cards into the slots.

- Before screwing down the new motherboard in the case, reinstall your peripheral cards. Make sure that the slots on the motherboard line up properly with the gaps on the back of the case. Try to reinstall the peripheral cards in the same order as you took them out. Doing so will reduce many types of compatibility problems.

The following tips are some things to keep in mind when you buy a replacement motherboard:

- Plan for the future. Is the computer going to be fast enough? A 20 MHz 80386SX is fine for most text-based programs, but it may be a little slow for heavy use of Windows applications. A 33 MHz 80386DX will accommodate Windows and desktop publishing but might not be fast enough for a CAD designer. If you work regularly with AutoCad or CorelDRAW, even a 33 MHz 80386 will be a bit draggy at times. When you consider speed, think about what you'll be using the computer for most of the time.

- Be sure to check the motherboard to see where the bus slots are positioned. You want at least six slots that can accommodate full-sized expansion cards. Some "baby" 80386 motherboards mount the expansion slots directly opposite the RAM sockets. The result of this is that when all of the memory banks are filled with chips, full-sized expansion cards won't fit into some of the slots.

- BIOS date and manufacturer. The BIOS used by the system should display a current date, preferably within the last six months. If the motherboard uses a BIOS from a well-established manufacturer, you can probably count on it to provide compatibility and bug-free performance. Phoenix Technology, Inc., AMI (American Megatrends, Inc.), and Award are the most well-known companies in this field. Some BIOS configurations from lesser-known companies work as well, and others are plagued by problems. If you don't recognize the name on the BIOS, you should "audition" the motherboard before buying it. Either arrange for a trial period to evaluate the motherboard, or bring your software into the store to test it.

80386 plug-in CPU cards

The state of the art for plug-in CPUs is evolving rapidly. At this writing, several companies are working on modules that plug into either an 80286 or 80386 motherboard, allowing any CPU type from a 16 MHz 80286 to 33 MHz 80486. The advantage of a plug-in processor is that it can be installed painlessly in about five minutes. You don't have to disconnect your power supply, remove cards from slots, or remove the motherboard from the case. The disadvantage of a plug-in module is that the new processor might not reach its full efficiency in your old system. Remember that it will be sitting in an old motherboard with a limited bus speed, using an older, slower hard drive.

An 80386SX plug-in unit costs slightly more money than an 80386SX motherboard. For twice the cost of either, you can buy a full 80386DX motherboard with a 32-bit CPU and 32-bit data bus. For just a little more than that, you can buy a complete, working, starter system including case, disk drives and a new hard disk controller. If you decide to buy the complete starter system, then you still have the old computer; two systems instead of one!

But buying a complete system is more expensive; performing a motherboard swap takes time and expertise. For some users, a plug-in upgrade makes more sense. This is particularly true for owners of IBM PS/2 machines. You can't just swap out the motherboard of PS/2 Models 50, 50Z, 55, 60, etc., like you can with an ISA or EISA clone.

Intel Snap-In 386 The Snap-In 386 is available in 16 MHz and 20 MHz versions. It can be used only with IBM's PS/2 Models 50 and 60, converting them from 80286 machines to 80386SX compatibility. The Snap-In module includes a 16K static RAM cache that effectively doubles performance speed. The Snap-In allows you to use an 80287 coprocessor, if one was previously installed on the machine.

ALL Computer Add-Ins The ALL Charge SX includes either a 16 MHz or 20 MHz 80386SX CPU. It replaces the 80286 chip on the motherboard and instantly converts the machine to a fully compatible 80386SX. The only limitation of this upgrade is that no support is offered for an 80287 math co-processor. A separate conversion module allows an 80387SX coprocessor to be inserted into the 80287 socket on the motherboard. The ALL SX card may be installed in either ISA or PS/2 motherboards with the use of an adaptor kit for PGA or LCC processor sockets. (PLCC sockets require no adaptor).

ALL's newer line of plug-in cards is more flexible. The ALL RPM (for RAM, Processor power, and Megahertz speed) modules come in two flavors. One can upgrade an 80286 to accept either an 80286 20/25 CPU or an 80386SX /16/ 20/25 CPU. The other module converts an 80286 or 80386 motherboard for use with 25/33 MHz 80486 or 80486SX CPU. The RPMs are sold without a specific CPU on the card. You can install any AMD or Intel CPU from 16 MHz 80286 to 25 MHz 80486 in the socket of the appropriate module. The RPMs also take a direct memory upgrade in 1M SIMMs. If you've got an older 80286 motherboard that's ordinarily limited to 1M, the RPM may accept additional memory. The RPM bypasses the slowdown that would occur if you added memory with an EMS card via a bus slot. Figure 5-14 shows the ALL 386SX plug-in module. Figure 5-15 shows the ALL RPM plug-in module.

At this writing, ALL Computers is preparing the debut of the RPM plug-in products. Owners of older ALL 286 ChargeCards and ALL SX cards will be able to trade them in and receive a rebate on the newer RPM modules.

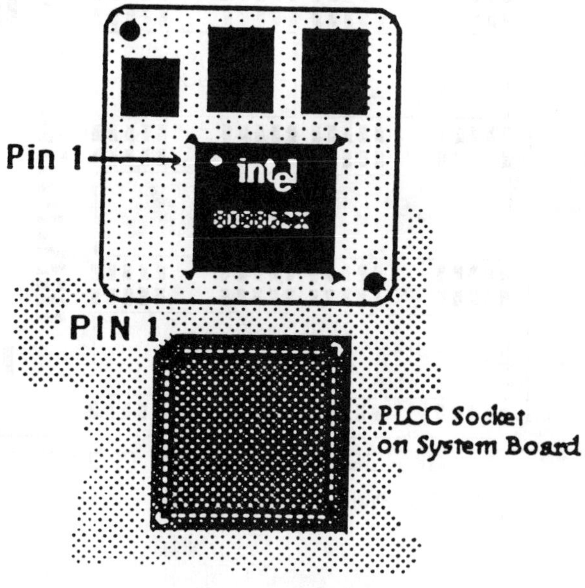

Fig. 5-14   ALL 80386SX Plug-in module. © 1989, ALL Computers, Inc.

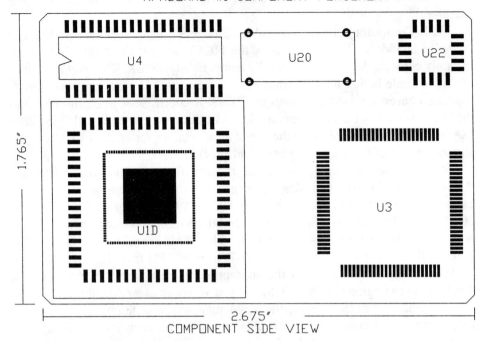

RPMBOARD #1 COMPONENT PLACEMENT

COMPONENT SIDE VIEW

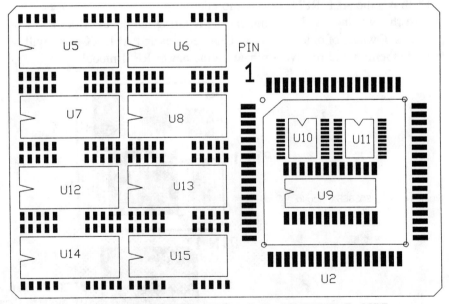

SOLDER-SIDE VIEWED FROM THE COMPONENT-SIDE

Fig. 5-15   ALL RPM Plug-in module. © 1989, ALL Computers, Inc.

Products from SOTA SOTA Technologies markets the SOTA Express 386SX plug-in. The SOTA Express comes in 16 MHz, 20 MHz, and 25 MHz flavors, and supports an 80387 coprocessor on the system. The SOTA 386SX cards have a slightly different design principle than ALL's. They include an 8K or 16K static RAM (SRAM) cache to increase the processor's performance. (SRAM is specialized RAM that does not require the refresh cycle of DRAM to maintain its contents. As a result, it provides much faster access times and does not require some of the support circuitry of DRAM.) This approach has both benefits and drawbacks. On the plus side, an older 6 MHz or 8 MHz IBM AT improves enormously, jumping to 20 MHz speeds and tripling performance on benchmarks like Norton's SysInfo. On the minus side, the SOTA card must add two or three wait states to maintain compatibility with the auxiliary motherboard chips and the bus. When the SRAM cache is enabled, the wait state slowdown is generally not noticed. Disable the SRAM cache and performance instantly reverts to 6 MHz.

For most tasks generated by your software, the SRAM cache keeps the machine performing at the 20 MHz level. Performance does break down if you multitask DOS applications under Windows. Apparently the 8K cache is insufficient to handle multiple virtual 8086 machines. The SOTA Express card permits multiple Windows applications to run concurrently at reasonable speed, but it's practically impossible to run three DOS programs at the same time under Windows no matter how much memory is present.

80486 upgrades

Consumers have had some happy fallout this year amidst the Intel-AMD processor wars. Prices for 80386/80486 processors and motherboards have been plummeting steadily since the spring. Whereas the average 33-MHz 80486 motherboard cost around $1800 before May of 1991 (including the processor), you might currently find them on sale for around half that price.

You may have heard 80486 war stories from consultants about hardware and software incompatibilities. There are a lot of vendors out there, and if you wind up with the wrong board, it could happen to you. 80486 machines can be a little bit more cantankerous than their 80386 counterparts. Yet, some of the clone boards selling for under $1000 work just as well as the $2000 and $3000 configurations from name brand manufacturers. Here are some tips on how to go shopping for an 80486 motherboard.

- A regular 80486 CPU has an internal math coprocessor built in. The math coprocessor speeds up the recalculation of spreadsheets, and the performance of CAD packages like AutoCad. Intel is now confusing the issue by marketing a chip called the 80486SX. The 80486SX is a slightly cheaper,

- slower version of the 80486 with the math coprocessor artificially disabled.

- The 80486 CPU has an internal SRAM cache of 8K. The SRAM cache speeds up the performance of all applications.

- Some 80486 motherboards have an additional (external) SRAM cache of 128K to 512K. The external SRAM cache is designed to further speed up application performance.

- The BIOS and setup configurations for 80486 machines might be more complex and/or advanced. The motherboard should automatically configure memory and recognize your video without setting jumpers. The setup options generally offer more sophisticated user features.

It pays to audition the motherboard in a working computer before you buy it. Some vendors have demonstration models set up running Microsoft Windows. This is a good compatibility test, but it's even better to bring in your own software and try it out on the vendor's machine. Alternatively, some vendors might allow you a one-week evaluation period with full refund if you encounter compatibility problems.

Igor's first law of transplant operations: back up your hard disk before you switch brains. In most cases, if you switch the same disk controller from one motherboard to another, the hard drive should boot without any problems—but not always. Another tip: if your system uses an older, MFM disk controller, ask the person who installs the motherboard to check the bus speed parameters of the new board. New, high-powered motherboards allow the bus speed to run as high as 33-MHz for modern disk controllers. MFM controllers require the traditional, slower 8-MHz bus speed.

Once the motherboard is installed and the computer starts properly, test it with both plain vanilla and complex boot configurations. If the machine won't start right off the bat, boot up from a floppy and inspect the CONFIG.SYS and AUTOEXEC.BAT on the hard drive. If the machine won't boot properly from the floppy, then watch out! The vendor might be able to get it to work by fiddling with internal setup parameters, but if the BIOS/motherboard designers have done their job, this shouldn't be necessary. If the system has built-in serial ports or an onboard video display adaptor, be sure to test those, too. (ChecKit and QAPlus, discussed in Chapter 2 are diagnostic utilities that can perform a thorough evaluation of all hardware functions.)

If you have an 80386/80486 memory manager, put it into the CONFIG.SYS and make sure it runs. The HIMEM.SYS driver included with Windows or MS-DOS 5 is a good place to start. Because you probably bought the 80486 to work with more than 1M of memory, the memory manager is crucial. If the system complains or locks up when your memory manager is installed, be wary. Calls for hardware and software technical support may resolve the problem, but a good motherboard/BIOS combination shouldn't put you through the wringer. If you have Windows, make sure you can run it in enhanced mode.

Conclusion

First, lets sum up what we've learned about expanded memory cards in this chapter:

- Memory added to an expanded memory card will run at the bus speed of the computer. If the motherboard memory is running at the 16 MHz of the CPU and the bus is running at 8 MHz, then memory accesses to the expanded memory card will take approximately twice as long.

- An 8088 machine requires an 8-bit card, while an 80286 machine will use either an 8- or 16-bit card. However, you always gain a speed advantage by using a 16-bit card on an 80286 because the data path is twice as large.

- On some machines, part of the motherboard's conventional memory must be removed or disabled to allow the EMS card backfill memory for multitasking.

- Some of the expanded memory cards on the market are not truly EMS 4.0 hardware compatible. These EMS cards are like the 80286 motherboards that won't multitask with EMS; their memory banks are not wired to map individual 16K pages.

New CPU technology from Intel

Very recently, Intel Corporation has announced implementation of several technological enhancements to their line of 486 processors. The first one that users will see is the "clock-doubled" 486SX2 and DX2 CPUs. The "clock doubled" CPUs will have two operating speeds, one for delivering data to the bus, and a higher speed (twice as fast) for internal register operations. Effectively, a 486SX 25/50 CPU will not only outperform a 25 MHz 486DX, but also come close to equalling a 50 MHz 486DX chip in some operations. The 33/66 and 50/100 486DX2s might very well lift the Intel PCs to the minicomputer workstation level.

Currently, AST Research, Advanced Logic Research, Northgate, Grid, and Unisys corporations have all announced computer models that can accommodate the new "clock-doubled" CPUs. The Northgate "Elegance" models are upgradable to any 486 CPU in the Intel series. In other words, users may buy a 486SX/16 entry level machine, and simply install a faster CPU on the motherboard at a later date.

Local bus disk access and graphics

The advent of disk-intensive and screen-intensive applications has focused attention on input/output bottlenecks in PC computing speed. Traditionally, disk read/write operations and screen redrawing have been limited to the speed of the motherboard's data bus (8 MHz to 16 MHz). Recently, several computer manufacturers have introduced the concept of a "Local Bus" that connects computer peripherals directly to the CPU.

Currently, clone manufacturers have implemented several proprietary technologies that allow SCSI controllers, network adapters, bus mastering devices, high performance graphics cards and other peripherals to function at the full clock speed of the CPU. This results in higher data transfer rates and more robust video performance. As we go to press, there is no universal standard for implementing this feature, but Intel Corporation has announced plans to publish one. By the time this book is in your hands, the Intel Local Bus standard might be a reality along with Intel's clock-doubled CPUs.

This completes the first part of this book, covering basic software and hardware issues in PC memory management. The rest of this book shows you how to put these concepts to work in your everyday productivity environment.

6
CHAPTER

Software strategies for improving performance

Increase conventional memory by eliminating unnecessary device drivers and TSRs from CONFIG.SYS and AUTOEXEC.BAT.

Increase conventional memory by changing the configuration of your applications.

Improve application performance by placing program overlay and data files on a RAM disk.

Command shells, TSR utilities, and task switching can provide flexibility and increased productivity.

Why optimize?

So far we've concentrated on hardware solutions to increase the amount of memory available to your applications. In many cases, we've also mentioned software required to make the hardware work. However, even without a hardware upgrade, you can get better performance out of your system. If you're up against RAM cram with your applications, you can configure them to use less memory. For example, instead of loading your word processor and spell checker, you might only want to load the word processor. You can also free up conventional memory by judicious editing of your CONFIG.SYS and AUTOEXEC.BAT. For example, reducing the number of files in your CONFIG.SYS can save a modicum of memory for your applications. Both of these solutions represent methods of optimizing your current environment.

Of course, many people not only optimize their environment for efficient use of memory but also for speed. If your application's performance is sluggish and you have some memory to spare, you might want to reverse the paring down process. Some applications can use the additional memory to speed up performance. For example, instead of storing an overlay on disk, the application might be able to store it in RAM. Because RAM is so much faster to access, you will notice a perceptible increase in performance. Even if your application doesn't store its overlays in memory, you might be able to store them on a RAM disk, essentially accomplishing the same results. We examined RAM disks, spoolers, and disk caches in Chapter 3. In this chapter, you'll see how to use them with your applications.

Retrieving conventional memory

One strategy for gaining conventional memory is to make DOS (and your applications) use less. Different versions of DOS take up different memory overheads. DOS 3.3 is an extremely stable operating system that consumes 10−15K less than DOS 4.01. PC- and MS-DOS 5, and DR DOS 5 & 6 use more memory than DOS 3.3 when loaded low but less memory when loaded high. Table 6-1 provides a more complete description of each version of DOS since 2.0. In addition, it provides you with the amount of memory used by each version.

Paring down the startup files

MS-DOS 4 & 5 and DR DOS 5 & 6 use an installation program to load the DOS files on your hard drive. In addition, these installation programs create a simple CONFIG.SYS and AUTOEXEC.BAT file based on your answers to questions it poses. No matter how you answer these questions, the installation program always places some entries in your startup files. As a result, the installation program might have placed some unnecessary commands in CONFIG.SYS or AUTO EXEC.BAT.

Table 6-1 DOS memory usage by version.

DOS version	Description	Kilobytes used
DOS 2.1	Introduced in 1983. This version of DOS does not provide network or file-sharing support. Disk partitions are limited to 15M. In some cases, it might be incompatible with current software. This was the first version of DOS to provide support for both foreign languages and the IBM PCjr.	41K
DOS 3.3	Introduced in 1987. DOS 3.3 does not provided expanded memory support. Hard disk partitions are limited to 32M. No command shell is included. This version of DOS does provide support for both 1.2M and 3.5" floppy drives. It also supports networks and disk drive aliases. In addition, this version allows the user set file attributes to read-only. Other enhancements include updated foreign language support, nested batch files, and the ability to use four serial ports at up to 19,200 baud.	55K
DOS 4.01	Introduced in 1988. This version of DOS provides limited expanded memory support. Disk partitions may exceed 32M. It includes a limited DOS shell. This is the first version of DOS to provide a utility (the MEM command) for determining where a program is loaded in memory.	69K
DOS 5.0	Introduced in 1991. DOS 5.0 provides full expanded memory support. Disk partitions may exceed 32M. The user may choose to load the operating system above 640 KB. A DOS shell with task switching is included. This is the first version of DOS to provide its own set of shells for Novell NetWare. It also provides an enhanced version of the MEM command. MS-DOS 5.0 comes with a copy of Storage Dimension's SpeedStor driver (not the entire product).	63K
DR DOS 5	DR DOS 5.0 provides limited expanded memory support. Disk partitions may exceed 32M. It provides a non-task switching, graphic file manager.	70.2K
DR DOS 6	Introduced in 1991. This version of DOS provides full expanded memory support. Disk partitions may exceed 32M. The user may choose to load the operating system above 640 KB. It includes the TASKMAX/VIEWMAX task switcher/ graphic file manager. DR DOS 6.0 comes bundled with PCKWIK disk cache and ADDSTOR disk compression utilities.	67K

Paring down MS-DOS

To begin to understand how you can eliminate some of the memory grabbers from your machine, you need to know what the CONFIG.SYS and AUTOEXEC.BAT files contain. The MS-DOS 5 installation program automatically adds the following statements to your CONFIG.SYS.

```
Device=SETVER.EXE
Device=HIMEM.SYS
DOS=HIGH
```

A DOS 4.01 installation might insert the following entries in addition to the ones just shown:

CONFIG.SYS
```
Device=ANSI.SYS
Device=PRINTER.SYS
Device=DISPLAY.SYS
Install=FASTOPEN.EXE
```

AUTOEXEC.BAT
```
Graphics
Print
```

BUFFERS and FILES are two other CONFIG.SYS statements that might consume conventional memory. A *buffer* is a form of primitive disk cache. DOS stores the most recently fetched data from the hard disk in these little pieces of RAM. Too many buffers will actually slow your machine down because DOS will have more RAM to search through. Too few buffers will make your machine run very slowly as DOS tries to fetch everything from disk. Each buffer occupies the same amount of space as one sector on your hard drive (usually 512 bytes). If you find yourself in a memory pinch, you may decrease the allocated number of buffers. When you install a disk cache to replace the buffers, you may set the buffer allocation to around 5 without detriment to hard disk performance speed. MS-DOS 4 & 5 and DR DOS 6 allow you to load buffers high—into the HMA. Loading buffers high frees up conventional memory without losing hard disk performance efficiency.

The FILES entry affects how many files you can have open at once. DOS always takes the first five files for itself, so you need to add five to whatever number of files you want to open. A minimum of FILES=25 is generally required to run most software. However, you can specify any number of files from 8 to 255. Windows and data processing programs require substantially more. Files don't take up as much memory as buffers, so there is little to gain in decreasing them.

Eliminating one or more of the commands automatically installed in your CONFIG.SYS and AUTOEXEC.BAT might free up to 30K of conventional memory. However, you can't simply remove the entries from AUTOEXEC.BAT or CONFIG.SYS without understanding what tasks the device drivers and TSRs perform. Here's a brief summary of what they do.

DEVICE=SETVER.EXE

This is a DOS 5 driver that allows some older programs to run under DOS 5. If the program would ordinarily complain that the system is running an "incorrect DOS version," SETVER intercepts requests for DOS version number and fools the program into thinking an older version of DOS is running. If you don't use any software that has this problem, you don't need SETVER in your CONFIG.SYS.

DEVICE=HIMEM.SYS/DOS=HIGH

HIMEM.SYS is the DOS 5 extended memory manager. It allows the DOS command kernel to be loaded above 640K on 80286/80386/80486 machines when used in conjunction with the DOS=HIGH statement. If DOS is loaded low, HIMEM allows other applications like Xerox Ventura Publisher to claim the 64K HMA area. HIMEM.SYS is also necessary to run Microsoft Windows in Standard or Enhanced modes. Unless you substitute another memory manager like QEMM or 386MAX on an 80386 machine, these statements should be left untouched. (If you run Quarterdeck's DESQview on an 80286 machine, the Quarterdeck driver, QEXT.SYS is equivalent to HIMEM.SYS. Using QEXT .SYS in place of HIMEM.SYS will provide more memory for DESQview.)

DEVICE=ANSI.SYS

ANSI.SYS is an extended screen driver that allows some software to display color text and perform tricks with the on-screen cursor position. If you are not running software that specifically requires ANSI.SYS, this statement may be deleted from the CONFIG.SYS.

Note   Many telecommunications programs have an ANSI driver built in and might read ANSI graphics from remote connections without ANSI.SYS.

DEVICE=PRINTER.SYS

PRINTER.SYS allows you to use code page switching[1] with the IBM Proprinter Models 4201, 4202, 4207, and 4208, or the IBM 5202 Quietwriter III. It has no function for other printers. PRINTER.SYS uses about 13K of conventional memory.

---

[1]A *code page* is the means used to support characters used by various countries. For example, if you lived in Portugal, your character set would vary from the character set used in the United States. Because most keyboards are hardwired to support the character set used by the United States, you must load the appropriate code page if you need the extended support for another language. You can provide drivers for many different types of printers, even though they are not supplied with MS-DOS.

DEVICE=DISPLAY.SYS

DISPLAY.SYS enables code page switching on EGA, VGA, and LCD displays. In essence, your screen will display the characters used by the specified country instead of the default character set. DISPLAY.SYS uses about 10K of conventional memory.

DEVICE=EGA.SYS

EGA.SYS allows the MS DOS 5 Task Switcher to restore the screen with EGA displays. EGA.SYS uses about 3.2K of conventional memory.

INSTALL=FASTOPEN.EXE

The Install command in the CONFIG.SYS loads the Fastopen hard disk utility. Fastopen sets up buffers in memory that might allow programs on your hard disk to start up more rapidly. It is often unnecessary or incompatible with disk-caching software and multitasking environments. Fastopen uses about 3K of conventional memory (plus 100 bytes for each file tracked).

GRAPHICS

The GRAPHICS command appears in AUTOEXEC.BAT. It allows IBM Proprinters and Epson 9-pin dot matrix printers to reproduce graphic screens when you use the Print Screen key. The GRAPHICS command uses about 2K of conventional memory with DOS 4 and 6K of conventional memory with DOS 5.

PRINT

The Print command sets up a TSR queue for spooling documents in the background from the DOS command line. It is unnecessary if you print directly from applications. Print uses about 6K of conventional memory.

Paring down DR DOS

DR DOS presents a few new entries for your AUTOEXEC.BAT and CONFIG.SYS. The installation program for DR DOS 6 might place the following commands in your AUTOEXEC.BAT:

```
SHARE /L : 20
TASKMAX /d : c : \
```

The installation program places these statements in the AUTOEXEC.BAT if you elect to configure the DR DOS task switcher. The SHARE command is unnecessary if you don't intend to use the task switcher. You may remove it without any loss of performance or functionality. SHARE is a special device driver that keeps track of which files are open, what mode they are opened in, and who opened them. If an application tries to use the file while it is open in the READ-WRITE or WRITE-ONLY modes, SHARE reports it as a sharing violation. This prevents two programs from updating the same file at the same time in either a task-switching or multitasking environment.

Reducing application size

One way to gain more conventional memory is to reduce the amount of memory consumed by your everyday applications. Many programs can be reconfigured to use less memory by changing their startup defaults. The conventional memory you liberate by paring down application requirements might allow you to load network drivers or TSR utilities. Some programs also allow you to load part of their code in expanded or extended memory. For example, the latest mouse drivers from Microsoft and Logitech can be loaded into upper memory or extended memory. Other programs allow you to disable features that are unnecessary for your work. Whatever technique you use, paring down an application's memory requirements means more memory for the things you really need to load. The following paragraphs describe ways to conserve memory by cutting down the default requirements of popular applications. You can use these same techniques to reduce the requirements of other applications as well.

WordStar v4-6

The WSCHANGE utility lets you control memory usage within WordStar. For example, you might choose to have the main dictionary and thesaurus loaded in memory or read from disk. When you first enter WSCHANGE, the program will ask what program you want to create. It's usually a good idea to name the file something different than WS.EXE. That way you can experiment with different settings without affecting your word processor adversely. You can also compare the performance of WordStar with and without the changes. Once you get the settings the way you want them, simply copy the new file to WS.EXE to make the changes permanent.

From the main WSCHANGE menu, type C to select computer and then C to choose memory options. Figure 6-1 shows the first WordStar memory management screen.

Use Option A to load WordStar memory resident. Setting this option ON makes WordStar a little faster but consumes a lot of conventional memory. Option B on this display allows you to determine whether or not WordStar loads the dictionary and thesaurus into memory. Setting the option OFF conserves conventional memory, setting it ON makes spelling checks much faster. Never touch option D; doing so might prevent the dictionary from functioning at all. Options E, F, H, and I represent the best places to shave off a few kilobytes of conventional memory usage. For example, instead of using a personal dictionary, use the main

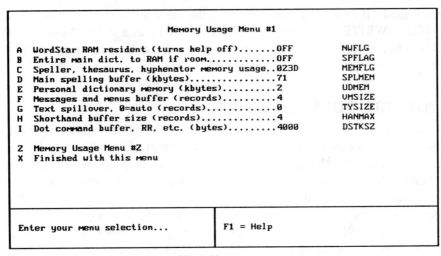

```
                    Memory Usage Menu #1

A   WordStar RAM resident (turns help off).......OFF        NWFLG
B   Entire main dict. to RAM if room............OFF         SPFLAG
C   Speller, thesaurus, hyphenator memory usage..023D       MEMFLG
D   Main spelling buffer (kbytes)...............71          SPLMEM
E   Personal dictionary memory (kbytes)..........2          UDMEM
F   Messages and menus buffer (records)..........4          VMSIZE
G   Text spillover, 0=auto (records).............0          TYSIZE
H   Shorthand buffer size (records)..............4          HANMAX
I   Dot command buffer, RR, etc. (bytes)........4000        DSTKSZ


Z   Memory Usage Menu #2
X   Finished with this menu




  Enter your menu selection...          F1 = Help
```

Fig. 6-1   WSChange Memory Usage Menu #1. © 1992, WordStar International, Inc.

one and set the personal dictionary to 0. That will shave 2K off the memory required by WordStar. If you don't use a lot of dot commands, you can probably shave a few kilobytes off there as well.

Figure 6-2 shows the second WordStar memory management screen. Notice that there are quite a few areas where you can shave a few kilobytes off WordStar's conventional memory requirement here as well. For example, if you don't use proportional fonts, then you don't need to reserve space for them. (Unfortunately, WordStar forces you to save room for at least one proportional space data table.) Many people will never perform a merge print. You can save 4K by setting Option

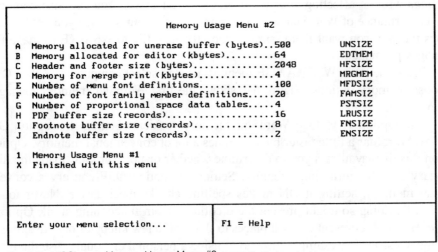

```
                    Memory Usage Menu #2

A   Memory allocated for unerase buffer (bytes)..500       UNSIZE
B   Memory allocated for editor (kbytes).........64        EDTMEM
C   Header and footer size (bytes)..............2048       HFSIZE
D   Memory for merge print (kbytes)..............4         MRGMEM
E   Number of menu font definitions............100         MFDSIZ
F   Number of font family member definitions.....20        FAMSIZ
G   Number of proportional space data tables.....4         PSTSIZ
H   PDF buffer size (records)...................16         LRUSIZ
I   Footnote buffer size (records)...............8         FNSIZE
J   Endnote buffer size (records)................2         ENSIZE


1   Memory Usage Menu #1
X   Finished with this menu




  Enter your menu selection...          F1 = Help
```

Fig. 6-2   WSChange Memory Usage Menu #2. © 1992, WordStar International, Inc.

D to 0. You should probably leave Option H—PDF Buffer Size—alone, however; changing this setting could inhibit WordStar from printing your document. You can save 22K of conventional memory by changing Option B—Memory Allocated for Editor—to 42K (the minimum allowed by WordStar). In total, you can probably reduce WordStar 6.0's default conventional memory requirements by at least 25K without affecting functionality. This means that you could load WordStar 6.0 on a system with 245K left after loading DOS.

Microsoft Word 5.5

Word takes slightly less memory when you run it in text mode (type WORD /C at the command line). You may also control the number of internal file buffers Word allocates for documents with the /Bnn switch. The default is to allocate 25% of available memory. Each buffer is 512 bytes. Starting Word with /B20 would reserve 10,240 bytes as file buffers. You can tell Word not to use expanded memory by including the /X switch.

WordPerfect 5.1

WordPerfect 5.1 requires around 384K of memory to start. You can divide the RAM requirement between conventional and expanded memory. This is useful if you are running WordPerfect in an environment with limited conventional memory available. The WP/W-n,n parameter sets the ratio of conventional to expanded memory used by WordPerfect. WP/W- 256,128 limits conventional memory usage to 256K, filling out the other 128K from EMS.

You may also conserve memory in WordPerfect by turning off the hyphenation feature or disabling an enhanced keyboard. The WP/32 switch tells WordPerfect that only the older LIM 3.2 type expanded memory is available. WP/NE disables the use of any expanded memory. WP/R loads additional WordPerfect modules into conventional or expanded memory, increasing performance speed by eliminating the need to access overlays on disk. (See the next section on using extra RAM to improve application performance.)

PCWrite

You can reduce PCWrite's overall memory requirement by omitting the spell check feature or loading a minimal on-line help file. Normally, PCWrite's minimum memory requirement is 384K. Quicksoft also distributes PCWrite Lite, a pared down version of PCWrite that can run in as little as 256K.

XYWrite III +

The spell checking and thesaurus features of XYWrite can be loaded into expanded memory. This greatly reduces the amount of conventional memory required for XYWrite to load.

Lotus 1-2-3 v2.xx

There are a number of ways to save conventional memory when using Lotus 1-2-3 v2.xx. For example, 1-2-3 loads from 256K to 384K of code (including add-ins) into expanded memory when available. You could reduce the size of a disk cache or print spooler to accommodate this requirement. Unfortunately, versions below 2.2 might have difficulty with some features or add-in modules running in expanded memory. Additionally, up to 2.5M of expanded memory may be used to store worksheet data, instead of trying to stuff it all into conventional memory. If your worksheets are larger than 2.5M, Beyond 640K from Intex Solutions will allow 1-2-3 to gain up to 4M of expanded memory for worksheets (up to 4M).

Besides using expanded memory, you can perform some additional paring of 1-2-3's memory requirements. For example, instead of automatically loading all your add-in modules, manually load only the ones you need to use. This can save a substantial amount of conventional memory. You can also break your worksheets into smaller pieces. Not only does this make the data you're looking for easier to find, but it reduces the memory required to load each worksheet.

Xerox Ventura Publisher (GEM Edition for DOS)

There are three GEM-based versions of Ventura Publisher that are still widely used: Ventura Publisher Standard 2.0, Ventura Professional Extension 2.0, and Ventura Publisher 3.0. (Ventura Publisher for Windows depends on Windows for its available memory.)

Ventura Publisher 2.0 (Standard Edition) may use only a small amount of expanded memory. With no expanded memory present, 550K of conventional memory is required to start the program. If 128K of EMS is present, VP 2.0 needs only 525K of conventional memory. Additionally, like DESQview, Windows, and Microsoft's DOS 5, VP 2.0 may use the first 64K of extended memory (HMA area) to load code. With Microsoft's HIMEM.SYS or a third party XMS driver, Ventura Publisher 2.0 may run in as little as 490K of conventional memory.

Ventura Professional Extension (2.0) and Ventura Publisher 3.0 (DOS version) may both use unlimited expanded memory. If 256K of EMS is available on the system, only 450K to 460K of conventional memory is required to start the program. (Note, you must have 256K of expanded memory free in addition to the expanded memory allotted for the EDCO hyphenation dictionary. The EDCO dictionary may be disabled to free up EMS.)

All GEM versions of Ventura Publisher allow you to control memory buffers for printing and screen fonts by setting command-line switches. The /A = switch allows the print and font buffer to be reduced within a range of 1K to 32K. You can edit the following line in VP.BAT or VPPROF.BAT:

```
DRVRMRGR VP [VPPROF] %1 /M = 02 /A = 32
```

Working down, you may replace /A = 32 with /A = 24, /A = 16, and so on, until a threshold is reached where the program starts.

Ventura Publisher uses approximately 10–15K more memory with VGA and Super-VGA screen drivers. If you have a video card that can display Hercules graphics, Ventura Publisher can be configured for a Hercules display as a last resort.

Ventura Publisher 3.0 and 4.0 for Windows gets its memory directly from Windows. See Chapter 9 on Windows Memory Management for details on how to fine tune Windows for your system.

Applying extra conventional memory

The last section showed us techniques for fine tuning DOS applications to conserve conventional memory. To gain this extra memory, you might need to disable program features or decrease a program's internal memory buffers. If you have sufficient conventional, extended, or expanded memory, you might want to apply the reverse procedure to improve performance. By increasing internal buffers and other features, you can fine tune both DOS and your applications to use any extra memory to improve performance and flexibility.

Some programs increase their performance speed dramatically when run with a disk cache or from a RAMdisk. All versions of DOS since v3 provide a RAMdisk utility that can use either conventional or extended memory. As we saw in Chapter 3, the RAMdisk is created by placing the appropriate device driver in the CONFIG.SYS. (In IBM DOS, the driver is called VDISK.SYS, while in Microsoft DOS it is RAMDRIVE.SYS.). Many applications include overlay files on the hard disk that must be accessed for supplementary program functions. If the main program and/or the overlays are copied to a RAMdisk, the various features may be accessed almost instantaneously. Additionally, some programs create temporary files while active. Allowing an application to write temporary files on a RAMdisk also improves performance speed. The following paragraphs illustrate how you can put this speed advantage to work with specific applications. By applying the principles shown, you can make almost any program faster.

> *Note* The RAMdisk supplied with MS-DOS 5 is limited to 4M as a maximum size. In actuality, this upper limit might not exist. We have included two shareware RAMdisks on our utilities diskette that may run at any size up to 32M if you have the memory for them.

WordStar

WordStar will run faster if WS.EXE (or whatever you named your WordStar executable file) and overlay files are copied to a RAMdisk. If the program is normally located on drive C: and the RAMdisk is drive E:, your batch file (let's call it WSRAM.BAT) might read as follows:

```
E:
COPY C:\WS\*.OVR
COPY C:\WS\*.CTL
COPY C:\WS\WS.EXE
WS.EXE
```

Note   You need to run WSCHANGE to tell WordStar where to find its overlay files. If you don't, WordStar will still look for them in the place you originally told it to look on your C: drive. You may do this by selecting C for computer and then D for WordStar files from the WSCHANGE main menu.

WordStar will also run faster if you set the RAM resident and main dictionary to RAM options on. This is done by running the WSCHANGE program, typing C for computer, and then C for memory options from the Main menu.

WordPerfect 5.1

There are several ways to improve the performance of WordPerfect. For example, you can direct WordPerfect's temporary files to a RAMdisk with the WP /D-X: parameter, where X is the RAMdisk letter. In addition, you can copy WordPerfect's macros, printer drivers, dictionary and thesaurus files to the RAMdisk. If the RAMdisk is drive E:, your batch file (let's call it WPRAM.BAT) might read as follows:

```
E:
MD WP51
CD WP51
COPY C:\WP51\*.PRS
COPY C:\WP51\*.WP{WP}US.*
COPY C:\WP51\*.WPM
WP /D-E:
```

If you do copy WordPerfect's auxiliary files to the RAMdisk, you might need to tell WordPerfect where to find the appropriate files by changing the setup options (hit Shift-F1 and then type 6, followed by 2,3,4,5 or 6).

Microsoft Word 5.5

To improve Microsoft Word's performance, copy the spelling checker, thesaurus, printer and font files to a RAMdisk. If the RAMdisk is drive E:, your batch file might read as follows:

```
E:
MD WORD
CD WORD
```

```
COPY C : \ WORD \ * . LEX
COPY C : \ WORD \ * . CMP
COPY C : \ WORD \ * . SYN
COPY C : \ WORD \ * . PRD
COPY C : \ WORD \ * . DAT
```

You'll need to tell Word where to find these files by changing the settings in the Options menu (Esc, then O).

Xerox Ventura Publisher

You can improve Ventura Publisher's performance by instructing it to write its temporary files to a RAMdisk. This is accomplished by placing the /O = d : parameter in VP.BAT as follows:

```
DRVRMRGR VP %1 /O = d :
```

[d :] is the drive letter of the RAMdisk. This parameter is not necessary with the Professional Extension and Ventura Publisher 3.0. Professional Extension and VP 3.0 automatically write temporary files to expanded memory.

Using TSR managers

TSR ("Terminate and Stay Resident") utilities fulfill a myriad of miscellaneous productivity chores including that of a desk calendar, auto-dialer, notepad, appointment scheduler, file manager, and more. With a simple press of some combination of keys (usually a control key and either a character or function key), the TSR pops over your current work, allowing you to look up an address, dial a number, or schedule an appointment. Some TSRs provide operating system functions, showing memory usage, providing a disk cache, intercepting and recording keystroke combinations, or loading a secondary command processor. Still other TSRs provide an interface between DOS and your hardware. These include products like Stacker and Speedstor for hard disk drives, or special drivers that allow you to use more than four serial ports on a PC.

Once you load a TSR, it consumes conventional memory even when you're not using it. Some of the more advanced TSRs include options to unload themselves from memory; but with most, the only way you can reclaim the memory they use without some type of external help is to reboot the system. Using a TSR manager, you can load and unload a series of programs by marking their location in memory. A TSR manager can keep track of your memory resident programs and remove them one by one.

INSTALL and REMOVE

INSTALL and REMOVE are a simple pair of PC Magazine utilities that let you regulate TSR programs. You run INSTALL prior to loading your TSR to set up a pointer to the TSR's memory location. A series of TSR programs can be loaded in layers, sandwiched in between instances of INSTALL.COM. When you want to remove a program, run REMOVE. Running REMOVE clears conventional memory of all TSR programs loaded after the last instance of INSTALL. Of course, if you have three programs loaded with INSTALL sandwiched between each one, and you want to remove the first one you loaded, then you will need to remove the other two first.

For a practical example of how you might use INSTALL and REMOVE, consider DOS utilities like APPEND or PRINT. APPEND consumes about 9K of memory, while the DOS PRINT utility consumes about 6K of memory. Normally, when you run either APPEND or PRINT, the resident portion of the code remains in memory until you reboot the machine. With INSTALL and REMOVE, you can load both APPEND and PRINT, and then remove them later on in your session to free memory for other applications. One loading sequence would be as follows:

```
INSTALL
APPEND /X:ON
INSTALL
PRINT
```

When you run REMOVE, it will eliminate the code for PRINT and the last loaded instance of INSTALL, freeing 6K and leaving APPEND resident. If you run REMOVE a second time, it will remove APPEND as well as the first instance of INSTALL.

The TSR utilities

This is a somewhat more sophisticated package of utilities released into the Public Domain by Kim Kokkonen of TurboPower Software. The TSR utilities contain MARK.COM and RELEASE.COM (RELEASE.EXE for v2.9 of the product), which perform functions analogous to INSTALL and REMOVE. The TSR utilities will also let you temporarily disable a TSR without removing it from memory, or load and remove specific TSR utilities from a menu. We have included the TSR utilities package on our Utilities Diskette.

Using file managers and command shells

Programs like XTree Gold, PC Tools, and the Norton Commander provide file management features and convenient access to other system utilities. The menu-driven interface provided by these utilities might provide file viewing, text editing, telecommunications, and disk maintenance options. File management shells can make DOS easier to use apart from multitasking environments like Windows and DESQview. A file manager might allow you to launch applications from a menu or associate specific file types with applications so that selecting a document or spreadsheet automatically runs the program that created it. Of course, these utilities provide an abundance of other miscellaneous features as well. For example, PC Tools includes a utility to measure your system's performance level.

MS-DOS 5 and DR DOS 5 & 6 provide a menu-driven file maintenance utility with their bundled graphic command shells. (MS-DOS 4 contains a command shell, but it did not include the file maintenance utilities.) These file managers don't offer as much flexibility as third-party packages, but DOSShell (included with MS-DOS 5) and VIEWMAX/TASKMAX (included in DR DOS 6) feature built-in task switchers. Third-party file managers can generally load only one program at a time. The following paragraphs present a comparison of the most popular PC command shell/file management packages.

Norton Commander

Figure 6-3 shows an example of the Norton Commander file display and a pull-down menu. Notice that the Norton Commander attaches some of the more important features to function keys. These keys are listed at the bottom of the display.

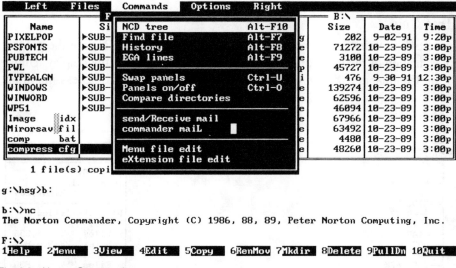

Fig. 6-3 Norton Commander.

The advantages of Norton Commander are the following:

- An easy method for building application menus. One interface provides a simple program launcher for novices as well as a flexible file manager for more advanced users.

- Useful telecommunications module. Norton Commander provides complete compatibility with MCI Mail. (Most current communications packages are not capable of using MCI for automated binary file transfers.)

- A well designed interface. Norton Commander allows simultaneous access to menu-driven features and the DOS command line.

Norton Commander shares the following features with other file management packages:

- A point-and-shoot application launch.
- A mouse-driven file management.
- A text editor
- An ASCII file viewer.
- Some specialized file filters for data files in popular application formats.
- A backup utility.

However, Norton Commander lacks the following features:

- A full-featured text editor.
- A system inventory/information utility.
- A pop-up shell within other applications.
- A task switcher.

XTree Gold

Figure 6-4 provides an example of XTree Gold's file display. Notice the graphic representation of the directory tree in the upper left corner of the display. Unlike Norton Commander, XTree Gold uses Alt key combinations to access important

```
Path: C:\                                          1-03-80 10:50:03 pm

C:\                                             FILE  *.*
 ├─AAA
 ├─BAT286                                       DISK  C:
 ├─BATDICK                                      Available
 ├─BATS                                           Bytes    2,187,264
 ├─BIOS
 │  └─DEMO                                       DISK Statistics
 ├─CRTL                                          Total
 ├─DIAG                                            Files          1,836
 ├─DOS                                             Bytes     28,974,867
 ├─DV                                            Matching
 ├─FASTBACK                                        Files          1,836
 ├─FONTS                                           Bytes     28,974,867
 ├─FOUNDRY                                       Tagged
                                                  Files              0
 !CARDS3 .GEM    AUTO20  .BAT    AUTOEXEC.QDK      Bytes              0
 A221130 .C00    AUTO21  .BAT    AUTOEXEC.SAV    Current Directory
 A22930  .C00    AUTOEXEC.BAT    AUTOEXEC.T2     C:\
 ANOTOPS .BAT    AUTOEXEC.ORG    AUTOEXEC.T21      Bytes        539,821

ALT DIR   Edit  File display  Graft  Hide/unhide  Log disk  Prune  Release disk
COMMANDS  Sort criteria  Tag  Untag  Wash disk  eXecute  Quit
          F2 format  F3 relog dir  F9 video mode  F10 configure
```

Fig. 6-4 XTree Gold.

features. XTree Gold also provides a constant display of disk statistics, allowing you to determine your hard drive's status at a glance.

The advantages of XTree Gold are as follows:

- The definitive interface for file location/file manipulation.
- Quick, well organized display of any drive or directory on your system.
- Comprehensive tools for moving, copying, and retrieving directories and files. This includes a clear statistical display of disk space allocation.
- A flexible text editor with many word processor-like features.

XTree Gold shares the following features with other file management packages:

- A point-and-shoot application launch.
- Associate data files with applications.
- An ASCII file viewer.
- Some specialized file filters for popular applications.
- Graphic viewers for AutoCad, Encapsulated Postscript, and most PC bit-mapped formats.

However, XTree Gold lacks the following:

- Application menus.
- Telecommunications.
- A backup utility.
- System information utility.
- A pop-up shell within other applications.

PC Tools

Figure 6-5 shows a typical PC Tools file display. Notice that like XTree Gold, PC Tools provides a graphic display of the directory tree. PC Tools uses function keys to provide ready access to its most important features. Like Norton Commander, these function key assignments appear along the bottom of the display. PC Tools allows you to change the function key assignments to any feature you desire, making the product very easy to configure. PC Tools also provides other windows not shown in this screen shot. For example, you can create a list of applications you want to run from within PC Tools, and then simply click on the application to start it. As an alternative, you can click on a file in the directory list that automatically starts the application you've associated with its extension.

The advantages of PC Tools are the following:

- Full-featured backup programs for both DOS and Windows environment.
- System inventory and performance benchmarks.
- Built-in disk maintenance utilities: Undelete, Unformat, and Diskfix.
- Pop-up file management, text editor, and telecommunications from within any other application.

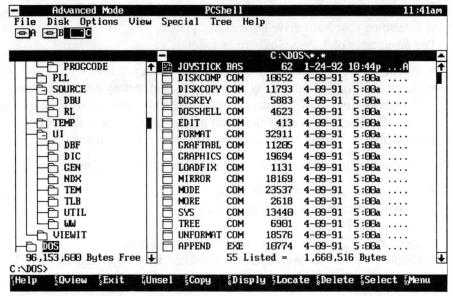

Fig. 6-5   Central Point's PCShell.

- Link to run remote computers.
- Extensive collection of file filters for viewing data files in multiple application formats.

PC Tools shares the following features with other file management packages:

- Point-and-shoot application menus.
- Tree-based file management (sort files by all standard criteria).
- Associate data files with applications.
- A text editor.

However, PC Tools lacks the following:

- Full support for MCI Mail.

DOSShell (MS-DOS 5)

Figure 6-6 shows a typical DOSShell file display. Notice that this utility also provides a directory tree, much like XTree Gold and PC Tools. A basic component of DOSShell is the list of applications in the lower left corner of the display, and the list of active applications in the lower right corner of the display. While DOSShell does make extensive use of pull-down menus, it does not provide function or Alt-key access to important features.

The advantages of MS DOS's DOSShell are the following:

- No extra cost, DOSShell comes bundled with the operating system.

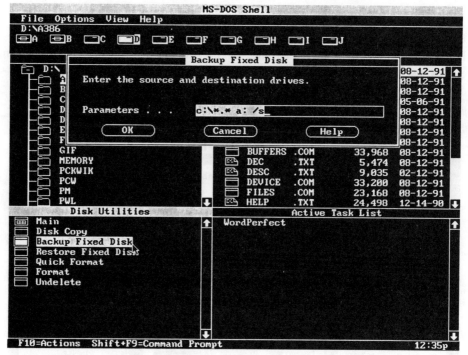

Fig. 6-6 Microsoft's DOSShell.

- Runs in 50 and 65-line VGA modes (which increases visible on-screen information).
- Extensive user-configurable menu options. The on-line help messages can be customized for novice users.
- Built-in task switcher allows user to load multiple applications and cycle between them.

DOSShell shares the following features with other file management packages:

- Tree-based file management.
- Sort files by all standard criteria.
- Menu-driven access to file maintenance functions.
- Mouse-driven file management.
- An ASCII file viewer.
- Backup, undelete, and unformat options can be built around included DOS 5 utilities.

However, DOSShell lacks the following:

- Added utility features.
- Telecommunications or specialized file viewers.
- A built-in text editor.

ViewMAX (DR DOS 6)

Figure 6-7 shows a typical ViewMAX file display. Notice that ViewMAX uses RAM fonts to enhance the appearance of the display. In addition, it provides an easy to use application launch display, similar to the ones provided by both Windows and the Macintosh (with obviously less utility).

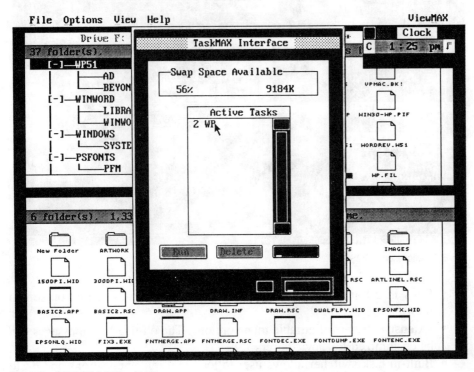

Fig. 6-7 DR DOS 6.0 ViewMAX.

The advantages of DR DOS's ViewMAX are the following:

- The task switcher included with DR DOS 6 can be run from within View-MAX. It is an improvement on the MS DOS 5 task swapper, for its ability to automatically recognize extended and expanded memory and to cut and paste text between applications.

ViewMAX shares the following features with other file management packages:

- Capability of sort file display by all standard criteria.
- A point-and-shoot application launch.
- Associate-specific data files with applications.
- Tree-based file management.

- An undelete utility.
- An ASCII/Hex file viewer.

However, ViewMAX lacks the following:

- A file search utility
- A text editor (although users can access the text-based DR DOS editor).

Working with DOSShell's task swapper (MS-DOS 5)

For some users, the DOS 5 command shell with its included task swapper might meet day-to-day computing needs. DOSShell allows a variety of different programs to be launched as islands unto themselves. If your computing style is to "take a break" from one application and switch over to the next, DOSShell's task switcher is useful. You won't have to quit one application to start the next. Instead, you can launch many programs and leave them open. The task switcher returns you to each application as you left it, allowing you to resume work on each preloaded document. If you add a third-party print spooler, you might be able to print in the background from one application while you use another. However, DOSShell does not provide inter-application connectivity. Text and graphics can't be transferred from one program to another.

To enable DOSShell's task swapper, you must choose Enable Task Swapper from the Options menu. An active task's window opens on the lower right. To run multiple applications, start each one by double clicking its name in the file list or program list menu. You may switch back from an application to DOSShell by pressing either Ctrl-Esc, Alt-Esc, or Alt-Tab.

Pressing Ctrl-Esc will always return you from the application to DOSShell. If you press Alt-Esc, the task swapper will alternate between open applications in the Active Task List. If you press Alt-Tab, the task swapper will return to the application that was active immediately prior to the current application. If you press Alt-Tab and don't release the Alt key, the task swapper will display the title bar of the prior active application. By continuing to press the Tab key, you may quickly cycle between the title bars of all open applications in the task list. When you release the Alt and Tab keys, the application corresponding to the displayed title bar will become active.

You may add a program to the Active Task List while remaining in DOSShell. Select the name of the program file, and double-click with the mouse while the Shift key is depressed (or press Shift-Enter). You can set up a series of applications in the task list in this way, and switch to each one at your convenience.

Tips for Improving Performance When DOSShell switches between applications, the inactive programs are swapped to a series of files on your hard disk. The default is to store the files in the same directory as DOSShell. There is no direct way to make DOSShell use expanded or extended memory for task swapping, but you can do it indirectly.

The location of the DOSShell swap files can be controlled with the DOS environment variable, SET TEMP. If you have sufficient extended or expanded memory, create a RAM disk larger than 512K. If the RAM disk is drive E, then place the following command in AUTOEXEC.BAT or enter it from the DOS command line:

```
Set TEMP = E : \
```

DOSShell will then swap out inactive applications to the RAM disk instead of to your hard disk. The result is much better efficiency in switching from one program to the next.

If you have enough extended or expanded memory for a 1M RAM disk, you can run the entire DOSShell program from it. The following batch file (let's call it RAMSHELL.BAT) copies the essential files to the RAM disk and launches DOS-Shell:

```
COPY C : \ DOS \ DOSSHELL . * E :
COPY C : \ DOS \ DOSSWAP . * E :
E :
DOS SHELL
```

Printing in the Background   Although DOSShell suspends inactive applications when you switch away, you can continue having a print job run in the background after you switch away to another program. Simply load a print spooler into memory before you start DOSShell.

First load your print spooler from the command line, and then start DOS-Shell. The spooler will be shared by all applications running under DOSShell. When you print from an application, wait until the data has been completely transferred into the spooler. You may then switch to another program, and printing in the background will continue.

Working with the ViewMAX and TaskMAX (DR DOS 6)

TaskMAX, the DR DOS task swapper can be either run as a text-based interface from the command-line or called from within ViewMAX. TaskMAX is slightly more powerful than the Microsoft task swapper. It can automatically recognize extended or expanded memory, and be popped up over applications running in text mode. Taskmax also offers application connectivity with a simple cut-and-paste utility. A rectangular box of text can be transferred from any text screen into either a text-based or graphic-based application in a different partition. There are three paste options: straight ASCII, spreadsheet text, or numeric spreadsheet formats. The spreadsheet options insert a down arrow character (ASCII character 25) to force each new line down to the next cell.

As with DOSShell, you can install a print spooler or other utilities before running TaskMAX to share them with all subsequent partitions. (See "Printing in the Background" in the "DOSShell" section.)

Software Carousel

Software Carousel is a third-party task switcher, less expensive than a full-fledged multitasking environment but more powerful than DOSShell or TaskMAX. By loading parts of itself into expanded or extended memory, Software Carousel might use as little as 4K of conventional memory overhead. You can open up to twelve separate program partitions. (Each program you run uses one partition.) Figure 6-8 shows a typical Software Carousel display. Notice that this product assigns function keys to each of the tasks, making switching between them much easier.

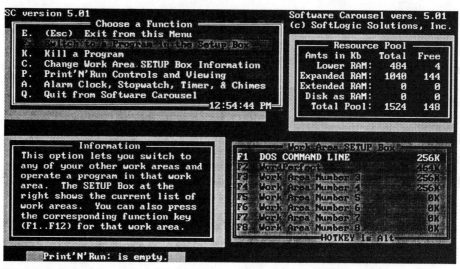

Fig. 6-8   Software Carousel Task Switcher. Softlogic Solutions.

Task switching with Software Carousel is faster and more flexible than with DOSShell. Built-in support for either extended or expanded memory allows a smooth transition between applications. Software Carousel can create a series of memory partitions with user-designated sizes. You can choose to run specific programs when Carousel starts or open new partitions on-the-fly. If extended or expanded memory is exhausted or not present, Carousel swaps inactive partitions to the hard disk.

The user can switch between different program partitions through configurable hot-key combinations. Alternatively, you can pop-up the Software Carousel main menu over any application. Programs in different memory partitions may access a common pool of extended or expanded memory. Thus, Windows in Standard Mode might co-exist with Lotus 1-2-3 version 3 or AutoCad in separate partitions. (DOSShell's task swapper does not permit program switching in and out of Windows.) If a program running in one partition locks up, Software Carousel allows you to close it without affecting programs running in other partitions.

Software Carousel works on all PC hardware platforms. If part of it is loaded into expanded memory, Software Carousel uses only 10K of conventional memory overhead. You can choose to load Software Carousel into the HMA on 80286/ 80386 systems with extended memory. When loaded in this manner, Software Carousel consumes only 4K of conventional memory.

Note   Remember that Software Carousel is a task switcher, not a multitasker. It uses extended and expanded memory transparently, but only one program is active at a time. All other partitions are frozen until you switch into them.

Software Carousel includes a built-in print spooler and a cut and paste utility for transferring text between applications. The Print'N'Run feature allows printing from one application while you work in another. (You must install the spooler utility before Software Carousel for this to work.) Software Carousel allows you to regulate print output from multiple partitions by popping up the Main menu.

Snip 'N' Snap is Software Carousel's text capture utility. Software Carousel's text transfer abilities are full featured. Some of the things you can do include the following:

- Capture text from a series of sources for automatic input into separate spreadsheet cells.
- Convert spreadsheet columns to rows, or rows to columns.
- Clip bits of the screen and save them as an ASCII file.

Once you capture a screen, Software Carousel allows you to alter the paste-in process to the next application. You can insert designated character strings, adjust line length, add lines, eliminate blank lines, remove character strings, and remove extra spaces.

Software Carousel is equipped with a series of alarm and timer utilities. This allows you to run programs or batch files at specified times. Screen messages and audible alarms notify you of impending events or appointments. One of the utilities allows you to time an individual event or sequence of commands. One use for these timer functions is to perform an automated backup at a designated time. Because you can switch between memory partitions with commands entered in batch files, various other unattended routines are possible—including controlling a telecommunications event or timing a program's execution and capturing its output to a disk file.

Tips for Productivity with Software Carousel

- You can start TSR programs before Software Carousel if you want to pop them up in all of your memory partitions. Alternatively, you can start a TSR program after Software Carousel in a partition of its own. For instance, you might want to load a keyboard macro utility like Prokey before Software Carousel. You may automate text transfers and other repetitious procedures with a shared set of keystrokes across all partitions.

- If you normally start your applications from a menu, you may substitute Software Carousel's menu feature or set up batch files to run your regular menu program in each memory partition.

- Don't define a RAM disk as a storage area with Software Carousel. This actually slows down performance. Instead, let Software Carousel access extended or expanded memory directly.

Task switching vs. multitasking— Which do you need?

If you follow the long term view of PC productivity espoused by Microsoft's chairman, Bill Gates, all individual applications will eventually cease to exist. The PC working environment will consist of a series of tools and modules attached to a single interface. Instead of using a separate spreadsheet, word processor, and drawing program, you'll calculate tables, type documents, or draw pictures within one common environment. Each new module, like a spelling checker, or table generator, will be available for use by all other modules in the system.

Applications written for Microsoft Windows are a preview of Bill Gates' vision of the future. The idea behind Windows is to give all applications a standard set of menus and provide a seamless way for programs to exchange data with one another.

Some computer users might be skeptical of Windows and mice. Many PC users have taught themselves to be productive with DOS applications. These power users typically master half a dozen different command sets and move from one to another without batting an eyelash. These people demand personal control of computing processes. They are willing to read manuals and think like programmers in order to gain computing power and efficiency. Computer users of this type prefer macros and automated batch procedures to pull-down menus and icons.

Somewhere in between these two poles (novices dependent on pull-down menus and PC power users) are the majority of PC users. Most MS-DOS users want to get their work done, but they always have one eye open for something to make their work go faster or easier. Task switching and multitasking environments are useful for all varieties of user.

Here are some good rules of thumb for choosing between task switchers and multitasking environments:

- Task switchers are less complicated. They are easy to use. Under a task switcher, applications are unlikely to interfere with one another and crash.

- Multitaskers may permit you to do more work in less time. You can type a document and use a modem simultaneously. You can lay out a page while you sort a database, or draw a picture while you recalculate a spreadsheet.

- Because a multitasker juggles several programs at once, it can require more setting adjustments than a task switcher. For instance, although Windows and DESQview both run many applications "out-of-the-box," you might have to make configuration changes for some applications. To keep two or three DOS programs running simultaneously might require additional adjustments. (Windows tends to be more transparent in this regard if it runs Windows applications exclusively.) Once a configuration is established for a suite of programs, the user may forget about the multitasking environment. The same programs can be multitasked day-in and day-out without fear of application failure. But the initial setup might require some time and study to get everything to run smoothly.

- As you might guess, heavy users of modems and fax boards are beneficiaries of a multitasking environment. If your computing work tends to be more sequential, a task switcher might be all you need. With a task switcher you might

  ~ Open a series of documents and paste text between them.
  ~ Draw a picture and place it in a page layout program.
  ~ Enter names in a database and generate a report.

For jobs like these, only one program needs to be active at a time. The other programs may be stored in the background, waiting for you on standby. There's no need for them to be active when you're working in another application.

- With a multitasker, a typical scenario might entail

  ~ activating an auto-login and downloading procedure with a telecommunications program.
  ~ opening a spreadsheet and performing a complex recalculation in the background.
  ~ opening a word processor and sending a series of mail-merged documents to a printer.

Conclusion

This chapter has provided three types of information. First, we looked at how you could make an application more memory conscious. Second, we looked at how you could use the memory freed by removing unneeded parts of an application. This increases the efficiency of the parts you use every day. Finally, we went past the improvements you could expect to obtain with a single application and looked at how task switching could improve your efficiency. All three pieces go hand-in-hand. Freeing memory that your application is not using creates more memory for multitasking and other speed enhancements. Making an application run more efficiently allows you to switch between tasks more quickly. Using a task switcher or multitasking environment allows you to reduce the time you spend waiting for applications to load. Your programs are always ready for your use.

The survey of file management and application management techniques provided in this chapter is intended as an overview to introduce readers to some of the possibilities latent in their computing environment. The next several chapters cover the nuts and bolts of memory configuration using Microsoft's DOS 5 and third-party memory management packages.

7
CHAPTER

Managing memory with MS-DOS 5

Take inventory of your applications to find out what kind of memory you should allocate for them.

The HIMEM.SYS and EMM386.EXE drivers allow MS-DOS 5 to control conventional, extended, and expanded memory.

The DOS=HIGH and DOS=UMB parameters in CONFIG.SYS control DOS 5's "load high" feature.

Specific strategies for memory allocation depend on your application requirements.

DOS 5 provides basic memory management but lacks the advanced features of third-party packages.

Introduction

There are two approaches that this chapter will give you to memory management with DOS 5. If you're in a hurry to get your applications up and running, you can take stock of what type of memory they need and refer to quickstart section to configure your CONFIG.SYS and AUTOEXEC.BAT.

Alternatively, you may read the sections that explain how managing memory works. A solid understanding of the theory can help you to achieve the best possible memory configuration on your system for all of your applications. This approach will require more detailed attention and some trial and error experimentation.

Three types of memory on your system can be allocated by DOS 5 for applications to recognize: conventional, expanded, and (on 80286/80386/80486 systems) extended. Additionally, 80386/80486 systems may load programs and drivers into upper memory (the range between 640K and 1M), even though no physical memory is installed there.

Making use of upper memory— How loadhigh works

As we saw in Chapter 3, there is no physical RAM wired into the motherboard for the address region from 640K to 1M on most PCs. Yet DOS has the ability to address this region, and does so for isolated areas of fixed ROM that are hardwired into the system. If the unused address space between 640K and 1M is mapped to (or filled by) physical RAM, it can also be used to load device drivers and TSR utilities.

The address space between 640K and 1M is mapped to (or filled by) physical RAM outside of DOS's normal 0K to 640K conventional limit. The physical RAM may come from several different places:

- EMS 4.0 memory installed on an external memory card.
- Extended memory (on 80286/80386/80486 machines).
- Dedicated shadow RAM on some 80286/80386/80486 machines.
- Unused video RAM on a VGA adaptor card.

MS-DOS 5 makes use of upper memory by borrowing RAM and fitting device drivers and TSRs into addresses around the reserved ROM areas. For MS-DOS 5, ROM areas are roped-off islands in upper memory. The most common address ranges reserved for ROM are

A000-AFFFh	EGA/VGA graphics memory
B000-B7FFh	Monochrome adaptor memory
B800-BFFFh	CGA/EGA/VGA text memory
C000-C7FFh	VGA BIOS on non-PS/2 systems

| E000-EFFFh | Video and extended BIOS on PS/2 systems. |
| F000-FFFFh | ROM BIOS |

More advanced memory managers can actually relocate some of these ROM addresses that appear fixed to MS-DOS 5. This can create more upper memory for loading device drivers and TSRs.

You might wonder why upper memory can't simply be added to DOS's conventional memory totals. In some cases, it can. But for DOS to use this area as conventional memory, the entire range must be one contiguous block, from 0K up to the top. The traditional top of conventional memory is 640K (A000h). DOS can't simply add an area from D000-DFFFh to its 640K total if there is no RAM mapped from A000h to CFFFh. We'll see in Chapter 8 that some memory managers can create an upper memory area contiguous with DOS, allowing conventional memory totals of 704K to 960K.

You might get a brief summary of memory usage on your machine with the MEM command. MEM will show you the used and free portions of conventional, upper, expanded and extended memory. (The report for extended memory will be divided into two sections if HIMEM.SYS is loaded.)

Quick start overview

The number of programs that require more than 640K to run is increasing every day. An even larger group of programs can run within 640K but also make use of extended or expanded memory to improve their functionality or performance efficiency. Some applications that require more than 640K to run include the following:

- Microsoft Windows 3.1 (And its supported third-party Windows applications) (Extended)
- AutoCAD 386 (version 11 and above) (EMS/Extended)
- Paradox 386 (version 3.5)(EMS/Extended)
- Lotus 1-2-3, (release 3.xx)(EMS/Extended)
- Xerox Ventura Publisher for DOS (v. 3.0) (EMS)

The following applications can make use of more than 640K of memory to enhance their performance:

- AutoCAD IV 1.1 (EMS/Extended)
- FoxBase Plus (EMS)
- FoxPro (EMS/Extended)
- Framework (EMS)
- Lotus Agenda (EMS)
- Q&A (EMS)
- R-BASE (EMS)

- AutoCAD 10 (EMS)
- Deluxe Paint (EMS)
- GEM Artline (EMS)
- Harvard Graphics version 3.0 (EMS)
- PC Paintbrush (EMS)
- Microsoft Assembler 6.0 (EMS/Extended)
- Microsoft C 6.0 (EMS/Extended)
- Turbo Pascal Pro (Extended)
- Lotus 1-2-3 release 2xx (EMS)
- QUATTRO PRO (EMS)
- Supercalc (EMS)
- DESQview (EMS)
- Microsoft Windows 3.0 (EMS/Extended)
- PCMOS 4.1 (Extended)
- Software Carousel (EMS)
- VM386 (EMS)
- Norton Commander (EMS)
- PCTools (EMS)
- WordPerfect Office (EMS)
- XTREE Gold (EMS)
- WordPerfect 5.0/5.1 (EMS)
- WordStar 6 (EMS)
- Xywrite III+ (EMS)

In this chapter, we deal with configuring memory for these applications with MS-DOS 5. Chapter 8 covers the use of DR DOS 6 and third-party memory management packages. MS-DOS 5 doesn't provide any tools for 8088 expanded memory management. If you need to run an EMS 4.0 application on an 8088, you must install a separate memory card with its own third-party memory manager. An 8088 is of no use for programs that require extended memory. (See Chapters 5 and 8 for information on EMS 4.0 hardware and software issues with 8088 machines.)

MS-DOS 5 provides extended memory management for 80286 machines but does not include any tools for 80286 expanded memory management. If you need to run an EMS 4.0 application on an 80286 machine, you will need additional software, and possibly additional hardware. (See Chapters 5 and 8 for information on EMS 4.0 hardware and software issues with 80286 machines.

For 80386/80486 machines, MS-DOS 5 provides both extended and expanded memory management tools. It emulates the popular feature developed by Quarterdeck for their QEMM memory manager. Users can choose to load device drivers and TSR utilities into upper memory between 640K and 1M.

HIMEM.SYS

The HIMEM.SYS driver is Microsoft's XMS (Extended Memory Specification) manager. It performs the following functions:

- Allocates XMS memory to applications.
- Allows DOS to load into the HMA on 80286/80386/80486 systems.
- Allows device drivers and TSRs on 80386/80486 systems to use part of upper memory.[1]

When you run the MEM command with HIMEM.SYS present in CONFIG.SYS, the extended memory report is divided into two sections: contiguous extended memory and available XMS memory. Usually, MEM will report contiguous extended memory as 0K. This doesn't mean that you lack extended memory on your system, it means that HIMEM.SYS has taken control of all of it and converted it to the newer extended memory standard. This is exactly what you want to do if your main working environment is Microsoft Windows.

EMM386.EXE

EMM386.EXE, the other DOS 5 memory manager, might use some of the XMS memory and convert it to EMS memory. EMM386 works only on 80386/80486 machines and appears in CONFIG.SYS. EMM386 converts XMS memory into expanded memory that is 100% compatible with the LIM 4.0 expanded memory specification. It is also the driver that controls loading programs high (that is, mapping drivers and TSR programs to address space in upper memory).

Loading DOS into the HMA

DOS 5 allows you to load the command processor (COMMAND.COM) and two hidden system files (IO.SYS, MSDOS.SYS) into the first 64K of extended memory (HMA). HIMEM.SYS must be present in CONFIG.SYS to allocate this memory. You must place the statement

```
DOS = HIGH
```

in CONFIG.SYS after the line that loads HIMEM.SYS. (The DOS 5 installation program does this by default, when you upgrade from an earlier version.) When the DOS command files are loaded high, memory for the Files and Buffers statements is also allocated from the HMA.

---

[1]If these memory acronyms are confusing you, you might want to go back and review Chapter 3.

Loading device drivers and TSRs into UMB

DOS 5 allows you to load both device drivers and small programs into upper memory. Both HIMEM.SYS and EMM386.EXE must be present in CONFIG.SYS in order to use upper memory. In addition, you must enable EMM386.EXE with the RAM parameter. The statement DOS = UMB must appear in CONFIG.SYS following the two device drivers. You can combine the two DOS statements as DOS = HIGH, UMB if you want to load DOS into the HMA and reserve the UMB for TSRs.

Sample configuration files

The following statements reflect the contents of a typical CONFIG.SYS and AUTOEXEC.BAT after the MS-DOS 5 Setup/Installation:

CONFIG.SYS
```
DEVICE = C : \ HIMEM . SYS
DEVICE = C : \ DOS \ SETVER . EXE
DOS = HIGH
DEVICE = C : \ UTIL \ MOUSE . SYS
FILES = 40
BUFFERS = 20
```

AUTOEXEC.BAT
```
PROMPT $P$G
PATH = C : \ DOS ; C : \ UTIL ; C : \ BAT
DOSKEY
PRINT
```

You may optimize your configuration by using the LOADHIGH and DEVICE-HIGH commands. This code loads the requested program into the UMBs:

CONFIG.SYS
```
DEVICE = C : \ HIMEM . SYS
DEVICE = C : \ DOS \ EMM386 . EXE RAM
DOS = HIGH, UMB
DEVICEHIGH = C : \ DOS \ SETVER . EXE
DEVICEHIGH = C : \ UTIL \ MOUSE . SYS
FILES = 40
BUFFERS = 20
```

AUTOEXEC.BAT
```
PROMPT $P$G
PATH = C : \ DOS ; C : \ UTIL ; C : \ BAT
LH DOSKEY
LH PRINT
```

The revised configuration reserves UMB RAM for device drivers and TSRs, as well as loading DOS into the HMA. In CONFIG.SYS, the statement DEVICE HIGH= replaces DEVICE= to load a specific driver above 640K. In AUTOEXEC.BAT, the command prefix "LOADHIGH" (or "LH") precedes the name of a program that should load above 640K.

Allocating expanded memory

The EMM386.EXE driver controls expanded memory allocation as well as managing upper memory. The statement

```
Device=EMM386.EXE [RAM] nnnn
```

sets the expanded memory size, where nnnn is a specified number of kilobytes. If nnnn is omitted, then EMM386 uses a default of 64K.

Note   You may omit the RAM parameter if you are not loading TSRs or device drivers into upper memory.

Allocating HMA for programs other than DOS

Microsoft Windows, Xerox Ventura Publisher, Norton's NDOS, and DESQview are all programs that can load code into the 64K HMA if it is not occupied by DOS. To keep the HMA free for other programs, keep the DEVICE=HIMEM.SYS statement in CONFIG.SYS, but delete the DOS=HIGH statement. The tradeoff is that while you will gain more memory for these programs to operate, the DOS window size for Windows might be smaller.

By trying four different configurations of CONFIG.SYS and AUTOEXEC.BAT, you can achieve varying amounts of memory for DOS within Windows. In the first configuration, we loaded DOS high and every device driver and TSR that would fit in the UMBs. Starting Windows showed 13,961K in the About dialog box. Opening a DOS window showed 572K for DOS programs. Removing the HIGH part of the DOS=UMB, HIGH statement in CONFIG.SYS and restarting the machine, Windows showed 14,408K in the About dialog box, while the DOS window showed 528K for DOS programs. Next we loaded all the TSRs and device drivers low. Windows still showed 14,408K, but the DOS window showed 524K. Finally, we eliminated both the DEVICE=EMM386.EXE RAM and DOS=UMB statements from CONFIG.SYS. The Windows About dialog box showed 18,342K for Windows, but the DOS window only showed 520K. (The reason for this drop was because SMARTDRV was no longer able to load part of itself high.) As you can see, there are a number of ways to configure your machine depending on the results you hope to achieve. In some cases, it is actually better to load DOS low and reserve the HMA for other programs. However, you can reach a halfway point by loading DOS low and your TSRs and device drivers high.

Allocating "Old Extended Memory" (non-XMS)

Some programs have not been updated to use Microsoft's XMS manager. (Microsoft Windows 386 2.1 is one example). If an older program requires extended memory and fails to find it, try using the /INT15 = xxxx parameter (where xxxx is the amount of memory in kilobytes you want HIMEM.SYS to reserve for the older program). Unfortunately, this switch doesn't work with every program; you might need to delete the DEVICE = HIMEM.SYS statement from the CONFIG.SYS to run some "old extended memory " programs.

Using Smartdrive disk cache

MS-DOS 5 includes the same Smartdrive disk cache that was originally bundled with Windows 3.0. (Windows 3.1 sports a newer, revised version.) You can configure Smartdrive to use either expanded or XMS memory. The SMARTDRV .SYS device driver is loaded in CONFIG.SYS after HIMEM.SYS and/or EMM386.EXE. The syntax is

DEVICE = [D : \PATH]SMARTDRV.SYS [XXXX] [YYYY] [/A]

where XXXX is the initial memory size of the cache and YYYY is the minimum memory size of the cache. The /A parameter builds the cache in expanded memory.

For example, DEVICE = D : \WINDOWS\SMARTDRV.SYS 1024 512 will establish an initial cache size of 1024K in XMS (extended) memory. In general, the cache will remain at the initial specified size until you run Microsoft Windows. The cache reverts to the minimum size (in this case, 512K) while Windows is running. The other memory (in this case 512K) is given back to Windows for running applications. When you exit Windows, the cache resumes its full initial size.

It is more efficient to use XMS memory for the Smartdrive cache. If you allocate expanded memory with EMM386 and use the /A parameter, then cache performance will suffer. Of course, converting the XMS memory to expanded memory does allow you to use it for other programs needing expanded memory.

Smartdrive's efficiency increases as you increase cache size to about 2M. Once you reach the 2M level, Smartdrive's overhead in managing the cache reduces the amount of performance improvement you can expect to see from an increase in cache size.

The cache size specified in CONFIG.SYS is rounded down to the nearest multiple of the track size of your hard disk. For example, if you have a standard RLL drive using 26 sectors/track and a sector size of 512 bytes, then each track provides 13K of memory. If you allocate a 1024K cache, then the actual cache size is 1014K, or 78 tracks.

Note Smartdrive consumes an overhead of 15K to 32K of conventional memory as the cache size increases. You may load the cache into upper memory using the "DEVICEHIGH" parameter.

Using the RAMdrive RAMdisk utility

MS-DOS 5 provides a RAMdisk utility that can use either conventional, expanded, or XMS memory. The RAMdrive is installed by adding the following line to CONFIG.SYS:

```
DEVICE = [D : \ PATH]RAMDRIVE . SYS [DISKSIZE SECTORSIZE
ENTRIES] [/E | /A]
```

The default settings (no parameters) create a 64K RAMdisk using conventional memory that can accept 64 directory entries and uses a 512K sector size. D : \ PATH is the location of the RAMDRIVE.SYS file on your hard disk. DISK-SIZE is the size (in kilobytes) of the RAMdisk. Values range from 16 through 4096, with a default of 64K. SECTORSIZE is the disk sector size (in bytes); valid values are 128, 256 and 512. A 512-byte sector size is the default. If you specify a SECTORSIZE, then you must also specify a value for DISKSIZE. ENTRIES is the number of files and/or directories you may create in the RAMdisk's root directory; valid values range from 2 through 1024, with the default being 64. If you want to specify the number of ENTRIES, then you must specify values for DISKSIZE and SECTORSIZE as well. /E loads the RAMdisk into XMS memory. (You must load HIMEM.SYS in CONFIG.SYS before RAMDRIVE.SYS.) /A loads the RAMdisk into expanded memory. (You must load HIMEM.SYS and EMM386.EXE, or an equivalent third-party EMS manager in CONFIG.SYS before RAMDRIVE.SYS.)

RAMDRIVE.SYS usually uses a drive letter for the RAMdisk one higher than your last physical drive. If you have more than five logical drives installed on the system, you might need to inform DOS by placing a LASTDRIVE = statement in CONFIG.SYS. For examples, a system with 2 floppies and one physical hard drive with one partition will typically include the following settings in CON-FIG.SYS:

```
DEVICE = C : \ HIMEM . SYS
DOS = HIGH
DEVICE = C : \ DOS \ RAMDRIVE . SYS 512 /E
FILES = 20
BUFFERS = 20
```

Using these settings, RAMDRIVE.SYS will allocate 512K from XMS memory for data storage. It will use the default sectorsize and dirsize allocations (512 bytes/sector, 64 entries). DOS will assign the RAMdisk drive letter D:. In a system with 2 floppies and one physical hard drive with multiple partitions (C, D and E), the CONFIG.SYS entries might appear as follows:

```
FILES = 20
BUFFERS = 30
LASTDRIVE = G
DEVICE = C : \ DOS \ RAMDRIVE . SYS 128 512 128
```

No XMS driver is loaded. RAMDRIVE.SYS allocates 128K of conventional memory for the RAMdisk. It uses a sector size of 512 bytes per sector, and 128 file entries in the root directory. The LASTDRIVE statement allows DOS to recognize drive letters as high as G. There are already two floppies and three logical hard disk partitions (total of logical drives A − E). DOS recognizes the RAMdisk as drive F. You can use drive letter G with the DOS SUBST or ASSIGN commands.

There are a few techniques for optimizing the use of RAMdrives. For example, if you expect to create a lot of small files, then it might be more efficient to use a sector size of 128 or 256 bytes. This allows you to place more files on the RAMdrive. For example, if you use a sector size of 512 bytes and copy a 2-byte file to the RAMdrive, it still takes 512 bytes. Of course, if you have a lot of small files like this, you might end up wasting more space than you use.

In addition, limit the number of root directory entries to a few more than the number of files you expect to copy to the RAMdrive. Each directory entry consumes some of the memory set aside for the RAMdrive. Obviously, the fewer directory entries you specify, the more space that is available for the RAMdrive.

Tip   As we saw in Chapter 6, many programs will perform faster if they are run from a RAMdisk. You can instruct some programs to use a RAMdisk for the temporary work files they create. For Microsoft applications (including DOSShell, Windows and Windows applications) the TEMP environment variable controls where spillover/work files are placed. The DOS SET command is used to set the TEMP variable to the desired drive letter. If the RAMdisk is drive F, then enter the following instruction from the command line or from a batch file:

```
SET TEMP = F : \ .
```

In some cases, there are advantages to creating a subdirectory on drive F first and then setting the TEMP variable to the subdirectory:

```
MD F : \ TEMP
SET TEMP = F : \ TEMP
```

This allows you to bypass the limit on the number of entries that the root directory will accept.

Programs from other vendors might have their own temporary environment variables, instead of TEMP. For instance, for ProComm+, SET PCPLUS = [d : \path] controls placement of work files. Consult the documentation of specific applications for details.

In general, RAMDRIVE.SYS is most efficient when you use XMS memory. Using conventional memory limits the applications you can load and the functionality they can provide. As with SMARTDRIVE, RAMDRIVE's performance in expanded memory is somewhat slower. RAMDRIVE.SYS consumes about 2K of conventional memory. You may eliminate this by using the DEVICEHIGH command to load the driver into upper memory. For example, the following CONFIG.SYS shows how you can load both SMARTDRIVE and RAMDRIVE above 640K:

```
DEVICE = HIMEM.SYS
DEVICE = C : \DOS \EMM386.EXE RAM
DOS = HIGH, UMB
DEVICEHIGH = C : \DOS \SMARTDRV.SYS 512
DEVICEHIGH = C : \DOS \RAMDRIVE.SYS 512 /E
FILES = 30
BUFFERS = 20
```

As you can see, both Smartdrive and RAMdrive are configured to load in upper memory and use XMS memory for data storage. Now that you're familiar with the basics of DOS 5's memory management features, you might want a closer look "behind the scenes" at how it works.

Strategies for DOS memory management

Our goals in memory management are to make more memory available for programs and/or improve the system's speed. We've seen that we can free up memory by loading the DOS system files above 1M (on 80286/80386/80486 systems), and by loading device drivers/TSRs into upper memory (on 80386/80486 systems).

The DOS 5 LOADHIGH command is a powerful way to free up conventional memory on an 80386. DOS reads the "LOADHIGH" command, and the EMM386 manager maps expanded memory to unused address space in the A000h-FFFFh range. You may arbitrarily insert DEVICEHIGH or LOADHIGH in front of every statement in your CONFIG.SYS and AUTOEXEC.BAT, but you might find that not all of the drivers and TSRs will actually load above 640K. [2] With DOS 5, you have to do a little trial-and-error experimentation to achieve an

---

[2]Some third-party 386 memory managers provide automatic optimization features. They test each statement in your CONFIG.SYS and AUTOEXEC.BAT files, and then automatically load as many as possible into the UMB. More on this in the next chapter.

optimal configuration. The MEM utility can provide the information you need on available upper memory, and the RAM requirements of individual device drivers and TSRs. Essential to this analysis is the /CLASSIFY switch, which provides you with an easy to use, plain English readout on your system.

Preparation for loadhigh

1. Back up your original CONFIG.SYS and AUTOEXEC.BAT on the hard disk. Make a floppy boot disk (FORMAT A: /S) for emergencies. If the machine fails to boot or locks up after you load a particular file high, you may reboot from the floppy and then edit CONFIG.SYS and/or AUTOEXEC.BAT. Remember to copy any device drivers that you need to make your hard disk work to the floppy. For example, if you use Stacker or Speedstor, make certain you copy the appropriate drivers to the floppy.

2. Make sure both HIMEM.SYS and EMM386.EXE are loaded in CONFIG.SYS. You must load EMM386.EXE with either the RAM or NOEMS parameter specified. Use the RAM parameter if you also want EMM386 to provide expanded memory. Use the NOEMS parameter to provide maximum memory for loading applications high without providing expanded memory for applications. The statement DOS = UMB must also appear in CONFIG.SYS.

3. Reboot the machine. Run MEM /C |MORE (/C is the classify parameter) to display a report of system memory usage one page at a time. To obtain a printout of the results, type MEM /C > PRN or MEM /C > LPT1. To save the results to an ASCII disk file type, type MEM /C > MEMC.FIL.

4. Examine the statistical report produced by MEM /C. The first section gives you the size of each driver or TSR present in conventional memory. The memory sizes are listed in decimal bytes, decimal kilobytes and hexadecimal bytes. Look for the largest driver or program in the list that will fit into Upper Memory.

Note   You cannot load the MS-DOS system files, HIMEM, and EMM386 into Upper Memory.

5. Now determine whether the driver or program you have selected will fit into Upper Memory. Compare its conventional memory usage with the size of the largest available Upper Memory Block. (You'll find this directly below the conventional memory report. If MEM /C didn't produce an Upper Memory Report, then EMM386.EXE is not loaded correctly.) If the item you chose is too big, look for the next largest entry in the list until you come to one that will fit.

6. Change the startup parameter for the chosen file in CONFIG.SYS or

AUTOEXEC.BAT. For drivers in CONFIG.SYS, change DEVICE = [FILENAME] to DEVICEHIGH = [FILENAME]. For TSRs in AUTOEXEC.BAT, insert the command LOADHIGH or LH in front of the program name.

7. Save the new CONFIG.SYS or AUTOEXEC.BAT file and reboot the machine. Run MEM /C again to confirm that the driver you chose is now loaded into Upper Memory.

8. Test the system for stability. This step is especially important if you increase upper memory size by adding an "INCLUDE" statement to EMM386. (See later.)

9. If there is sufficient Upper Memory left, repeat steps 4 through 8 for the next driver or TSR you want to load high.

If you want to expedite this procedure, you may attempt to change more than one item at a time and test a group of drivers in one pass. If there is insufficient Upper Memory available, then HIMEM.SYS loads the files low. You can always verify which items are loaded into Upper Memory with the MEM /C command. Remember to keep a floppy boot disk on hand. If the system refuses to boot or locks up after a specific load high attempt, you can boot from the floppy and retrace your steps to isolate the incompatible item.

Gaining more UMB for loadhigh

EMM386.EXE inspects Upper Memory for reserved blocks of ROM code. If you configure it with the RAM parameter, EMM386 establishes a 64K pageframe (usually at segment D000h). Specific address ranges between A000h and D000h are included or excluded depending on the video cards and peripherals installed in your system. Systems with VGA cards will typically show 32K of Upper Memory available between C800 and D000.

To check the amount of UMBs available for loading applications high, you must use the MEM command. EMM386.EXE generates its own memory report, but it will always tell you that there is no Upper Memory available if the DOS = UMB statement appears in CONFIG.SYS. Figure 7-1 shows a typical EMM386 report, while Fig. 7-2 shows a typical MEM /C report. Notice that the MEM /C report provides more information about your system than the EMM386 report.

If EMM386.EXE is run with the NOEMS parameter, the address range from D000 to E000 is added to Upper Memory instead of being configured as an EMS pageframe. You will get no expanded memory for applications, but you will add 64K to the largest available Upper Memory Block.

```
C:\>EMM386

MICROSOFT Expanded Memory Manager 386   Version 4.41
Copyright Microsoft Corporation 1986, 1991

      Available expanded memory . . . . . . . .   1024 KB

      LIM/EMS version . . . . . . . . . . . . .    4.0
      Total expanded memory pages . . . . . . .     88
      Available expanded memory pages . . . . .     64
      Total handles . . . . . . . . . . . . . .     64
      Active handles  . . . . . . . . . . . . .      1
      Page frame segment  . . . . . . . . . . .   C800 H

      Total upper memory available  . . . . . .      0 KB
      Largest Upper Memory Block available  . .      0 KB
      Upper memory starting address . . . . . .   D800 H

EMM386 Active.

C:\>
```

Fig. 7-1   EMM386 Expanded Memory display.

```
Name                Size in Decimal          Size in Hex
------              ------------------       ------------

SYSTEM              232992   (227.5K)          38E20
ANSI                  4192   (  4.1K)           1060
SMARTDRV             22976   ( 22.4K)           59C0
LMOUSE               15648   ( 15.3K)           3D20
SHARE                 5232   (  5.1K)           1470
FREE                 46496   ( 45.4K)           B5A0

Total  FREE :        46496   ( 45.4K)

Total bytes available to programs (Conventional+Upper) :    656160   (640.8K)
Largest executable program size :                           609296   (595.0K)
Largest available upper memory block :                       46496   ( 45.4K)

   1441792 bytes total EMS memory
   1048576 bytes free EMS memory

   7340032 bytes total contiguous extended memory
         0 bytes available contiguous extended memory
   1785856 bytes available XMS memory
         MS-DOS resident in High Memory Area

C:\>
```

Fig. 7-2   MEM /C display.

Using the EMM386 Include parameter

By default, EMM386.EXE ignores all memory above address E000h, basically
because IBM PS/2 systems and some clones reserve this space for extended BIOS
routines. This address range is also used by many network adapter BIOS routines.
However, a large number of ISA and EISA machines make no use of the E000h-
EFFFh address range. (Make certain this address area is clear before you use it by
checking with one of the utilities mentioned in Chapter 2.) You can force
EMM386.EXE to recognize this memory by using the Include switch as follows:

```
Device = EMM386.EXE [RAM or NOEMS] I = E000-EFFFh
```

Using the Include switch (abbreviated as I =) might add yet another 64K (or more) to the total Upper Memory available for loading applications high. If you try this, be prepared with your boot floppy boot disk. Some machines might use this area for other purposes.[3]

If you're adventurous, you might try to further increase available Upper Memory by using the Include switch to extend the load high area into the F block. There is a lot of variation with individual BIOS manufacturers as to which sections of the F000h-FFFFh range actually contain ROM code. Many older ISA clones leave the range from F000h to F7FFh unoccupied. Newer machines tend to intersperse the BIOS instructions throughout the entire range. You might try including individual 4K segments one at a time: I = F000-F0FF, then I = F100-F1FF, etc. Some of these Include attempts will cause the machine to lock up or fail to boot properly. If you find an area in the F block that does not appear to affect performance adversely, you can include it in the EMM386.EXE statement and try loading programs into it.

A step-by-step loadhigh example

Here's a step-by-step illustration of how to use loadhigh, based on a real-world example. Let's assume that the following configuration files exist after a default upgrade from DOS 3.3:

CONFIG.SYS
```
DEVICE = C:\HIMEM.SYS
DEVICE = C:\EMM386.EXE 4096
DOS = HIGH
FILES = 60
BUFFERS = 5
BREAK ON
DEVICE = C:\UTIL\NJRAMD.SYS /P25 /S
DEVICE = C:\FAX\SATISFAX.SYS IOADDR = 0350
```

AUTOEXEC.BAT
```
PROMPT $P$G
COPY COMMAND.COM E:\
SET COMSPEC = E:\COMMAND.COM
```

---

[3]As you can see by now, loading high with MS-DOS 5 is essentially a trial-and-error process. If you own a third-party memory inventory utility like Quarterdeck's Manifest, you may examine the UMB directly to identify the address ranges of all ROM chips, video memory, and other code/data located in the upper memory area. Microsoft's MSD and Qualitas' ASQ provide slightly less specific listings. In the next chapter, you'll see that you can save time and trouble with a third-party memory manager. The good third-party packages automate most of the manual procedures outlined in this chapter.

```
PATH = C : \ DOS ; C : \ UTIL ; C : \ NORTON ; C : \ BAT ; C : \ UTIL \
FONT ; D : \ WINDOWS
HYPERDKE C : 1024 S V XI : -
MOUSE . COM
APPEND C : \ DOS
PROMPT $P$G
CD \
SET TEMP = E : \
NCC /START
```

The user added only one DOS 5 specific enhancement. CONFIG.SYS contains the EMM386 driver. This supplies 4096K of expanded memory. The DOS 5 installation program adds the DOS = HIGH statement as a default.

There are a few third-party enhancement entries in both CONFIG.SYS and AUTOEXEC.BAT. NJRAMD.SYS is an expanded memory RAM disk. On this system it is initialized as drive E:. (The hard disk is partitioned into drives C and D.) SATISFAX.SYS is a device driver that enables the Intel SATISFAXION Fax/Modem board, an installed peripheral.

In AUTOEXEC.BAT, HYPERDKE is a command file that allocates 1024K of expanded memory for the Hyperdisk disk cache. AUTOEXEC.BAT also includes statements that load a mouse driver and append a DOS directory. NCC is a Norton Utilities feature that displays the date and time. Following our step-by-step procedure, we make the following changes in CONFIG.SYS (the additions appear in bold type.):

```
DEVICE = C : \ HIMEM . SYS
DEVICE = C : \ EMM386 . EXE RAM 4096
DOS = HIGH , UMB
FILES = 60
BUFFERS = 5
BREAK ON
DEVICE = C : \ UTIL \ NJRAMD . SYS /P25 /S
DEVICE = C : \ FAX \ SATISFAX . SYS IOADDR = 0350
```

The user reboots the machine and runs MEM /C. Figure 7-3 shows the results.

Notice that MEM lists the upper memory area but doesn't list any of our programs there. Looking at the list of items in the conventional memory section, we find that HYPERDKE uses 23,072 bytes. We can tell DOS to place HYPERDKE in Upper Memory by inserting an LH command on the line that loads HYPERDKE in AUTOEXEC.BAT as follows (the additions appear in bold type):

```
PROMPT $P$G
COPY COMMAND . COM E : \
SET COMSPEC = E : \ COMMAND . COM
```

```
PATH = C : \ DOS ; C : \ UTIL ; C : \ NORTON ; C : \ BAT ; C : \ UTIL \
FONT ; D : \ WINDOWS
LH HYPERDKE C : 1024 S V XI : -
MOUSE . COM
APPEND C : \ DOS
PROMPT $P$G
CD \
SET TEMP = E : \
NCC /START
```

Conventional Memory

Name	Size in Decimal		Size in Hex
MSDOS	14864	(14.5K)	3A10
HIMEM	1184	(1.2K)	4A0
EMM386	8400	(8.2K)	20D0
NJRAMD	768	(0.8K)	300
SATISFAX	4016	(3.9K)	FB0
COMMAND	2624	(2.6K)	A40
MOUSE	10720	(10.5K)	29E0
HYPERDKE	23072	(22.5K)	5A20
APPEND	9024	(8.8K)	2340
FREE	64	(0.1K)	40
FREE	64	(0.1K)	40
FREE	580256	(566.7K)	8DAA0

Total FREE 580384 (566.8K)

Upper Memory

Name	Size in Decimal		Size in Hex
SYSTEM	163840	(160.0K)	28000
FREE	32736	(32.0K)	7FE0

Total FREE 32736 (32.0K)

Total bytes available to programs
(Conventional + Upper)   613120 (598.8K)
Largest executable program size   580096 (566.5K)
Largest available upper memory block   32736 (32.0K)

4587520   bytes total EMS memory
2736128   bytes free EMS memory

9699328   bytes total contiguous extended memory

Fig. 7-3 Initial Upper Memory Block Optimization display.

```
        0    bytes available contiguous extended memory
  5304320    bytes available XMS memory
             MS-DOS resident in High Memory Area
```

Fig. 7-3   Continued

On rebooting the machine, we run MEM /C again to see whether Hyperdisk is now loaded into upper memory. Actually, in this particular teaching example, MEM's report will still show HYPERDKE loaded in conventional memory. The load high attempt has failed. Let us temporarily accept this bit of bad news and try the next largest item on the list. Remember, we can't load MSDOS, HIMEM or EMM386.EXE high, so the next thing to try is Mouse at 10,720 bytes. Edit AUTOEXEC.BAT, remove the "LH" from the line containing HYPERDKE, and insert the "LH" before MOUSE. Figure 7-4 shows the results.

Conventional Memory

...

Total FREE   591136   (577.3K)

Upper Memory

Name	Size in Decimal		Size in Hex
SYSTEM	163840	(160.0K)	28000
MOUSE	10720	(10.5K)	29E0
FREE	21984	(21.5K)	55E0

Total FREE   21984   (21.5K)

Total bytes available to programs		
(Conventional + Upper)	613120	(598.8K)
Largest executable program size	590848	(577.0K)
Largest available upper memory block	21984	(21.5K)

Fig. 7-4   Results of loading the mouse driver into upper memory.

This time when we reboot and run MEM /C, it confirms that the mouse driver has been loaded high. As a result, we gained 10K of additional conventional memory.

We might continue in this way, choosing the next item on the list. (There are now 21,984 bytes of Upper Memory left). Instead, let's scratch our heads a bit about why HYPERDKE wouldn't load into Upper Memory. According to MEM's report, we had 32K of Upper Memory available, and HYPERDKE uses only 23,072 bytes. Why didn't it fit into Upper Memory? The answer to this question is that some device drivers and TSRs require more code when they are loaded initially than the resident code they leave in memory. So HYPERDKE's startup requirements are greater than 32K, even though only 23,032 bytes of resident code are left behind it.

Is there anything we can do about this? If we could somehow get enough Upper Memory to initially load HYPERDKE, then it would be satisfied with only 23,072 bytes afterward. Let's try adding an "INCLUDE" statement to EMM386.EXE for the E000h block:

CONFIG.SYS
```
DEVICE = HIMEM.SYS
DEVICE = EMM386.EXE RAM I = E000-EFFFH 4096   . . .
```

Let's try loading HYPERDKE into Upper Memory again. Reboot the machine and run MEM /C. Figure 7-5 shows the results.

Conventional Memory

Name	Size in Decimal		Size in Hex
MSDOS	14864	(14.5K)	3A10
HIMEM	1184	(1.2K)	4A0
EMM386	8400	(8.2K)	20D0
NJRAMD	768	(0.8K)	300
SATISFAX	4016	(3.9K)	FB0
COMMAND	2624	(2.6K)	A40
MOUSE	10720	(10.5K)	29E0
APPEND	9024	(8.8K)	2340
FREE	64	(0.1K)	40
FREE	64	(0.1K)	40
FREE	144	(0.1K)	90
FREE	603184	(589.0K)	93430

Total FREE   603456   (589.3K)

Upper Memory

Name	Size in Decimal		Size in Hex
SYSTEM	229408	(224.0K)	38020
HYPERDKE	23072	(22.5K)	5A20
FREE	144	(0.1K)	90
FREE	32544	(31.8K)	7F20
FREE	42416	(41.4K)	A5B0

Total FREE   75104   (73.3K)

Fig. 7-5   Getting the HYPERDKE driver to load in upper memory.

Total bytes available to programs
(Conventional + Upper)   678560   (662.7K)
Largest executable program size   603184   (589.0K)
Largest available upper memory block   42416   (41.4K)

    4587520   bytes total EMS memory
    2736128   bytes free EMS memory

    9699328   bytes total contiguous extended memory
           0   bytes available contiguous extended memory
    5238784   bytes available XMS memory
              MS-DOS resident in High Memory Area

Fig. 7-5   Continued

This does the trick. HYPERDKE now fits into the UMB, and we have much more Upper Memory left to load other programs. To be completely safe, we should run a few applications and test the system. If everything works properly, then we can "go for broke" and load all of the remaining drivers and TSRs high:

CONFIG.SYS
```
DEVICE = C : \ HIMEM . SYS
DEVICE = C : \ EMM386 . EXE RAM I = E000-EFFFH 4096
DOS = HIGH , UMB
FILES = 60
BUFFERS = 5
BREAK ON
STACKS = 0 , 0
DEVICEHIGH = C : \ UTIL \ NJRAMD . SYS /P25 /S
DEVICEHIGH = C : \ FAX \ SATISFAX . SYS IOADDR = 0350
```

AUTOEXEC.BAT
```
PROMPT $P$G
COPY COMMAND . COM E : \
SET COMSPEC = E : \ COMMAND . COM
PATH = C : \ DOS ; C : \ UTIL ; C : \ NORTON ; C : \ BAT ; C : \ UTIL \
FONT ; D : \ WINDOWS ;
LH HYPERDKE C : 1024 S V XI : -
LH MOUSE . COM
LH APPEND C : \ DOS
PROMPT $P$G
CD \
SET TEMP = F : \
NCC /START
```

Note   There is no reason to load NCC high because it is not a TSR utility. It did not consume any memory on the original MEM report.

Once we complete our edits, we reboot the machine. If we run MEM /C again, we get the results shown in Figure 7-6. Quite a difference. Conventional memory increased from the original 580,384 bytes to 628,096 bytes. There is still 26.4K of Upper Memory available to load device drivers or TSR utilities.

Conventional Memory

Name	Size in Decimal		Size in Hex
MSDOS	14864	(14.5K)	3A10
HIMEM	1184	(1.2K)	4A0
EMM386	8400	(8.2K)	20D0
COMMAND	2624	(2.6K)	A40
FREE	64	(0.1K)	40
FREE	628032	(613.3K)	99540
Total FREE	628096	(613.4K)	

Upper Memory

Name	Size in Decimal		Size in Hex
SYSTEM	229408	(224.0K)	38020
MOUSE	10720	(10.5K)	29E0
APPEND	9024	(8.8K)	2340
NJRAMD	768	(0.8K)	300
SATISFAX	4016	(3.9K)	FB0
HYPERDKE	23072	(22.5K)	5A20
FREE	144	(0.1K)	90
FREE	23344	(22.8K)	5B30
FREE	26992	(26.4K)	6970
Total FREE	50480	(49.3K)	

Total bytes available to programs (Conventional + Upper)	678576	(662.7K)
Largest executable program size	627872	(613.2K)
Largest available upper memory block	26992	(26.4K)

4587520	bytes total EMS memory
2736128	bytes free EMS memory
9699328	bytes total contiguous extended memory
0	bytes available contiguous extended memory
5238784	bytes available XMS memory
	MS-DOS resident in High Memory Area

Fig. 7-6   End result of upper memory block optimization.

Using multiple configuration files

While MS-DOS 5 provides more user options than any previous Microsoft release, you might still find you need to reconfigure the system to deal with individual applications. The following examples illustrate scenarios where this might occur:

- If you are going to use Windows, then you probably want all of the memory above 1M reserved by HIMEM.SYS for Windows' use. This is a good configuration until you need to run AutoCad 386, a program that uses both expanded memory and extended memory. For AutoCad, you'll want to split the expanded/extended memory allocation in CONFIG.SYS.
- You'll probably load DOS above 1M for most situations, but some programs might want the HMA for their own use. Quarterdeck's DESQview and the GEM version of Xerox Ventura Publisher both gain more memory if DOS is loaded low. This is because DOS uses only 38−48K of the HMA. Other programs can use the entire 64K. In other words, you might waste 16−24K of the HMA when loading DOS high with these applications.

One solution to these problems is to compose multiple sets of CONFIG.SYS and AUTOEXEC.BAT. For each separate session, boot the system with the appropriate startup files. The traditional way to do this is to name each set of startup files with a different extension, and then copy the appropriate pair to the root directory when you want to use it. Fortunately, there's a better way to handle the problem with a shareware program included on our utilities disk.

First the traditional method. Let's decide that we'll encounter the following three scenarios on a regular basis.

- The user wants to go directly into Windows for the entire session.
- The user wants to stay in DOS to run Paradox, 1-2-3 release 3, AutoCad 386, and other programs that use both extended and expanded memory.
- The user wants to run Ventura Publisher for GEM, and other expanded memory applications from DOS. We'll want to load DOS low to reclaim the HMA. We'll want as much RAM as possible configured as expanded memory.

For a 386 system with 8M of RAM, we'll need the following three sets of startup files:

```
CONFIG.WIN
DEVICE=HIMEM.SYS
DEVICE=EMM386.EXE NOEMS I=E000-EFFFH
DOS=HIGH,UMB
FILES=50
BUFFERS=15
```

```
DEVICEHIGH=C:\UTIL\MOUSE.SYS
DEVICEHIGH=C:\DOS\SMARTDRV.SYS 2048
```

AUTOEXEC.WIN
```
PROMPT $P$G
PATH=C:\DOS;C:\BATCH;C:\UTIL;C:\WINDOWS;C:\
WINWORD
LH GRAPHICS
CD \WINDOWS
WIN
```

CONFIG.CAD
```
DEVICE=HIMEM.SYS
DEVICE=EMM386.EXE RAM I=E000-EFFFH 3844
DOS=HIGH,UMB
FILES=50
BUFFERS=15
DEVICEHIGH=C:\UTIL\MOUSE.SYS
DEVICEHIGH=C:\DOS\SMARTDRV.SYS 1024
```

AUTOEXEC.CAD
```
PROMPT $P$G
PATH=C:\DOS;C:\BATCH;C:\UTIL;C:\ACAD;C:\123R3
LH DOSKEY
LH APPEND C:\DRAFT;C:\ACCOUNT
CD \ACAD
ACAD
```

CONFIG.EMS
```
DEVICE=HIMEM.SYS
DEVICE=EMM386.EXE RAM I=E000-EFFFH 6992
DOS=LOW,UMB
FILES=50
BUFFERS=15
DEVICEHIGH=C:\UTIL\MOUSE.SYS
DEVICEHIGH=C:\DOS\SMARTDRV.SYS 1024
```

AUTOEXEC.EMS
```
PROMPT $P$G
PATH=C:\DOS;C:\BATCH;C:\UTIL;C:\VENTURA;C:\
WP51
LH DOSKEY
LH APPEND C:\TYPESET;C:\DOC
```

In addition to this set of three startup files, you might set up the following series of batch files. They allow you to choose a configuration (by copying the appropriate files to AUTOEXEC.BAT and CONFIG.SYS automatically) and reboot the machine.

WIN.BAT
```
COPY C:\BATCH\CONFIG.WIN C:\CONFIG.SYS
COPY C:\BATCH\AUTOEXEC.WIN C:\AUTOEXEC.BAT
REM REBOOT THE MACHINE TO RUN WINDOWS
```

CAD.BAT
```
COPY C:\BATCH\CONFIG.CAD C:\CONFIG.SYS
COPY C:\BATCH\AUTOEXEC.CAD C:\AUTOEXEC.BAT
REM REBOOT THE MACHINE TO RUN AUTOCAD
```

EMS.BAT
```
COPY C:\BATCH\CONFIG.EMS C:\CONFIG.SYS
COPY C:\BATCH\AUTOEXEC.EMS C:\AUTOEXEC.BAT
REM REBOOT THE MACHINE TO RUN DESQVIEW OR VENTURA
PUBLISHER
```

The BOOT.SYS utility included on our utilities disk can streamline this procedure for you. BOOT.SYS is a shareware package that displays a menu of choices before CONFIG.SYS and AUTOEXEC.BAT are executed. When the machine starts, the menu appears. The user chooses a configuration from the menu and the system boots using the appropriate configuration. This is all accomplished in one step without rebooting the machine. You don't have to copy or rename any files. With BOOT.SYS installed, the following screen might greet the user on startup.

```
Which of these configurations do you want?
   1. Load DOS high, configure all RAM above 1M as XMS for
      Windows.
   2. Load DOS high, split RAM above 1M 50/50 between
      Extended and Expanded Memory.
   3. Load DOS low (Save HMA for another program). Set up
      disk cache, then configure all remaining RAM above
      1M as Expanded Memory.
```

In other words:

1. DOS High / Run Windows
2. DOS High 50/50 EMS/Ext (Run AutoCad 386)
3. DOS Low / Max EMS (Run Ventura Publisher)

The best part of using BOOT.SYS is ease of operation. You point the arrow selector at the appropriate choice with the cursor keys and press Enter.

Setting up BOOT.SYS requires some experience with DOS batch files. It is an extremely flexible utility that can present a series of nested menus. The documentation included on the diskette provides a quick start template. While a complete discussion of how to use BOOT.SYS is beyond the scope of this book, here are the CONFIG.SYS and AUTOEXEC.BAT files necessary to implement the menu just shown[4]:

```
CONFIG.SYS
BUFFERS = 20
FILES = 40
DEVICE = C: \ BOOT . SYS
DEVICE = TOP WHICH OF THESE CONFIGURATIONS DO YOU WANT?
DEVICE = TOP
DEVICE = TOP 1.  Load DOS high, configure all RAM above 1M
DEVICE = TOP as XMS for Windows
DEVICE = TOP
DEVICE = TOP 2.  Load DOS high, split RAM above 1M 50/50
DEVICE = TOP between Extended and Expanded Memory
DEVICE = TOP
DEVICE = TOP 3.  Load DOS low (Save HMA for another program)
DEVICE = TOP Set up disk cache, and then configure all
DEVICE = TOP remaining RAM above 1M as Expanded Memory.
DEVICE = TOP
DEVICE = BOOT . 1 DOS High / Run Windows
DEVICE = C: \ HIMEM . SYS
DEVICE = C: \ EMM386 . EXE NOEMS I = E000 - EFFFH
DEVICEHIGH = C: \ UTIL \ MOUSE400 . SYS
DEVICEHIGH = C: \ DOS \ SMARTDRV . SYS 2048
DEVICE = BOOT . SET AUTO = WIN
DEVICE = BOOT . 2 DOS High 50/50 EMS/Ext (Run Autocad 386)
DEVICE = C: \ HIMEM . SYS
DEVICE = C: \ EMM386 . EXE RAM I = E000 - EFFFH 3488
DEVICEHIGH = C: \ UTIL \ MOUSE400 . SYS
DEVICEHIGH = C: \ DOS \ SMARTDRV . SYS 1024
DEVICE = BOOT . SET AUTO = CAD
DEVICE = BOOT . 3 DOS Low / Max EMS (Run Ventura Publisher)
DEVICE = C: \ HIMEM . SYS
DEVICE = C: \ EMM386 . EXE RAM I = E000 - EFFFH 6992
DOS = LOW
DEVICE = C: \ UTIL \ MOUSE400 . SYS
```

---

[4]Note that you must place the files BOOT.SYS and BOOT.COM in an accessible directory.

```
DEVICE = C : \ DOS \ SMARTDRV . SYS 1024
DEVICE = BOOT . SET AUTO = EMS
DEVICE = BOOT . END
DOS = HIGH , UMB
```

AUTOEXEC.BAT
```
PROMPT $P$G
C : \ BOOT SET
IF ERRORLEVEL 10 GOTO NOT_INSTALLED
GOTO %AUTO%
: WIN
PATH = C : \ DOS ; C : \ BATCH ; C : \ UTIL ; C : \ WINDOWS ; C : \
 WINWORD
LH GRAPHICS
CD \ WINDOWS
WIN
GOTO DONE
: CAD
PATH = C : \ DOS ; C : \ BATCH ; C : \ UTIL ; C : \ ACAD ; C : \ 123R3
LH DOSKEY
LH APPEND C : \ DRAFT ; C : \ ACCOUNT
CD \ ACAD
ACAD
GOTO DONE
: EMS
PATH = C : \ DOS ; C : \ BATCH ; C : \ UTIL ; C : \ VENTURA ; C : \
 WP51
LH DOSKEY
LH APPEND C : \ TYPESET ; C : \ DOC
GOTO DONE
: NOT_INSTALLED
ECHO BOOT . SYS IS NOT INSTALLED!
: DONE
```

A brief description of how BOOT.SYS and BOOT.COM work with this particular AUTOEXEC.BAT and CONFIG.SYS is as follows. (We start with CONFIG.SYS.) All material entered in CONFIG.SYS between the DEVICE = BOOT . SYS line and the DEVICE = BOOT . END line are controlled by the BOOT.SYS driver. All commands we want to run regardless of configuration are entered above the DEVICE = BOOT . SYS line and below the DEVICE = BOOT . END line. All text entered on the DEVICE = TOP lines appears as text at the top of the user menu that BOOT . SYS displays on screen. The DEVICE =

BOOT.1, DEVICE=BOOT.2, and DEVICE=BOOT.3 sections control the three customized CONFIG.SYS choices. The three DEVICE=BOOT set lines define three environment variables that will be used later to control what happens in AUTOEXEC.BAT. DEVICE=BOOT.SET AUTO=WIN, for example, defines a DOS environment variable named AUTO and sets its value to WIN.

In AUTOEXEC.BAT, the GOTO %AUTO% line plugs in the value for the environment variable selected by the user. If the user chooses run Windows from the configuration menu, then we run the BOOT.1 CONFIG.SYS commands. This is because the AUTO variable is set equal to WIN. In AUTOEXEC.BAT, GOTO %AUTO% jumps to the portion of the batch file under the :WIN label.

DOS 5 memory management command reference

HIMEM.SYS
DEVICE=[D:\PATH] HIMEM.SYS [/HMAMIN=M] [/NUMHANDLES=N]
        [/INT15=XXX] [MACHINE:XXXX] [/A20CONTROLON|OFF]
        [/SHADOWRAM:ON|OFF] [CPUCLOCK:ON|OFF]

/HMAMIN   Controls the minimum memory allocation a program must request in the HMA area (for example, device =himem.sys /hmamin=36). If a program tries to load less than 36K in the HMA, the request will be refused with this setting. The program will have to load all of its code in conventional memory. The default value is 0 (i.e., any program request for HMA memory will be honored.)

                       The /hmamin setting might be useful if you want to reserve the HMA for a program that will use it most effectively. For instance, MS-DOS 5 uses only 32−48K to load the command kernel high. Ventura Publisher for GEM and DESQview both use the entire 64K. With a setting of /hmamin=64, the HMA will remain empty, until a program asks to use all of it.

/NUMHANDLES   Specifies the maximum number of extended-memory-block (EMB) handles provided by HIMEM.SYS. Each time a program requests a block of XMS memory, HIMEM.SYS assigns it an EMB handle. Valid settings range from 1 through 128, with a default setting of 32. (Each handle uses 6 bytes of conventional memory.)

/INT15 = XXXX   Allocates a portion of extended memory (in kilobytes) for use by older programs that don't recognize Microsoft's newer XMS memory standard. For example, if you have an older disk cache, print spooler, or RAM disk, the following setting would reserve 1024K of extended memory for use with non-XMS software: DEVICE = HIMEM.SYS /INT15 = 1024. If there is 4096K of extended memory on your system, then HIMEM.SYS would still allocate 3072K as XMS memory (for use by XMS programs such as Windows). Valid values for XXXX range from 64 through 65535. HIMEM.SYS automatically rounds the value to the nearest multiple of 64.

/MACHINE : XXXX and
/A20CONTROL : ON|OFF   These two parameters control the use of the A20 handler for extended memory. The A20 handler is a hardware-dependent feature that varies on different types of machines. You can use any of the codes or equivalent numbers listed in Table 7-1 for the XXXX value. HIMEM.SYS will display the A20 handler on the screen as it loads from CONFIG.SYS. If you receive an error message stating that HIMEM.SYS won't install the selected A20 handler, you can always specify a different machine type. (The default is type 1, PC AT.)

The A20CONTROL : ON|OFF switch specifies whether HIMEM.SYS will install itself if your computer's BIOS pre-enables the A20 line. The default is "on," instructing HIMEM to install itself no matter what the pre-existing state of the A20 line. This switch occasionally fails to work even if your computer actually pre-enables the A20 line. If you continue to get an error message from HIMEM.SYS, it may be necessary to alter the status of the A20 line in your computer's setup program. Access the setup program according to the instructions that came with the computer and search for an "A20 always enabled" option. This option is offered on some machines, because it speeds up performance of extended memory. If HIMEM.SYS will not load, turn this option off.

/SHADOWRAM:ON|OFF   This switch specifies whether HIMEM.SYS should switch off a system's internal shadow RAM and add the RAM to the extended memory pool. It doesn't work on many systems. (The default is /shadow ram:off)

/CPUCLOCK:ON|OFF   On a few systems HIMEM.SYS can affect the clock speed of the computer. This switch may correct problems by slowing HIMEM down.

Table 7-1 Machine codes for HIMEM.SYS.

Code	Number	A20 handler
AT	1	IBM PC/AT
PS2	2	IBM PS/2
PT1CASCADE	3	Phoenix Cascade BIOS
HPVectra	4	HP Vectra (A and A+)
ATT6300Plus	5	AT&T 6300 Plus
Acer1100	6	Acer 1100
Toshiba	7	Toshiba 1600 and 1200XE
Wyse	8	Wyse 12.5 MHz 286
Tulip	9	Tulip SX
Zenith	10	Zenith ZBIOS
AT1	11	IBM PC/AT
AT2	12	IBM PC/AT (Alternative Delay)
CSS	12	CSS Labs
AT3	13	IBM PC/AT (alternative delay)
Philips	13	Philips
FastHP	14	HP Vectra
	8	Bull Micral 60
	1 or 8	COMPUADD 386 Systems
	2	Datamedia 386/486
	8	Hitachi HL500C
	8	Intel 301z or 302
	1	JDR 386/33
	7	Toshiba 5100
	2	UNISYS PowerPort

EMM386.EXE
DEVICE=[DRIVE:][PATH]EMM386.EXE [ON|OFF|AUTO] [MEMORY]
[W=ON|W=OFF] [MX|FRAME=ADDRESS|/PMMMM] [PN=AD
DRESS [X=MMMM-NNNN] [I=MMMM-NNNN] [[B=ADDRESS]
[L=MINXMS] [A=ALTREGS] [H=HANDLES] [D=NNN] [RAM]
[NOEMS]

ON|OFF|AUTO	The default value for EMM386 is on. Enabling the expanded memory management for the amount of memory specified with the MEMORY parameter (see later). If EMM386 is set to off, expanded memory management is suspended until the "On" parameter is invoked from the DOS command line. The Auto switch enables expanded memory support only when it is requested from DOS by another program. You cannot switch EMM386 off or into auto mode if programs have been loaded high or if expanded memory has been allocated for a cache, RAM-disk, or spooler.
MEMORY	Indicates the amount of memory (in kilobytes) that EMM386 allocates as Expanded Memory. Values range from 16 through 32,768. EMM386 rounds the specified value down to the nearest multiple of 16. (The default value is 256K.)
W = ON|OFF	Switches support for a Weitek coprocessor on or off. (A Weitek coprocessor is similar to an Intel 287 or 387 chip; it speeds up floating point numerical calculations.) The default setting is w = o f f.
MX	Allows you to specify the address of the pageframe with a preset code. On most systems, EMM386 sets the page-frame to D000h by default. You might find it convenient to relocate the pageframe address to obtain more memory for loadhigh, or to make room for a network adaptor. Table 7-2 contains a list of values you can assign to X. Microsoft recommends using values 10 through 14 only on computers with 512K of conventional memory. You may also specify the address of the EMS pageframe directly (see later).
FRAME = ADDRESS	Allows you to specify the pageframe address directly using a four-digit hexadecimal number. Valid addresses are in the range 8000h through 9000h and C000h through E000h in 400h increments. You use this parameter in place of the /MX parameter. For example, the following two statements are equivalent:

```
DEVICE = EMM386 . EXE /M2
DEVICE = EMM386 . EXE FRAME = C400
```

/PMMMM	This parameter provides another way to specify the page-frame address. Valid ranges are the same as the FRAME =

Table 7-2   Page frame values for EMM386.

MX value	Page frame location
1	C000h
2	C400h
3	C800h
4	CC00h
5	D000h
6	D400h
7	D800h
8	DC00h
9	E000h
10	8000h
11	8400h
12	8800h
13	8C00h
14	9000h

parameter. For example, you may specify a pageframe as follows:

DEVICE = EMM386.EXE /PC400

PN = ADDRESS

On rare occasions, you might want to specify the address of a single page of EMS memory. For example, if you have areas too small to place the entire pageframe, but large enough to specify 16K pages, then you could still use expanded memory by specifying the locations of the individual pages. Valid values for n (the page number) are 0 to 255. Valid values for address are 8000h through 9C00h and C000h through EC00h, in 400h increments. Addresses for EMS pages 0 through 3 must remain contiguous in order to maintain support for the LIM 3.2 expanded memory standard. If the /Pn switch is used in conjunction with the Mx, frame = 5, or /Pmmm switches, then individual addresses may not be specified for EMS pages 0 through 3.

X = MMMM - NNNN

The X parameter excludes a specific range of UMB memory from use by EMM386.EXE. This parameter may be useful to avoid conflicts with video cards and other adaptors that are not detected by EMM386 automatically. Valid values for MMMM and NNNN are in the range A000h to FFFFh. Addresses are rounded down to the nearest 4K boundary. If you use both the X switch and the I switch (see below), the X switch takes precedence over an overlapping I = range. (In other words, you cannot both include and exclude a memory address range. EMM386 favors the safety of excluding the range rather than including it and causing conflicts.)

I = MMMM - NNNN   Use the I parameter to include specific UMB address ranges for loading programs high or expanded memory pages. Normally, EMM386 does not use any addresses above the pageframe. If your pageframe is set to D000h, on many machines, you may use the I = switch to include the range E000h-EFFFh. For example, if you wanted to include the E000h to EFFFh range, then you would use the I parameter as follows:

```
DEVICE = EMM386 . EXE FRAME = D000 RAM
I = E000 - EFFFH
```

Use of the I = parameter in this example adds 64K to the UMB total available for loading programs high. (Note that some machines have ROM code in the E000 block. You must use a trial and error process to determine which areas of upper memory may be specified with the I(nclude) parameter.

B = ADDRESS   This parameter is important for users of Quarterdeck's DESQview. B = ADDRESS specifies the lowest memory segment available for EMS page swapping. Valid ranges include 1000h (64K) to 4000h (256K). The default value is 4000h. DESQview is the most common program that takes advantage of EMS page swapping below 640K. Using the EMM386 default setting, DESQview's secondary windows attain a maximum size of 384K. A setting of B = 1000 sets the lowest memory address for EMS page swapping to 64K. This causes the size of secondary DESQview windows to jump to 512K.

L = M I NXMS   This parameter reserves a minimum amount of XMS memory (in kilobytes) after running EMM386. The L parameter overrides the memory parameter if the two are in conflict. The total amount of EMS allocated by the memory parameter is offset. . . . to accommodate the amount of extended memory allocated with L = parameter. The default value for L is 0.

A = ALTREGS   This parameter specifies how many alternate register sets for multitasking EMM386 will allocate. (See the explanation in Chapter 5, page 90). Valid ranges include 0 through

254. The default value is 7. The more alternate registers allocated, the faster EMM386 can swap individual EMS pages in and out of conventional memory. Each alternate register set allocated adds approximately 200 bytes to the memory overhead of EMM386.EXE.

H = HANDLES   This parameter specifies how many expanded memory handles EMM386 can establish. Generally each handle is used to contain the code and/or data for an individual device driver or program running in expanded memory. However, some programs require multiple handles. For example, many print spoolers and RAM disks that allow you to dynamically resize the amount of memory used require multiple handles. Values for H range from 2 through 255. The default value is 64.

D = NNN   This parameter specifies the amount of memory (in kilobytes) that EMM386 reserves for DMA (direct memory access) buffers. Direct Memory Access is a method of sidestepping the CPU in reading and writing to disk or memory. Many backup programs use this technique to establish a direct link between your hard drive and backup device. Sidestepping the CPU greatly improves the speed of these utilities. Microsoft recommends that this value reflect the largest single DMA transfer that will occur while EMM386.EXE is active. Valid values range from 16 to 256. Most backup programs use a default of a 64K DMA buffer. Setting D = 32 or D = 64 might resolve problems with some SCSI controller interfaces.

RAM   This parameter turns on access to upper memory for loading programs high. It also permits EMM386 to allocate some XMS as expanded memory for programs.

NOEMS   This parameter allows access to upper memory for loading programs high, but disables the use of expanded memory. This frees the use of the 64K pageframe for loading programs high.

Using Norton's NDOS

NDOS, included with the Norton Utilities 6.0 and above, is a substitute command processor for Microsoft's COMMAND.COM. NDOS includes all of the commands and functions associated with MS-DOS 5, plus a superset of enhanced batch capabilities and utilities. NDOS can be loaded as the start-up command processor for a DOS session by invoking it with the Shell command in CON-FIG.SYS.

One of the advantages of using NDOS is that you can configure it to use less conventional memory than COMMAND.COM. It requires only 3K of conventional memory for its resident portion. (You can pare this requirement down to less than 1K by moving the resident portion and environment space to upper memory.) The DOS = HIGH command in CONFIG.SYS works in the usual way with NDOS. If DOS is loaded low with NDOS as the command processor, only the NDOS kernel, and its related environment are placed above 640K. If DOS is loaded high with NDOS as the command processor, the system files IO.SYS and MSDOS.SYS are loaded into the HMA. The DOS = LOW/DOS = HIGH commands in CONFIG.SYS work the same way with NDOS, as they would without it. Entering the following command in CONFIG.SYS installs NDOS as the resident command processor.:

SHELL = [D :][\ PATH]NDOS . COM /S : B /P

This is a basic configuration that tells NDOS to swap most of itself to the optimal location for your individual computer. NDOS has five swapping modes:

- /S : B[D : \ PATH] (*Best guess swapping*). This is the default mode. NDOS tries XMS memory swapping first on an 80286/80386/80486 computer. If no XMS memory is found, NDOS looks for EMS 4.0 memory. If no expanded memory is found, NDOS swaps part of itself to the specified drive and directory.

- /S : D[D : \ PATH] *(Swap to disk)*. NDOS creates a swapfile, NDOSSWAP.XXX, where XXX represents the current shell nesting level (000 for the primary shell). The swapfile is created in the root directory of the boot drive if no drive/path statement is included. (The swapfile for secondary shells defaults to the location specified in the COMSPEC variable.)

- /S : E *(Swap to expanded memory)*. There must be 80K of free EMS memory for the primary shell, or around 32K for a secondary shell.

- /S : N *(Disables swapping)*. NDOS is loaded in memory-resident mode, only.

- /S : X *(Swap to XMS memory)*. There must be 80K of free XMS memory for swapping to occur.

To gain even more conventional memory, the 3K resident portion of NDOS may be moved into an Upper Memory Block as follows:

SHELL = [D :][\ PATH]NDOS . COM /S : B /U /E : NNN[U] /P

The /U switch places most of the resident code for NDOS between 640K and 1M. HIMEM.SYS and EMM386.EXE or a third-party load high driver must precede the shell statement in CONFIG.SYS for this to work. The /E switch allocates the size of the DOS environment, where NNN is the size in bytes. Adding a U to the environment size places the environment space in UMB along with the resident command kernel. Substituting NDOS for the usual DOS command processor gains from 4K to 6K of additional conventional memory for application use.

Limitations of DOS 5 memory management

DOS 5 provides basic memory management features. We've already seen that you must overcome one of these limitations by setting up multiple system configurations. Another limitation of DOS 5's memory management is that Microsoft Windows 3.0 will not run in Standard Mode when the loadhigh features are used (Windows 3.1 has been rewritten to solve this problem). To generalize, the limitations of DOS 5's memory management are as follows.

- Expanded/XMS memory allocation is not controlled dynamically. The system must be rebooted to change the memory configuration.
- Drivers must be loaded into Upper Memory by a manual, trial-and-error procedure.
- The amount of Upper Memory available for loadhigh is limited because the address space must be shared by peripherals and extended ROM BIOS code.
- The XMS and Expanded Memory drivers themselves consume conventional memory resources.
- The XMS and Expanded Memory drivers lack sophisticated control features available in third-party packages.

Conclusion

In this chapter, you learned about the various memory management capabilities provided by DOS 5. Even though these capabilities are limited, they do come bundled with DOS 5. The second section of this chapter pointed out how you can fully exploit these capabilities to enhance your programming environment. The third section provided you with a quick reference to the two most important of the memory management utilities, HIMEM.SYS and EMM386.EXE. An understanding of these two utilities is essential to fully utilizing the DOS 5 environment. Finally, we looked at Norton's NDOS, one of the command shells that can be used in place of Microsoft's COMMAND.COM.

Some third-party packages offer more flexibility in their memory management features than DOS 5. For example, instead of going through a trial-and-error procedure to load files above 640K, you can accomplish it automatically. More load-high memory can be configured in upper memory, leaving more conventional memory for running applications. The more advanced third-party managers don't have to be reconfigured to adjust XMS/Expanded memory allocation. We'll learn about these features and other advanced memory management options in the next chapter.

8
CHAPTER

Third-party memory management

Expanded memory cards use a special memory manager shipped with the card. Most EMS cards can provide both extended and expanded memory on 80286 and above platforms.

Specialized third-party hardware and software allow you to load programs on 8088/80286 computers.

DR DOS 6 has both advantages and drawbacks, compared to MS-DOS 5.

Third-party packages for 80386 and above machines allow more control of the machine, providing a wider range of options. Automatic memory optimization can eliminate some of the trial-and-error procedures necessary in configuring MS-DOS 5 and DR DOS 6.

Introduction

We saw in Chapter 7 that MS-DOS 5 offers basic memory management tools for 80386 and above computers. Even though these tools are better than what was provided in previous versions of DOS, third-party memory managers offer more options and greater flexibility. In this chapter, we review a wide variety of memory management tools for all PC platforms. You'll find out how to load drivers and TSRs high on 8088 and 80286 machines, as well as on 80386/486 computing platforms. Microsoft's MS-DOS 5 provides expanded memory management on 80386-and-above CPUs, but includes no support for 8088/80286 machines. Fortunately, packages from third-party vendors allow EMS 4.0 memory management on 8088 and 80286 machines. In some cases, they even allow you to load device drivers and TSRs high on those platforms.

ATLAST! The lazy man's loadhigh solution

If you're the type of computer user who doesn't want to be reading this chapter in the first place, ATLAST! might be your solution for optimizing memory with MS-DOS 5 or DR DOS 6. ATLAST!, distributed by RYBS Electronics, is a memory watchdog utility. It keeps track of the contents of your CONFIG.SYS and AUTOEXEC.BAT, and then automatically figures out how to load programs into upper memory. With ATLAST!, you don't have any "LOADHIGH" or "DEVICEHIGH" statements to add to your configuration. ATLAST! keeps track of which drivers and TSRs it should load high or low in a separate file in its own directory.

ATLAST! does not provide independent expanded/extended memory management but instead cooperates with whatever memory management package you already have. With MS-DOS 5, ATLAST! automatically installs and configures the EMM386.EXE memory manager. With other memory management packages, ATLAST! works with the configuration already set up for the memory manager. Only one line is added to CONFIG.SYS to load the ATLAST!.EXE device driver. All third-party "LOADHIGH" statements are removed from your startup files. You may enter simple changes to your CONFIG.SYS and AUTOEXEC .BAT at will. ATLAST! reboots the system one time, reoptimizing your upper memory configuration. Any drivers and TSRs that will fit into upper memory are placed there automatically.

The installation procedure for ATLAST! is painless. With MS-DOS 5 and DR DOS 6, ATLAST! automatically installs the 386 memory manager included with the operating system. A configuration menu lets you override ATLAST!'s automatic defaults, but this will probably be unnecessary. ATLAST! performs a scan of upper memory and adds optimal parameters to the EMM386 command line. If ATLAST! detects the presence of QEMM, 386MAX or NETROOM, it accepts the command line parameters already set for those memory managers.

(On 8088/80286 machines, ATLAST! cooperates with the third-party EMS 4.0 memory managers.)

ATLAST! reboots the machine and loads programs high without inserting additional commands into CONFIG.SYS and AUTOEXEC.BAT. If the startup configuration changes, ATLAST! detects this, requests permission to reboot the machine once, and optimizes upper memory usage again. Figure 8-1 shows a typical ATLAST! configuration file under MS-DOS 5. ATLAST!.INI is created automatically and stored in the \ATLAST! directory on your hard drive. You may add or delete commands from CONFIG.SYS and AUTOEXEC.BAT without worrying about upper memory.

```
[pif.advice]

command.com=low,  locked
keyrepet.com=low,locked
command.com=low,  locked
command.com=low,  locked

[pif]

atlast!=         high=F700,  need=528,      keep=528
atlast!=         high=F700,  need=176,      keep=176
atlast!=         high=CC0C,  need=8560,     keep=8560
hyperstb.exe=    high=CC0C,  need=7584,     keep=240,     size=7072
hyper386.exe=    high=CC0C,  need=51984,    keep=28336,   size=43536
njramdxp.sys=    high=CA06,  need=2944,     keep=704,     size=1917
satisfax.sys=    high=CC0C,  need=29072,    keep=4016,    size=28042
files=           high=CC0C,  need=2672,     keep=2672
fcbs=            high=F700,  need=256,      keep=256
buffers=         high=CC0C,  need=2672,     keep=2672
drives=          high=F200,  need=880,      keep=880
stacks=          high=F700,  need=624,      keep=624
stacks=          high=F200,  need=1232,     keep=1232
ndos.com=        high=CC0C,  need=13408,    keep=3824,    size=11855
vshield.exe=     low,        need=290432,   keep=3424,    size=37559
ansi.com=        high=CC0C,  need=3088,     keep=1808,    size=1799
mouse.com=       high=CC0C,  need=57296,    keep=17104,   size=55804,   ems
dvansi.com=      high=CC0C,  need=3312,     keep=2480,    size=2032
atlast!.exe=     low,        need=90784,    keep=105392,  size=85312
```

Fig. 8-1 ATLAST! configuration file.

Users who have some familiarity with memory management techniques may customize ATLAST!'s performance by manually editing the settings in the ATLAST!.INI file, but the program is designed to be as completely user-transparent as possible. A single-user license for ATLAST! costs approximately $79, but a network site license might greatly reduce the cost per workstation for large corporate environments. This package might save MIS managers considerable time because they won't have to tinker with individual workstations each time a new program is added.

ATLAST! is not quite as rugged as the full-featured memory managers we will examine in this chapter. It won't always yield as much conventional memory as

QEMM or 386MAX, or allow as much control of your system. Some fine-tuning might be required with the following problem configurations:

- You might have to disable the delayed write feature in some advanced disk cache programs for ATLAST! to successfully recognize changes in CONFIG.SYS and reboot correctly.

- You must manually check AUTOEXEC.BAT for certain utilities that take over the keyboard. For instance, ATLAST! fails in its automatic reboot/reconfiguration process when the Norton Utilities' Control Center module is invoked to display the date and time. Enter the following statement manually to force termination of the optimization process before ATLAST! reaches the "problem" utility: [d :] \ ATLAST! \ ATLAST! COMPLETE must precede a problem line like [d :] \ NORTON \ NCC /START.

- Some simple TSR utilities might cause the system to crash if ATLAST! attempts to load them high. If the system hangs, edit the ATLAST!.INI file manually to force those programs to load in conventional memory.

Considered generically, ATLAST! is a simple, transparent solution with a minimal learning curve. For network managers who need to get 20 to 50 client workstations up and running with MS-DOS 5, it might be the quickest, most cost-effective solution. ATLAST! is also compatible on 8088 and 80286 platforms with EMS 4.0 memory cards.

8088 vs. 80286 vs. 80386 overview

EMS 4.0 memory is always managed by a device driver placed in CONFIG.SYS. There are three different levels of expanded memory manager support based on the processor used in your machine. On 8088 machines, the only way to get expanded memory is by adding an EMS card to a slot on the bus. Each brand of add-on EMS card has its own memory manager.

On 80286 machines, expanded memory can be added in three ways:

- An EMS card in a bus slot.
- A special 80286 memory management unit inserted in the CPU slot.
- An expanded memory manager supplied with the motherboard.

As we saw in Chapter 5, the EMS options supplied by motherboard manufacturers usually don't provide "true" hardware compatible expanded memory.

80386 and above machines do not require additional hardware to use expanded memory. The expanded memory manager converts the extended memory on the motherboard directly to EMS 4.0. Both MS-DOS 5 and DR DOS 6 include EMS drivers that perform this conversion. The MS-DOS 5 and DR DOS 6 EMS drivers provide basic functionality. They allow programs like 1-2-3, release 2, WordPerfect, etc., to use expanded memory for storage. The MS-DOS 5 driver even allows limited EMS multitasking under DESQview.

Third-party memory managers provide more flexibility than the drivers included with the DOS operating systems. They allow you to sort the memory by speed, reassign unused video address space to conventional memory, and fine tune the allocation of expanded memory for individual programs. Perhaps the most important feature offered by third-party packages is their ability to load programs above 640K without tedious user intervention.

It is possible to load device drivers and TSR's above 640K on all PC platforms. A prevailing misconception in the computer world is that this can be accomplished only on 80386 machines. However, the process is somewhat trickier on 8088/80286 platforms. DR DOS 6 even allows you to load the operating system above 640K on 8088 machines. MS-DOS 5 only provides this capability on 80386 and above machines. You must install separate hardware-compatible EMS 4.0 memory on your system for 8088 and most 80286 machines to perform their "load high" magic. (Some 80286 machines can load programs high in Shadow RAM. See the 80286 section later).

8088 systems

You generally purchase the EMS 4.0 memory hardware and software for 8088 machines separately from "above-640K" loadhigh utilities. Fortunately, some 80386 memory management packages do include loadhigh utilities for 8088 and 80286 machines (Qualitas' 386MAX and Helix's NETROOM are examples). Quarterdeck's QRAM is an 8088/80286 loadhigh package marketed separately from their QEMM 386 memory manager. DR DOS 6 from Digital Research includes 8088/80286 loadhigh utilities as part of the operating system. While MS-DOS 5 does not include loadhigh utilities that work on 8088/80286 machines, it will cooperate with 8088/80286 loadhigh products marketed by third-party vendors.

80286 systems

Like 8088s, 80286 machines use loadhigh utilities in conjunction with add-on EMS 4.0 memory cards. Some 80286 systems can load programs high without expanded memory. These machines use special chip sets that can load device drivers and TSR programs high by borrowing from the area reserved for Shadow RAM. Any 80286 system with 64K or more of extended memory can load the operating system above 1M with MS-DOS 5 and DR DOS 6. Finally, an 80286 system equipped with an ALL ChargeCard or SOTA plug-in module may convert extended memory directly to EMS 4.0. These modules are referred to as Memory Management Units (MMUs). The software supplied with an MMU includes both expanded memory management and load high utilities.

80386 and above systems

80386 and above systems require only an appropriate software driver and some extended memory to load programs above 640K. Third-party memory managers for 80386 and above machines also allow many fine-tuning options. The system can sort memory by speed, shadow system ROM into expanded or extended memory, and relocate the addresses of system ROM code. The last option allows you to configure more upper memory as "high-RAM" for device drivers and TSR utilities.

Tips for smooth installation of an expanded memory manager

The first thing you have to do to access expanded memory is make sure that the physical RAM is available on your machine. We presented a detailed explanation of the logistics of this process in Chapter 5. 8088 and 80286 users might need to do an installation of an add-on hardware board; 80386 and above users might need to add additional memory chips to the motherboard. No matter what platform you use or which memory manager you install, you might find the following suggestions useful:

1. Take inventory of how your computer uses memory before you install the memory manager. This step is optional. You can run CHKDSK, MEM or another memory-checking utility to determine your default system configuration.

2. Back up your AUTOEXEC.BAT and CONFIG.SYS. Doing this ensures you can get back to a default condition should something go wrong with your installation. It also allows you to monitor the changes made by automatic installation software.

3. Make a floppy boot diskette. The process of testing and loading programs above 640K is not always foolproof. The memory manager might cause your computer to hang when it starts up. If you have a floppy system diskette handy, you can always reboot the machine from a floppy. Then you can edit CONFIG.SYS and AUTOEXEC.BAT on your hard disk, and start again. It's a good idea to include a small text editor on the floppy boot disk. (We've provided one called TED on our bundled utilities diskette.) Copy the default CONFIG.SYS and AUTOEXEC.BAT you backed up in Step 2 to the floppy under different names (CONFIG.BAK and AUTOEXEC.BAK) so that you'll be able to restore them to the hard drive if necessary.

4. Install the memory management software. This step might entail copying files to the hard disk or running a setup program. If you copy the files

manually, you might need to edit CONFIG.SYS to install the device driver. Most memory management packages will do this for you. The setup program might detect the presence of other memory management software in CONFIG.SYS and ask for permission to remove it. In some cases, CONFIG.SYS is automatically stripped of old memory management drivers, while in other cases you must remove the old drivers manually. More sophisticated memory managers will also offer to optimize your AUTOEXEC.BAT and CONFIG.SYS. The optimization process tests your configuration and directs device drivers and TSR's to load into high memory. The memory optimization process might reboot your machine several times before it's through. This is where the machine is most likely to hang. If the computer does hang, don't panic. Just reboot from a floppy diskette, restore your original CONFIG.SYS and AUTOEXEC.BAT to the hard drive, and start over. (This is why Steps 2 and 3 are of critical importance.) If your memory management package doesn't complete its automatic optimization process, you might need to strip lines from CONFIG.SYS or AUTOEXEC.BAT until you see where the problem lies.

5. Reboot the machine (if the installation process has not already done this). The most likely scenario is that all will be well and you can proceed to Step 6. If you do see error messages displayed on the screen, write them down. (You can pause the execution of CONFIG.SYS or AUTOEXEC .BAT by pressing the Pause key on your keyboard.) If the machine hangs up during the boot process, try to determine from the messages displayed on screen what was going on when the freeze occurred.

6. Take Inventory. Now that you've successfully installed the memory manager, run CHKDSK, DOS 5's MEM, or a memory utility included with the memory management software. Make note of the amount of conventional, extended and expanded memory available. Check to see that all of your device drivers and TSR's have been loaded. In MS-DOS 5, MEM /C will display all programs loaded into conventional, upper, and HMA memory. (For DR DOS 6, the syntax is MEM /B /U /F.)

7. Test your applications. If you own Microsoft Windows, start it in both Standard and Enhanced modes. If you own DESQview, start it and run the Memory Status utility to see if you have expanded memory for multitasking. If you own Lotus 1-2-3, open a large spreadsheet and check the memory usage statistics.

As you become more proficient in working with memory management software, you might want to manually reconfigure the EMS 4.0 device driver. You can fine tune expanded memory managers by editing their command line parameters. (See the command reference section at the end of this chapter.)

DR DOS 6 (HIDOS.SYS/EMM386.SYS)

Before we look at the more advanced third-party packages, we'll devote some space to Digital Research's DR DOS 6. DR DOS 6 includes basic memory management functions, much like those in MS-DOS 5. Unlike MS-DOS 5, DR DOS 6 does offer shared XMS/Expanded Memory management on 80386-and-above platforms. Both MS-DOS 5 and DR DOS 6 permit device drivers and programs to load above 640K, in upper memory. With both operating systems, loading programs above 640K is a manual process, executed through trial and error. MS-DOS 5 and DR DOS 6 have the following memory management features in common:

- The command kernel of the operating system can load above 1M on 80286 and above systems with extended memory.
- Both operating systems provide an XMS memory manager for Microsoft Windows, and other XMS-aware programs.
- They both include expanded memory emulators for use with 80386-and-above systems.
- You can load drivers and TSRs into upper memory (640K to 1M) manually on 80386-and-above machines equipped with more than 1M of RAM.
- The disk cache included with the operating system may use either XMS or expanded memory to improve hard disk performance.

These memory management features are available only in DR DOS 6:

- The command kernel of the operating system may load into upper memory, as well as above 1M. This feature works on 80386 and above machines with extended memory, 8088/80286 machines with hardware compatible EMS 4.0 memory, or 80286 and above machines with a supported chip set for Shadow RAM.

- On 80286 and above machines with more than 1M, Files and Buffers may load above 1M, regardless of where the operating system is placed.

- You can load programs and drivers into upper memory manually on 8088/80286 machines with hardware-compatible EMS 4.0 memory. This feature also works on 80286-and-above machines with a supported chip set for Shadow RAM, or any 80386-and-above machines with more than 1M of user-RAM.

- On 80386 and above machines, memory above 1M may be allocated dynamically to applications as either XMS memory, or expanded memory. Users may run applications like AUTOCAD, Lotus 1-2-3, or Windows during the same session without the need for separate configuration files and rebooting the machine.

Setting Up DR DOS

DR DOS's setup program (see Fig. 8-2) presents a choice between three scenarios: maximum application memory, balanced application memory and functionality, or maximum performance and functionality. The user's selection affects the installation of the memory manager, disk cache software, and DR DOS disk utilities. The setup program also allows the user to choose whether to configure the system for expanded memory or loading programs above 640K (as shown in Fig. 8-3). On 8088/80286 systems, the setup program installs HIDOS.SYS as the memory manager. It installs EMM386.SYS on 80386 and above systems.

```
 Digital Research                                    DR DOS 6.0 SETUP

         If you wish you can reset your configuration to one of the three
         default settings listed below. This will result in the loss of any
         non-default settings you may have entered previously. If you do not
         wish to do this select the 'Continue without changing' option.


       * Maximum application memory at the expense of functionality.


       ▌ Balance application memory and functionality.


       * Maximum performance and functionality at the expense of
         application memory.

       * Continue without changing any current settings.



 F1=Help  ↕=next/prev line  <Enter>=select option  <Esc>=prev screen  F10=abort
```

Fig. 8-2   DR DOS's Setup program.

```
 Digital Research                                    DR DOS 6.0 INSTALL


       The following MemoryMAX options will be included:

        - 80386 Memory support (EMM386.SYS)          YES   [YES/NO]

        - Relocate DR DOS data areas                 YES   [YES/NO]
          and device drivers

      Move the cursor to any field and enter a new value, if required.

         * Your computer contains an 80386/386SX/486 cpu.
         * You have 9472K of extended memory available.

         ▐ Accept current settings and continue

 F1=Help  ↕=next/prev line  <Enter>=select option  <Esc>=prev screen  F10=abort
```

Fig. 8-3   DR DOS's System Loading selection.

Using HIDOS.SYS

DR DOS 6 includes an XMS memory manager that provides a superset of the features included in Microsoft's HIMEM.SYS. Besides converting extended memory for use with Windows, Digital's HIDOS.SYS allows the operating system, device drivers, and TSR programs to load above 640K. This feature works on any 8088 or 80286 computer equipped with fully EMS 4.0 compatible expanded memory. On 80286 machines without expanded memory, the operating system can load above 1M if some extended memory is present. If the 80286 has neither expanded nor extended memory, then the operating system, device drivers, and TSR's may load into upper memory if the 80286 uses a special NEAT chipset for shadow RAM.

On 80286 systems with more than 1M, DR DOS 6 automatically configures itself to load the DR DOS operating system above 1M in the HMA. You can control the placement of the operating system using the DEVICE = HIDOS.SYS /BDOS = parameter. When NEAT shadow-RAM or EMS 4.0 memory is present, you can use HIDOS in conjunction with DR's HIDEVICE and HILOAD options to place device drivers or programs in UMB memory. (This also works for 8088 machines with EMS 4.0 memory). The statement DEVICE = HIDOS.SYS /BDOS = AUTO in CONFIG.SYS tells DR DOS to determine optimum placement for the operating system. On 8088/80286 systems equipped with expanded memory, the HIDOS.SYS statement should be placed after the DEVICE = line that loads your EMS 4.0 expanded memory manager. For example,

```
DEVICE = REMM451 . SYS /C = 16 /P = 16 /S = E000
DEVICE = HIDOS . SYS /BDOS = AUTO
```

would load HIDOS on a machine running DR DOS with one of AST's expanded memory cards (See the section on AST's memory management for details on configuring REMM.SYS.)

The HIBUFFERS = statement places DOS buffers in the HMA area on machines with extended memory. The HIDEVICE and HILOAD statements are used to load device drivers and programs, respectively, into upper memory. (See the section on using EMM386.SYS, and the DR DOS command reference later in this chapter for more details.)

Using EMM386.SYS

On 80386-and-above systems, DR DOS's EMM386.SYS driver handles XMS, EMS, and loadhigh functions. If your goal is to load programs above 640K while running Microsoft Windows or other DOS extended programs, EMM386.SYS can accomplish this. Configuration of expanded memory outside of Windows is optional.

Like HIDOS.SYS, EMM386.SYS uses the HIBUFFERS command to allocate DOS buffers above 640K. Device drivers are loaded into upper memory with the HIDEVICE command. You can load TSRs into upper memory with the HILOAD command. For example,

CONFIG.SYS
```
DEVICE = EMM386.SYS /BDOS = AUTO /ROM = AUTO
HIBUFFERS = 40
HIDEVICE = MOUSE.SYS
```
AUTOEXEC.BAT
```
PROMPT $P$G
PATH = C:\DRDOS
HILOAD C:\SK\SK.EXE
```

instructs DR DOS to determine the optimum placement for the operating system. DR DOS loads the operating system either into the HMA (at address FFFFh), or into upper memory (between A000h and EFFFh). The /ROM = AUTO switch instructs DR DOS to automatically shadow all ROMs found in upper memory to RAM above 1M. The statement HIDEVICE = MOUSE.SYS loads a mouse driver into upper memory. The statement HILOAD SK.EXE in AUTOEXEC.BAT would load Borland's SideKick into upper memory.

The flexibility provided by DR DOS's memory management can free additional conventional memory. Loading DOS high into the HMA, gains only 37–48K of conventional memory. 16K or more of the 64K HMA remains unused. Applications like DESQview, Ventura Publisher for DOS, and Windows can use the full 64K of the HMA. You can load DR DOS high in upper memory (between 640K and 1M). This saves the HMA for use by another application. The net gain in conventional memory, for users of HMA-aware programs, can be as high as 101K. (An HMA-aware program gains 64K, plus the 37K saved by loading DOS in upper memory.) You can regulate ROM shadowing and the placement of the command kernel by replacing "AUTO" with specific addresses for /ROM = and /BDOS = . For example,

```
DEVICE = EMM386.SYS /BDOS = C800 /ROM = C000-C7FF
              /ROM = F000-FFFF
```

This statement forces the DOS command kernel to load in upper memory at address C800h. The ROM BIOS is shadowed in the region from F000h to FFFFh. The video BIOS (from C000h to C7FFh) is also shadowed. In this instance, DOS is loaded above 640K, but the 64K HMA area is still free for use by another program. You can load additional device drivers and programs into upper memory alongside of the operating system kernel if they will fit. (Running DR DOS's MEM /U command will reveal if any upper memory remains.)

Your memory management goals might include

- Loading programs above 640K.
- Running Microsoft Windows.

- Running a DOS-extended program like Lotus 1-2-3 release 3.1.
- Allocating expanded memory to programs outside of Windows.

You can accomplish these goals by using the /KB = nnnn switch to allocate a specific portion of your total memory as expanded memory. The DR DOS default is to place all memory above 1MB into a common pool. Any application that wants the memory can request it as either XMS or EMS 4.0.

Adding the /Winstd parameter to the EMM386 command line permits Windows 3.0 to run in Standard Mode, while still providing expanded memory support for DOS applications outside of Windows. With Windows 3.1, this parameter is unnecessary. For more details about EMM386 command line parameters, see the DR DOS reference section at the end of this chapter.

Survey of 8088/80286 memory managers

AST Research—EMS Cards/AST Premium 286

EMS drivers from AST research are named REMMxxx.SYS. Starting with v4.00, an odd version number is used for AST memory boards (RAMpage +, SixPak Plus, etc.). The even numbered versions of REMM.SYS are used with AST Premium Computer Systems (AST Premium 286, AST Premium 386, etc.). You would use REMM45.SYS with an AST EMS card, and REMM46.SYS with an AST computer. AST also issues frequent updates of its memory management software. You can order the current driver versions directly from AST or download them from their bulletin board. AST drivers can also appear on many public bulletin board systems.

Memory installed on an AST card can be divided between "backfilled" conventional memory, extended memory, and expanded memory. This is done by setting a series of switches on the card, or handled automatically by the installation software. The installation program might display a graphic figure of the dip switch settings on your screen with the older cards. Copying the switch settings will help you to set the card up properly before inserting it into the computer. For AST Premium Computers, the division of memory is set with jumpers on the special FASTRAM memory cards included with the motherboard. (See the command reference at the end of this chapter for details on configuring AST's REMM.SYS memory manager.)

Intel AboveBoard, AboveBoard+, and AboveBoard 286

Like the AST package, the Intel AboveBoard+ includes an automatic setup program. It also includes RAMdisk and print spooler utilities. You set up the Intel memory manager by running INSTALL. The RAMdisk and print spooler may use either conventional or expanded memory. Intel also supplies several diagnostic utilities. You can check the integrity of the chips installed on the AboveBoard by running TESTAB.EXE.

Intel memory management is slightly less flexible than its AST counterpart. The AboveBoard series does not use built-in alternate mapping registers for multi-tasking. Instead, the alternate registers are simulated in software. Once you finish installing the AboveBoard+, you can fine tune its memory usage by editing the line that loads EMM.SYS in CONFIG.SYS. (See the Command Reference at the end of the chapter for details.)

All ChargeCard 286

After you insert the ChargeCard into a CPU slot (see Chapter 5), it remains dormant until you load the ALLEMM4 device driver. The software for the Charge-Card provides expanded memory management and loadhigh capability on 80286 machines under all versions of DOS; it is not dependent on MS-DOS 5. The All installation program allows three choices for memory management:

- Maximum EMS Configuration.
- Both EMS and High Memory Available.
- Maximum High Memory Configuration.

"High memory" in the All documentation refers to UMB memory, not to Microsoft's HMA. The three install choices control the added parameters placed on the DEVICE = ALLEMM4.SYS line in CONFIG.SYS. Users who want expanded memory, but have no need to load programs high should pick the first choice. Users who want expanded memory and want to load programs above 640K should pick the second option. Network users and others who need the maximum possible load high area should pick the last one.

You may fine tune any of the three choices selected from the install procedure by editing the ALLEMM4 command line parameters. The ChargeCard allows many memory options; it is almost as powerful as an 80386 memory manager. The AllOpt program will automatically analyze your AUTOEXEC.BAT and CONFIG.SYS, reboot the computer, and load programs and drivers into upper memory. You may examine the contents of memory with Allmenu. Allmenu is a memory diagnostic utility, similar to Quarterdeck's Manifest. You may use it to get a complete picture of how memory in the system is being used.

The ChargeCard software offers specific advanced memory management features. These include loading files and buffers into upper memory with FILES .COM and BUFFERS.COM. Instead of loading device drivers into UMB memory from CONFIG.SYS, All's DEVICE.COM allows you to load device drivers from AUTOEXEC.BAT. Use ALLOAD.EXE to load executable programs high from within AUTOEXEC.BAT.

The All loadhigh utilities are more powerful than features included with MS-DOS 5 or DR DOS 6. You can also use them to place programs at specific UMB addresses. The art of shoehorning as many programs as possible into upper memory involves placing programs in the smallest available contiguous block, the largest block, or from the top of the largest block down. Additionally, some device drivers explode upon loading, demanding up to two or three times the amount of memory that they will actually use. The All utilities can temporarily allocate additional memory space to allow these files to load. The All memory manager can also provide expanded memory shadowing for any ROM area in upper memory. The All shadowing feature may either replace, or be used in conjunction with, dedicated shadow RAM.

Because the ChargeCard uses software to distinguish between extended and expanded memory, you may allocate both for your system without reconfiguring dip switch settings or jumpers. This is useful if you want to run programs like Lotus 1-2-3, DESQview, or Windows 3.0/3.1 during the same session and not have to reboot the machine.

Note If you use the ChargeCard with a print spooler, RAMdisk, or with an extended memory disk cache, you must allocate extended memory on the ALLEMM4 command line with the EXTMEM= parameter. The ALLEMM4.SYS driver should be the first line in CONFIG.SYS. If you use Quarterdeck's DESQview, you can gain an extra 64K for DESQview windows by allocating 64K for Quarterdeck's QEXT.SYS driver. For example:

```
DEVICE = [d : \ path] ALLEMM4 . SYS RAM EXT = 64
DEVICE = [d : \ path] QEXT . SYS
```

If you plan to run Windows 3.0 or 3.1, you must set aside sufficient extended memory for Windows with the EXTMEM parameter. You must also run either Microsoft's HIMEM.SYS driver or Quarterdeck's QEXT .SYS driver. Here's a sample configuration for Windows 3:

CONFIG.SYS
```
DEVICE = ALLEMM4 . SYS FR = C800 EXTMEM = 2048
         I = C800 - F7FF RAM = D800 - E7FF ROM = C000 -
         C7FF ROM = F800 - FFFF
DEVICE = HIMEM . SYS
FILES = 15
BUFFERS = 2
```

AUTOEXEC.BAT
```
PROMPT $P$G
PATH = C : \ DOS ; C : \ ALL ; C : \ UTIL ; C : \ WINDOWS
DEVICE = C : \ WINDOWS \ SMARTDRV . SYS 512 /E
ALLOAD MOUSE
BUFFERS = 15
FILES = 50
```

The ChargeCard software permits you to load device drivers, files, and buffers from AUTOEXEC.BAT with All's special utilities (DEVICE .COM, FILES.COM, BUFFERS.COM).

On systems running CGA or Hercules graphics cards, you can configure the ALLEMM4 device driver to annex the EGA\VGA video area as part of conventional memory. This adds 64−96K to the available conventional memory. For CGA systems, add the following parameter to the ALLEMM4 line in CONFIG.SYS:

```
DEVICE=ALLEMM4.SYS I=A000-B7FF
```

For Hercules systems:

```
DEVICE=ALLEMM4.SYS I=A000-AFFF
```

Quarterdeck's QRAM/Qualitas' Move'Em

Third-party packages from Quarterdeck and Qualitas allow device drivers and TSR's to load into UMB memory on any 8088 or 80286 machine equipped with separate expanded memory. These utilities will also work with some variants of 80286 NEAT shadow RAM. QRAM and Move'EM are device drivers placed in CONFIG.SYS after the expanded memory manager. These third-party packages contain powerful loadhigh options equivalent to those available with the All ChargeCard. (They do not permit the operating system to load above 1M, and they are not expanded memory managers; they must be used in conjunction with expanded memory or NEAT Shadow RAM. The current version of Qualitas' 386 product, 386MAX, includes Move'Em as a bundled utility. The Move'Em utility supports 8088 and 80286 machines, but the 386MAX expanded memory manager does not. The following example shows a typical configuration for Quarterdeck's QRAM on an AST 286 Premium:

CONFIG.SYS
```
DEVICE=REMM.SYS /P=32 /C=16 /S=E000
DEVICE=C:\QRAM\QRAM.SYS
DEVICE=C:\QRAM\LOADHI.SYS C:\DOS\SETVER.EXE
FILES=20
BUFFERS=5
```

AUTOEXEC.BAT
```
PROMPT $P$G
PATH=C:\DOS;C:\QRAM;C:\UTIL
BUFFERS=25
FILES=30
LOADHI C:\DOS\MOUSE.COM
```

Note that QRAM permits DOS FILES and BUFFERS to load into upper memory from AUTOEXEC.BAT. To maintain compatibility with Microsoft Windows, DOS must have the capacity to open 18 files set in CONFIG.SYS. (See the Command Reference on QRAM for more details.) The following example shows a typical Move'Em configuration:

CONFIG.SYS
```
DEVICE = REMM.SYS /P = 32 /C = 16 /S = E000
DEVICE = C:\MOVE'EM\MOVE'EM.MGR
DEVICE = C:\MOVE'EM\MOVE'EM.SYS PROG = C:\DOS
  \SETVER.EXE
FILES = 30
BUFFERS = 25
```

AUTOEXEC.BAT
```
PROMPT $P$G
PATH = C:\DOS;C:\MOVE'EM;C:\UTIL
MOVE'EM PROG = C:\DOS\MOUSE.COM
```

Survey of 80386 and above memory managers

The question that may come to your mind if you own an 80386 and above system is "Do I really need to buy a third-party memory manager? Can't I get by with MS-DOS 5 or DR DOS 6?" The answer to this question depends on how you intend to use the computer. Some users might go directly into Lotus 1-2-3 or WordPerfect after turning on the machine. Others will launch multitasking environments like DESQview or Windows. Some users will have a variety of applications to run, all of which have different memory requirements. Someone who intends to run DOS versions of Paradox, AutoCAD, 1-2-3, and Windows as well, is certainly not going to have an easy time making do with MS-DOS 5. Quarterdeck's QEMM is probably a far better choice. A programmer who makes use of the software version of the Periscope Debugger will probably want to investigate Qualitas' 386MAX. Users who want to run applications on a server under Novell Netware 386, Microsoft's Lan Manager or BANYAN might do well to investigate Helix Software's NETROOM. The following section presents a survey of third-party packages.

Introduction to advanced 80386 memory management

You can divide memory managers for 80386 and above systems into two main types: those that handle extended and expanded memory as separate resources, and those that combine all system memory above 640K into a shared pool. MS-DOS 5's bundled memory management is an example of the first type. With MS-DOS 5's HIMEM.SYS and EMM386.EXE, you must preconfigure the amounts of extended and expanded memory available to applications. As we saw in Chapter 7, you must maintain alternate system configurations to accommodate programs with different memory requirements.

The second type of memory manager makes the entire shared memory pool available for any requesting program. If you have 8M of memory on the machine, AutoCAD gets 8M of expanded memory when you run it. When you run Windows, it gets 8M of XMS memory. The memory is allocated automatically, conforming to the demands of the application. Digital Research's DR DOS 6 takes a hybrid approach to this problem: Digital's EMM386.SYS driver essentially converts all RAM above 1M to XMS memory. Programs that want expanded memory get an emulation of true EMS 4.0. This works fine with single applications like 1-2-3, release 2.xx, but Quarterdeck's DESQview can't use the memory for multitasking. This is because Digital's EMS 4.0 emulation does not allow mapping of memory pages below 640K.

Basic common features

The memory managers explored in this section have many features and even command-line parameters in common. In Chapter 7, we learned how some of the basic control functions apply to MS-DOS 5's memory management. As you read the sections on the advanced memory managers, watch for the following key elements in each one:

- How to include or exclude upper memory ranges from the memory manager's control: (INCLUDE=, EXCLUDE=).
- How to set the address for the Expanded Memory Pageframe (FRAME=).
- How to map upper memory areas with ROM code into faster RAM (ROM=).
- How to designate specific upper memory addresses for use as high RAM (QEMM: RAM= 386MAX: USE= NETROOM: XMS= or EMS=).
- How does the memory manager actually load programs into upper memory. (Utilities placed in CONFIG.SYS and AUTOEXEC.BAT precede the name of the program to load high.)

Which advanced package is the best?

You might wonder how the various third-party memory managers compare in features and performance with DR DOS 6.0 and MS-DOS 5.0. The following tables are reprinted with permission from PC Week. Table 8-1 provides a comparison of the features and specifications for various 80386 memory managers. Table 8-2 shows conventional memory you can expect to receive from various memory managers on an ISA machine. Table 8-3 shows the same figures for a PS/2 machine. Table 8-4 shows the speed differential between various memory

Table 8-1 Memory Manager features and specifications. PC WEEK, December 23, 1991.

Memory Manager	EMS 4.0/XMS Support	Shared Memory Pool	Automatic Loadhigh	Maximum UMB Available /w EMS 4.0 & VGA ISA	PS/2	Relocates UMB ROMS	Added Enhancements
MS DOS 5	Yes	No	No	168K	128K	No	Disk cache
DR DOS 6	Yes[1]	No	No	168K	128K	No	Disk cache
386MAX 6.0	Yes	Yes	Yes	168K	128K	Yes	Disk cache, RAM disk, System Inventory utility, online tutorial
BLUEMAX 6.0	Yes	Yes	Yes	168K	168K	Yes	Disk Cache, System Inventory utility, online tutorial
QEMM 6.01	Yes	Yes	Yes	224K[2]	224K	Yes	System Inventory utility
NETROOM 2.10	Yes	Yes	Yes	224K[3]	192K	Yes	System Inventory utility, network loader, HMA loader
MEMORY COMMANDER 2.18	Yes	No[4]	Partial[5]	128K	96K	No[6]	RAM disk
QMAPS 2.0	Yes	Yes	Yes	168K	128K	No	RAM disk, Disk Cache, print spooler
ALL386	Yes	Yes	Yes	168K	128K	No	System Inventory utility

[1] DR DOS does not support bank-switched EMS 4.0 for multitasking.

[2] With ROM areas remapped to EMS by Stealth. Otherwise, 160K maximum.

[3] With ROM areas compressed & remapped to HMA. Otherwise, 160K maximum (Note, ROM compression on PC Week's test machines provided only 192K)

[4] Memory Commander maintains separate EMS and XMS memory pools, but allows Windows in enhanced mode to reclaim all allocated expanded memory.

[5] Applications must be entered into a database in order to load above 640K.

[6] Remapped ROM capability planned for version to be released in January, 1992.

Table 8-2 Memory on ISA machines. PC WEEK, December 23, 1991.

Memory Manager[1]	DOS Loaded LOW	DOS Loaded HIGH	DOS in WINDOWS (w/DOS HIGH)	Loaded in UMB
MS DOS 5	496,900[2]	545,900[2]	525,200	122,600
DR DOS 6	463,408[3]	520,288[3]	510,064	101,900
386MAX	533,024	580,000	546,512	145,000
BLUE MAX	--	--	--	--
QEMM	576,000[4]	613,000[4]	562,000	205,000
NETROOM	518,000[5]	565,500[5]	549,500	150,000[6]
MEMORY COMMANDER	508,000 -- 631,000[7]	557,000 -- 650,000[7]	537,000	124,126
QMAPS	498,160[8]	545,136[8]	529,360	123,500
ALL386	499,408[9]	543,728[9]	529,360	124,000

[1](Memory size in bytes)

[2]36K recovered manually after straight sequential load high process.

[3]DR DOS run without the Norton NDOS shell in order to use its HILOAD command to place programs above 640K.

[4]35K recovered manually after auto-optimization process.

[5]22K recovered manually, after auto-customization process.

[6]This was the best configuration on the test machine, loading DOS high instead of compressing BIOS.

[7]Memory Commander provides a variable amount of conventional memory depending on an application's video requirements (see review). Also excluded Norton's NDOS Shell.

[8]60K recovered manually.

[9]26K recovered manually.

managers. We used the following configuration to obtain these test results (except where noted in the tables):

CONFIG.SYS
```
SHELL = E : \ NORTON \ NDOS . COM E : \ NORTON /E : 512U /S : B /U /P
BUFFERS = 20
FILES = 25
```

Table 8-3 Memory on PS/2 machines. PC WEEK, December 23, 1991.

Memory Manager[1]	DOS Loaded LOW	DOS Loaded HIGH	DOS in WINDOWS (w/DOS HIGH)	Loaded in UMB
MS DOS 5	485,296	534,280	467,792	96,000
DR DOS 6	466,624	500,896	432,000	82,804
386MAX	--	--	--	--
BLUE MAX	535,088	582,064	515,600	153,000
QEMM	575,392	612,272	545,808	202,000
NETROOM	514,704	552,112	520,464	104,500
MEMORY COMMANDER	478,960 -- 536,496	520,016 -- 585,552	449,800	84,800
QMAPS	467,328	514,304	448,016	92,504
ALL386	451,456	495,776	429,488	65,535

[1](Memory size in bytes)

Table 8-4 Memory Manager speed differences. PC WEEK, December 23, 1991.

Memory Manager	PCWeek Benchmarks		WP51 Disk Access[1]	Spreadsheet Recalc[2]
	Text Scroll	*Graphics*		
DOS 5(No Shadow)	57.19	10.60	1 min 26 sec	2min 26sec
DOS 5(Shadowed)	12.41	10.27	1 min 7 sec	2min 21sec
DR DOS 6	10.16	10.00	1 min 14 sec	2min 21sec
386MAX	10.93	10.38	1 min 12 sec	
BLUE MAX			----------	----
QEMM	12.41	10.43	1 min 9 sec	2min 39sec
NETROOM	10.49	10.43	1 min 12.3 sec	2min 38sec
MEMORY COMMANDER	12.96	10.71	1 min 15.5 sec	2min 31sec
QMAPS	10.54	10.05	1 min 6 sec	2min 31sec
ALL386	10.60	10.27	1 min 7 sec	2min 38sec

[1]WordPerfect Macro loads 300K document and prints it to a disk file.

[2]LOTUS macro sets up 100 col by 100 row spreadsheet, generates random numerical entries, and performs 100 iterations of a series of recalculations.

```
DEVICEH=C:\DOS\ANSI.SYS
BREAK ON
DEVICE=E:\WINDOWS\EGA.SYS
DEVICE=C:\UTIL\NJRAMDXP.SYS /P25 /S
DEVICE=F:\DR6\SSTORDRV.SYS
DEVICE=F:\DR6\DEVSWAP.COM
```

AUTOEXEC.BAT
```
PATH=C:\DOS;C:\UTIL;E:\NORTON;C:\BAT;
      F:\WINDOWS;
C:
VSHIELD.EXE /LH
LH VSHIELD1.EXE
HYPERDKX C:2048 S V
LH APPEND C:\DOS
LH DOSKEY
KEYREPET A 1
PROMPT $P$G
CD \
EP /ON
DISKMON /PROTECT+
LH G:\HSG\GRAB.EXE
LH C:\DOS\MOUSE.COM
LH C:\DOS\MIRROR /TC
LH RMAP.COM
SEL /15/5
```

Tables 8-2 and 8-3 illustrate the differences in conventional memory obtained using various memory managers with a typical configuration. One factor that contributes to the amount of conventional memory you see at the DOS prompt is how well the memory manager loads applications into upper memory. Three problems can arise in the load high process that account for the disparity in conventional memory totals with different memory managers.

First, both MS-DOS 5 and DR DOS 6 take a basic approach to loading programs into the upper memory block. The first driver encountered is placed into the first available space above 640K, the second driver is placed into the second available space, followed by the third, etc. Because each driver is loaded in order, this simple procedure can fail to load large drivers listed near the end of CONFIG.SYS or AUTOEXEC.BAT into upper memory, which might result in less than optimal usage of the upper memory area.

Third-party memory managers are usually a little smarter than either MS-DOS 5 or DR DOS 6. For example, when a large program is listed near the end of AUTOEXEC.BAT, QEMM, 386MAX, NETROOM, and other memory managers have algorithms that take inventory of the size of all programs listed. They can then load programs into designated regions of upper memory, not necessarily in linear sequence. The result is a more efficient use of the upper memory area with less effort on the part of the user. This directly translates into a larger conventional memory area without the necessity of hand tuning either AUTOEXEC .BAT or CONFIG.SYS.

A second problem that arises in loading programs high comes from "exploding device drivers." These programs require a large amount of free memory on initial loading (sometimes as much as 120K). After initialization, the programs shrink, leaving a resident stub of 6K to 32K in upper memory. Neither MS-DOS 5 or DR DOS 6 can compensate for this situation. Fortunately, QEMM, 386MAX, and NETROOM can compensate for "exploding device drivers" by temporarily allowing these programs to use the EMS 4.0 pageframe when they load. Of course, the amount they compensate for the problem is related to how well the memory manager actually controls memory usage.

The third problem relates to a lack of sufficient contiguous address space to load a driver high, even with the temporary loan of the EMS pageframe. On most ordinary 80386 systems, the VGA card and the PC's ROM BIOS occupy up to 96K of upper memory. On IBM PS/2 systems, the BIOS takes up 128K. The reserved ROM address space in upper memory is an immovable island for some memory managers, resulting in an inability to load some drivers high. If one memory manager can get around this problem and another cannot, you will see differences in the amount of conventional memory provided.

Quarterdeck's QEMM386

Many savvy users consider Quarterdeck's QEMM one of the best 80386 memory managers available. Quarterdeck has been in the memory management business almost since the inception of the PC. It was the first company to market a memory manager specifically designed for 80386 machines.

QEMM can create up to 225K of high RAM from upper memory—more than any competing memory management package. (This assumes that you are using the newest version of QEMM and implement the Stealth feature.) The authors have found that QEMM is stable and reliable with a wide range of PC applications. Although, the Stealth feature does not work well with some applications or specific machine configurations. QEMM's sophisticated memory management allows you to take advantage of the following advanced capabilities:

- QEMM allows you to load drivers and TSRs into upper memory and still run Windows version 3.0/3.00a in standard mode. (Microsoft rewrote Windows 3.1 so that QEMM's competitors can also run it in Standard Mode.)

- You can launch DOS-Extended VCPI applications like Lotus 1-2-3 3.0, AutoCad 11, and Paradox 3.5 as single DOS tasks from Windows running in Standard Mode.

- Quarterdeck's DESQview can run VGA graphics-based and ill-behaved text applications in "virtualized" Windows.

Quarterdeck allows you to install QEMM automatically using a preconfigured set of defaults, or a setup customized by the user. It's usually a good idea to strip references to other memory management utilities from your CONFIG.SYS and AUTOEXEC.BAT prior to installing QEMM. The installation program provided with QEMM won't automatically remove every memory manager related statement. For example, you must delete the DEVICEHIGH and LOADHIGH statements for MS-DOS 5's memory manager manually.

The default QEMM setup will accommodate most generic 80386 configurations. If you decide to choose your own defaults, you might want to keep the QEMM manual handy to look up the effects of the various options. You can change any choices you make later by manually editing the DEVICE = QEMM 386SYS line in CONFIG.SYS. If you do decide to modify QEMM's default setup, then the install program displays the dialog box shown in Fig. 8-4. (Your display may differ depending on which version of QEMM you own.)

The following paragraphs explain the entries you can expect to see on the dialog box.

```
        Quarterdeck Office Systems
        DESQview-386 Installation
        Serial No: XXX-XX-XXXX-XXXXXX


                Current QEMM Switch Settings:

        Extended Memory for QEMM Use . . . .    ALL
        Page Frame Address . . . . . . . . .    AUTO
        DESQview 1.3 and 2.00 Compatible ? .    No
        Fill Conventional Memory ? . . . . .    Yes
        Fill Video Memory ?. . . . . . . . .    Yes
        Replace Slow Memory with Fast ?. . .    No
        Fill All High Memory with RAM ?. . .    Yes
        Copy All ROMs to RAM ? . . . . . . .    No
        Initial QEMM Mode. . . . . . . . . .    ON
        Alternate Maps . . . . . . . . . . .    8
        Total Handles. . . . . . . . . . . .    64
        Other:


        Enter when complete    ↑↓    Space to edit value
```

Fig. 8-4 QEMM Custom Setup display.

Extended Memory for QEMM Use By default, QEMM places all extended memory in your system in a common, shared pool. Some programs might require extended memory outside of QEMM (for instance, older applications that don't follow Microsoft's XMS memory management). This option allows you to reserve a designated portion of extended memory to leave outside of QEMM's control.

Set Page Frame Address By default, QEMM attempts to select an optimum upper memory address for the EMS 4.0 page frame. You can override this option by providing a user-specified address. A user-specified page frame must have a hexadecimal address that ends in two zeros. Newer versions of the QEMM installation program provide you with a list of acceptable page frame addresses.

DESQview 1.3 and 2.00 Compatible The default is off. Change this parameter if you plan to run an older version of Quarterdeck's DESQview.

Fill Conventional Memory This setting applies only if there is less than 640K of conventional memory installed on the machine. By default, QEMM will backfill memory up to 640K from the extended memory pool. On monochrome and CGA systems, some versions of QEMM will also fill in the video memory area reserved for VGA graphics. (Newer versions provide a separate selection for this option.) This brings the conventional memory total to 704K for monochrome machines, and 736K for CGA machines.

Fill Video Memory Newer versions of QEMM provide this option so you can determine whether or not you want to use the video memory area to provide additional conventional memory on monochrome and CGA equipped machines or configure it as mappable EMS. This allows you to decide how to use this area independently of the decision to backfill conventional memory. This option provides up to 736K of conventional memory on a CGA machine and up to 704K of conventional memory on a monochrome machine.

Replace Slow Memory with Fast The default is no. On systems that have memory modules with different speeds, QEMM can order all of the "fast" memory first and leave the "slow" memory at the top of the pool. This option can improve performance on systems that use RAM with different speeds. For instance, you might have 8M of "fast" RAM on the motherboard, and 2M of "slow" RAM on an add-on memory card.

Fill all High Memory with RAM The default is yes. QEMM automatically seeks the maximum available upper memory space for use in loading drivers and TSR's. The user has the option to limit high RAM by specifying a smaller address range.

Copy All ROMs to RAM The default is no. QEMM can shadow any specified ROM address in upper memory, mapping the ROM information to faster RAM. Selecting yes on this option can speed up system performance on machines that don't offer their own internal ROM shadowing.

Initial QEMM Mode The default is on. QEMM has three operating modes. If QEMM loads programs into upper memory, the default is on. QEMM memory management is always available. The AUTO mode activates QEMM memory management only when a specific application requests expanded or XMS memory. In the OFF mode, QEMM remains dormant.

Alternate Maps The default is 8. Alternate maps consist of memory reserved by QEMM to speed up EMS 4.0 memory swapping. A good rule of thumb is to allocate one alternate map for each EMS 4.0 program you plan to run concurrently under QEMM.

EMS Handles The default is 64. QEMM assigns a separate EMS 4.0 handle to each program or process that requests expanded memory. The default of 64 is usually more than enough.

Other This option only appears if you previously installed QEMM in CONFIG.SYS on older versions. Newer versions of QEMM always provide this option. This option allows you to change, keep, or add parameters already present on the QEMM command line.

After selecting automatic setup or changing the previously described QEMM defaults, the installation program shows you the QEMM command line as it will appear in CONFIG.SYS. You may tell the installation program to place QEMM in CONFIG.SYS or manually install it, later. The installation program copies the QEMM files to the hard disk. Next, the installation program searches your hard disk for Microsoft Windows. If it finds Windows 3 (or later), you are prompted to modify Windows for compatibility with QEMM. (You can skip this step and modify the Windows configuration later with Quarterdeck's QWINFIX utility.

If you choose to display the READ.ME file included with QEMM, you will get information about the latest minor changes to the program, and possible problems arising from specific hardware and software. At this point, you may complete the installation process by running Quarterdeck's OPTIMIZE utility, or exit back to DOS. OPTIMIZE is QEMM's automatic process for loading drivers and TSR utilities into upper memory. If you choose to exit to DOS at this point, you can run the OPTIMIZE process whenever you choose, by invoking it from the DOS command line.

If you like, you can have QEMM go into the OPTIMIZE process directly after installation. If all goes well, OPTIMIZE will reboot your computer three times and complete its cycle. However, if you have "problem" drivers in your configuration, the OPTIMIZE process might cause the machine to lock up. (WordPerfect's Repeat Performance keyboard utility is one such example.) If the system crashes running OPTIMIZE, then reboot from a floppy disk and restore the original CONFIG.SYS and AUTOEXEC.BAT.

Note   That's why it's important to back up your startup files and make emergency boot disks.

When OPTIMIZE can't complete its cycle due to problem utilities, you need to inspect your CONFIG.SYS and AUTOEXEC.BAT file by file to find them. If you are uncertain about whether a program in your startup configuration can be loaded in upper memory, check the program's documentation and the QEMM READ.ME file. It might be a good idea to inspect your CONFIG.SYS and AUTOEXEC.BAT before invoking OPTIMIZE. The reasons for this are as follows:

- You might want to create a special list of programs that OPTIMIZE should not try to load high.
- You might want to reconfigure some programs that try to load themselves into upper memory to load themselves low. If OPTIMIZE handles sizing and placing for these programs, they might load into upper memory more efficiently.

Quarterdeck allows users to create a special exception list for programs that can't load high. Program names are entered (without their file extensions) into an ASCII file called OPTIMIZE.EXC. This file should reside in your QEMM directory. OPTIMIZE will skip over any drivers or programs named in this list. For example, if you want OPTIMIZE to ignore Repeat Performance (RP.SYS) and Superstor (SSTORDRV.SYS), the OPTIMIZE.EXC text file would contain two lines:

```
RP
SSTORDRV
```

Another optimization problem is caused by programs that attempt to load into upper memory without QEMM's assistance. Quarterdeck mentions Multisoft's PC-Kwik disk cache, and Norton Utilities' NCache in the READ.ME file. Disk Monitor and Erase Protect are two other programs from the Norton Utilities that behave in this way. Disk compression software like Superstor, Stacker, and Doubledisk might also thwart Quarterdeck's load high procedure. Again, if you don't know whether a particular program in CONFIG.SYS or AUTOEXEC.BAT loads itself into upper memory, you might be able to find out by reading the program's documentation. Some of these programs can be configured to load themselves low, allowing QEMM to handle their placement in upper memory.

In its final phase, OPTIMIZE permits the user to invoke several options. One of these options allows you to toggle "problem" drivers to load low before OPTIMIZE completes its final pass. To reach the "Data Collection" screen in OPTIMIZE, select O for Options at the screen prompt presented after the OPTIMIZE "Detection Phase" (shown in Fig. 8-5). Three menu choices appear (see Fig. 8-6). Select Choice 2, "Modify data collected..." The next screen displays a list of all the programs and drivers that OPTIMIZE has analyzed (see Fig. 8-7). You can set individual programs to load low (below 640K) by changing the "Y" to "N" in the "Try to Load High" column.

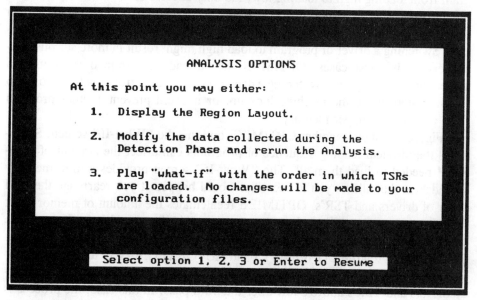

Quarterdeck OPTIMIZE

```
                    ANALYSIS COMPLETE

        OPTIMIZE has tried all combinations of loading 9
        resident programs into 1 high RAM regions.  The
        best configuration found was:

             Resident programs loaded high:      8
             Conventional memory used:           1 K
             High RAM used:                     89 K

             Largest free block of high RAM:   103 K
             Total free high RAM:              103 K
             Total combinations:               512


        Enter to Continue    0 for Options    Esc to Quit
```

Fig. 8-5   QEMM OPTIMIZE Detection Phase display. Quarterdeck Office Systems.

Quarterdeck OPTIMIZE

```
                    ANALYSIS OPTIONS

        At this point you may either:

            1.   Display the Region Layout.

            2.   Modify the data collected during the
                 Detection Phase and rerun the Analysis.

            3.   Play "what-if" with the order in which TSRs
                 are loaded.  No changes will be made to your
                 configuration files.


        Select option 1, 2, 3 or Enter to Resume
```

Fig. 8-6   QEMM OPTIMIZE menu. Quarterdeck Office Systems.

DATA FOR THE OPTIMIZE PROCESS

Program	Try to Load High?	SQUEEZE Frame?	Temp?	Initial Size	Final Size
QEMM386.SYS	Y	–	–	13232	13232
HYPERSTB.EXE	Y	–	Y	6656	288
EGA.SYS	Y	–	Y	4896	3296
NJRAMDXP.SYS	Y	–	Y	1936	720
SATISFAX.SYS	Y	–	Y	28064	4032
SSTORDRV.SYS	N	–	N	55872	22736
APPEND	Y	–	Y	12992	9280
GRAB.EXE	Y	–	Y	24112	23872
MOUSE.COM	Y	–	Y	40544	13952

Arrow keys to select or Space to toggle
CAUTION: Changing this data might have adverse affects

Enter to Accept Changes   Esc to Undo Changes

Fig. 8-7   QEMM OPTIMIZE Analysis display. Quarterdeck Office Systems.

A message at the bottom of the "Modify data" screen warns you that changes may have adverse effects on your configuration. In general, if you switch a program from loading high to loading low, the only adverse effect will be a decrease in the final total of available conventional memory. (The last column on the screen shows the amount of memory that each program will consume after initial loading.) Switching a driver or program to load high might result in more serious consequences. In most cases, OPTIMIZE has already determined the optimum placement for a program. Switching a driver on this screen from loading "low" to "high" might make the machine lock up, or it could prevent another program from loading into upper memory.

Figure 8-8 shows another OPTIMIZE option—the "What-If" screen. Sometimes the physical loading sequence of programs can affect the amount of high-RAM needed to load them all. The "What-If" screen provides a mini-memory spreadsheet that allows you to see what would happen if you rearrange the load order of drivers and TSR's. OPTIMIZE recalculates the amount of memory that your programs use to reflect changes you propose in the spreadsheet. If you come up with a sequence that produces more conventional memory, you can direct OPTIMIZE to rewrite CONFIG.SYS and AUTOEXEC.BAT in its third pass.

Stealth   OPTIMIZE will tell you if it is successful in loading all of your startup drivers and TSR's above 640K after the third pass. In this case, the process is complete; you may exit to DOS or restart the machine with your new configuration. If OPTIMIZE has not successfully placed all of your drivers and programs

```
                "WHAT-IF" THE ORDER IS CHANGED

      Device Drivers                      TSRs
   Program        Initial  Final    Program        Initial  Final
   QEMM386.SYS     13232   13232    APPEND           12992    9280
   HYPERSTB.EXE     6656     288    GRAB.EXE         24112   23872
   EGA.SYS          4896    3296    MOUSE.COM        40544   13952
   NJRAMDXP.SYS     1936     720
   SATISFAX.SYS    28064    4032
   SSTORDRV.SYS    55872   22736


                              Original    Best    Current
        Conventional RAM Used:    1 K      1 K       1 K
        Largest Free High RAM:  103 K    103 K     103 K
          Arrow keys to Select, Enter to Pick Up

        F1 to Recalculate    Esc to Return
```

Fig. 8-8   QEMM OPTIMIZE What If display. Quarterdeck Office Systems.

in upper memory, it will prompt you for permission to test the system for Stealth compatibility. The Stealth testing and reconfiguration is an additional process that is not necessary in all configurations.

QEMM's Stealth feature creates additional high RAM in upper memory by juggling video and BIOS ROM in and out of their customary address space. It maps the ROM address space to high RAM as though it were free. When a program needs to make a low-level request to a ROM address, QEMM reroutes the request to the EMS pageframe and temporarily swaps the appropriate ROM into the pageframe. Once completed, the ROM code carries the instruction out. If you choose to invoke Stealth testing, OPTIMIZE reboots your computer again to see whether each Stealth mode works on your machine. Most 80386 and above systems can accept the "stealthing" of upper memory ROMs. Stealth has two compatibility modes and will try the most generous mode first. OPTIMIZE will tell you if your system is compatible with Stealth-M (Mapping). If the system is incompatible, OPTIMIZE will test compatibility with Stealth-F (Frame). Stealth-F creates less high RAM than Stealth-M because it remaps only those ROM addresses that already lie within the EMS pageframe. If QEMM can use its stealth feature on all or part of your system's ROM, OPTIMIZE offers to run through the analysis and configuration procedure again. The additional high RAM will often allow QEMM to load the remainder of your drivers and TSRs in upper memory.

Using Manifest and LOADHI   With most common user setups the optimize algorithm achieves a maximum of conventional memory without user intervention. In some cases, though, the user might want to fine tune the loadhigh process manually. The user might find additional upper memory not automatically recognized by QEMM. In addition, some programs and drivers might force themselves into upper memory, causing OPTIMIZE to work around them in its calculations. What OPTIMIZE really does to your CONFIG.SYS and AUTOEXEC.BAT is preface eligible programs and drivers with appropriate LOADHI statements. LOADHI.SYS (for device drivers in CONFIG.SYS) and LOADHI.COM (for programs in AUTOEXEC.BAT) are the two utilities that actually load drivers/programs into upper memory. LOADHI.SYS and LOADHI.COM reside in the QEMM directory. A series of command line options allow the LOADHI utilities to pinpoint an upper memory location, and deal with problems that may arise with specific drivers/TSRs.

Effect of Stealth on Upper Memory Blocks Remember that the upper memory blocks available between 640K and 1M might be broken up by the presence of ROM code for peripherals and adaptors. For instance, on a VGA system, there might be one block in the unused monochrome video area (B000h to B7FFh) and another in between the VGA ROM and the EMS pageframe (C800h to DFFFh). Each contiguous block is assigned a region number by QEMM. QEMM assigns a number to each block that it can use as high RAM (hold programs/drivers loaded high). If QEMM is running with the Stealth-M parameter enabled, the high RAM area may contain one large contiguous block (the ROM areas are swapped into the EMS page frame). Without Stealth, or when Stealth-F is used, there might be several smaller available upper memory regions interspersed with unmappable ROM regions. We can use Quarterdeck's Manifest utility to discover what's actually going on in our system.

Using Manifest Manifest presents a dynamic display of memory usage. It can show which upper memory addresses are free to accept additional programs or TSR drivers after the computer boots. Manifest lets you discover the size of each available high RAM region, and how much memory remains free.

The Manifest interface is a grid of nine information categories running down the left-hand side of the screen. Moving the cursor left-to-right displays topic information screens for each category. You may scroll to any information screen by choosing a category with the up/down cursor keys and using the left/right cursor keys to select a topic.

Manifest's First Meg feature might help you track down the usage of upper memory by a network card. Notice in Fig. 8-9 that the First Meg overview screen provides a segment by segment list of memory usage. The DOS overview screen lets you see the total memory allocated to the operating system. The Expanded Memory screens provide a detailed map of EMS usage and some useful performance benchmarks. For instance, if you plan to do high speed telecommunications in expanded memory, check the Timer Interrupt Latency in the Expanded

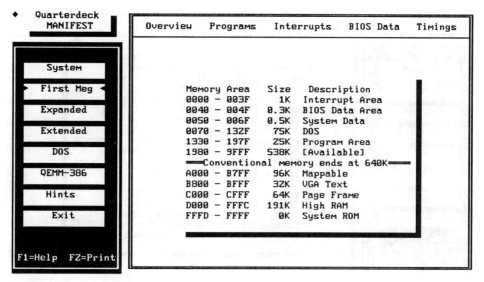

Fig. 8-9   Manifest's First Meg display with Stealth.

Memory Benchmarks screen. Timer Interrupt Latency should register at 400 or less to perform 9600 baud file transfers in the background.

The QEMM-386 *Type* screen in Manifest presents a graphic depiction of how DOS, programs, and peripherals use each 4K segment in the first megabyte. It shows memory allocated for programs, reserved for ROM devices, configured as an EMS Page Frame, mapped for loading drivers above the contiguous DOS region, or excluded entirely from QEMM's control. The QEMM-386 *Analysis* screen can alert you to conflicts in your current configuration.

Note   If you are not using the Stealth feature, Manifest's QEMM-Analysis screen can help you to include or exclude memory under QEMM's control. If any 4K segment in the first megabyte is X'd, then you should exclude that segment from QEMM's control. An "I" in a 4K segment indicates that QEMM may use it as mappable RAM. Be on the lookout for X's and I's in the region from F000h to FFFFh.

The First Meg category's *Overview* and *Program* screens are useful for determining the status and usage of upper memory. Figure 8-9 shows a First Meg *Overview* for a 80486 system running QEMM's Stealth feature. Note that in this configuration, there is only one high RAM region. Figure 8-10 shows a First Meg overview for a 80486 system running QEMM without Stealth. Manifest tells us that there are three individual high RAM regions. QEMM numbers these regions 1 through 3. We can see how the various loadhigh regions are used by selecting Manifest's First Meg *Program* window. This display presents a complete list of all

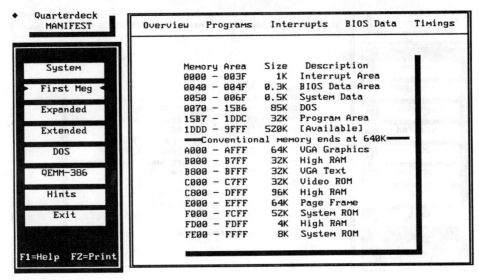

Fig. 8-10   Manifest's First Meg display without Stealth.

resident programs and drivers in both conventional and upper memory (Fig. 8-11 and Fig. 8-12). Next to each program listing on the left is its address range and size. Available memory in a particular high RAM region is highlighted in brackets.

Working with LOADHI   Let's assume that we have already run OPTIMIZE, and want to add Microsoft's DOSKEY utility to our default configuration. Using one approach, we could place DOSKEY at the bottom of AUTOEXEC

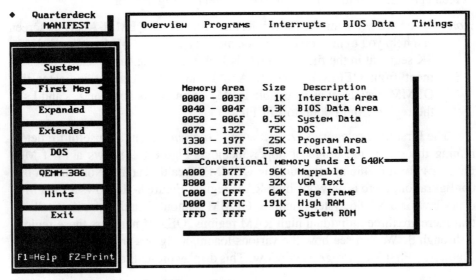

Fig. 8-11   Manifest's Conventional Memory display.

212   *Third-party memory management*

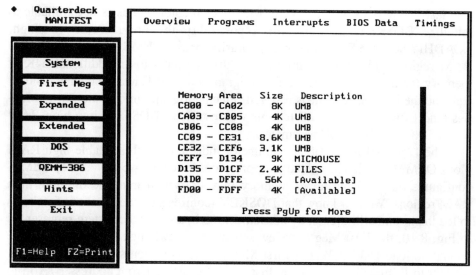

Fig. 8-12 Manifest's Upper Memory display.

.BAT and rerun the entire OPTIMIZE process. Alternatively, we could use Manifest and LOADHI to help us add a line for DOSKEY manually. Manifest can show us what upper memory regions are configured as high RAM and how much of each is still available. LOADHI will tell us how much memory DOSKEY requires, and place the program into a specific available region.

LOADHI has a large number of command line options. You don't need to learn all of them to fine-tune the memory optimization process. (Quarterdeck does provide thorough documentation for each parameter in the QEMM manual.) For this example, we will need two important LOADHI features: /GETSIZE and /REGION.

/GETSIZE (GS) determines the actual amount of memory a program needs to load and to remain resident. You can invoke /GETSIZE in either the CONFIG .SYS (DEVICE = [d : \ ]PATH \ LOADHI . SYS /GS [d : \ ][PATH] \ [driver name]) or in AUTOEXEC.BAT (LOADHI /GS [d : \ ][PATH] [\ program name). The /GS switch forces the designated driver or program to load low (in conventional memory). LOADHI reports both the amount of memory the program needs to load and the resident program stub. For example:

```
C : \ QEMM \ LOADHI /GS C : \ DOS \ DOSKEY
DOSKEY INSTALLED.
LOADHI : 6560 RUN-TIME BYTES (7K)
LOADHI : 4368 RESIDENT BYTES (5K)
LOADHI : THIS PROGRAM MAY USE SQUEEZEF
```

LOADHI reports that the DOSKEY utility requires 6560 bytes of memory to start up (line 3), and will leave a resident stub in memory of 4368 bytes (line 4).

The last line tells us that if a 6560-byte upper memory block is not available to initialize DOSKEY, there is still a possibility the program can loadhigh. LOADHI's Squeeze Frame option temporarily loans the EMS Pageframe to a high RAM region. This allows a program or driver access to an additional 64K of memory for initialization. Once the program loads, it leaves a smaller resident stub and the EMS pageframe is restored. Piecing together information from Manifest and LOADHI /GETSIZE tells us where to load DOSKEY into high RAM with LOADHI's /REGION parameter.

The LOADHI /REGION:n parameter indicates which available high RAM block QEMM should use to load your program/driver. As we saw above, QEMM configures the available upper memory in your system into one or more high RAM regions. We now know that DOSKEY requires an initial total of 6560 bytes to loadhigh, and will eventually consume 4368 bytes. For the system represented in Fig. 8-10, the First Meg overview screen shows two high RAM regions large enough to load DOSKEY. The First Meg programs screen shows that Region 1 (B000h to B7FFh) has only 1.3K that is still available (from address B7ABh to B7FEh). Thus, we won't be able to load DOSKEY into Region 1 without reshuffling the work that OPTIMIZE completed. However, Region 2 (C800h to DFFFh) has 56K available (from D1D0h to DFFEh). Therefore, we will be able to load DOSKEY into Region 2. To accomplish this, we insert a line into AUTOEXEC.BAT manually using a text editor.

LOADHI /r:2 C:\DOS\DOSKEY

You may insert this line anywhere in AUTOEXEC.BAT. However, you should insert it as the last LOADHI statement in the file in most cases. (By placing the DOSKEY as the last driver to loadhigh, we ensure that DOSKEY will not displace a previous driver from Region 2.)

Note   You can always try a "quick and dirty" way to load a new program into upper memory by omitting the /REGION parameter from any LOADHI statement. Without a /REGION:n instruction, QEMM will try to shoehorn the program into the first available high RAM area. If Manifest displays a large amount of available high RAM, you might want to take the risk of simply adding generic LOADHI statements to CONFIG.SYS or AUTOEXEC.BAT. You might be able to place new programs into high RAM without a detailed analysis. Unfortunately, by using this approach you run the risk that the new program(s) will dislodge other programs from upper memory or fail to loadhigh themselves. You can always confirm the changes made in memory usage by running Manifest both before and after attempting to install a new program.

Undocumented QEMM Features and Command Switches   In addition to the two documented Stealth modes, QEMM contains a third, undocumented,

Stealth feature that swaps upper memory ROMs into extended memory using Intel's protected mode. During the beta testing of v6.0, the ST:P (protected mode) feature didn't work as well as expected. As a result, Quarterdeck dropped it from the documented feature list. However, you can still use the feature by adding the parameter ST : P to the QEMM command line. Future versions of QEMM may contain documentation for the advantages and uses of this parameter.

Fine Tuning QEMM QEMM's performance is controlled by a series of parameters entered on the QEMM386 command line in CONFIG.SYS. You can modify any QEMM option by editing CONFIG.SYS with a text editor. A complete discussion of all QEMM command parameters is beyond the scope of this book. Such a discussion is one of the strong points of Quarterdeck's own documentation for QEMM. The following material might serve as a rough and ready guide to fine-tuning QEMM's most important features.

How do I get my system to boot with QEMM loaded?

The following parameters are standard fixes to try adding to the QEMM command line to resolve machine-specific incompatibilities:

    DEVICE = QEMM386 . SYS IA NRH NS NOSH NX

IA (IgnoreA20) tells QEMM not to trap the system's 8042 keyboard controller.

NRH (NoRomHoles) disables QEMM's automatic detection of unused address areas in upper memory.

NS (NoSort) tells QEMM not to sort the memory on your system by speed. (This is the default in version 6.00 and above).

NOSH (NoShadowRAM) tells QEMM not to use the Shadow RAM available on PCs with Chips & Technologies LEAP, SCAT or NEAT chipsets.

NX (NoExtendedBIOSData) tells QEMM not to move extended BIOS data into upper memory on machines that store BIOS information stored in the last kilobyte of conventional memory.

I've used the automatic optimize feature to get the maximum amount of memory. Are there ways to get more memory?

There are three standard methods to get additional memory with QEMM. First, the Stealth feature generally takes advantage of any memory available in the C000h to FFFFh address range. You can create an additional 32K of high memory on some VGA systems by using the monochrome video area. QEMM might not automatically use this region. Add the following line to the QEMM386 command line to use the monochrome video area as high RAM:

    DEVICE = QEMM386 . SYS RAM RAM = B000-B7FF

Second, you can gain an additional 64−96K for text applications on VGA systems. Quarterdeck's VIDRAM utility can borrow the A000h to B7FFh address range normally reserved for monochrome video and EGA/VGA graphics. It adds that additional RAM to conventional memory. You cannot run EGA and VGA graphics while VIDRAM is active, but text applications can use the additional memory. VIDRAM may borrow RAM to fill the A000h block from either expanded memory, or the RAM on a VGA graphics card. The syntax to accomplish this is as follows:

VIDRAM [ON][EMS][EGA][OVERRIDE][OFF]

ON specifies that VIDRAM should disable EGA and VGA graphics. This provides an additional 64K for text applications.

EGA specifies that VIDRAM should use video RAM instead of EMS memory to extend DOS memory.

EMS specifies that VIDRAM should use EMS memory to extend DOS memory.

The OVERRIDE parameter is necessary on some systems to force VIDRAM on. For instance, the OVERRIDE parameter is necessary to turn VIDRAM on with dual-monitor configurations that use both VGA and monochrome graphics.

OFF re-enables EGA and VGA graphics and resets the top of conventional memory on a VGA system to 640K.

Finally, QEMM automatically annexes 64−96K of reserved video memory to DOS on systems that use MDA, Hercules, or CGA graphic adaptors. If you have such a system and still show only 640K of conventional memory, you may add an INCLUDE parameter to the QEMM line to force mapping of the video area.

On Hercules monochrome and MDA systems:

DEVICE = QEMM386.SYS I = A000-AFFF

On CGA systems:

DEVICE = QEMM386.SYS I = A000-B7FF

If you prefer, the reserved video area can be used as high RAM.

DEVICE = QEMM386.SYS NV RAM

The No Video (NV) parameter instructs QEMM not to annex video RAM to conventional memory. If the reserved video area is unused on your system, the NV parameter tells QEMM to map it as high RAM, instead.

How do I get Windows to start in Enhanced Mode when I use QEMM on my 80386?

First, make sure you have a version of QEMM that supports your version of Windows. You must patch (update the executable code) QEMM 5.10 and 5.11 in order to run Windows 3.00a. Windows 3.1 requires QEMM version 6.00 or above.

If you are using QEMM 6.xx, make sure that you have run the included QWINFIX utility to modify Windows' SYSTEM.INI configuration file. If Windows still doesn't run in Enhanced Mode, there might be a conflict between Windows and QEMM over the B000h to B7FFh monochrome video region. You can exclude this region from QEMM's control by adding an EXCLUDE statement to the QEMM386 command line.

```
DEVICE = QEMM386.SYS X = B000-B7FF
```

Windows loads in enhanced mode when I use QEMM, but soon crashes. What causes this to happen?

Some VGA video adaptor ROMs might cause conflicts between Windows and QEMM. You can remedy this by excluding the video ROM from QEMM's control using an EXCLUDE statement as follows:

```
DEVICE = QEMM386.SYS X = C000-C7FF
```

Refer to the QEMM READ.ME file for additional information on video cards from specific vendors. (Some cards may not require that you exclude the entire 32K region.)

Another common problem occurs Windows when you load an expanded memory disk cache. Windows users should configure disk caching software to use extended memory instead of EMS 4.0 whenever possible.

If difficulty with Windows persists, try removing all LOADHI statements from CONFIG.SYS and AUTOEXEC.BAT. In addition, pare your QEMM command line as follows:

```
DEVICE = [D:][\PATH]QEMM386.SYS RAM X = B000-B7FF
X = C000-C7FF NOSH IA
```

If this works, restore the LOADHI statements to the startup files on a line-by-line basis to search for possible conflicts. If no conflicts are found, you may restore any Stealth parameter to the QEMM command line and test again. See the Appendix for a step by step troubleshooting procedure for QEMM's Stealth parameter. Also see Chapter 9 on Windows for a discussion on editing Windows' SYSTEM.INI parameters.

My system hangs with QEMM, version 6 and my disk cache loaded. What method should I use to correct this?

Try removing any Stealth parameter from the QEMM command line and see if the problem goes away. The Stealth feature provided with version 6.00 is unstable with some disk cache software that uses advanced write caching. The problem is corrected in QEMM 6.01.

How do I get my network to work when I use QEMM?

QEMM attempts to keep all PC interrupts enabled during DMA (Direct Memory Access) disk transfers. This can conflict with the performance of some networking software (10NET, TOPS, and FARALLON PHONENET are known examples). You can instruct QEMM to disable interrupts during DMA transfers by adding the LOCKDMA parameter to the QEMM command line as follows:

    DEVICE = QEMM386 . SYS LD

For TOPS networking software, you might also have to configure the network card to use IRQ 3 instead of IRQ 2. (See Chapter 11 for more details.)

How do I load a device driver before QEMM in CONFIG.SYS without disabling Stealth?

The HOOKROM.SYS device driver allows you to load other drivers before QEMM386.SYS in CONFIG.SYS, yet maintain compatibility with Stealth. Enter HOOKROM.SYS as the first line in CONFIG.SYS when using either the Intel Inboard accelerator (PC or AT) or SOTA Express 386 plug-in module. Use the following configuration with the SOTA EXPRESS card:

    DEVICE = HOOKROM . SYS
    DEVICE = SOTAX386 . SYS
    DEVICE = QEMM386 . SYS RAM ST : M

How to I get QEMM to work with Ventura Publisher 2.0 and 3.0?

The DOS-based version of Ventura Publisher requires that the EMS pageframe be set no higher than E000h. If Manifest reports the pageframe at E800h or EC00h, reset the pageframe address on the QEMM command line as follows:

    DEVICE = QEMM386 . SYS FR = E000 (or FR = D000)

Ventura Publisher 2.0 will not operate properly if the statement STACKS = 0 , 0 is present in CONFIG.SYS while any QEMM Stealth parameters are operative. Removing the STACKS = 0 , 0 statement solves the problem.

How do I load more programs above 640K when I don't need expanded memory?

Add the parameter FR = NONE to the QEMM command line. This provides an additional 64K of high RAM by disabling the EMS pageframe. Cancelling the EMS pageframe will prohibit the use of EMS 4.0 memory by most applications, although Quarterdeck's DESQview can remain operative for multitasking.

How do I get the Ctrl-Alt-Del warm reboot to work when I use QEMM?

The most common reason for this is that you have configured QEMM to use the portion of the F000h block that contains the keyboard BIOS. Try excluding the region from FB00h to FBFFh from QEMM's control. In addition, add the IA (IgnoreA20) parameter to the QEMM command line.

I have "fast" memory installed on my motherboard and "slower" memory installed on an external card mounted on the bus. How can I boost the overall performance of my applications?

If your system uses an add-on memory card in addition to the RAM installed on the motherboard, the speed of read/write operations will vary as different sections of memory are accessed. The RAM on the motherboard operates at the full speed of the CPU. In contrast, the memory card is limited to the 8MHz or 12MHz speed of the data bus. QEMM can arrange the RAM in your system so that the computer accesses the fastest memory first and uses the slowest memory last. If you have a system with 4M on the motherboard and 2M on an old Intel or AST card, you may configure the "slow" memory as a disk cache and save the "fast" memory for applications. The following paragraphs tell you how using the EMS.COM utility included with QEMM. This utility temporarily assigns memory to an EMS handle, and later releases it.

1. Place the SORT = Y parameter on the QEMM386 command line to enable sorting of memory by speed.
2. Use a disk cache that loads from AUTOEXEC.BAT rather than CONFIG.SYS. (Examples of such caches are the Windows 3.1 version of Smartdrive, Hyperdisk, and Multisoft's Super PCKwik.)
3. Before loading the disk cache in AUTOEXEC.BAT, use EMS.COM to temporarily reserve all of the available "fast" memory.
4. Load the disk cache. It will configure itself to use the remaining "slow" memory.
5. Once you've loaded the disk cache, use EMS.COM to release the fast memory you reserved. This memory will now be available for Windows and DOS applications to use.

The following example shows how to implement this procedure in your AUTOEXEC.BAT. The example uses the Windows 3.1 version of Smartdrive as a cache. Let's assume that you have 5M of extended memory and only 3M of it is mounted on the motherboard.

```
C:\QEMM\EMS CFAST BLOCK1 3096
C:\WINDOWS\SMARTDRV
C:\QEMM\EMS free block1
```

EMS.COM creates a temporary EMS handle called "Block1" out of the 3096K of "fast" RAM on the motherboard. SMARTDRIVE loads, using the remaining "slow" memory for its cache. EMS.COM then frees "Block1," restoring the 3096K of fast memory to the available pool.

Differences between 5.xx and 6.xx Versions of QEMM Quarterdeck added a number of significant upgrades between version 5.xx and 6.xx of QEMM. Table 8-5 provides a brief summary of these changes.

Table 8-5   QEMM inter-version differences.

Version	Change
5.00	This version added the OPTIMIZE utility and various machine-specific control parameters.
5.10	First version to support MS Windows 3.0 in Standard and Enhanced modes.
5.11	This version provides more stable support for MS Windows 3.0. You must patch it in order to run Windows maintenance release 3.00a or above.
5.12	Adds built-in support for Windows maintenance release 3.00a.
5.13	Adds a series of patches for problems with 0 byte EMS handles and programs that dynamically resize EMS or XMS handles.
6.00	This major upgrade adds the Stealth feature. It also provides a more sophisticated OPTIMIZE user-interface. Improves support for MS-DOS 5, allowing buffers to load into upper memory.
6.01	Fixes the conflicts between Stealth and the write features of advanced disk caching software. It also fixes bugs in OPTIMIZE procedure related to nested batch files.
6.02	This version fixes conflicts between VIDRAM and DOS 5 when no UMBs are available. It adds command switches to support IBM SCSI interface, extends the range of the EMBMEM parameter and fixes bugs found in the LOADHI Unlink parameter. A revised version of Manifest provides a more accurate report of EMS usage.

Getting Further Help with QEMM Quarterdeck Office Systems has compiled a database of technical notes concerning QEMM and DESQview called the Quarterdeck White Papers. This file is available on many public bulletin board systems. You can also download it from Quarterdeck's own support BBS. Additionally, Quarterdeck maintains a 24-hour FAX line that allows you to request FAX copies of individual technical support bulletins.

Qualitas' 386MAX

Qualitas' 386MAX certainly qualifies as a memory manager with a pleasant, user-friendly interface. Although MAX can't create as much high memory for loading programs, it does provide one or two features that QEMM lacks. 386MAX includes an OEM version of Multisoft's PC-Kwik disk cache, and an XMS/EMS RAMdisk. 386MAX also supports device instancing under Windows, whereas QEMM does not. Device instancing means that 386MAX maintains separate copies of shared TSRs and device drivers loaded before Windows. Each Windows virtual machine can use an instanced device with different settings. For instance, with ANSI.SYS loaded, you may assign different screen colors and keyboard mappings in each multitasking window. Without device instancing, the settings for ANSI.SYS in one window bleed through to all other DOS windows. The 386MAX package also includes Move'Em, an 80286 memory management utility similar to Quarterdeck's QRAM. If you have both 80286 and 80386 systems at your worksite, 386MAX provides load high support for both platforms in one package.

Note   Windows 3.1 can allow device instancing with other memory managers by invoking the LocalTSRs = parameter in SYSTEM.INI. (See page 281 for details.)

The 386MAX user interface provides a step-by-step depiction display of every move the memory manager makes during installation. If you see something you don't understand, you can stop the process and select a help menu for an explanation. The STRIPMGR subprogram recognizes when you've configured your system with another memory manager. If STRIPMGR finds another memory manager installed, it asks whether you want the other manager removed. If you answer yes, STRIPMGR automatically removes AUTOEXEC.BAT and CONFIG.SYS commands associated with other memory managers. The next installation phase allows you to choose between automatic load high configuration or an interactive process. The interactive installation prompts the user for input before starting each new task. If you choose interactive installation, 386MAX displays a list of all of the load high candidates in your CONFIG.SYS and AUTOEXEC .BAT. You can place the cursor on any program in the list and use the space bar to toggle between loading it high or loading it low.

Although 386MAX lacks QEMM's "Stealth Technology," it makes good use of the memory that it can control. The MAXIMIZE load high utility affords one level of sophistication not implemented in QEMM's OPTIMIZE. MAXIMIZE can rearrange the physical order of the files in CONFIG.SYS and AUTOEXEC

.BAT. This allows you to economically package TSRs into high RAM. Maximize makes more programs fit into the same available upper memory space by loading "exploding" device drivers first. (Of course, as we mentioned in the last section, QEMM's Stealth feature frees up more high RAM to begin with, but not all systems can take advantage of QEMM's Stealth.)

386MAX has a unique feature for users of Microsoft Windows 3.0/3.1. "Virtual loadhigh technology" allows you to place separate drivers and TSR's above 640K while running a DOS virtual machine inside of Windows. If you have a DOS application that requires a special TSR to function, you can run that program inside of Windows and load the program into upper memory. After opening the first window, you can open another DOS window and load a different TSR into upper memory. 386MAX will allow you to switch back and forth between the two DOS applications under Windows without getting confused. The TSR loaded in the first window will not affect the second window and vice versa.

386MAX's VGASWAP option can gain 32K of additional high RAM on ISA and EISA VGA systems. VGASWAP moves the video BIOS from its customary location at C000h to the unused monochrome video area at B000. (This creates more contiguous upper memory for loading programs high.) Unfortunately, this option could produce unexpected results with some super VGA display adapters or with software that uses ROM fonts to produce a graphics-like effect.

For IBM Microchannel systems, Qualitas offers a "twin memory manager" called BLUEMAX. BLUEMAX performs remapping and rearranging of PS/2 ROMs to maximize upper memory on IBM PS/2 systems. When installing BLUEMAX on a PS/2 system, the user is prompted to insert the IBM Reference diskette. BLUEMAX compresses the extended IBM BIOS in the E000h block and continues with the installation. BLUEMAX substitutes the ROM compression feature for the 386MAX's optional VGASWAP option. Aside from this, BLUEMAX uses the same command syntax as 386MAX. Unless otherwise noted, the information presented in the following paragraphs about 386MAX applies to BLUEMAX as well.

Once you finish installing 386MAX, Qualitas' MAX control interface offers access to a series of options. You can display system information in a quick-view window, or invoke ASQ, the extensive inventory utility. A built-in text editor makes it easy to modify configuration parameters.

Fine Tuning 386MAX Many of the parameters used by 386MAX are similar to the QEMM features examined in the last section. 386MAX differs from QEMM in that the command line parameters are not entered directly into CONFIG.SYS. 386MAX reads them from an ASCII configuration file that resides in the 386MAX directory on your hard disk instead. The installation and MAXIMIZE programs create the 386MAX.PRO file automatically when you run them. The 386MAX.PRO file contains information about which areas of memory to include or exclude, EMS ROM shadowing, etc.

To change the 386MAX parameters established on configuration, you can edit 386MAX.PRO with any ASCII text-editor. To help with fine-tuning memory management, Qualitas includes a feature called the Option Editor within the MAX text editor. While editing the 386MAX.PRO file, you can open a window on the left of the screen that displays each possible 386MAX command line option. The window on the right details the purpose of the selected feature with its command syntax. For instance, Fig. 8-13 shows that if you place the cursor on the VGASWAP parameter, the window on the right tells you that on a system using a VGA video display, "VGASWAP reduces fragmentation in high DOS memory. It increases the size of the largest contiguous region of high DOS memory." If you decide that VGASWAP is a desirable feature, you can install it by hitting the OK/Enter button at the bottom of the screen.

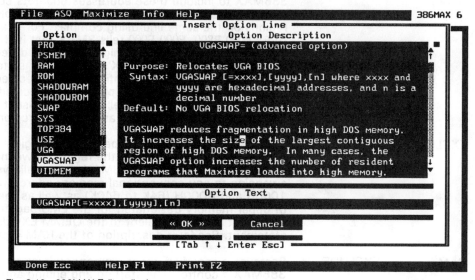

Fig. 8-13   386MAX Editor display.

Upper memory address ranges are specified in a slightly different format for 386MAX than for QEMM. 386MAX includes the boundary of the next address segment in the specified range. For instance, with QEMM the upper memory area reserved for monochrome video is indicated by the range B000h—B7FFh. For 386MAX, the same range is written B000h—B800h.

A complete explanation of the 386MAX/BLUEMAX command parameters is beyond the scope of this book. They are all documented in the reference manual provided by Qualitas. Table 8-6 provides a summary of the most important functions.

386MAX Loadhigh Utilities   386MAX loads drivers and programs into upper memory just as QEMM does. The 386LOAD.SYS and 386LOAD.COM utilities are equivalent to Quarterdeck's LOADHI.SYS and LOADHI.COM.

Table 8-6 386MAX function summary.

Function	QEMM Equivalent	Description
INCLUDE=	RAM	Specifies an upper memory address range to use as high RAM for loading drivers and TSRs. For example, the statement INCLUDE=F700-FB00 adds the specified address range to the upper memory blocks when you enter it into the 386MAX.PRO file. It is then available for loading drivers and TSR's.
USE= INCLUDE=	RAM= INCLUDE=	Use these options to override the default upper memory address range selected for use by 386MAX during installation. Some systems have free regions in upper memory that appear to be in use. The USE option tells 386MAX to include these addresses under its control and map them as high RAM. You can include multiple address regions on the same line using commas. For example, USE=B000-B800, E000-F000 tells 3MAX that it should map the two specified ranges to high RAM. The difference between USE= and 386MAX's INCLUDE= statements is that USE= automatically configures the specified region for loading high. INCLUDE= places the specified region under 386MAX control and allows you to use it as an EMS-mappable area, as well as a loadhigh region.
EXCLUDE=		Decreases the size of the upper memory region used for EMS swapping by excluding the region between the specified addresses. The 386MAX default allows for EMS swapping to any conventional memory address between 1000H and A000H (64K to 640K) as well as the portion of upper memory designated for the EMS pageframe. This statement is not equivalent to the QEMM EXCLUDE statement. See later description of the RAM= parameter.
RAM=	EXCLUDE=	Removes a specified upper memory address region from 386MAX's control. The starting and ending addresses must lie on 4K boundaries. For example, if you are having video problems with a VGA system, the statement EXCLUDE=C000-C800 places the VGA video ROM outside of 386MAX control.
FRAME=	FRAME=	Specifies the starting address for the 64K upper memory area to use as the EMS pageframe.
NOFRAME	FRAME=NONE	Disables the use of EMS 4.0. This provides an additional 64K of upper memory to use for loading device drivers and TSRs high.
EMS=	EMS=	Designates the amount of extended memory (in kilobytes) to make available to applications as EMS 4.0 Expanded Memory.
EXT=	EXT=	Designates the amount extended memory (in kilobytes) to be make available as "old extended memory" for

		applications that don't support Microsoft's newer XMS standard.
PRGREG =	REGION =	By default, 386MAX may define several areas for loading drivers and utilities in upper memory. PRGREG=1 refers to the first region, PRGREG=2, to the second, and so on. The statement PRGREG=1 in the 386MAX.PRO file tells 386^MAX to load its internal program code into the first available region of upper memory.
ROM =	ROM =	Specifies an upper memory address range that 386MAX shadows in EMS memory. If you disabled your system's internal ROM shadowing feature, you probably want to specify two address ranges for 386^MAX to shadow: the VGA video area and the ROM BIOS. When you designate a specific address for ROM shadowing, this turns off default shadowing of the system BIOS, so you will want to add another ROM= statement to restore it. To cover both video and system ROM bios, insert the following statements: ROM=C000-C800, F000-10000 ROM=C000-C800, F000-10000
VGASWAP		Use this parameter with VGA graphics cards to get a larger contiguous block of upper memory. This statement swaps the VGA BIOS address space from C000h into the unused monochrome area at B000h. This allows 386MAX to use the address space from C000h-C800h as part of the EMS pageframe or as a high RAM upper memory block.

Placed in front of drivers and TSRs in CONFIG.SYS and AUTOEXEC.BAT, they load programs into specified upper memory blocks. You can apply the same techniques outlined for use with Quarterdeck's OPTIMIZE to Qualitas' MAXIMIZE.

- You might want MAXIMIZE to ignore a program in your startup files during the memory optimization process. Do this by adding the program to the special MAXIMIZE exception list—386LOAD.CFG—found in the 386MAX directory.

- Use the GETSIZE parameter with the 386LOAD utilities to determine the initial memory required for loading a TSR and the stub left resident after loading. For instance, to determine the amount of upper memory space required for Microsoft's MOUSE.COM, type

386LOAD GETSIZE PROG = [d:][path]\MOUSE.COM

MOUSE.COM will load into conventional memory. You can display both the initial and resident memory requirements for the driver by running the MAX interface and inspecting the Resident Program Summary under the INFO menu. Figure 8-14 shows the RAM requirements for Microsoft's version 8.00 mouse driver.

Load Sizes
RESIDENT PROGRAM MEMORY SUMMARY

Device or Program Name	Size Parameters		Allow Flex Frame?	Suggested Action
	Initial	Resident		
386MAX.SYS	2,768	2,768	No	No SIZE parameter needed
ANSI.SYS	9,040	4,192	Yes	Remove GETSIZE; no SIZE needed
NJRAMDXP.SYS	1,920	704	Yes	No SIZE parameter needed
UMB	8,304	8,304	No	No SIZE parameter needed
UMB	4,208	4,208	No	No SIZE parameter needed
UMB	4,208	4,208	No	No SIZE parameter needed
UMB	8,912	8,912	No	No SIZE parameter needed
UMB	3,216	3,216	No	No SIZE parameter needed
UMB	592	592	No	No SIZE parameter needed
MOUSE.COM	44,272	13,776	Yes	Remove GETSIZE; use SIZE=13,776

All programs/environments fit   Prog/env in use   51,08

Menu Esc   Help F1   Print F2

Fig. 8-14   Microsoft Mouse Driver v8.00 memory requirements.

You can invoke 386MAX from the DOS command line for a quick display of system memory usage. Invoking ASQ gives you more extensive information. Launch ASQ from the DOS command line or enter it through the integrated MAX control interface.

Working with ASQ   ASQ is Qualitas' system inventory utility. You can use it to display information about system configuration and memory usage. ASQ also includes an interactive tutorial section. Tutorial lessons are accessed through a topic index (Fig. 8-15) or called up as help screens while the user is in the inventory and benchmark area of the program. For instance, if you are looking at the usage map for extended memory, pressing F3 switches you to the tutorial screen devoted to extended memory (see Fig. 8-16).

Like Quarterdeck's Manifest, ASQ can display the current state of the first megabyte of memory, and system usage of hardware and software interrupts. ASQ's display of upper memory usage can help you determine whether additional drivers or TSRs can load above 640K. The EMS memory handle list shows how resident programs use memory. For instance, if the list says that EMS handle 2 allocated 2048K, it's very likely that this handle corresponds to a 2048K disk cache loaded in CONFIG.SYS. You can save any ASQ information screen to disk or print it by selecting "Snapshot" from the File Menu. The version of ASQ included with this book on our utilities disk is an earlier generation of the program that Qualitas has consented to distribute as shareware.

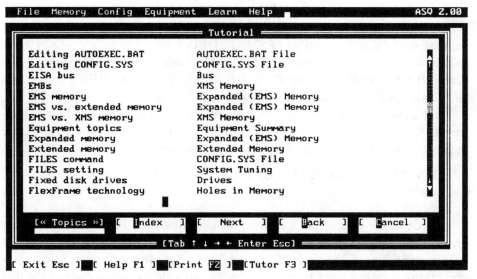

Fig. 8-15   Qualitas' ASQ Tutorial Index.

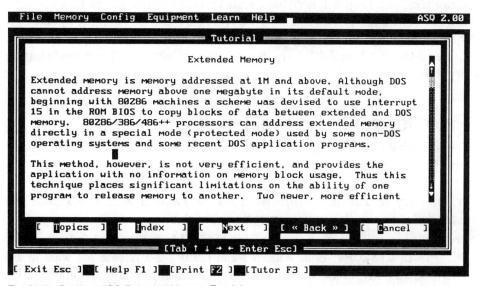

Fig. 8-16   Qualitas' ASQ Extended Memory Tutorial.

QCACHE and 386DISK   The QCACHE utility supplied with 386MAX/BLUEMAX 6 is an OEM version of Multisoft's PC-Kwik disk cache. It contains a subset of the standard Multisoft features. (For example, it doesn't provide the Powerwrite advanced write-cache option.) QCACHE can use either extended or expanded memory. By default, QCACHE loads its housekeeping code into upper memory, although you can disable this feature with command-line options. You can automatically install QCACHE during the 386MAX setup or load it later from the command line. In performance and flexibility, QCACHE rates somewhat more powerful than the versions of SMARTDRIVE included with MS-DOS 5 and Windows 3.0, but less versatile than the Multisoft's complete version of PC-Kwik, HYPERDISK, PC Tools PCACHE, NORTON's NCACHE, or the version of SMARTDRIVE included with Windows 3.1.

386DISK is an extended/expanded memory RAMdisk that Qualitas recommends you substitute for the DOS VDISK or RAMDRIVE software if you are running 386MAX or BLUEMAX. The command for using 386DISK is

```
DEVICE = 386[MAX]DISK.SYS <SIZE> <SECTOR> <DIR>
<MEM>
```

SIZE is the size of the RAMdisk in kilobytes. SECTOR is the number of bytes in each disk sector, with the default sector size being 128 bytes. You may also specify sizes of 256, 512, 1024, and 2048 bytes. The sector size affects how much space is taken every time DOS needs to allocate another section of the disk to a file. For example, if your file consumes 129 bytes and you use a 128 byte sector size, then DOS will need to allocate two sectors (one for the first 128 bytes and another for the 1 byte remaining). DIR is the maximum number of entries in the root directory (default = 64). MEM specifies the type of memory to use for the cache (/EMS, /EXT, and /XMS are the permitted values.) /XMS is extended memory through an XMS driver.

Fixes for common problems

The following material might serve as a rough and ready guide to finding problems you might have with 386MAX.

When I try to run Microsoft Windows or Lotus 1-2-3, r. 3.1 with my extended memory disk cache, everything crashes.

Try adding the following parameter to the 386MAX.PRO configuration file: DEBUG = DPMIXCOPY. Both Windows and Lotus 1-2-3 release 3.1 want to use Microsoft's DPMI for extended memory, rather than the more common VCPI. Adding this parameter to 386MAX.PRO alerts 386MAX to honor the DPMI instruction calls.

If you use a disk cache that employs a double-buffering scheme (such as the Windows 3.1 version of Smartdrive), load the cache into conventional memory rather than high DOS memory. Microsoft also recommends that you delete the following lines in the 386MAX.PRO file if present:

```
XMSHNDL = 2 or XMSHNDL = 3
LOAD = WINDOWS.LOD
```

The latter is a parameter from older versions of 386MAX/BLUEMAX that might not be removed by the version 6.0 setup program.

My hard disk doesn't work correctly with 386MAX installed.

Check the documentation for your disk controller card to see if the controller must have a section of upper memory reserved for its internal BIOS. For instance, Storage Dimension SCSI drives must use the address range C800−CC00h or CC00−D000h. Add a RAM statement to 386MAX.PRO to exclude the appropriate region (e.g., RAM = CC00-D000h).

Differences in 386MAX/BLUEMAX 5.xx to 6.xx Table 8-7 provides a brief summary of enhancements added to 386MAX/BLUEMAX from version 5.00 to the current version.

Table 8-7   386MAX/BLUEMAX inter-version differences.

Version	Change
5.00	Added MAXIMIZE utility to place drivers and TSRs above 640K.
5.1	Implemented support for DOS 5. In adddition, this version provides support for Windows 3.0 in Real or Enhanced modes.
6.0	Added support for Windows 3.1. This includes a smoother load high process and an improved, integrated MAX control interface. An OEM version of Multisoft's PCKWIK disk cache is bundled along with Qualitas' Move'EM 286 load-high utility.
6.01	Increased the amount of memory available for DOS programs running inside of Windows 3.0/3.1 and fixed incompatibility with Quarterdeck's QEXT.SYS for DESQview users. Also corrects minor hardware-specificproblems in version 6.0

Helix's NETROOM

NETROOM is a memory management package that sports some unique features. Originally designed as a tool to gain memory in networked environments, NETROOM supports three different techniques for loading programs and drivers above 640K.

- The NETROOM installation program automatically detects Novell networking software. The NETHMA utility places NETxx drivers and the network shell above 1M in the HMA. When appropriate, NETROOM transplants the DOS command kernel, usually placed in the HMA under MS-DOS 5, into upper memory. NETROOM's HMALOAD utility can load other network drivers and TSRs compiled as .COM files into the HMA.

- The NETSWAP utility allows you to swap huge blocks of code transparently in and out of expanded memory. Consequently, as much as 576K of drivers and TSRs can also load outside of the 640K conventional memory range. Helix recommends that you use this feature with IBM TOKEN RING, 3COM, and BANYAN networks. You can also use NETSWAP with some success on ordinary TSR utilities, providing supplementary support in addition to the standard upper memory load-high options.

- NETROOM provides standard EMS 4.0 and upper memory loadhigh functions offered by other 80386 memory management packages. Like 386MAX, NETROOM includes separate support for loading high on 8088/80286 machines. NETROOM does not have QEMM's all-inclusive Stealth remapping feature, so it attempts to create more upper memory through a series of other options. NETROOM can compress and relocate part of the ROM BIOS above 1M to the HMA on 80386 and above machines. You have a choice between filling the HMA with network drivers, the DOS operating system, remapped ROM BIOS code, or remapping other TSR .COM files and drivers.

NETROOM's DISCOVER interface is a hybrid of Quarterdeck's Manifest and Qualitas' 386MAX. A series of pulldown menus allow you to display system information, edit system configuration files or begin the automatic load-high process (called CUSTOMIZE). The CUSTOMIZE process allows you to view a step-by-step summary of NETROOM's load high moves, or speedily reboot the machine to complete the configuration. The user may also select an advanced options screen to modify a series of configuration options:

Disable EMS page frame?
Disable Token-Ring adapter detection?
Disable High-DOS scan?
Enable support for SCSI adapters?
Disable automatic SCSI detection?
Enable EGA/VGA BIOS relocation?
Disable protected mode memory test?
Disable trapping of reset vector?
Disable EBDA (extended bios data) relocation?
Disable Windows 3.x support?
Disable interrupt controller virtualization?

Each option corresponds to a parameter entered on the RM386.SYS command line. (RM386.SYS is the name of NETROOM's expanded/extended memory device driver.) Some of these parameters are spin-offs of options offered in QEMM and 386MAX. The Token-Ring option searches upper memory for ROM reserved by a network card. The SCSI detection feature tests your hard disk for the presence of a bus-mastering controller. "Enable EGA/VGA BIOS relocation" is equivalent to 386MAX's VGASWAP. Interrupt controller virtualization is a compatibility safeguard for programs that take over DOS interrupts. Disabling this feature might speed up performance at the risk of incompatibilities with programs like Quarterdeck's DESQview.

After a preliminary check of CONFIG.SYS and AUTOEXEC.BAT, CUSTOMIZE reboots the computer. CUSTOMIZE automatically strips memory management statements and loadhigh utilities left by QEMM, 386MAX, and MS-DOS 5. If you selected the step-through process, CUSTOMIZE displays each line of the new CONFIG.SYS and AUTOEXEC.BAT for your inspection before rebooting. Two other option prompts ask whether NETROOM should try to reclaim upper memory in the BIOS area (F Block), and whether NETROOM should compress the BIOS and video ROM and load them into the HMA. When you get these prompts, CUSTOMIZE highlights a preferred "Yes" or "No" response that the user can override. CUSTOMIZE automatically loads NOVELL drivers that it detects in your startup files in the HMA. NETROOM automatically attempts to load the DOS operating system into upper memory when using the HMA for network drivers or compressed, remapped BIOS code. After a series of reboots, CUSTOMIZE completes the upper memory optimization, displaying before and after conventional memory totals.

CUSTOMIZE's approach differs from the QEMM or 386MAX utilities for handling nested batch files found in AUTOEXEC.BAT. Because NETROOM is primarily designed to place network software above 640K, it analyzes nested batch files and loads them high on an all-or-nothing basis. For instance, if you have an AUTOEXEC.BAT that reads

```
PROMPT $P$G
PATH=C:\DOS;C:\BAT;C:\UTIL
CALL TSR.BAT
```

CUSTOMIZE attempts to load all of the drivers in TSR.BAT into upper memory. If only some of the programs listed in TSR.BAT fit above 640K, CUSTOMIZE makes the decision to load everything in the batch file low.

Note   If you want CUSTOMIZE to load as many programs as possible above 640K, then don't nest batch files in AUTOEXEC.BAT. Place everything in AUTOEXEC.BAT instead. For instance, if TSR.BAT consists of

```
APPEND C:\DOS
MOUSE.COM
DOSKEY
MIRROR /T:C
```

then place all of these statements directly into AUTOEXEC.BAT instead of calling TSR.BAT as follows:

```
PROMPT $P$G
PATH=C:\DOS;C:\BAT;C:\UTIL
APPEND C:\DOS
MOUSE.COM
DOSKEY
MIRROR /T:C
```

NETROOM'S DISCOVER Control Interface DISCOVER offers six pull-down menus that allow the user to display system information, print or save information screens to disk, edit configuration files, or to begin the CUSTOMIZE loadhigh process. The View menu provides extensive information about the system memory usage and hardware configuration. Screens for extended memory, high-DOS, resident program display, and benchmarks are similar to the ones offered in Quarterdeck's Manifest. DISCOVER goes one step farther than Manifest by allowing users to select a hexadecimal dump of any 64K segment within the first megabyte. The user places the cursor on any driver or program listed on the memory map screen and presses Enter to initiate a hex dump starting at the address of the selected driver. Figure 8-17 shows DISCOVER's detailed and well-organized listing of system interrupt usage.

```
                              DISCOVER v2.20
View        File      Print      Customize     Edit      Options        Quit
┌─────────────────────────────────────────────────────────────────────────┐
│                          Interrupt Table                                  │
│     #     Name         Address      Description                           │
│ ┌─                                                                        │
│ │ 0    DISCOVER      51D6:00BA    Divide By Zero                          │
│ │ 1    DOS           0070:06F4    Debug Exception                         │
│ │ 2    DOS           12DF:0016    NMI                                     │
│ │ 3    DOS           0070:06F4    Breakpoint                              │
│ │ 4    DOS           0070:06F4    Overflow                                │
│ │ 5    BIOS          F000:3C60    Print Screen                            │
│ │ 6    BIOS          F000:3D10    Invalid Opcode Exception                │
│ │ 7    BIOS          F000:3E10    Coprocessor Not Present                 │
│ │ 8    GRAB.EXE      1455:1831    IRQ 0 - Timer                           │
│ │ 9    GRAB.EXE      1455:18CD    IRQ 1 - Keyboard                        │
│ │ A    BIOS          F000:66E0    IRQ 2 - Slave/Available                 │
│ │ B    BIOS          F000:66E0    IRQ 3 - COM2                            │
│ │ C    MOUSE         CF6E:02BC    IRQ 4 - COM1                            │
│ ▼ D    BIOS          F000:66E0    IRQ 5 - Available/XT-Hard Disk          │
└─────────────────────────────────────────────────────────────────────────┘
                             <F1>=HELP
```

Fig. 8-17   Discover's System Interrupt Usage display.

DISCOVER's File and Print menus allow you to send information screens to the printer or saved them to disk. The Edit menu displays CONFIG.SYS, AUTOEXEC.BAT, or any user-specified text file in DISCOVER's internal text editor. The Customize menu initiates the memory optimization process we've already described.

NETROOM's Upper Memory Loadhigh Utilities NETROOM uses two utilities—XLOAD.SYS and XLOAD.EXE—to place drivers and TSRs into upper memory. These are similar to the drivers included with QEMM and 386MAX. XLOAD.EXE precedes the name of a program to be load high in AUTOEXEC .BAT. DEVICE = XLOAD.SYS precedes the name of a device driver to load high in CONFIG.SYS.

You can invoke XLOAD.SYS or XLOAD.EXE with the -D parameter to determine the amount of RAM a driver or TSR program requires for loading high. For example, to determine the requirements for loading Microsoft's MOUSE .SYS driver, you would enter the following line into CONFIG.SYS:

```
DEVICE = [D:\PATH]XLOAD.SYS -D [D:\PATH] MOUSE.SYS
```

When you reboot the machine, XLOAD.SYS will pause and display the following message:

```
DEVICE = XLOAD.SYS -D E:\WINDOWS\MOUSE.SYS
XLOAD v2.20-TSR High-DOS Loader
Copyright (c) 1990,91 Helix Software Company, Inc.
All rights reserved.
Loading program: E:\WINDOWS\MOUSE.SYS
Loading program low.
Microsoft (R) Mouse Driver Version 8.20.01 Beta
Copyright (C) Microsoft Corp. 1983-1991. All rights
reserved.
Mouse driver installed
Resident size: 16976 bytes.
Maximum size: 56064 bytes.
Press F1 to continue...
```

NETROOM's 80386 memory manager can map upper memory addresses to either XMS or Expanded Memory to create high RAM. Mapping upper memory addresses to XMS allows slightly faster execution of code, improving system performance. (This is NETROOM's default.) Mapping upper memory addresses to EMS allows specified regions to be used as EMS 4.0 pages or as high RAM. NETROOM uses XMS mapping for high RAM if the command line appears as follows:

```
DEVICE = RM386.SYS AUTO
```

or as

```
DEVICE = RM386.SYS XMS = C800-DFFF XMS = F200-F2FF
```

NETROOM uses Expanded Memory (EMS) mapping for high RAM if the command line appears as follows:

DEVICE = RM386 . SYS EMS = C800 - DFFF

You can combine the options and designate both XMS and EMS upper memory blocks on the same command line as follows:

DEVICE = RM386 . SYS XMS = C800 - DFFF EMS = F700 - FAFF

The XLOAD utilities require slightly different parameters to control the load high region depending on which method you use to create the high RAM. If the RM386.SYS command line contains the AUTO parameter, it uses automatically recognized upper memory blocks as XMS high RAM.

- Designate the region used by XLOAD with the -S parameter followed by a hex address ending in "01" when using XMS memory mapping. For instance, XLOAD . EXE -SC801 DOSKEY would load the DOSKEY.EXE utility into an XMS region beginning at address C800h.

- Designate the region used by XLOAD with the -S parameter followed by a hex address ending in "00" when using EMS memory mapping. For instance, XLOAD . EXE -SD000 MIRROR /T:C would load the DOS 5 MIRROR utility into an EMS region beginning at address D000h.

Fine Tuning NETROOM/RM386.SYS If you have drivers you want CUSTOMIZE to ignore, add them to the CUSTOMIZE.DAT file using the internal text editor included in the DISCOVER control interface. Enter the program or driver name without the three-letter file extension. Program names preceded by an asterisk are loaded low during the CUSTOMIZE process and ignored. Program names not preceded by an asterisk are remarked out; they are not loaded into memory at all during the CUSTOMIZE process. Remarked out programs are restored to AUTOEXEC.BAT and CONFIG.SYS after the CUSTOMIZE process completes.

NETROOM's MOVEVBIOS parameter is similar to 386MAX's VGASWAP. It relocates VGA BIOS code from the C000h − C800h region to unused monochrome video space at B000 − B800. NETROOM's BIOSHMA parameter searches for ROM in the C000h − C800h region, and in the F000h − 10000h region. When invoked, BIOSHMA compresses as much as 96K of ROM code and transfers it above 1M to the HMA. This allows you to use the C000h − C800h and F000h − 10000h address ranges as high RAM for loading drivers and TSRs. NETROOM asks the user about using the compression feature during the CUSTOMIZE setup routine.

Note BIOSHMA is not 100% compatible with all 80386 BIOS setups. NETROOM tests the upper memory area to determine how much of the BIOS it can compress and relocate if you invoke BIOSHMA. NETROOM can compress only 32 − 64K on some systems.

If NETROOM uses the HMA for network drivers or compressed BIOS code, it can load the DOS operating system into upper memory instead of above 1M. This is controlled by a parameter automatically entered as the last line of CONFIG.SYS as follows:

INSTALL = [D : \ PATH]XLOAD . EXE [D : \ PATH]DOSUMB . COM

Users may force DOS to load in upper memory and leave the HMA vacant by manually appending this parameter as the last line of CONFIG.SYS. The DOS = HIGH parameter must also appear in CONFIG.SYS before this line.

A complete explanation of RM386.SYS (RAM-MAN) command line options is beyond the scope of this book. Table 8-8 provides a summary of the more important parameters.

Table 8-8 NETROOM parameter summary.

Parameter	Description
AUTO	The AUTO parameter automatically configures high DOS memory for NETROOM's XLOAD utilities. The RAM-MAN (RM386.SYS) memory manager attempts to set up an optimal high DOS memory configuration mapped to XMS memory when using this parameter.
XMS = ADDR1-ADDR2	Use this parameter to manually define upper memory address regions mapped as XMS high RAM. The starting address must begin on an even 16K segment (C800h, C900h, CA00h, etc.). The ending address should end in "FF" (C8FFh, C9FFh, CAFFh, etc.)
EMS = ADDR1-ADDR2	Use this parameter to manually define upper memory address regions mapped as EMS high RAM. The starting address must begin on an even 16K segment and the ending address should end in "FF" as above.
INCLUDE = ADDR1-ADDR2	This parameter places specific upper memory regions under RAM-MAN's control. When used with the AUTO parameter, the specified regions are automatically configured as XMS high DOS memory.
EXCLUDE = ADDR1-ADDR2	This parameter excludes the specified address region from RAM-MAN's control.
BIOSHMA [FULL] [HALF][VIDEO]	This parameter compresses and relocates portions of BIOS code to the high memory area. FULL copies BIOS code from the F000h to FFFFh region. HALF copies only half of the "F" block (the 32K region from F800h to FFFFh) to the high memory area. VIDEO copies both the System BIOS from F000H to FFFFH and the VGA video BIOS from C000H to C7FFH to the high memory area. NETROOM compresses this 96K of ROM code to 64K to occupy the 64K HMA. **Note** It's generally best to let NETROOM determine

Table 8-8 Continued

which parameter to use internally. Attempts to force video compression with some BIOS setups will cause the system to crash.

MOVEVBIOS	This option is the same as 386MAX's VGASWAP. Rather than compress BIOS code, MOVEVBIOS simply shifts 32K of VGA video ROM from C000H to C7FFH into the monochrome address area [B000H to B7FFH]. This does not actually gain any new memory, but it allows you to use a larger contiguous area as high RAM.
ROM = ADDR1-ADDR2	The ROM code in the specified upper memory address is shadowed in faster RAM to improve performance.
FRAME =	Designates starting address for the EMS 4.0 pageframe (must lie on an even 16K address boundary).
NOFRAME	Disables the use of an EMS pageframe, providing an additional 64K address range for use as high RAM.
NOTEST	Disables RAM-MAN's start-up extended memory test, which speeds the boot sequence slightly.

NETROOM's Network Loaders In addition to loading code between 640K and 1M, NETROOM provides two extra methods for fighting RAM cram.

The NETHMA and HMALOAD utilities can place up to 64K of user-designated device drivers or .COM format programs into the HMA. NETHMA loads Novell's NETxxx workstation shells (which are compiled in .EXE format). HMALOAD allows you to load one generic network shell, device driver, or TSR program compiled in the .SYS or .COM format. For more information on using NETHMA and HMALOAD, see the chapter on networking.

The NETSWAP and NETSWAP4 utilities allow programs and drivers to load into expanded memory. NETSWAP.EXE is limited to the 64K mapped by the EMS 3.2 pageframe. Use it on 8088/80286 machines with EMS 3.2/EMS4.0 memory. NETSWAP4.EXE provides access to 576K of EMS 4.0 memory that is switched in and out of DOS's conventional area on an as needed basis. NETSWAP4 creates a virtual machine in expanded memory that can load up to 576K of drivers and TSRs while consuming only 32K of conventional memory for housekeeping. The virtual machine is swapped into conventional memory whenever DOS calls one of the programs it contains. Network drivers, disk caching software and many types of TSR utilities can load into a NETSWAP4 virtual machine. Multitasking environments like DESQview and Windows can run with a full complement of conventional memory, paging the virtual machine when an application requires information on a network drive or disk cache. To load programs into a virtual machine, the user simply invokes the appropriate NETSWAP loader followed by the name of a batch file. For example, if you normally initialize a LANTASTIC server with a file called STARTNET.BAT, you invoke the NETSWAP4 loader to load all of the commands within AUTOEXEC.BAT as follows:

```
PROMPT $P$G
PATH=C:\DOS;C:\LANTASTI;C:\NETROOM
NETSWAP4 STARTNET.BAT
```

NETSWAP4 can relocate TSRs as well as network files. NETROOM's DEVLOAD command even makes it possible to load device drivers from a batch file instead of placing them in CONFIG.SYS. There is a performance penalty when using NETSWAP because the code loaded in the virtual machine is paged in and out of conventional memory. The performance penalty for disk accesses and memory reads ranges from 10 to 20 percent. You can find ways to optimize performance and reduce the impact on system speed. For a more extensive explanation of NETROOM's NETSWAP feature, see the chapter on Networks.

Tips on Optimizing NETROOM's Performance   The following text provides you with some insights into optimizing NETROOM's performance:

- NETROOM's STRETCH.EXE utility can furnish 64−96K of conventional memory for text applications on VGA systems by disabling EGA/VGA graphic modes. This feature is analogous to Quarterdeck's VIDRAM. Just type STRETCH at the command prompt. To run graphics-based applications, type STRETCH OFF to re-enable the use of EGA/VGA video memory.

- When running Windows 3.0/3.1 in Enhanced Mode, do not define EMS high-RAM for RAM-MAN. Use the "AUTO" or XMS= parameters to define high-RAM regions.

- To make NETROOM work with DR DOS 6, you must manually remove the following statements from the DR DOS 6 CONFIG.SYS file:

```
DEVICE=EMM386.SYS
DEVICE=HIDOS.SYS
HIDOS=
```

and manually insert the following NETROOM commands:

```
DEVICE=[d:\path]\RM386.SYS AUTO ROM
DEVICE-[d:\path]\XLOAD.SYS -O
DOS=HIGH
```

Other third-party loadhigh tools and memory managers

ALLCHARGE 386   The ALL386 memory management package is bundled with special 80386 and above hardware enhancements manufactured by ALL

Computer Company. It is optimized to work with their special hardware. ALL-CHARGE contains an automatic loadhigh configuration utility and supports a shared XMS/EMS memory pool. The package includes a system inventory utility similar to Quarterdeck's Manifest. You must have at least 412K of conventional memory free to use the ALLMENU utility. ALL386's operation and command-line options are very similar to the ones found in Quarterdeck's QEMM.

Memory Commander Memory Commander's approach to managing DOS memory is slightly different than other memory managers. It varies the amount of conventional memory available to individual applications based on how they use the system's video memory. This approach is only partially successful in practice. While some text based applications load and function in an environment that provides 800K or more of conventional memory, performance with graphics-based applications might be erratic and unreliable in Memory Commander's special enhanced modes. You can configure Memory Commander to provide 800K+ of conventional memory for text-based applications by decreasing the amount of UMB reserved for loading TSR's. This feature might come in handy for users of text-based programs without EMS/Extended memory support or disk swapping capability. Programs in this category include Borland's Turbo Pascal 6 and Software Publishing Corporation's Harvard Graphics 2.3.

The authors were unsuccessful in getting Memory Commander's graphic Mode C to work with Ventura Publisher 2.0, GeoWorks, or other tested VGA paint programs. Graphic applications are compatible with Memory Commander's conventional Mode A, where video memory is not relocated.

Memory Commander also offers the option of configuring upper memory as "high RAM." There is a maximum of 128K available for loading programs high with Memory Commander configured for both expanded memory support and upper memory. You must enter the names of programs and drivers into a special database to tell Memory Commander to load them into upper memory.

Users of Memory Commander might experience some incompatibilities. For instance, Norton's NDOS shell interferes with the operation of Memory Commander's control interface. The package does include a RAM disk and built-in ANSI driver. Users may display upper memory statistics, but the package does not include a system inventory utility like the ones bundled with QEMM, 386MAX and NETROOM.

QMAPS 2.0 Quadtel's QMAPS provides a pleasant installation interface, but users might encounter some difficulty running its automatic loadhigh utility. QMAPS presents basic, standard and advanced setup choices. The advanced setup walks the user through an exhaustive list of command parameters. Choosing an inappropriate configuration option can cause the installation program to lock up. (For example, choosing "Modify current installation" will lock up the machine if you're installing the program for the first time.) QMAPS does not automatically scan and recover ROM regions, but it does offer users an opportunity to include or exclude specific addresses if known in advance.

QMAPS' SMARTMOV memory optimization utility provides inconsistent results when it processes nested batch files. SMARTMOV functions correctly when using a basic set of configuration files, but you can probably product more memory by manually editing the CONFIG.SYS and AUTOEXEC.BAT.

QMAPS does not accommodate exploding device drivers by loaning the EMS pageframe, nor does it support separate device instancing under Windows. QMAPS 2.0 does not provide a completely reliable environment for running Windows and some network software. Versions subsequent to 2.0 may be more stable.

Dynamic Memory Control (DMC)—A Conventional/UMB Memory Referee DMC is a device driver/TSR watcher that expands on the capabilities of the TSR referees discussed in Chapter 6. Using DMC, you can load any driver, TSR-utility or even a full-featured memory manager from a DOS batch file into conventional or upper memory. You can remove any program loaded with DMC from upper memory in the same way that the TSR utilities on our utilities diskette remove programs from conventional memory.

The ability to dynamically load and remove TSR's and device drivers from upper memory allows considerable flexibility for users who need to manage complex system configurations. Instead of creating multiple startup configurations and rebooting, DMC allows you to create a series of batch files to manage various workstation scenarios. For instance, you could set up a batch file that loads a series of Novell network drivers into upper memory. If you subsequently log off the network, you can construct a batch file that unloads all of the Novell software from upper memory, and replaces it with a screen-grabbing utility and device driver for a scanner. DMC even lets you switch memory managers on the fly. The RTSR utility can convert any device driver into an executable program that you can load and unload at will from the command-line. This means that you can load DOS 5's HIMEM.SYS from AUTOEXEC.BAT, then write a batch file that removes the DOS 5 memory manager and switches to Quarterdeck's QEMM without rebooting the system.

DMC can run interactively or through a batch process. Figure 8-18 shows how to load and unload drivers or TSRs in memory through the DMC control interface. As with the shareware MARK/REPLACE utilities, DMC loads place marking "Notes" into memory between individual drivers. You can load either executable programs or DOS device drivers into conventional or upper memory sandwiched between the Notes. In Fig. 8-18, DMC is set to record the choices you make into a batch file called LOAD.BAT. Figure 8-19 shows DMC's Unload options screen. QEMM386 was loaded as a removable TSR followed by a Note, and two utility programs. Use the menu or the mouse to remove the utility programs QEMM loaded high, or even remove QEMM itself from memory.

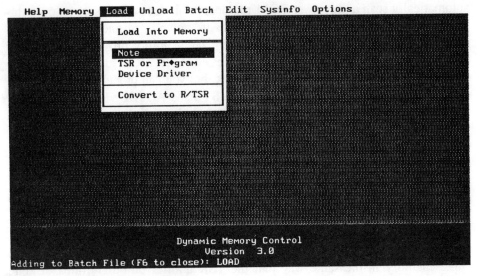

Fig. 8-18   DMC Control Interface display.

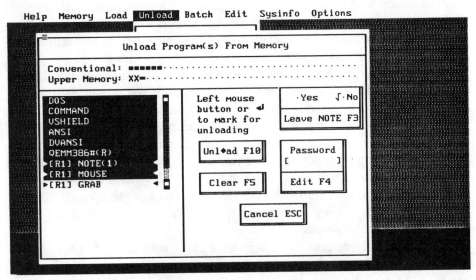

Fig. 8-19   DMC Unload Options screen.

DMC also offers an alternative method for watchdogging TSR's. In addition to the NOTE and FREENOTE memory bookmarks, you can recompile any program or device driver as a removable TSR utility. Figure 8-19 shows that this was performed on Quarterdeck's QEMM. DMC's RTSR feature compiled QEMM-386.SYS into a TSR program called QEMM386#.EXE. You can install QEMM386#.EXE from the DOS command line. Conversely, you remove it from memory by typing QEMM386# . EXE /U (for "Un-install"). You can remove programs and drivers compiled with RTSR from memory in any order without using the NOTE place marker between programs.

Note If you use DMC's more sophisticated method of removing programs from memory, removing one program out-of-sequence might cause problems for a subsequently loaded utility that depended on the first program.

DMC's control interface also includes an excellent set of system inventory and memory display utilities, as shown in Fig. 8-20.

```
Help  Memory  Load  Unload  Batch  Edit  Sysinfo  Options

      Memory Map Display

   Summ

   Summary      10144K Physical Memory    DOS 5.00
   Conv   Memory Type      Size      Free     (% Free)
   expA
   extE   Conventional    655360    572336     87.3%
   Uppe   Expanded       9846784   5832704     59.2%
          Extended       9633792   5767168     59.8%
   Run    UMB Region 1    130816     25536     19.5%
          UMB Region 2     40◆2      1456      36.1%
          UMB Region 3    24480      2736      11.1%
```

Fig. 8-20   DMC Inventory and Memory Display Utility display.

Installing QEMM, 386MAX, or NETROOM with Stacker

STACKER is a disk compression utility. In most cases, it creates a second partition on your drive, compresses the information in the original (first) partition, and places it in the second partition. Once STACKER finishes its installation and compression, it rearranges the drive letters on your hard disk. The original partition becomes drive D, while the second partition becomes drive C. This rearrangement of drive letters takes place each time you boot up your machine. If you have STACKER loaded on your boot drive, this can cause a conflict with the optimization utilities supplied with various memory managers. For example, if the optimization utility expects to find its batch file on drive C, then it will fail as soon as STACKER loads. Unfortunately, you must load STACKER to use your applications.

The best way to solve this problem is not to use STACKER to compress your boot drive and to make certain that the directory and files for the memory manager reside on an uncompressed drive. Of course, this assumes you have two physical drives in your machine. If necessity requires that you use STACKER on your boot drive, you may still get the various optimization utilities to work by temporarily disabling STACKER's drive-swapping feature. Use the following procedure:

1. Locate the following line in CONFIG.SYS:

   DEVICE = [d: \ path] SSWAP.COM C: D:

   Temporarily disable this line by placing a ":" or "REM" statement in front of the word "DEVICE."

2. Make sure that both the STACKER software and the memory manager software reside on an uncompressed drive.

3. Reverse all references between the uncompressed drive and the STACKER volume in AUTOEXEC.BAT of the original (uncompressed) boot drive. For example, if your AUTOEXEC.BAT under STACKER contains the statement C: \ UTIL \ MOUSE.COM, change this to read D: \ UTIL \ MOUSE.COM. If there is a statement that reads D: \ PCTOOLS \ PC-CACHE, change this to read C: \ PCTOOLS \ PC-CACHE.

4. You may now run OPTIMIZE, MAXIMIZE, or DISCOVER, and they should work correctly.

5. Once you complete the optimization, re-enable the DEVICE = SSWAP .COM statement in CONFIG.SYS. Change the drive references in your AUTOEXEC.BAT to reflect the original STACKER designations. For example, you would change D: \ UTIL \ MOUSE.COM back to C: \ UTIL \ MOUSE.COM.

Command reference

AST Research—EMS Cards/AST Premium 286

The following paragraphs describe the configuration options provided with AST Research's EMS Cards. The REMM.SYS command line options are as follows:

DEVICE = REMM.SYS /P = NN /C = NN /LMMMM-NNNN /X = MMMM-NNNN
/S = MMMM /M = NN

/P = NN   Process IDs. This option is analogous to setting EMS handles. A setting of /P = 32 will usually ensure good performance. You can use a setting of /P = 16 to conserve memory.

/C = NN   Contexts. This option is similar to mapping registers. A setting of /C = 16 is usually adequate. A setting of /C = 32 might result in slightly faster performance on some systems but could cause compatibility problems with some video cards.

/L = MMMM - NNNN

Include. By default, REMM.SYS ignores certain areas of upper memory. The /L switch forces REMM to include the specified address range. Values range from A000h to EFFFh. On EGA/VGA computers, you gain 32K of mappable EMS using the setting /L = B000 - B7FF. If you use a Monochrome or Hercules adaptor, include A000h to AFFFh to gain an additional 64K. CGA systems gain as much as 96K using the setting /L = A000 - B7FF. The added memory does not show up as conventional memory when you run CHKDSK but as mappable EMS for use by loadhigh utilities or multitasking programs.

/X = MMMM - NNNN

Exclude. This parameter is the opposite of the /L switch. Use /X to exclude specified address ranges in upper memory. The /X parameter helps avoid memory conflicts with network adaptors or other add-in peripherals that reserve part of upper memory for their own use.

/S = MMMM   Set pageframe. REMM automatically establishes an EMS pageframe in the first convenient UMB area that it finds. You can gain additional loadhigh memory by overriding the automatic setting and specifying a specific address for the pageframe using the /S parameter. A setting of /S = E000 provides the maximum amount of contiguous UMB space for loading high and multitasking on machines that permit it.

/M = nn   Use this parameter to force REMM.SYS to operate in 16-bit address mode. Normally REMM operates in 8-bit mode to avoid conflict with other adaptor cards. You can use REMM in 16-bit mode if it occupies a 128K UMB segment by itself, or shares the segment only with other 16-bit devices. 8-bit and 16-bit devices can't occupy the same 128K segment. The default for REMM.SYS is to treat the first 640K as 16-bit memory and recognize upper memory as 8-bit memory. The following paragraphs explain how to enable a 128K segment in upper memory as 16-bit memory.

You can divide the DOS addressable megabyte into eight 128K segments. When you use REMM.SYS, each segment is assigned a default binary value of 1 for 16-bit memory or 0 for 8-bit memory. REMM.SYS uses the defaults shown in Table 8-9.

The /M parameter provides the means of changing these defaults. If you change its hexadecimal value to a binary value, then the default of 1Fh looks like the pattern in Table 8-9 (00011111b). Each position in the binary conversion translates to one of the 128K

Table 8-9   REMM.SYS 128K segment
memory type defaults.

128K segments	Binary (Default)[1]
E000h-EFFFh	0
C000h-DFFFh	0
A000h-BFFFh	0
8000h-9FFFh	1
6000h-7FFFh	1
4000h-5FFFh	1
2000h-3FFFh	1
0000h-1FFFh	1

[1]Type 0 memory is 8-bit access. Type
1 memory is 16-bit access.

segments. To change a 128K segment in upper memory to 16-bit memory, change the corresponding digit from 0 to 1. For example, if you have a 16-bit video card on an 80286 and above machine, then you can configure the C000h−DFFFh block as 16-bit memory. If you place the EMS pageframe in this region, the speed of EMS read/write operations will increase. The new value for M is 01011111 or 7fh. For a 16-bit AST VGA video adaptor and REMM, add the following statement to CONFIG.SYS:

```
DEVICE = EMM.SYS COMPUTER MEMORY_ADDRESS I/O_ADDRESS
   [EXP = X] [ND] [NP] [NE] [H = X]
```

/N   (Nomenclature). Appending the /N parameter tells REMM to display a verbose report of the system's expanded memory allocation.

Intel Above Board/Above Board+/AboveBoard 286, etc. (Intel Corp.)

The Intel memory manager is called EMM.SYS. The EMM.SYS configuration options are as follows (the parameters in brackets are optional):

```
DEVICE = EMM.SYS COMPUTER MEMORY_ADDRESS I/O_ADDRESS
   [EXP = X] [ND]  [NP] [NE] [H = X]
```

COMPUTER   Specified by a two-letter code, the Computer parameter defines the type of computer in which the Above Board is installed. Table 8-10 provides a list of valid computer types.

MEMORY_ADDRESS This parameter sets the address of the EMS pageframe. Table 8-11 provides a list of valid pageframe values.

I/O_ADDRESS This parameter specifies the port address for the memory card. You can vary the port address on Intel memory cards using dip switch settings or automated installation software. Each Above Board installed in the computer must use a different I/O port. The line in CONFIG.SYS must correspond to the port address for each card. Table 8-12 provides a listing of valid I/O port values.

Table 8-10 EMM.SYS computer types.

EMM.SYS parameter	Type of Computer
PC	COMPAQ DESKPRO, IBM PC, IBM PC XT, IBM PC or PC XT and compatibles
AT	COMPAQ DESKPRO 286, COMPAQ DESKPRO 386, IBM PC AT, IBM PC XT 286, IBM PC AT and compatibles
MOD30	IBM Personal System/2

Table 8-11 AboveBoard pageframe values.

Above Board PC & PS/PC	Above Board AT,PS/AT, 286 & PS/286 in 80286-based computers)	Above Board 286 & PS/286 (in 8088- or 8086-based computers)
C400h	C000h	C800h
C800h	C400h	CC00h
CC00h	C800h	D000h
D000h	CC00h	D400h
D400h	D000h	D800h
D800h	DC00h	
DC00h	E000h	
E000h		

Table 8-12   AboveBoard I/O address parameter choices.

AboveBoard PC & PS/PC	AboveBoard AT & PS/AT	AboveBoard 286 & PS/286
208	208	208
218	218	218
258	258	248
268	268	258
2A8	2A8	2A8
2B8	2B8	2B8
2E8	2E8	2E8

Above board configuration examples

DEVICE = EMM.SYS AT D000 208

> The Above Board card is installed in an IBM AT-compatible computer with the EMS pageframe at D000h and I/O port at 208.

DEVICE = EMM.SYS PC E000 208 258

> Two Above Board cards are installed in an IBM XT-compatible computer. The pageframe is shared by both boards at E000h. The first board uses I/O port 208, the second board uses I/O port 258.

Above board optional parameters

EXP = X   Verifies the amount of expanded memory by comparing the specified value with the physical amount of memory installed on the memory card. Values for x are multiples of 16 up to 32,768. The EMM software generates an error if the number doesn't correspond to the physical memory on the card. (This parameter does not increase or decrease the amount of memory recognized by the device driver, it is only a diagnostic tool.)

ND   No Diagnostics. Speeds boot-up by skipping the Above Board memory tests.

NP   No Pause. Forces EMM.SYS to ignore error or advisory messages. The default setting will pause the system for user input after the software displays a message.

NE   No Extended memory tests. Forces EMM.SYS to skip extended memory diagnostic tests. This parameter speeds the boot process when the AboveBoard is not configured to provide extended memory. Do not use this parameter if the AboveBoard is configured to provide extended memory.

H = X   Controls the number of allocated EMS memory handles. The default value is 64.

AllChargeCard 286 (All Computer Company)

The All memory manager is called ALLEMM4.SYS. The command syntax is as follows:

```
DEVICE = ALLEMM4 . SYS [ I O = ][FRAME = ][RAM = ][ROM = ][EXTMEM = ]
          [MEMORY = ][ I NCLUDE = ][EXCLUDE = ][HANDLES = ]
          [NAMES = ][MAPS = ][CONTEXTS = ][NOF I LL][NOV I DEOF I LL]
```

The following paragraphs provide a summary of the most important options and how to use them:

FRAME = XXXX   Designates a hexadecimal address between A000h and E800h for the 64K EMS pageframe. The EMM chooses a pageframe automatically when this parameter is omitted. A setting of FR = NONE disables the pageframe to provide more UMB memory as a loadhigh area.

RAM = MM00 - NNFF

Designates a UMB region to use for loading programs high. You can specify multiple regions by including multiple RAM statements. If RAM is used with no region specified, the memory manager will use all available UMB memory excluding the pageframe for load high. Note that you must specify regions in 4K increments. The starting address must end with two 0's and the upper boundary ends with two F's.

ROM = MM00 - NNFF

Designates a ROM address in hexadecimal that the EMM shadows in expanded memory. Typical regions containing ROM code include C000h – C7FFh (VGA video) and F000h – FFFFh (ROM BIOS).

EXTMEM = XXXX   Designates the total amount of extended memory (in kilobytes) which ALLEMM4 will not use. XXXX is specified as a decimal number.

MEMORY = XXXX   Designates the total amount of extended memory (in kilobytes) that ALLEMM4 should convert to expanded memory. The ME and EXT functions are converses of one another. Use only one of them. XXXX is specified as decimal number.

INCLUDE = MM00-NNFF

    Designates a UMB memory range in hexadecimal that you want ALLEMM4 to control. This parameter is useful when you discover areas of upper memory that do not contain ROM code but are not recognized by ALLEMM4 on startup.

EXCLUDE = MM00-NNFF

    Designates a UMB memory range in hexadecimal that you want excluded from ALLEMM4's control. This parameter is useful if the system locks up on startup and you trace the problem to a ROM address that ALLEMM4 does not see. If you also entered the RAM parameter, ALLEMM4 might attempt to control some UMB memory that contains ROM instructions.

HANDLES = XXX   Specifies the total number of EMS handles available . XXX is a decimal number between 16 and 255. The default is 64 handles.

MAPS = XX   Specifies the total number of alternate mapping registers made available for EMS page swapping. XX is a decimal number between 0 and 64. The default is 8 alternate maps.

NOVIDEOFILL   (NV). Inhibits ALLEMM4 from annexing the EGA/VGA video area (A000h – AFFFh) to conventional memory. This parameter is applicable with MDA, Hercules and CGA graphic adaptors only. Instead of increasing conventional memory to 704K, ALLEMM4 uses the A000h block as UMB load-high memory or mappable EMS pages.

QRAM 2.0 (Quarterdeck Office Systems)

Quarterdeck Office System's QRAM loads drivers and TSR's into upper memory in cooperation with third-party EMS 4.0 memory support, or special Chips & Technologies Shadow RAM. The package consists of a device driver (QRAM .SYS) that is loaded after any EMS 4.0 memory manager in CONFIG.SYS, and a series of LOADHI utilities. The syntax for QRAM.SYS is as follows:

```
DEVICE = [D:][PATH]QRAM.SYS [RAM[ = MMMM-NNNN]
         [INCLUDE = MM00-NNFF] [EXCLUDE = MM00-NNFF]
```

[FORCEEMS] [FRAMELENGTH = X] [NOFILL]
[NOVIDEOFILL] NOXBDA] [NOSHADOWRAM]
[NOPAUSEONERROR] [PAUSE] [HELP]

RAM

Using the RAM parameter by itself instructs QRAM to use any upper memory under its control as high RAM for loading drivers and programs. MM00−NNFF specifies an upper memory address range in hexadecimal to use as high RAM.

INCLUDE =

(I). Instructs QRAM to include a portion of upper memory under its control that it would otherwise ignore.

EXCLUDE =

(E). Instructs QRAM to exclude a portion of upper memory from its control. MM00−NNFF specifies the specific upper memory address range to exclude (in hexadecimal).

FORCEEMS

(FEMS). This parameter forces QRAM to honor EMS memory requests when the EMS pageframe is set to a value less than four with the FRAMELENGTH parameter (see below). This allows some programs access to expanded memory even without a full pageframe.

FRAMELENGTH = X

(FL). Tells QRAM to assume an EMS pageframe of X pages, where X is a number from 0 to 4. Setting X to 0 disables the pageframe. The EMS pageframe is normally established by the expanded memory manager (it uses a default of four 16K pages). This parameter lets you free up one or more of those pages for use as high RAM. Use this parameter in conjunction with the FORCEEMS parameter. You can use the FORCEEMS and FRAMELENGTH parameters to establish a limited amount of high RAM with expanded memory cards that are not completely EMS 4.0 hardware compatible. A setting of FL = 0 will enable 64K of high RAM on these systems, though it will disable use of any expanded memory.

NOFILL

(NO). Instructs QRAM not to backfill conventional memory below 640K from an add-on memory card. This parameter also prevents filling the A000h segment (640−704K) on systems with monochrome and CGA video adaptors.

NOVIDEOFILL

(NV). Instructs QRAM not to fill the memory area from A000h to B7FFh with memory. On monochrome systems, the default setting fills the area from A000h−AFFFh from expanded memory, increasing DOS conventional memory to

704K. On CGA systems, the default setting fills the area from A000h – B7FFh from expanded memory, increasing DOS conventional memory to 736K.

NOXBDA   (NX). Instructs QRAM not to relocate extended BIOS data. On some machines, the last kilobyte of conventional memory at 639K is used to store extended BIOS information. By default, QRAM relocates this information to provide contiguous conventional memory up to 704K.

NOSHADOWRAM

(NOSH). Instructs QRAM not to try and recover proprietary shadow RAM. Use of this parameter might cause QRAM to function on an otherwise incompatible system.

NOPAUSEONERROR

(NOPE). Instructs QRAM not to pause on an error. By default, QRAM displays a "Press any key to continue, ESC to abort" message if it encounters any errors while reading the command line instructions.

PAUSE   Instructs QRAM to pause the display when outputting messages.

For a detailed reference on the use of Manifest, Optimize, LOADHI.SYS and LOADHI.COM, see the section on Quarterdeck's QEMM. These utilities have identical syntax and function with both products.

DR DOS 6 (HIDOS.SYS, EMM386.SYS) (Digital Research, Inc.)

Digital Research's DOS 6 includes two memory management drivers. HIDOS .SYS is used on 8088 and 80286 systems equipped with expanded memory and/or 80286 systems equipped with NEAT shadow RAM. EMM386.SYS is used on 80386 and above systems. The syntax for HIDOS.SYS is as follows:

```
DEVICE = [D:][PATH]HIDOS.SYS [/AUTOSCAN = MMMM-NNNN]
         [/INCLUDE = MMMM-NNNN] [/EXCLUDE = MMMM-NNNN]
         [/VIDEO[MMMM-NNNN]] [BDOS = AUTO|FFFF|MMMM]
         [/USE = MMMM-NNNN] [/ROM = AUTO|MMMM-NNNN|NONE]
         [/XBDA][/CHIPSET = AUTO|CHIPSET|NONE]
```

/AUTOSCAN   Instructs HIDOS.SYS to scan upper memory in 4K blocks to determine which areas are free. MMMM-NNNN may specify a hexadecimal UMB range to scan. The Autoscan procedure is sensitive to areas of upper memory that might contain ROM and will ordinarily exclude any segment that is questionable.

/INCLUDE   Instructs HIDOS.SYS to include a portion of UMB memory in the SCAN procedure that it would otherwise ignore. MMMM-NNNN specifies a hexadecimal range to include in the scan procedure.

Note DR's use of "Include" does not automatically make the region available for loading code, it merely performs memory tests. The /USE parameter opens the region for use as high DOS memory.

/EXCLUDE   This parameter instructs HIDOS.SYS to exclude an area of upper memory from the SCAN procedure. EXCLUDE overrides the results of AUTOSCAN, and excludes a region used by a network card or other ROM adaptor. MMMM-NNNN specifies the starting and ending segment addresses in hexadecimal.

/VIDEO   This parameter allows HIDOS.SYS to extend conventional memory past 640K by releasing space normally reserved for the video display adaptor. The default setting uses the memory from A000h to AFFFh on monochrome systems and A000h to B7FFh on CGA systems. MMMM-NNNN allows you to specify a smaller range, where MMMM must equal A000h and NNNN equals any hex value from A001h to B7FFh.

/BDOS = XXXX   This parameter specifies where HIDOS.SYS relocates the DR DOS command kernel above 640K in conjunction with the HIDOS = ON statement in CONFIG.SYS. Values for XXXX include AUTO (lets DR DOS determine the optimum area to load the command kernel), FFFF (relocates the command kernel to the HMA), and NNNN (relocates the command kernel to a specified segment address in upper memory). Your system must provide enough contiguous upper memory to hold the DR DOS command kernel for the NNNN option to work.

/USE = MMMM-NNNN
                This parameter overrides the automatic HIDOS memory tests, forcing the use of the specified upper memory address. MMMM-NNNN specifies a hexadecimal starting and ending address for the address range.

/ROM = XXXX   This parameter copies the specified ROM address into RAM, speeding up the performance of programs that make use of ROM routines in the specified area. XXXX may contain MMMM-NNNN (the starting and ending address of ROM segment in upper memory), AUTO (copies all ROMS in upper memory that

HIDOS.SYS can locate), or NONE (ROMs are not copied to RAM). HIDOS.SYS uses a default value of NONE.

/XBDA Some systems locate extended BIOS data just below the top of conventional memory at 638−640K. HIDOS.SYS automatically relocates this code to the bottom of conventional memory in order to create a contiguous free area near the top. HIDOS .SYS can use the /XBDA parameter in conjunction with the /VIDEO parameter to annex 64K of video memory. The /XBDA parameter disables the default relocation of extended BIOS data for programs that require this code at the top of conventional memory.

/CHIPSET = CHIPSET

This parameter specifies the method HIDOS.SYS uses to gain extra memory on your computer. On 80286 systems, the name of a particular chipset allows DR DOS to borrow shadow RAM. The EMS options allow HIDOS to use expanded memory instead of shadow RAM. The recognized chipsets include AUTO (HIDOS.SYS detects the type of chipset in the machine automatically), NEAT (HIDOS.SYS looks for Chips and Technologies NEAT chipset), SCAT (HIDOS.SYS looks for Chips and Technologies SCAT chipset), EMSUMB (HIDOS.SYS uses EMS 4.0 or EEMS memory), and EMSALL (HIDOS.SYS disables the EMS pageframe, mapping an additional 64K of upper memory but disabling expanded memory for all other programs). When using the EMSUMB option, you must provide the expanded memory first by adding an expanded memory manager to CONFIG.SYS.

The syntax for EMM386.SYS is as follows:

```
DEVICE = [D:][PATH]EMM386.SYS [/FRAME = AUTO|NONE|NNNN]
         [/KB = 0|AUTO|NONE|NNNN] [/AUTOSCAN = MMMM-NNNN]
         [/INCLUDE = MMMM-NNNN] [/EXCLUDE = MMMM-NNNN]
         [/VIDEO[MMMM-NNNN]] [BDOS = AUTO|FFFF|MMMM]
         [/USE = MMMM-NNNN] [/ROM = AUTO|MMMM-NNNN|NONE]
         [/COMPAQ] [/LOWEMM] [/XBDA] [/WINSTD]
```

The /AUTOSCAN, /INCLUDE, /EXCLUDE, /VIDEO, /BDOS, /USE, /ROM, and /XBDA parameters have the same use and syntax as listed for HIDOS.SYS. The additional parameters provide the following features:

/FRAME = XXXX	This parameter controls the location of the EMS pageframe in upper memory. XXXX can have the following values: AUTO (lets DR DOS scan upper memory and assign a pageframe address automatically), NONE (disables support for expanded memory), and NNNN (specifies a hexadecimal upper memory starting address for the EMS pageframe). The NONE option provides an additional 64K of upper memory to use as high RAM for loading drivers and TSRs.
/KB =	Specifies the amount of expanded memory allocated to applications.
/COMPAQ	Makes an extra 256K of extended memory available by reclaiming Shadow RAM on COMPAQ 80386 and 80486 systems.
/LOWEMM	Instructs DR DOS to load the bulk of the code for the EMM386.SYS driver into conventional memory instead of the default, which is to load about 24K of EMM386 into upper memory.
/WINSTD	Allows Windows 3.0 to run in its Standard Mode while EMM386 provides expanded memory for other programs.

Conclusion

Now that you've reached the end of this chapter, you might want to re-examine Table 8-1, Table 8-2, and Table 8-3, which all display a features list and series of benchmarks for all of the advanced memory management packages examined. The data provided by the charts reflects the rigorous testing procedure used to stretch each memory manager to its limits. Most users won't tax these packages to the extent that these tests did performing everyday tasks. Any of the top three, QEMM, 386MAX or NETROOM will meet the average user's needs, yet the results set the performance of the various memory managers in perspective.

This chapter concludes Part Two of this book on PC operating strategies. In the next part, "Enhancing Productivity with Multitasking," we'll see how to apply the memory management techniques we've learned to multitasking systems like Microsoft Windows and DESQview and also present strategies for fine tuning multitasking systems in networked environments.

9
CHAPTER

Multitasking with Microsoft Windows

How do you configure your memory management software for Windows? Specific configurations can lead to improved Windows application performance. Other strategies can increase the memory available to multitask DOS applications.

What are the differences in the three Windows operating modes? Each mode can provide you with an edge in using DOS applications. Enhanced mode is best for 80386 and above machines, while 80286 machines normally use Standard mode.

How does Windows perform on 80286 versus 80386 and higher systems?

Use Windows' multitasking capabilities to improve your productivity.

Specific strategies for coordinating Windows and DOS applications to build a productive environment.

Comments about Windows

A lot of people feel that Windows is either too unstable, too slow, or too difficult to use. Except for the last complaint, most of these problems are not based on Windows' capabilities but on inadequate or incomplete installation and optimization. The focus of this chapter is not only to help you get the best performance and stability from Windows but to show you how you can use it as well. Like many multitasking environments, Windows is an order of magnitude harder to install than DOS. However, the results are well worth the effort you expend.

Preparing DOS for Windows

Your first step in preparing to use Windows efficiently is to prepare DOS. The better you prepare DOS, the easier it is for you to set up Windows. Of course, you must consider the obvious things that affect both DOS and Windows like AUTOEXEC.BAT and CONFIG.SYS; the settings in these two files are probably the most important. Then come the subtle considerations. For example, while DOS is relatively impervious to TSRs, how will Windows react to a character mode TSR popping up over its graphics display? Is it even important to load the TSR before you start Windows? Another subtle area is the settings you use with disk caches. Using the same setting with Windows that you use for DOS might prove less than optimal. These are low-key issues you must consider to obtain maximum performance and stability from Windows.

Setting up CONFIG.SYS and AUTOEXEC.BAT

Getting great performance from either DOS or Windows requires a little work with both the CONFIG.SYS and AUTOEXEC.BAT files. For example, how many files and buffers do you need to allocate in a standard DOS environment versus a Windows environment? Some people would simply use the same setup for both environments, never realizing that Windows has special needs that DOS doesn't.

Let's start with the number of files. Because DOS is a single tasking environment, it usually doesn't require a large number of files. After all, how many files will the average single application open? (Many database managers open a lot of files, even in a single tasking environment.) Windows, on the other hand, is a multitasking environment. As a result, you could have many programs open simultaneously, which causes a need to set the number of files higher.

For example, say you were able to run four programs concurrently, and each program opened three files (one for the program itself, one for an overlay file, and a third for a data file), then you would need a minimum of 25 files. (DOS requires five of the files and Windows requires at least eight in Standard mode.) Because most applications are not satisfied opening a paltry three files, you can see that the number of files required grows quickly. Many Windows installations can achieve a good balance between memory usage and flexibility by allocating between 50 and 70 files. Depending on the applications you run, you might need to allocate an even greater number of files.

Note   Using a utility like the one supplied with QEMM to load files in AUTO EXEC.BAT might cause problems with Windows. Microsoft recommends placing at least 20 files in CONFIG.SYS to allow Windows to start properly. You may use a memory manager utility to augment the minimum of 20 files loaded in CONFIG.SYS.

Now that we have had a chance to look at the number of files, let's look at the number of buffers you must allocate—a question much more complex than it first appears. Many people automatically say that you need a higher number of buffers with Windows than with DOS, but this is only true if you don't plan to use a disk cache with Windows. The truth of the matter is that the number of buffers needed varies with the type and number of other devices you have installed. For example, if you use a high speed disk cache, then it is probably better to allocate only a few buffers (10, unless the vendor recommends a specific number of buffers). Allocating a larger number of buffers will actually result in poorer, not better performance from Windows.

You must also consider the size of any permanent swap file you create. The larger the swap file, the more RAM that will appear in the Windows About dialog box and the more disk accesses that Windows will make. While it might first appear that you could achieve better performance by allocating more buffers (or a larger disk cache), you must consider the point of diminishing returns. Because the disk cache uses RAM that Windows would otherwise use for applications, you must experiment to find the point where increasing the size of a disk cache no longer produces an equivalent increase in performance.

Of course, there are some CONFIG.SYS and AUTOEXEC.BAT entries that remain the same no matter which environment you use. For example, you normally use the SHELL statement in CONFIG.SYS to either load a replacement for COMMAND.COM (see Chapter 7) or to change the parameters of the standard command processor. For example, SHELL = COMMAND.COM /E:1024 /P allocates a 1024-byte area for the environment (the place used to store the path and SET statements in AUTOEXEC.BAT). Many people use the same environment for DOS and Windows, just combining the requirements of both. However, you can save a few bytes of RAM by keeping the environments separate. In almost every case, the Windows path and SET statements are larger than those used by DOS, which means that Windows requires a larger environment as well.

Windows 3.1 will introduce yet another factor in the decision of how many buffers to allocate. This version provides an advanced 32-bit access driver that runs in protected mode, bypassing DOS. As a result, the number of buffers you allocate will not affect performance at all. Every access to the disk drive is intercepted by the protected mode driver. Of course, this will probably affect most disk caches as well. If the disk cache provides an option to use one amount of memory when you're in DOS and another when you're in Windows, then you should probably set the amount of memory in Windows to zero. Both PC Kwik 2.1 & higher and SuperDRV provide this capability. (This assumes that you have at least 30 buffers allocated in CONFIG.SYS.)

Loading applications high

Many people automatically load as many of their favorite TSRs and device drivers as high as possible when invoking a DOS session. To make the best use of Windows and its capabilities, you have to follow a different strategy. Because Windows can use the load high area to good advantage in speeding up some routines, you must balance the need to conserve conventional memory with the need to provide Windows with as much memory as possible. Instead of loading programs high or in conventional memory, you could start them within a DOS window after you start Windows. In this way, you still get access to your DOS programs without penalizing Windows' use of conventional and high memory.

You can call some of your favorite TSRs (PC Tools Shell, Sidekick, etc.) from within Windows. One advantage to this approach is that you don't suffer the problems inherent with TSR usage. Each program uses its own DOS session and loads into a conventional memory area. In fact, some programs like PC Tools automatically create the PIF files, Groups, and other files you need to implement this strategy. Even if your program doesn't provide these files automatically, you can create them using the utilities provided by Windows. (See the following section on understanding PIF files.) Other programs—including device drivers like mouse drivers and ANSI.SYS—should be loaded before Windows because the device driver affects the operation of hardware required by Windows as well as the DOS sessions you might open within Windows. Remember this when deciding whether or not to load a TSR or device driver before you enter Windows.

The decision of whether or not to load programs high before entering Windows is fairly easy. All you need to do is decide whether you want Windows to use more high memory to optimize for speed or provide more conventional memory for DOS applications. If conventional memory is the main emphasis, then you will want to load as many device drivers and TSRs as possible high. Otherwise, load only enough programs high to provide the conventional memory required by your DOS applications within Windows.

Using a third-party memory manager

The decision to use a third-party memory manager is fairly easy if you use versions of DOS older than 5.0. However, DOS 5.0 makes the decision a little more difficult. The question you need to ask yourself is whether DOS 5.0 is providing the level of performance and flexibility that you need to get the job done. For example, you might find QEMM necessary if you plan to launch DOS-extended applications in Windows' Standard Mode, while 386MAX or NETROOM might be a better choice if you plan to run multiple DOS sessions that require device instancing (such as setting multiple ANSI.SYS definitions). You might even want to consider using QEMM's Stealth capability to obtain maximum memory. Unfortunately, Stealth will slow Windows down by about 10% on disk and screen writes. However, the capabilities inherent in DOS 5.0 provide the least expensive solution, at least in the short term. Whether or not you will ever recoup the expense (both in cost and setup time) of using a third-party memory manager is a decision you need to base on the complexity of your environment and the performance you expect from Windows.

Using Smartdrive Smartdrive is the disk cache provided with Windows. You can load it by placing a statement like C:\WINDOWS\SMARTDRV in AUTOEXEC.BAT. The version of Smartdrive provided with Windows 3.1 uses the command line parameters shown in Table 9-1.

You start Smartdrive as follows:

```
SMARTDRV [[/E:ELEMENTSIZE] [/B:BUFFERSIZE] [DRIVE [+]|[-]]
         [SIZE] [WINSIZE]]...
```

Table 9-1   Smartdrive command line parameters.

Parameter	Description
/E: *Element Size*	Specifies the size of the cache elements in bytes. You can use this parameter to optimize the cache. For example, if you tend to use a lot of applications with small files, then you might want the cache to read one cluster of data at a time. Many of the utilities mentioned in previous chapters can provide this parameter for you. In most cases, it is a value of 2048 bytes for MFM drives. If you use a lot of large files in your applications, then reading an entire track at once might be more efficient. For example, if your driver uses 17 sectors per track (all MFM drives), then you would use a value of 8704 bytes.
/B: *Buffer Size*	Specifies the size of the read buffer in bytes. In most cases, you'll want to leave this parameter at its default value.
Drive + *Add Drive*	Tells Smartdrive which drives you want to cache.
Drive - *Subtract Drive*	Tells Smartdrive which drives you do not want cached.
Size	Specifies the amount of XMS memory (in K) to use while in DOS. Always makes this value a multiple of the element size. For example, if you wanted to cache 480 tracks of data on an MFM drive, then you would specify

Table 9-1 Continued

Parameter	Description
	a size of 4080K. Smartdrive appears to work best with a cache size between 2M and 4M, although performance will vary based on your machine type and installed memory.
Windows Size	Specifies how much XMS memory (in K) you want Smartdrive to use within Windows. Always makes this value a multiple of the element size. For example, if you wanted to cache 512 clusters of data on a standard MFM drive, you would specify a value of 1024K. Smartdrive appears to work best with a cache size between 1M and 4M within Windows, although performance will vary based on your machine type and installed memory. The standard arrangement is to use 1/2 the memory you use under DOS for Windows. Always weigh the performance increase you'll receive from Smartdrive against the memory requirements of the applications you run under Windows.
/C Clear Buffer	Tells Smartdrive to write all data in the cache to the hard drive.
/R Reset Buffer	Tells Smartdrive to write all data in the cache to the hard drive, clear all data contained in the buffer, and restart Smartdrive.
/L Load Smartdrive Low	Normally Smartdrive loads into upper memory, if possible. This parameter allows you to load Smartdrive in low memory and reserve upper memory for other drivers and TSRs.
/Q Quiet	Suppresses the display of loading information on screen.
/S Status	Displays the number of cache hits and misses on screen along with the standard Smartdrive status information.

The version of Smartdrive provided with Windows 3.0 didn't perform as well as many third-party disk caches. As a result, many people replaced it with products like PC Kwik. The version of Smartdrive provided with Windows 3.1 is much faster than its predecessor and is designed to fully integrate itself with the Windows 3.1 environment. It even comes with a program for monitoring cache efficiency within Windows. The monitoring program allows you to change cache configuration and to flush the cache to disk. As a result, you will probably not need to use a third-party manager if you plan to use Windows 3.1 exclusively. (You may still want a third-party manager if you plan to use a combination of DOS and Windows.)

Understanding 32-bit drive access

Windows 3.1 provides a new feature called 32-bit access. The following paragraphs provide a complete picture of how this feature can affect the multitasking
environment provided by Windows. However, before we examine how 32-bit
access affects your computing environment, we'll explain what it is.

If you tried to figure out what 32-bit access is by its name, you might suspect
that it's some new technique for accessing the data on your drive 32 bits at a time.
What 32-bit access actually provides is a little more complex, however. Figure 9-1
shows the hard disk drive access method used by Windows in a standard configuration.

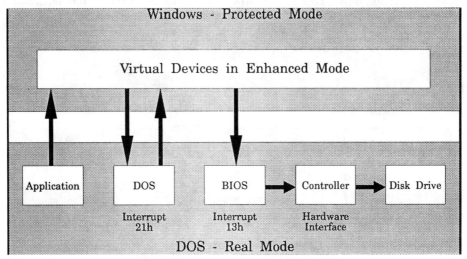

Fig. 9-1   Windows hard drive access method using standard configuration.

Every time an application requests data from the hard drive, Windows intercepts the request to see if it can fulfill it. Usually this request asks to open a file or
requests specific byte ranges of data. Once Windows determines that it can't fulfill
the request, it switches to real mode and passes the request to the DOS interrupt
21h handler. This handler looks at the request and starts to take care of it by issuing interrupt 13h requests. You can look at interrupt 21h as the manager and interrupt 13h as the worker. Interrupt 21h gets the whole problem in one big chunk. It
breaks the problem up into chunks that interrupt 13h can handle. As a result, each
interrupt 21h call can result in a lot of interrupt 13h calls.

Once again, Windows intercepts each interrupt 13h call and sees if it can handle it. If not, Windows switches back to real mode and allows the BIOS to handle
the call. The BIOS performs the work required to fulfill the call and passes the
information back to Windows, which passes it back to DOS, which passes back to
Windows, which finally passes it back to the application.

This is a lot of work to go through to open a file or read a few bytes of data from the hard drive. The worst part, though, is that this is only a portion of the problem. Even though Windows is supposed to multitask, everything stops during a disk access because Windows switches to real mode to allow DOS and the BIOS to handle the call. This means that you really multitask when there is no disk activity—not all the time.

Figure 9-2 shows the new 32-bit access method used by Windows. Notice that the BIOS is completely cut out of the picture. That's because FastDisk emulates the BIOS using protected mode code. This means that you not only eliminate two mode transitions but that you can effectively multitask during more of the disk access cycle. We only lose the DOS processing time instead of both DOS and BIOS processing time. This improvement accounts for part of the noticeable speed-up in Windows 3.1.

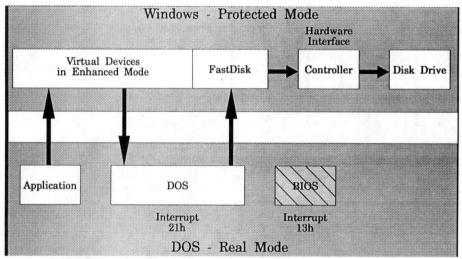

Fig. 9-2   Windows hard drive access method using 32-bit access.

Knowing if you can use 32-bit access

Because the 32-bit driver is not automatically installed, you can probably assume that you're not using it if you didn't install it. You can also check the status of this feature by running the 386 Enhanced option of the Control Panel. The Virtual Memory option displays a dialog box similar to the one shown in Fig. 9-3. The type entry tells you what type of swap file Windows is using (temporary or permanent) and whether or not Windows is using 32-bit access to speed disk access.

Determining whether or not you can use 32-bit access is relatively easy. Simply select the Change button and the additional information shown in Fig. 9-4 appears. Notice the "Use 32-bit Access" check box in the lower left corner of the display. If you see this entry highlighted, then you can use 32-bit access to greatly

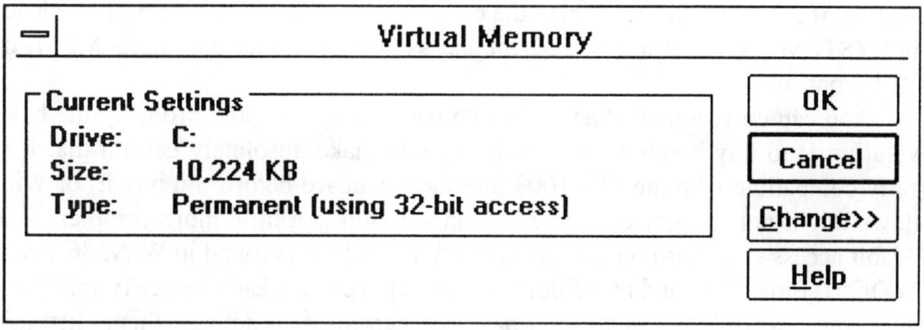

```
┌─────────────────────────────────────────────────────────────┐
│ ──│              Virtual Memory                              │
│  ┌─ Current Settings ──────────────────────┐  ┌───────────┐ │
│  │  Drive:   C:                            │  │    OK     │ │
│  │  Size:    10,224 KB                     │  ├───────────┤ │
│  │  Type:    Permanent (using 32-bit access) │ │  Cancel   │ │
│  │                                         │  ├───────────┤ │
│  └─────────────────────────────────────────┘  │ Change>>  │ │
│                                                ├───────────┤ │
│                                                │   Help    │ │
│                                                └───────────┘ │
└─────────────────────────────────────────────────────────────┘
```

Fig. 9-3   Windows Virtual Memory Configuration dialog box.

```
┌─────────────────────────────────────────────────────────────┐
│ ▷─│                                                          │
│  ┌─ Current Settings ──────────────────────┐  ┌───────────┐ │
│  │  Drive:   C:                            │  │    OK     │ │
│  │  Size:    5,112 KB                      │  ├───────────┤ │
│  │  Type:    Permanent (using 32-bit access) │ │  Cancel   │ │
│  │                                         │  ├───────────┤ │
│  └─────────────────────────────────────────┘  │ Change>>  │ │
│                                                ├───────────┤ │
│                                                │   Help    │ │
│  ┌─ New Settings ──────────────────────────┐  └───────────┘ │
│  │                                         │                │
│  │  Drive:   │▭ c: [john's data]       │▼│ │                │
│  │  Type:    │ Temporary                │▼│ │                │
│  │                                         │                │
│  │  Space Available:          106,116 KB   │                │
│  │  Recommended Maximum Size:  19,696 KB   │                │
│  │                                         │                │
│  │  New Size:              │ 19696 │ KB    │                │
│  └─────────────────────────────────────────┘                │
│  ☒ Use 32-Bit Disk Access                                   │
└─────────────────────────────────────────────────────────────┘
```

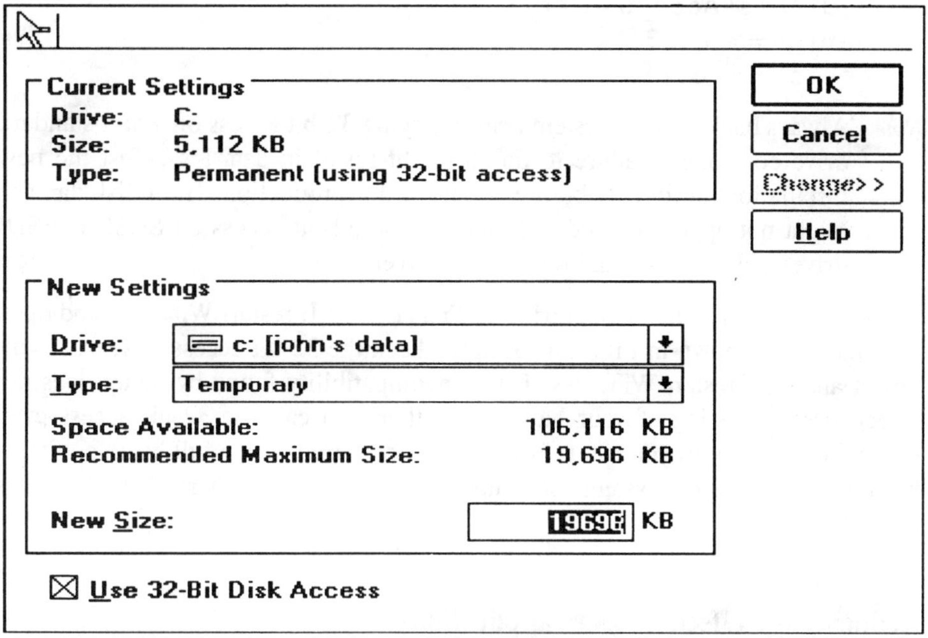

Fig. 9-4   Windows Change Virtual Memory Configuration dialog box.

enhance the performance of Windows, especially if you use a lot of DOS applications.

There are a few rules of thumb that you need to know about 32-bit access. First, Microsoft is working with most hard drive manufacturers to produce the drivers required for every hard drive currently available. Unfortunately, the current driver only works with IDE, MFM, and most RLL drives coupled with a Western Digital controller. The important factor is the controller. Many controller cards claim Western Digital compatibility but do not fully implement Western Digital's standard WD 1003 interface. As a result, the Window's Setup program does not recognize the controller or the drive during Windows installation. Of course, if Setup doesn't recognize the controller, it won't make the proper entries in SYSTEM.INI for you to use 32-bit access even if you have an IDE, MFM, or RLL controller.

You can correct this situation in two ways. The first (and probably the best) solution is to buy a new controller card. Just make absolutely certain that it is fully compatible with the WD 1003 interface standard before you buy it, or Windows might not recognize it. The second solution is a little more complex. The 32-bit access system is composed of three virtual devices found in WIN386.EXE: WDCtrl, BlockDev, and PageFile. The actual purpose of each device is unimportant; you must only worry about what you need to do to activate them. Just add three entries to SYSTEM.INI as follows:

```
32BitDiskAccess=off
device=*int13
device=wdctrl
```

Note Always back up your system prior to trying 32-bit access on a non-standard drive controller. Failure to do so might result in data loss. Test the new installation thoroughly before you use it for production. Hard disk damage might not appear immediately. Never use 32-bit access on SCSI or ESDI drives unless you install the proper driver.

Once you place the three entries in SYSTEM.INI, restart Windows and open the dialog box shown in Fig. 9-4. Simply check the 32-bit access box, exit Windows, and then restart Windows. If the incompatibility found by Setup does not affect the functioning of your hard drive, then you can use 32-bit access even though Windows says you can't. However, be prepared with a full backup of your hard drive in case the system locks up, or worse yet, your hard drive becomes corrupted.

Reducing the effects of DOS applications

Prior to 32-bit access, every DOS application had to remain in physical memory at all times. Windows could not use virtual memory management techniques on DOS programs. The reason is simple: you can't determine exactly when a DOS program will request data from the hard drive. Because of this, you can't ensure the integrity of the Windows environment either.

For example, if Windows places part of the data area a DOS application is using on the hard disk, and then the DOS application decides to get some information from the hard drive and place it in this data area, the DOS application will actually end up writing over another application. Of course, the logical answer would be to pause the DOS application, read the data area from the hard drive, and replace it in memory. While this works fine in theory, however, it doesn't work in practice. DOS and the system BIOS are not re-entrant—you can only run one copy at a time. Therefore, even if Windows detected that the DOS application wanted to write to its data area, it could not read the data area from disk and place it back in memory; the DOS and BIOS routines are already in use by the application.

This whole scenario changes when you use 32-bit access. Because the BIOS gets replaced by a protected mode driver, you can pause the application and get whatever it needs from disk before letting it write to memory. The 32-bit driver supplied with Windows is fully re-entrant. Windows can safely use virtual memory management techniques with DOS applications, even if they are active in the background. Thus, you cannot only load more DOS applications into memory, but these applications will run more reliably and much faster as well. 32-bit access allows Windows to maintain firmer control over the DOS applications you ask it to manage.

Understanding the About box

The About box is more than a dialog box telling you the name of a program, its creator, and the version you're using; it also tells you a lot about the current memory status of Windows. Figure 9-5 shows a typical Enhanced Mode About box. You should know about three entries.

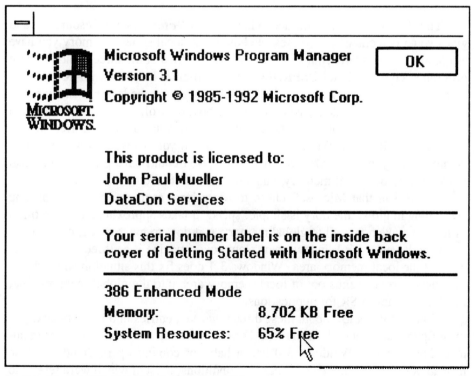

Fig. 9-5   Windows Enhanced Mode About dialog box.

The first entry is the Windows mode. Windows 3.0 has three modes: Real, Standard, and Enhanced. Real mode uses only conventional memory and does not support multitasking or virtual memory. Standard mode uses both conventional and extended memory but does not support multitasking or virtual memory. Enhanced mode uses conventional, extended, and virtual memory, and it also supports true multitasking. Windows 3.1 supports only Standard and Enhanced modes. In essence, the loss of real mode support allowed the developers at Microsoft to provide a more stable environment for this release. The mode tells you how your environment is configured and what capabilities your environment possesses.

The second entry you need to know about is memory, which doesn't necessarily represent the amount of physical RAM you have in your machine but the amount of virtual memory available for applications. The distinction is less important if you can make use of 32-bit access for DOS applications but is of paramount importance otherwise. Because Windows must keep all DOS applications physically loaded in RAM without 32-bit access, you can get an "Out of memory" error message even though the About box says that you have plenty of virtual memory left. What this means is that if you have 4M of RAM on your machine, you can probably run six 512K DOS sessions without running out of memory. (This assumes that you have not loaded a disk cache or other extended memory program.)

The third entry is a little deceiving. It says "Free System Resources" and gives you a percentage that represents how much local system memory you have available. This is a 64K chunk of memory used by two of the three Windows core programs: GDI.EXE and USER.EXE. Each program has its own 64K data segment (the local system memory). The About box reports the lesser of the two percentages. Every icon, menu, window, dialog box, control, cursor, and bitmap you see in Windows is stored in these segments. If you run out of free system resources (FSR), then Windows will lock up and you'll lose everything you've created since your last save. In other words, you could have plenty of physical RAM, plenty of virtual memory, and still run out of resources.

The reason that Microsoft chose to use a local segment instead of placing everything in global memory is simple: speed. It takes approximately three times as long to make a far call to global memory as it does to make a near call to local memory. If you think Windows runs slow now, imagine it as three times slower without the local memory area. Windows 3.1 does fix this situation somewhat—Microsoft moved menus out of local memory area into the global memory area, resulting in more FSR for applications.

Now that you know about these three important entries in the About box, you must figure out what to do with them. For one, these three entries can act as monitors. For example, Windows 3.0 had a habit of coming up in Standard mode instead of Enhanced mode under certain conditions, most of which were related to the memory manager you used. By checking the About box, you could ensure that Windows comes up in the correct mode. If it doesn't, then you can start to troubleshoot the cause. Checking both the memory and FSR entries can help you avoid system crashes. If you're running low on either quantity, you can close an application before starting a new one.

You can also use the memory and FSR indicators to balance your Windows environment. For example, if you consistently find that you run low on FSRs and still have a lot of memory left, you might want to reduce the amount of virtual memory by changing the size of your swap file. This will free some FSR and reduce the amount of system overhead required to manage the swap space. You can also increase your FSRs by reducing the number of groups in program manager and eliminating unnecessary programs from each group. Then your system will run faster and use less resources to perform the same tasks.

Optimizing WIN.INI

WIN.INI is the Windows environment initialization file. In other words, it's the file that most directly affects the appearance and usability of your Windows environment. For example, all the color and sound settings for Windows appear in WIN.INI. It is also the file that produces the most visible system performance enhancements. This doesn't mean that these enhancements will produce the greatest actual change; they are simply the ones that you'll notice. In fact, many of the parameters in SYSTEM.INI produce better results once you optimize them.

Table 9-2 provides a listing and description of the most common WIN.INI entries. (Almost every application you install will make some changes to WIN.INI as well.) In some cases, you can change these entries using one of the programs in the control panel or by changing the defaults of your applications. In other cases, you will need to make the changes using a text editor like Notepad. Never use a word processor that produces formatted files as an editor; the WIN.INI file must remain in ASCII text format.

One of the problem areas experienced by users is the time required to boot Windows. Part of this problem might stem from an excess of entries in your WIN.INI file. Windows reads and acts on every line in the file, even if the application that created it is no longer active. Unfortunately, while every Windows application provides an installation program, few provide a deinstallation program. As a result, all the entries that the program made in WIN.INI remain after you remove the program from your drive. Carefully editing WIN.INI to remove these entries can often improve overall execution speed of Windows, albeit slightly.

You can make other enhancements through WIN.INI. For example, you will notice a significant speed improvement if you refrain from using wallpaper or patterns as a background. Windows refreshes the background even if it is not visible.

Table 9-2 WIN.INI standard entries.

Entry	Description
Windows	
Beep = *[Yes|No]*	This entry determines if Windows sounds a beep when you make an error.
BorderWidth = *<Number>*	This entry determines the width of the border around all windows. 1 is the narrowest width, while 49 is the widest.
CoolSwitch = *[0|1]*	(Windows 3.1.) Use this entry to control fast switching (Alt-Tab). The default is 1, which enables fast switching. Disabling fast switching may clear some control key conflicts with DOS programs. It may provide you with some additional memory as well. Of course, this will greatly increase the time required to go from one task to another as well.
CursorBlinkRate = *<ms>*	Specifies the cursor blink rate in milliseconds.
DefaultQueueSize = *<number>*	(Windows 3.1) This entry determines the number of messages an applications message queue can hold. Windows uses messages to tell an application when it has data to process or when it has the input focus. An application must respond to many messages. The queue holds these messages until the application has time to service them. Decreasing the number of message slots could free some memory, but it might also cause the application to hang. You should never need to change this entry.
Device = *<DeviceName>* , *<DeviceDriver>* , *<PortConnection>*	The device entry specifies a printer or other output device, the device driver used to create the output, and the port the device is connected to.
DeviceNotSelectedTimeout = *<Seconds>*	Determines how long Windows will wait between the time an output request is made and the device is turned on (made available for output). If this time lapses, Windows displays an error message stating the device is not available. The default time of 15 seconds is sufficient for a printer attached to a local workstation. You might want to increase this time for network printers.
Documents = *<Extensions>*	(Windows 3.1) Use this entry to increase the number of file extensions that Windows looks at as document files.

For example, you might want to include .ME as a document file. Many vendors include a READ.ME file on disk to reflect the latest changes to a product. Normally this entry is blank. You must manually edit

WIN.INI to add document extensions.

DosPrint = *[Yes|No]*

(Windows 3.1) Determines if Windows uses DOS interrupts or prints directly to the printer port. Using DOS interrupts might reduce compatibility problems with some printers. However, like 32-bit access, direct printing greatly enhances Windows ability to monitor the printer and increases overall execution speed. The default setting is no; do not use DOS interrupts.

DoubleClickHeight = *<Pixel>*
DoubleClickWidth = *<Pixel>*

(Windows 3.1) Use this entry to set the distance the mouse cursor can move between clicks on a double click. For example, if you set the distance to two pixels and move the mouse cursor three between clicks, Windows will count the clicks as two separate clicks even if you meet the double click time requirement. The default setting is 4 pixels.

DoubleClickSpeed = *<ms>*

Determines the maximum number of milliseconds that can elapse between the clicks of a double click. The default setting is 452 milliseconds.

DragFullWindow = *[0|1]*

(Windows 3.1) Setting this value to 1 tells Windows to display the full Window rather than a gray outline when you drag it. The default setting is 0 (show gray outline only). You must edit WIN.INI manually to change the setting. However, displaying the full image rather than an outline will adversely affect the speed of your application, especially tasks running in the background. Using the gray outline is much faster.

KeyboardDelay = *<ms>*

(Windows 3.1) Determines the number of milliseconds you must hold a keyboard key down before it begins to repeat. The default setting is 2 milliseconds.

KeyboardSpeed = *<ms>*

Determines the number of milliseconds between repetitions of a key when you press the key down. This setting does not work with all keyboards. The default setting is 31 milliseconds between keys.

Load = *<Filenames>*

Tells Windows which programs to automatically execute as icons. These program run before the programs in your start up group in Windows 3.1. You must manually edit WIN.INI to add programs to this list. Some programs automatically install a program in the list. (For example, PC Tools Deluxe automatically install the TSR Manager in this list.) In many cases you can install a

Table 9-2   Continued

Entry	Description
	program more easily using the start up group in Windows 3.1. You can change the run minimized property to run the program as an icon.
MenuDropAlignment = *[0 | 1]*	(Windows 3.1) Specifies whether menus open right or left aligned with the menu title. The default of 0 opens menus left aligned. A setting of 1 opens menus right aligned. You must manually edit WIN.INI to change this setting.
MouseSpeed = *[0 | 1 | 2]*	Determines how Windows accelerates the mouse for a given level of movement. A value of 0 never accelerates the mouse. A value of 1 accelerates the mouse to twice normal speed when mouse speed reaches MouseThreshold1. A value of 2 accelerates the mouse to twice normal speed when mouse speed reaches MouseThreshold1 and four times normal speed the mouse speed reaches MouseThreshold2.
MouseThreshold1 = *< Pixels >* MouseThreshold2 = *< Pixels >*	Determines the level at which the mouse cursor speed accelerates with regard to mouse movement.
MouseTrails = *< Number >*	(Windows 3.1) Specifies the number of mouse pointers displayed when you select the mouse trails option in the control panel. You may select from a range of 1 to seven pointers. The mouse trails option will not appear in the control panel until you add this entry to WIN.INI. This option is only applicable to EGA, VGA and Super VGA displays. Using mouse trails does not significantly impact Windows application execution speed, but it does affect it slightly.
NetWarn = *[0 | 1]*	Setting this parameter to 0 suppresses the network warning message that normally appears when Windows is setup to run a network, and either the wrong network is running or no network is running at all. The default value is 1.
NullPort = *< String >*	Use this entry to specify the port name used for a null port. This is the name that appears in the Printers-Configure dialog box when you install an output device, but do not assign it a port.
Programs = *< Extension >*	This entry tells Windows which file extensions it should treat as executable programs. The default extensions are: BAT, EXE, COM, and PIF. You must manually edit WIN.INI to change this entry.
Run = *< Filenames >*	Use this entry to tell Windows which programs to run on start up. While you had to use this entry with Windows 3.0, it is far easier to use the start up group in Windows 3.1.

ScreenSaveActive = [0 | 1]

(Windows 3.1) Determines if the screen saver supplied with Windows 3.1 is active. Setting this value to 0 turns off the screen saver (the default condition).

ScreenSaveTimeOut = <Secs>

Specifies the timeout period for the screen saver in seconds. For example, if you set this value to 60, then the screen saver becomes active after 1 minute of keyboard and mouse inactivity.

Spooler = [Yes | No]

Setting this value to 0 deactivates the Print Manager.

SwapMouseButton = [0 | 1]

Provides the means for exchanging the right and left mouse buttons. The default setting is 0.

TransmissionRetryTimeout = <Secs>

Determines the amount of time that Windows will try to send information to the printer. If Windows is not successful within the specified time, then it displays an error message on screen. The default setting is 45 seconds. In most cases you can reduce this setting to 30, effectively reducing the time you must wait for an error indication. Network setups might require a longer interval.

Desktop

GridGranularity = <Number>

Specifies the grid size Windows uses to position Windows on the display. The default setting is 0. The range is from 0 to 49 pixels in units of 8 pixels.

IconSpacing = <Pixels>

Determines the spacing between icons in pixels. The default setting is 77.

IconTitleFaceName = <Font>

(Windows 3.1) This entry determines the typeface used for icon titles. The default setting is MS Sans Serif. You must change the setting by editing WIN.INI manually.

IconTitleSize = <Number>

(Windows 3.1) This entry determines the size of the typeface used for icon titles in points. The default size is 8.

IconTitleWrap = [0 | 1]

(Windows 3.1) Determines whether Windows wraps icon titles that will not fit on one line. The default setting of 1 sets this feature on.

IconVerticalSpacing = <Pixels>

(Windows 3.1) Determines the vertical spacing between icons. Windows uses a default value based on the size and type font you use for the icon title. You must manually edit WIN.INI to change this setting.

MenuHideDelay = <ms>

(Windows 3.1) Specifies the time interval Windows waits before it hides a cascading menu. The default is 0

Table 9-2   Continued

Entry	Description
	milliseconds for an **80386** computer and **400** milliseconds for an **80286** computer. You must manually edit WIN.INI to change this setting.
MenuShowDelay = *<ms>*	(Windows 3.1) Specifies the time interval Windows waits before it displays a cascading menu. The default is **0** milliseconds for an **80386** computer and **400** milliseconds for an **80286** computer. You must manually edit WIN.INI to change this setting.
Pattern = *<b1> <b2> <b3> <b4> <b5> <b6> <b7> <b8>*	(Windows 3.1) Defines a bitmap pattern for the screen background. The bitmap is eight pixels high by eight pixels wide Each entry represents 1 row of the bitmap. A 1 in a bit position turns on the foreground color, while a 0 turns on the background color.
Wallpaper = *<Filename>*	Specifies the bitmap filename used as a screen background.
WallpaperOriginX = *<Coord>* WallpaperOriginY = *<Coord>*	(Windows 3.1) Allows you to adjust the starting offset for tiled wallpaper. X is the left side of the display, Y is the top of the display. The default setting is 0 for both coordinates. You must manually edit WIN.INI to change this setting.

Extensions

<Extension> = *<Command Line>*	Each entry contains a file extension and the command line to execute for that extension. For example, if you want to include a CorelDRAW! file extension, you would use *CDR = CORELDRW.EXE ^.CDR* as the entry. The carrot (^) replaces the filename with the filename you double click. You may only enter one line per extension. Some programs enter these extensions automatically.

Intl

Entry	Description
iCountry = *<Country>*	Specifies the country code.
iCurrDigits = *<Number>*	Specifies the number of digits to put after the decimal separator in currency.
iCurrency = *<Number>*	Specifies a currency format.
iDate = *<Number>*	Specifies a numerical date format for compatibility with Windows 2.x

iDigits = *<Number>*	Specifies the number of digits to display after the decimal separator in numbers.
iLZero = *[0|1]*	Specifies whether to put leading zeros in decimal numbers. 1 is the default of no leading zeros.
iMeasure = *[0|1]*	Specifies the measurement systems as metric or English. 1 is the default of English measurement.
iNegCurr = *<Number>*	Specifies a negative number format.
iTime = *<Number>*	Specifies whether to format time using a 12-hour or 24-hour clock.
iTLZero = *<Number>*	Specifies whether to put leading zeros in time.
s1159 = *<String>*	Specifies the string that follows times before noon in the 12-hour time format.
s2359 = *<String>*	Specifies the string that follows times after noon in the 12-hour format or that follows all times in the 24-hour format.
sCountry = *<String>*	Specifies the name of the country whose standard value you want to use.
sCurrency = *<String>*	Specifies the currency symbol you want to use.
sDecimal = *<String>*	Specifies the punctuation used to separate the fractional part of a decimal number from the whole number part.
sLanguage = *<String>*	Specifies the language you use. Windows applications that provide language specific tasks, such as sorting or spell checking use this entry.
sList = *<String>*	Specifies the character used to separate items in a list. The most common separator in US English is the comma.
sLongDate = *<Date>* sShortDate = *<Date>*	Specifies your choices for the long and short date formats. This includes abbreviations for the words and different separators. Windows will only accept certain picture combinations. Therefore, you should always use the control panel to change this entry.
sThousand = *<String>*	Specifies the symbol used to separate thousands. For example, the US uses the comma, while many European countries use the period.
sTime = *<String>*	Specifies the character used to separate the hours, minutes, and seconds in time. Most countries use the colon as a separator.

Table 9-2 Continued

Entry	Description

Ports

<PortName> : = *<Baud-Rate>* , *<Parity>* , *<Word-Length>* , *<Stop-Bits>* [,P]

This section contains a list of port names and their parameters. Normally, only the communications (COM) ports contain any information. Applicable ports include: COMx:, LPTx:, EPTx: (IBM specific printers), FILE: = (or a filename with a PRN extension), LPTx.DOS (for a parallel printer that bypasses Windows handling).

Fonts

<FontName> = *<Filename>*

Specifies the font name used by Windows and the font file that contains the description for that font. Never change this entry manually.

FontSubstitutes

<FontName> = *<FontName>*

(Windows 3.1) Equates the Windows 3.1 font name on the right with the Windows 3.0 font name on the left. This is especially useful for documents that used a font supported by Windows 3.0 but not by 3.1.

TrueType

nonTTCaps = *[0| 1]*

(Windows 3.1) Setting this entry to 1 displays all non-TrueType fonts in all capital letters. 0 is the default setting (display in initial capital letters).

TTEnable = *[0| 1]*

(Windows 3.1) Determines if Windows applications can access TrueType fonts. The default setting of 1 enables all Windows applications to use TrueType fonts.

TTOnly = *[0| 1]*

(Windows 3.1) Setting this entry to 1 disables non-TrueType font usage. The default setting is 0 (use all available fonts).

MCI Extension

<Extension> = *<MCI Driver Name>* (Windows 3.1) Associates a media file with a specific Multimedia Command interface (MCI) driver.

Network

<Port> = *<Network Printer Path>* (Windows 3.1) Associates a port with a network printer path. These connections are restored each time you start Windows.

< Drive > = *< Network Server and Share >*
  (Windows 3.1) Associates a drive (mapped or physical) with a file server and path. These connections are restored each time you start Windows.

Embedding

< Object > = *< Description >* , *< Description >* , *< Program File >* , *< Format >*
  (Windows 3.1) Lists the Object Linking and Embedding (OLE) objects, their descriptions, the programs used to create them, and their format. Never modify this section without using the Registration Info Editor.

Windows Help

M_WindowPosition = *< Number >* , *< Number >* , *< Number >* , *< Number >* , *< Number >*
H_WindowPosition = *< Number >* , *< Number >* , *< Number >* , *< Number >* , *< Number >*
A_WindowPosition = *< Number >* , *< Number >* , *< Number >* , *< Number >* , *< Number >*
C_WindowPosition = *< Number >* , *< Number >* , *< Number >* , *< Number >* , *< Number >*

  (Windows 3.1) These four entries determine the default size and position of the Main Help Window, and the History, Annotate, and Copy dialog boxes. The first two numbers determining the upper left X and Y coordinates. The second two numbers determine the height and width of the window and dialog boxes. The fifth parameter determines if Windows maximizes the window and dialog boxes. A value of 1 maximizes, while a value of zero presents the Main Help Window in its default size. The fifth parameter does not affect the size of the dialog boxes.

IFJumpColor = *< Red Value >* *< Green Value >* *< Blue Value >*
  (Windows 3.1) Specifies the color of text that leads to a new panel of help information located in a different file. You must change this value by manually editing WIN.INI.

IFPopupColor = *< Red Value >* *< Green Value >* *< Blue Value >*
  (Windows 3.1) Specifies the color of text that displays a pop-up panel of help information (glossary definitions) located in a different file. You must change this value by manually editing WIN.INI.

JumpColor = *< Red Value >* *< Green Value >* *< Blue Value >*
  (Windows 3.1) Specifies the color of text that leads to a new panel of help information. You must change this value by manually editing WIN.INI.

MacroColor = *< Red Value >* *< Green Value >* *< Blue Value >*
  (Windows 3.1) Specifies the color of text that executes a help macro. You must change this value by manually editing WIN.INI.

Table 9-2   Continued

Entry	Description

PopupColor = <*Red Value*> <*Green Value*> <*Blue Value*>
> (Windows 3.1) Specifies the color of text that displays a pop-up panel of help information (glossary definitions). You must change this value by manually editing WIN.INI.

Sound

<*System Event*> = <*Filename*>, <*Description*>
> (Windows 3.1) Associates a sound file (WAV format) with a specific system event. The description key name describes the system event.

PrinterPorts

<*Device*> = <*Driver*>, <*Port*>, <*Device Timeout*>,
<*Retry Timeout*>, [<*Other Ports*>..]
> Associates an output device with the driver and parameters required to use it. You may associate a device with more than one driver and output port. The device timeout and retry timeout settings tell Windows how long to wait for device acknowledgment and the interval between retries. Network devices usually require a higher setting than the local defaults of 15 seconds for device timeout and 45 seconds for retry timeout.

Devices

<*Device*> = <*Driver*>, <*Port*> Associates an output device with a driver and port. Windows provides this section for Windows 2.x compatibility purposes.

Programs

<*Program File*> = <*Drive*>: <*Directory*>
> (Windows 3.1) Provides a listing of programs and where Windows can find them. This entry is an alternative to listing every program in the path. Using the program entry increases the DOS window size by reducing the size of the environment variables.

The more complex the background, the longer it takes Windows to refresh it. As a result, all your applications slow down when you use a complex background. Because a pattern requires little memory and less resources to redraw than wallpaper, you might want to use it instead if speed is your main concern but you don't want to see a blank background.

Optimizing SYSTEM.INI

The SYSTEM.INI file initializes the underlying Windows system. In essence, this file directly affects the part of Windows that you can't see. This file contains the controls that determine what screen driver you use, the drivers used to talk with the hardware in your system, and many of the mode-specific settings. Because you can't see much of what goes on with the SYSTEM.INI file, you should make any changes one at a time and observe Windows for any adverse reactions to the change. For example, changing your screen driver can cause compatibility problems with the display adaptor. Windows may still work, but it might not work fully.

Some entries in SYSTEM.INI produce significant increases in speed, one such entry being the 32-bit access examined previously. Other enhancements deal with Windows interface with the hardware. For example, installing a 256-color driver for your display greatly reduces overall system speed. The mathematics of this are simple. If you use a $640 \times 480 \times 16$ color VGA display, Windows moves 153,600 bytes every screen redraw. Using a $640 \times 480 \times 256$ color VGA display means that Windows moves 307,200 bytes every screen redraw. In other words, you effectively double screen redraw time. Because screen redraws are a major source of speed problems in Windows, reducing the number of bytes that Windows must move is a foremost consideration.

On the other hand, many people complain that Windows does not provide the resolution and screen real estate required to fully implement a GUI environment. Alternately, you could install an $800 \times 600 \times 16$ color driver for your Super VGA adaptor. Using this screen configuration, you obtain an incremental increase in resolution while increasing screen redraw time by a mere 56%. (Windows needs to move 240,000 bytes for every redraw on an $800 \times 600 \times 16$ color Super VGA display.) The BigDesk program provided on our utilities diskette is another way to increase your screen real estate. BigDesk creates a grid ranging from 2×2 to 8×8 of virtual screens equivalent to your basic resolution. Using its panning tool, you can place applications or icons on several virtual screens, and then pan to that area when you want to see them.

Table 9-3 presents many of the common SYSTEM.INI files. Unlike WIN.INI, the SYSTEM.INI file receives most of its input directly from the Windows core applications. Some programs like Adobe Type Manager make entries in this file, but these applications are few. As a result, you will find most of the entries that appear in your SYSTEM.INI in the table. Always make changes to SYSTEM.INI using a text editor like Notepad. Never use a word processor that produces formatted files as an editor—the SYSTEM.INI file must remain in ASCII text format.

Table 9-3   SYSTEM.INI standard entries.

Entry	Description
Boot	
286grabber = *<Filename>*	This entry contains the filename of a grabber that makes non-Windows applications visible when you run Windows in standard mode. The default entry is blank.
386grabber = *<Filename>*	This entry contains the filename of a grabber that makes non-Windows applications visible when you run Windows in enhanced mode. The default entry is blank.
CachedFileHandles = *<Number>*	(Windows 3.1) Use this entry to specify the number of most recently used executable (EXE) and dynamic link library (DLL) files to keep open for quick access. The valid range for this entry is 2 to 12 files. Windows uses a default of 12, but you might need to reduce it in some network environments. Some networks limit the number of files that the server can open at one time. Therefore, the server might not have enough file handle capacity to support all 12 open files (besides the application and Windows file handles) at once. You must edit SYSTEM.INI manually to change this setting.
COMM.DRV = *<Filename>*	Determines which serial communication driver that Windows uses. The default setting is blank. You must edit SYSTEM.INI manually to change this setting.
DISPLAY.DRV = *<Filename>*	Specifies the name of the display driver used by Windows. The default setting is blank. Never change this setting manually; always use the Windows Setup program.
<Drivers> = *<Filename>* | *<Alias Name>*	(Windows 3.1) These entries contain the filenames or aliases of DLLs Windows loads during start-up. Each DLL acts as a device driver. Always allow the setup programs provided with your application to change these entries. Making manual changes could have unpredictable results.
FIXEDFON.FON = *<Filename>*	Determines which font file Windows 2.x uses. The default setting is blank. Never change this setting manually; always use the Windows Setup program.
FONTS.FON = *<Filename>*	Determines the proportionally spaced font file used by Windows 3.x. The default setting is blank. Never change this setting manually; always use the Windows Setup program or select the Windows Setup icon from the Main group.

KEYBOARD.DRV = < *Filename* > Specifies the keyboard driver used by Windows. The default setting is blank. Never change this setting manually; always use the Windows Setup program or select the Windows Setup icon from the Main group.

LANGUAGE.DLL = < *Filename* > Specifies the language DLL used for language specific function. If you do not specify a language DLL, Windows uses the built-in US English library. The default setting is blank. Never change this setting manually; always select the International icon from the Control Panel.

MOUSE.DRV = < *Filename* > Specifies the filename of the Windows mouse driver. Never change this setting manually; always use the Windows Setup program or select the Windows Setup icon from the Main group.

NETWORK.DRV = < *Filename* > Specifies the filename of the Windows network driver. Never change this setting manually; always use the Windows Setup program or select the Windows Setup icon from the Main group.

OEMFONTS.FON = < *Filename* > Determines the original equipment manufacturer (OEM) font used with the display driver. Never change this setting manually; always use the Windows Setup program.

Shell = < *Filename* > Determines the shell program displayed when Windows starts. The Windows setup program automatically selects PROGMAN.EXE for this entry. You must manually edit SYSTEM.INI to change this entry.

SOUND.DRV = < *Filename* > Specifies the filename of the Windows sound driver. The default is blank. Never change this setting manually; always select the Sound icon from the Control Panel.

SYSTEM.DRV = < *Filename* > Specifies the filename of the Windows system hardware driver. The default is blank. Never change this setting manually; always use the Windows Setup program.

TASKMAN.EXE = < *Filename* > (Windows 3.1) The task manager is the program used to switch between Windows tasks. Each time you press Ctrl-Esc, the task manager display pops up. The default filename is TASKMAN.EXE. You must edit SYSTEM.INI to change this setting.

Boot.Description

< *String* > This section contains a list of strings that describe devices you can install during setup. Never modify this section.

Drivers

< *alias* > = < *Driver Filename* > [< *Parameters* >]
Each entry associates a driver with an alias. You may

Table 9-3   Continued

Entry	Description
	provide optional parameters for each driver. The intent of this section is to provide a means of describing non-standard drivers. In most cases, the setup program provided with your application makes these entries automatically.

Keyboard

Entry	Description
KEYBOARD.DLL = *< Filename >*	Specifies the filename of the Windows keyboard driver. Never change this setting manually; always use the Windows Setup program, select the International icon from the Control Panel, or select the Windows Setup icon from the Main group.
OEMANSI.BIN = *< Filename >*	Specifies the ANSI code page table for systems not using code page 437 (the US OEM character set). You must manually edit SYSTEM.INI to change this entry.
SubType = *< Number >*	Determines the subtype of keyboards that have the same layout. Never change this setting manually; always use the Windows Setup program.
Type = *< Number >*	Determines the keyboard type. Never change this setting manually; always use the Windows Setup program. Common keyboard types include the following: 1 IBM PC or XT compatible (83 keys) 2 Olivetti 102-key ICO 3 IBM AT compatible (84 or 86 keys) 4 IBM compatible enhanced (101 or 102 keys)

MCI

Entry	Description
< Device Filename >	This section contains a list of multimedia drivers. Setup automatically enters any required filenames. Select the Driver icon of the Control Panel to change entries in this section.

NonWindowsApp

Entry	Description
CommandEnvSize = *< Number >*	Specifies the size of the DOS environment. The default setting is the environment size prior to entering Windows. You must manually edit SYSTEM.INI to change this setting.
DisablePositionSave = *< 0| 1 >*	(Windows 3.1) The default setting of 0 saves the position and font information for a DOS application each time you exit. A setting of 1 disables automatic saving. You may still choose to save manually. You must manually edit SYSTEM.INI to change this setting.

FontChangeEnable = *< 0 | 1 >* (Windows 3.1) Provides the means for changing the font size of a DOS application running in a window. Setting the entry to 1 adds a font entry to the control menu. A setting of 0 disables font changes. The default setting is 1, unless you configure Windows with an older 3.0 video driver. You may manually edit SYSTEM.INI to change this setting.

LocalTSRs = *< list of TSR applications >*
(Windows 3.1) You can use this option to specify that terminate-and-stay-resident programs (TSRs) work properly when loaded in separate instances for multiple virtual machines. By default, DOSEDIT and CED are named in SYSTEM.INI. Adding ANSI.SYS to the LocalTSRs program list performs the same device instancing built into Qualitas' 386MAX with any other memory Windows-compatible memory manager.

MouseInDOSBox = *< 0 | 1 >* (Windows 3.1) Displays a usable mouse cursor in DOS applications that use the mouse when the application is running in a Window. The default setting is 1 if a DOS mouse driver was present when Windows was installed; otherwise, the default setting is 0 (no mouse cursor for DOS applications in Windows). You may manually edit SYSTEM.INI to change this setting.

NetAsyncSwitching = *< 0 | 1 >* Indicates whether the user can switch to another application once the current application makes an asynchronous network BIOS call while in standard mode. In some cases, switching away from the current application will cause system errors. A setting of 1 prevents the application from switching, even if it doesn't make another call. A setting of 0 allows the application to switch. The default setting is blank. You must manually edit SYSTEM.INI to change this setting.

ScreenLines = *< Number >* Determines the maximum number of lines displayed for a DOS application. The default setting is 25. You must manually edit SYSTEM.INI to change this setting.

SwapDisk = *< Drive >* : *< Path >* Specifies the location of the swap area used by Windows in standard mode. If this entry is missing, Windows uses the directory indicated by the TEMP environment variable. If the TEMP environment variable is undefined, Windows uses the Windows directory. You must manually edit SYSTEM.INI to change this setting.

Standard

FasterModeSwitch = *< 0 | 1 >* (Windows 3.1) Use this entry only if you own a Zenith Z-248 or Olivetti M-250-E keyboard and lose characters or control of the mouse when

Table 9-3   Continued

Entry	Description
	typing. The default setting is False. You must manually edit SYSTEM.INI to change this setting.
Int28Filter = <*Number*>	Interrupt 28h is the Idle Interrupt. It indicates an idle status on the machine. Many pieces of software use this interrupt to determine when they should perform work. Categories of software that use this interrupt include disk caches, print spoolers, network interfaces, and many TSRs. The number indicates how Windows reacts to the interrupt. Windows makes every nth interrupt 28h visible to software running on your machine. The default value is 10. A higher value will improve Windows performance, while a lower value will increase overhead, decreasing Windows performance. Using a value of 0 will prevent any interrupt 28h generation. Lowering the number on a network might decrease the incidence of network errors. Increasing the number on a stand-alone workstation should greatly enhance system performance. Set this value to 0 if you do not use any TSRs that rely on interrupt 28h. You must manually edit SYSTEM.INI to change this setting.
NetHeapSize = <*Number*>	Indicates the number of 4K buffers that Windows allocates from conventional memory for network data transfers. Increasing the number of buffers enhances network performance, but decreases the amount of RAM available to DOS applications. The default setting is 8 (32K buffer). You must manually edit SYSTEM.INI to change this setting.
PadCodeSegments = <*0*|*1*>	Setting this entry to 1 tells Windows to pad each code segment with 16 bytes. While this reduces the amount of memory left for applications and data, it does resolve the hanging experienced by some 80286 machines with C2 stepping. If your machine hands in standard mode, try setting this value to 1 to relieve the situation. The default value is 0. You must manually edit SYSTEM.INI to change this setting.
ReservedLowMemory = <*K*>	Specifies the amount of memory in K that you want reserved for applications other than Windows. There is no reason to change this value from the default setting of 0. You must manually edit SYSTEM.INI to change this setting.
Stacks = <*Number*>	(Windows 3.1) Determines the amount of stack space you have available for the Windows DOS extender,

DOSX. The extender uses this space to map a DOS or BIOS API from real mode to protected mode. If you receive a Standard Mode: Stack Overflow message, try increasing this number. The default setting is 12. You must manually edit SYSTEM.INI to change this setting.

StackSize = <*K*>   (Windows 3.1) Determines the size of the stack in K. The default size is 384K. You must manually edit SYSTEM.INI to change this setting.

386Enh

A20EnableCount = <*Number*>   (Windows 3.1) Specifies the initial A20 count, which tells HIMEM.SYS which A20 handler to use to access extended memory. The WIN386 loader normally computes this value. Never change it unless otherwise instructed by the vendor of your extended memory manager. Changing this value could produce unexpected results. You must manually edit SYSTEM.INI to change this setting.

AllVMsExclusive = <*0|1*>   Forces all applications to run in the exclusive full screen mode when set to true. This might prevent UAEs from non-Windows compatible applications. The default setting is false. You must manually edit SYSTEM.INI to change this setting.

AltKeyDelay = <*Seconds*>   Changes the keyboard interrupt processing rate between an Alt key and the next key in the keyboard buffer. Some applications require a slower response time than the standard .005 seconds used by Windows. You must manually edit SYSTEM.INI to change this setting.

AltPasteDelay = <*Seconds*>   Changes the time Windows waits before pasting any characters once it pastes an Alt key. Some applications require more time to recognize the Alt key than the standard .025 seconds used by Windows. You must manually edit SYSTEM.INI to change this setting.

AllEMSLocked = <*0|1*>   (Windows 3.1) Determines whether Windows locks all EMS memory instead of swapping it to disk. This setting overrides any PIF settings. Set this value to 1 if you use a disk cache that uses expanded memory. Failure to do so may result in hard disk corruption. This setting is also useful to speed applications that make extensive use of expanded memory. For example, the performance of some spreadsheet applications is greatly enhanced when you set this value to true. However, it also means that the physical RAM used by the application is unavailable for any other purpose. the default setting is 0. You must manually edit SYSTEM.INI to change this setting.

Table 9-3 Continued

Entry	Description
AllXMSLocked = <0|1>	(Windows 3.1) Determines whether Windows locks all XMS memory instead of swapping it to disk. This setting overrides any PIF settings. Use this setting to speed applications that make extensive use of XMS memory. For example, the performance of some spreadsheet applications is greatly enhanced when you set this value to 1 (true). However, it also means that the physical RAM used by the application is unavailable for any other purpose. The default setting is 0. You must manually edit SYSTEM.INI to change this setting.
AutoRestoreScreen = <0|1>	(Windows 3.1) Determines if Windows stores the display of a DOS application when you switch to another DOS application or back to Windows. Storing the display requires more memory than allowing the application to repaint the display. However, Windows can usually restore the screen faster than the application. The tradeoff is time versus memory. Setting the entry to 1 (true) enables screen storing. This is the default state. You must manually edit SYSTEM.INI to change this setting.
AutoRestoreWindows = <0|1>	(Windows 3.1) Determines if Windows stores the latest Windows display when you switch to a full screen DOS application. Storing the display requires more memory than allowing Windows to repaint the display. However, Windows can usually restore the screen faster than repainting it--especially true if you use a high resolution display with more than 16 colors. The tradeoff is time versus memory. Setting the entry to 1 (true) enables screen storing. The default state is 0 (false). You must manually edit SYSTEM.INI to change this setting.
BkGndNotifyAtPFault = <0|1>	(Windows 3.1) Determines if Windows sends notification to the current application when you switch to another application. This prevents the current application from updating the screen in mid-transition. The default setting for coprocessor-equipped displays is 0 (false). The default setting for standard displays is 1 (true). You must manually edit SYSTEM.INI to change this setting.
CGA40WOA.FON = <Filename>	Specifies the filename of the fixed pitch font used for DOS applications with a 40 x 25 character display. You must manually edit SYSTEM.INI to change this setting.
CGA80WOA.FON = <Filename>	Specifies the filename of the fixed pitch font used for DOS applications with a 80 x 25 character display. You must manually edit SYSTEM.INI to change this setting.

CGANoSnow = <*0	1*>	Setting this entry to 1 (true) tells Windows to perform special handling on CGA displays to prevent snow. However, setting this value to 1 (true) also slows displays times. You must manually edit SYSTEM.INI to change this setting.
COMxAutoAssign = <*Seconds*>	This entry determines how Windows handles contention for a serial port between two or more applications. If the number of seconds equals -1, then Windows asks if you want to give an application control over a port that another application recently used. If the number of seconds equal 0, then Windows never asks about device contention. Setting the value within the range of 1 to 1000 tells Windows to wait that number of seconds before allowing another application to use the port. The default is 2 seconds. Never change this setting manually; always select the 386 Enhanced icon from the Control Panel.
COMxBasePort = <*Port*>	Assigns a specific port number (I/O address) to the specified COM port. The default settings are COM1BasePort = 3F8h, COM2BasePort = 2F8h, COM3BasePort = 3E8h, and COM4BasePort = 2E8h. Check your hardware manual for the values of other settings. Never change this setting manually; always select the Ports icon from the Control Panel.
COMBoostTime = <*ms*>	Specifies the time Windows allows a communications application to process an interrupt in milliseconds. If you find that your application is losing characters, you can increase this value to remedy the situation. However, increasing the time from the default value of 2 will also affect the processing speed of other applications. You must manually edit SYSTEM.INI to change this setting.
COMxBuffer = <*Number*>	Specifies the size of the buffer for the communications port. Buffering the port may slow transmission speed. However, it also prevents loss of characters at high baud rates. The default setting is 128 characters. Make certain to coordinate this setting with the COMxProtocol setting. You must manually edit SYSTEM.INI to change this setting.
COMdrv30 = <*0	1*>	(Windows 3.1) Set this entry to 1 (true) if you are using the Windows 3.0 communications driver, 0 (false) if you are using the Windows 3.1 communications driver. You must manually edit SYSTEM.INI to change this setting.
COMxFIFO = <*0	1*>	(Windows 3.1) Set this entry to 1 (true) to fully utilize the FIFO capability of the 16550A UART (universal asynchronous receiver/transmitter) used by some communication ports. The main advantage in doing this

Table 9-3 Continued

Entry	Description
	is to enable the COM port's caching ability, effectively reducing the chance of lost characters when the communication program loses focus. The default setting is true for ports COM1 through COM4. You must manually edit SYSTEM.INI to change this setting.
COMxIRQ = <Number>	This entry determines the interrupt request line (IRQ) used by a communications port. While each port must use a unique I/O address, some technicians allow communication ports to share an IRQ. The disadvantage to this approach is that you cannot use the two ports simultaneously. The standard settings are COM1IRQ = 4, COM2IRQ = 3, COM3IRQ = 4, and COM4IRQ = 3. Many I/O cards now allow you to use settings other than IRQ 3 or 4. Setting the port to one of the alternate settings (5 if you don't have a second parallel port, for example) might allow you to use all four ports simultaneously. Never edit this entry manually; always select the Ports icon from the Control Panel and click on the Advanced button.
COMIRQSharing = <0|1>	Specifies that two or more COM ports share the same IRQ. The default setting is 0 (false) for all standard ISA machines and 1 (true) for EISA and MCA machines. Never set more than one COM port to the same IRQ on an ISA machine since ISA machines do not have the required arbitration chips. Never edit this entry manually; always select the Ports icon from the Control Panel and click on the Advanced button.
COMxProtocol = <XOFF|Blank>	Determines if Windows uses XON/XOFF protocol for data transfers over a communications port. The XON/XOFF protocol can help prevent data overflow at either the sending or receiving terminal. Never use XON/XOFF protocol for binary transfers. Windows 3.1 provides an additional hardware setting, which uses special hardware lines to control data flow. When using Windows 3.0 or below, you must edit SYSTEM.INI manually to change this setting. Never edit this entry manually in Windows 3.1; always select the Ports icon from the Control Panel and click on the Advanced button.
Device = <Filename> | *<Device Name>	Specifies a virtual device driver used with Windows in enhanced mode. There are two types of drivers. The first resides as a separate file on disk. You must specify the path, filename, and extension. The second resides within WIN386.EXE. You need only specify the device name to use this driver. Synonyms for Device = include Display =,

EBIOS =, Keyboard =, Network =, and Mouse =. Setup usually adds all the entries required to run Windows. You must manually edit SYSTEM.INI to change this setting.

Display = *<Filename>* | * *<Device Name>*
See Device =.

DMABufferIn1MB = *<0|1>*   Set this entry to 1 (true) to locate the DMA buffer within the first megabyte of RAM for 8-bit bus master compatibility. The default setting is 0 (false). You must manually edit SYSTEM.INI to change this setting.

DOSPromptExitInstruc = *<0|1>* (Windows 3.1) Determines if Windows displays a message telling how to exit from the DOS prompt back to Windows. The default setting of 1 (true) displays the message. Setting this entry to 0 (false) prevents Windows from displaying the message. You must manually edit SYSTEM.INI to change this setting.

DualDisplay = *<0|1>*   Windows normally uses the area between B000:0000 and B7FF:0000 on EGA and CGA when in enhanced mode unless it detects a secondary display. Setting this value to 1 (true) makes the address range available for a secondary display even if undetected. Setting it to 0 (false) allows Windows to use the address range. You must manually edit SYSTEM.INI to change this setting.

EBIOS = *<Filename>* | * *<Device Name>*
See Device =.

EGA40WOA.FON = *<Filename>* Specifies the name of the fixed pitch font used for non-Windows application with a screen size of 40 characters and more than 25 lines. The default setting is none. You must manually edit SYSTEM.INI to change this setting.

EGA80WOA.FON = *<Filename>* Specifies the name of the fixed pitch font used for non-Windows application with a screen size of 80 characters and more than 25 lines. The default setting is none. You must manually edit SYSTEM.INI to change this setting.

EISADMA = *<Boolean>* | *<Channel, Size>*
Determines the mode of DMA channel operation on an EISA machine. Setting the value to false tells Windows to treat the machine as an ISA machine. Setting the value to true allows you to change the mode of each channel. There area four DMA modes: 8-bit (8), 16-bit specified in words (16W), 16-bit specified in bytes (16B), and 32-bit (32). Windows ignores this entry on non-EISA machines. The default settings are 0,8, 1,8, 2,8, 3,8, 5,16W, 6,16W, and 7,16W. You must manually edit SYSTEM.INI to change this setting.

Table 9-3 Continued

Entry	Description
EMMExclude = <*Paragraph Range*>	Specifies what range of addresses Windows should ignore in the upper memory area. For example, you can exclude the video adapter data range by adding the entry *EMMExclude=A000-B7FF*. You must manually edit SYSTEM.INI to change this setting.
EMMInclude = <*Paragraph Range*>	Specifies what range of addresses Windows should use in the upper memory area. For example, you can include part of the normal BIOS address range by adding the entry *EMMInclude=F000-F7FF*. You must manually edit SYSTEM.INI to change this setting.
EMMPageFrame = <*Paragraph*>	Determines where Windows places the EMMPageFrame. Normally, Windows automatically attempts to find a 64K area to place the page frame. You must manually edit SYSTEM.INI to change this setting.
EMMSize = <*K*>	This entry specifies the total amount of EMS memory that Windows makes available to applications. The default setting is 65,536K. Use this entry if you have an application that allocates all of expanded memory for itself. This situation becomes apparent if Windows will not allow you to run another DOS application once the offending application loads. You must manually edit SYSTEM.INI to change this setting.
FileSysChange = <*0|1*>	This entry determines if the File Manager automatically receives messages whenever a non-Windows application creates, renames, or deletes a file. The default setting of 1 (On) constantly updates File Manager. While this does keep File Manager up to date, it severely impacts system speed. Setup automatically place the entry *FileSysChange=Off* in SYSTEM.INI. You must manually edit SYSTEM.INI to change this setting.
Global = <*Device Name*>	Defines device drivers loaded in CONFIG.SYS as global rather than local. For example, the MS$MOUSE driver automatically loads as local. You must use the exact spelling and case for the device you want to make global. Most device drivers use all uppercase letters. The default setting is to make all device drivers in CONFIG.SYS global. You must manually edit SYSTEM.INI to change this setting.
HardDiskDMABuffer = <*K*>	(Windows 3.1) Determines the amount of memory set aside for the DMA buffer used with the hard disk. Smartdrive determines this setting automatically when you turn double buffering on. You might need to change this value if you use a hard drive controller

that supports DMA transfers but you don't have double buffering turned on. The default value is OK for AT machines and 64K for micro-channel machines. You must manually edit SYSTEM.INI to change this setting.

HighFloppyReads = *< 0| 1 >* Windows normally turns a DMA verify for the address range E000:0000-EFFF:000F into a read to work around problems experienced by certain machines. In some cases, this causes the system to freeze when some software writes over the system shadow RAM. If your machine freezes and your manufacturer's manual states that the shadow RAM appears in this area, set this entry to No (0) and the EMMExlude entry to E000-EFFF. The default setting is yes (1). You must manually edit SYSTEM.INI to change this setting.

IdleVMWakeUpTime = *< Secs >* (Windows 3.1) This entry specifies the time interval (in seconds) between idle virtual machine wake-ups. Windows does not normally wake-up virtual machines that do not use interrupts 8h or 1Ch. The wake-ups force these interrupts to occur in the idle virtual machines. The value for this entry is expressed as a power of 2 (for example 1, 2, 4, 8, 16). The default setting is 8. You must manually edit SYSTEM.INI to change this setting.

IgnoreInstalledEMM = *< 0| 1 >* Setting this entry to yes (1) allows Windows to start even if there is an unknown EMM running. Using this entry may cause the machine to freeze if the EMM is incompatible with Windows or if a memory resident TSR was using expanded memory when you started Windows. The default setting is no (0). You must manually edit SYSTEM.INI to change this setting.

InDOSPolling = *< 0| 1 >* This entry prevents Windows from running other applications when a memory resident application sets the InDOS flag when set to yes (1). Many applications set this flag during critical interrupt 21h operations or when hooking interrupt 21h. The default setting is no (0). You must manually edit SYSTEM.INI to change this setting.

INT28Critical = *< 0| 1 >* Many pieces of network and memory resident software use interrupt 28h to detect machine idle times. Setting this entry to true (1) tells Windows to fully process the interrupt 28h call prior to executing any other calls. Setting the entry to false (0) ensures that Windows maintains full multitasking even though the software issues an interrupt 28h call. The advantage to setting the entry to true is that you should experience fewer network problems and a reduction of memory resident induced failures. The advantage to setting the entry to false is that you will experience

Table 9-3 Continued

Entry	Description
	better task switching times. You must manually edit SYSTEM.INI to change this setting.
IRQ9Global = <0|1>	Setting this entry to yes will prevent some systems from hanging when you try to read from a floppy drive. (Most floppy drive controllers use interrupt 6, so this setting is not necessary. To check your floppy drive, use a utility program like CheckIt.) The default setting is no. You must manually edit SYSTEM.INI to change this setting.
Keyboard = <Filename> | *<Device Name>	See Device = .
KeyBoostTime = <Secs>	Use this entry to specify how long an application operates at an increased priority when it receives a keystroke. For example, you could use this with a word processing program to increase its priority while you type and still allow several background application to operate. The default setting is .001 seconds. A setting of .1 is good if you type at approximately 50 words per minute. You must manually edit SYSTEM.INI to change this setting.
KeyBufferDelay = <Secs>	Specifies the time to delay pasting keyboard input when the keyboard buffer is full. Some applications require more than the default of .2 seconds. You must manually edit SYSTEM.INI to change this setting.
KeyIdleDelay = <Secs>	Use this entry to tell Windows how long to ignore idle calls after sending a keystroke to a virtual machine. Setting this value to 0 will greatly enhance keyboard speed, but may cause some applications to respond sluggishly. The default setting is .5 seconds. You must manually edit SYSTEM.INI to change this setting.
KeyPasteDelay = <Secs>	Use this entry to specify the wait between a key paste and the time Windows actually pastes it. Some applications may require more than the default of .003 seconds to recognize a keystroke. You must manually edit SYSTEM.INI to change this setting.
KeyPasteTimeout = <Secs>	Specifies the time Windows allows an application to make the necessary BIOS calls before it switches from the fast paste (interrupt 16h) to the slow paste (interrupt 9h). The default setting is 1 second. You must manually edit SYSTEM.INI to change this setting.

KybdPasswd = <0|1>

(Windows 3.1) Determines if the virtual keyboard device (VKD) supports the PS/2 8042 commands for password security. This setting defaults to true (1) for PS/2 machines and false (0) for all other machines. You must manually edit SYSTEM.INI to change this setting.

KybdReboot = <0|1>

(Windows 3.1) Windows attempts to reboot the virtual machine in response to a Ctrl-Alt-Del when this entry is true (1). Some computers reboot unreliably or hang using this method. Set the entry to false (0) to handle this condition. The default setting is true. You must manually edit SYSTEM.INI to change this setting.

Local = <Device Name>

Use this entry to define DOS device drivers that are local to each virtual machine. The entry must match the device driver spelling and capitalization exactly. For example, most device drivers use all upper case letters. The default setting is none. However, the Windows Setup program makes the entry Local=CON in SYSTEM.INI automatically. You must manually edit SYSTEM.INI to change this setting.

LocalLoadHigh = <0|1>

(Windows 3.1) Windows normally uses all of the UMB area for itself. However, by setting this entry to true (1), you can reserve UMB for each virtual machine. The advantage to allowing Windows to use the UMB is an increase in overall system performance. The advantage to leaving UMB for your DOS applications is that you free more conventional memory for each application. The default setting is false (0), Windows allocates all UMB for itself. You must manually edit SYSTEM.INI to change this setting.

LPTxAutoAssign = <Secs>

This value determines the time between the last use of a parallel port by one application and its use by another application. If you set this value to -1, then Windows will always ask if the new application should receive control of the port. If you set this value to 0, the Windows automatically gives each application control of the port as it requests it. Assigning a value between 1 and 1000 means that Windows will wait that many seconds between the end of one application's use of the port and its use by another application. The default setting is 60. Never change this setting manually; always choose the 386 Enhanced icon from the Control Panel.

LRULowRateMult = <Number>

(Windows 3.1) Specifies part of the value used to determine the Least Recently Used (LRU) low paging rate sweep frequency in milliseconds. You compute the value by multiplying the LRUSweepFreq by the LRULowRateMult. Essentially, this specifies an interval between garbage collection sessions. You may use values between 1 and 65535. The default setting is 10 (which, when coupled with the

Table 9-3 Continued

Entry	Description
	LRUSweepFreq specifies an interval of 2500 milliseconds). Increasing this setting might enhance Windows performance by reducing overhead. You must manually edit SYSTEM.INI to change this setting.
LRURateChngTime = *<ms>*	(Windows 3.1) This entry specifies the time that the VMM remains at the high LRU sweep rate with no page requests before switching to the low rate. It also specifies the time that VMM will stay at the low rate with no page requests before turning the LRU seep off. The default setting is 10,000 milliseconds. Setting this value lower could reduce system overhead more quickly. You must anually edit SYSTEM.INI to change this setting.
LRUSweepFreq = *<ms>*	(Windows 3.1) Specifies the time between LRU sweep passes. When taken by itself, this setting specifies the high sweep rate. When multiplied by the LRULowRateMult setting, it specifies the low sweep rate. The default setting is 250 milliseconds. You must manually edit SYSTEM.INI to change this setting.
LRUSweepLen = *<Pages>*	(Windows 3.1) Determines the size of the region swept on each pass. Windows determine this value by dividing the LRUSweepReset value by the LRUSweepFreq. This value must lie between 1 and 1024. You must manually edit SYSTEM.INI to change this setting.
LRUSweepLowWater = *<Number>*	(Windows 3.1) When the number of free pages drops below the specified value, Windows turns the LRU sweeper on. The default value is 24 pages. There is no reason to change the value of this entry. Setting to different value appears to have little effect on overall system performance. You must manually edit SYSTEM.INI to change this setting.
LRUSweepReset = *<ms>*	(Windows 3.1) Specifies the time required for an ACC bit reset divided by the number of 4M pages. Therefore, the time to reset all ACC bits is the number of pages in **system** + 1023/1024, where **1024 pages** = 4M. The minimum value is 100. The default value is 500. There is no reason to change the value of this entry. You must manually edit SYSTEM.INI to change this setting.
MapPhysAddress = *<Range>*	Use this entry to specify a range of physical page-table entries and linear address space for a device driver that must remain in physical RAM. For example, older versions of RAMDrive require

physical RAM to operate correctly. The default is none. You must manually edit SYSTEM.INI to change this setting.

MaxBPs = <*Number*>   (Windows 3.1) Use this entry to specify the maximum number of break points required by the VMM. A break point represents a method of transferring control to the Windows enhanced mode driver. You might need to change this value if you use a third party virtual device driver that requires more break points than the default value. The default setting is 200. You must manually edit SYSTEM.INI to change this setting.

MaxCOMPort = <*Number*>   (Windows 3.1) This entry determines the maximum number of communication ports supported in enhanced mode. The default setting is 4. You must manually edit SYSTEM.INI to change this setting.

MaxDMAPGAddress = <*Address*>   (Windows 3.1) Specifies the maximum physical page address that Windows can use for DMA. This entry works only with hard drive controllers that support DMA transfers. The default settings are: OFFFh for non-EISA machines and OFFFFFh for EISA machines. You must manually edit SYSTEM.INI to change this setting.

MaxPagingFileSize = <*K*>   Specifies the size of the swap file in K. The default setting is none (use a temporary swap file size determined by Windows). Never change this entry manually; always select the 386 Enhanced icon from the Control Panel, and then click the Virtual Memory button to set a value.

MaxPhysPage = <*Page Number*>   (Windows 3.1) Use this entry to specify the maximum physical page that the VMM can access. This is useful when the memory in your computer exceeds the value that devices attached to your computer can handle. For example, some network cards cannot access memory above 16M. By default, Windows allows VMM to access every page of memory your machine contains. You must manually edit SYSTEM.INI to change this setting.

MCADMA = <*0|1*>   (Windows 3.1) Setting this entry to true (1) allows Windows to use DMA extensions available on MCA machines. Never set this value to true on an ISA or EISA machine. The default setting is true on MCA machines and false on all other machines. You must manually edit SYSTEM.INI to change this setting.

MinTimeSlice = <*ms*>   Determines the minimum amount of time allocated to each application. A small value makes multitasking appear smoother but diminishes overall system performance. A higher value might interfere with the proper operation of some communication programs, especially at higher baud rates. The default setting

Table 9-3 Continued

Entry	Description
	is 20. Never change this setting manually; always select the 386 Enhanced icon from the Control Panel.
MinUnlockMem = < K >	(Windows 3.1) This entry specifies the minimum amount of physical RAM that remains unlocked when two or more virtual machines are running. The default setting is 40K. You must manually edit SYSTEM.INI to change this setting.
MinUserDiskSpace = < K >	Use this entry to specify the minimum amount of disk space that must remain after Windows allocates a temporary swap space. Leaving more disk space free allows you to store larger data files. Allowing Windows to allocate more disk space provides more virtual memory for applications. The default setting is 500K. You must manually edit SYSTEM.INI to change this setting.
Mouse = < Filename > | * < Device Name >	See Device = .
MouseSoftInit = < 0|1 >	Windows does not usually perform a hard rest of the mouse to ensure it will work when you switch to a non-Windows application. However, this might cause problems with some mouse software because it leaves the mouse in an unknown state. Setting this value to false ensures that the mouse is always reset, but will not allow you to use the mouse with a windowed non-Windows application. The default setting is true (1). You must manually edit SYSTEM.INI to change this setting.
NetAsyncFallback = < 0|1 >	Windows will normally fail a NetBIOS request if it runs out of global buffer space. When you set this entry to true (1), Windows allocates the buffer out of local memory instead. It will not allow any other virtual machines to start until the data is received the timeout period specified by NetAsyncTimeout expires. The default setting is false (0). You must manually edit SYSTEM.INI to change this setting.
NetAsyncTimeout = < Secs >	Use this entry to specify the time Windows needs to enter a critical section to service a failing NetBIOS request. This value is only used when you set NetAsyncFallback. The default setting is 5.0 seconds. You must manually edit SYSTEM.INI to change this setting.
NetDMASize = < K >	Specifies the size of the DMA buffer if a network is installed. The default setting on MCA machines is 32K

and OK on all other machine types. You must manually edit SYSTEM.INI to change this setting.

NetHeapSize = <*Number*>   Determines the size of the buffer (in 4K increments) that Windows allocates for transferring data over a network. The default setting is 12K. You must manually edit SYSTEM.INI to change this setting.

Network = <*Filename*> | * <*Device Name*>
                        See Device = .

NMIReboot = <*0|1*>   Set this entry to yes if you want your machine to reboot when it receives the non-maskable interrupt. For example, many memory errors (especially parity errors) generate a NMI. The default setting is no. You must manually edit SYSTEM.INI to change this setting.

NoEMMDriver = <*0|1*>   Setting this entry to true (1) prevents Windows from installing the EMM driver in enhanced mode. The advantages to not loading the EMM driver are a slight increase in available system memory and a noticeable increase in system performance. However, this also means that you cannot run DOS applications that require expanded memory. This setting differs from EMMSize = 0, which frees UMB for DOS applications but does not prevent the EMM driver from loading. The default setting is false (0). You must manually edit SYSTEM.INI to change this setting.

OverlappedIO = <*0|1*>   (Windows 3.1) Allows several virtual machines to make read and write requests to disk before the first request is serviced when set to true (1). The default setting is true unless InDOSPolling is true. You should never need to change this entry. You must manually edit SYSTEM.INI to change this setting.

PageOverCommit = <*M*>   (Windows 3.1) This entry determines the multiplier used by VMM to create system memory. To compute system memory round the amount of available memory to the nearest 4M and multiply by the value specified for PageOverCommit. Increasing this value increases the amount of linear memory. It also increase the size of the data structures and therefore paging activity. Therefore, you give up some system speed to increase available memory by increasing this value. You may specify a value between 1 and 20. The default value is 4. You must manually edit SYSTEM.INI to change this setting.

Paging = <*0|1*>   Set this value to no (0) if you want to set demand paging off. This prevents Windows from allocating a temporary swap file (or using the permanent swap file). It also means that memory available for application is limited to

Table 9-3   Continued

Entry	Description
	the physical RAM installed in your machine. You must manually edit SYSTEM.INI to change this setting.
PagingDrive = <*Drive Letter*>	Determines the drive used to create the temporary swap file. Windows ignores this entry if you have a permanent swap file. If you do not specify a swap drive, Windows attempts to use the drive containing SYSTEM.INI. If this drive is full, then Windows turns paging off. The default setting is none. You must manually edit SYSTEM.INI to change this setting.
PerformBackfill = <*Auto|Yes|No*>	(Windows 3.1) Use this entry to specify if Windows should backfill memory on machines containing less than 640K of conventional memory. You should only need to change this setting on diskless workstations because Windows can automatically detect the memory on a stand-alone workstation. The default setting is auto. Setting the entry to yes backfills memory. Setting it to no prevents backfilling. You must manually edit SYSTEM.INI to change this setting.
PerVMFiles = <*Number*>	This entry determines the number of private file handles allocated to each virtual machine. The number of private and global file handles (including those specified in CONFIG.SYS) cannot exceed 255. If you specify a number which exceeds 255, Windows automatically rounds the number down. The default setting is 10. You must manually edit SYSTEM.INI to change this setting.
PSPIncrement = <*Number*>	Specifies the amount of memory in 16-byte increments that Windows should reserve for each successive virtual machine when UniqueDOSPSP is set. Values may range from 2 to 61. The default setting is 2. You must manually edit SYSTEM.INI to change this setting.
ReflectDOSInt2A = <*0|1*>	Determines whether Windows consumes or reflects DOS interrupt 2Ah (Network Redirector) signals. Setting this entry to false (0) allows Windows to consume the signals and run more efficiently. Set the entry to true if you have network specific software that relies on the 2Ah signals. The default setting is false. You must manually edit SYSTEM.INI to change this setting.
ReservedHighArea = <*Paragraph Range*>	(Windows 3.1) Use this entry to prevent Windows scanning of a specified upper memory range for unused memory. The range must appear between A000h and EFFFh. For example, if you wanted to reserve the VGA ROM area, you would specify a range of C000-C7FF.

You may specify more than one range by using more than one ReservedHighArea statement. You must manually edit SYSTEM.INI to change this setting.

ReservePageFrame = <*0*|*1*> Setting this entry to false (0) removes the automatic page frame reservation and frees additional conventional memory for DOS applications. The default setting is true (1). You must manually edit SYSTEM.INI to change this setting.

ReserveVideoROM = <*0*|*1*> (Windows 3.1) This entry tells Windows that the video ROM resides in pages C600h and C700h. If the text displayed by non-Windows applications appears scrambled, set this entry to true (1). The default setting is false (0). You must manually edit SYSTEM.INI to change this setting.

ROMScanThreshold = <*Number*> (Windows 3.1) This entry determines the number of memory transitions that Windows must encounter before it declares an area as ROM. Setting the value to 0 causes Windows to declare all areas as ROM. The default setting is 20. You may need to set this value lower if Windows does not correctly recognize all the ROM in your system. Setting it higher might free some areas that Windows currently declares as ROM. You will not need to change this entry in most cases. You must manually edit SYSTEM.INI to change this setting.

SGrabLPT = <*Port Number*> This entry routes all printer interrupts on the specified port to the system virtual machine rather than the current virtual machine. The default setting is none. You must manually edit SYSTEM.INI to change this setting.

SyncTime = <*0*|*1*> (Windows 3.1) Setting this entry to true (1) causes Windows to synchronize itself with the CMOS timer at a regular interval. Windows usually maintains the correct time unless you set TrapTimerPorts to false and you run application which cause variances in the system time. The default setting is true (1). Setting this value to false (0) does not appreciably increase system performance. You must manually edit SYSTEM.INI to change this setting.

SystemROMBreakPoint = <*0*|*1*> Windows normally searches the area between F000:0000 and 1M for a special system break point instruction. Set this entry to false (0) if your system does not contain a permanent ROM between these address ranges. The default setting is true. You must manually edit SYSTEM.INI to change this setting.

SysVMEMSLimit = <*K*> Specifies the amount of EMS memory that Windows can use. The default setting is 2048K. Using a setting

Table 9-3   Continued

Entry	Description
	of -1 allocates all EMS for Windows use. A setting of OK prevents Windows from using any EMS. Any other setting allows Windows to use up to that amount of EMS. You must manually edit SYSTEM.INI to change this setting.
SysVMEMSLocked = <0|1>	Specifies if the system can swap Windows EMS to disk. Locking memory can increase the performance of a single application, but slows the rest of the system. The default setting is no (0). You must manually edit SYSTEM.INI to change this setting.
SysVMEMSRequired = <K>	Determines the amount of EMS required to start Windows. Leave this value at 0 if no Windows applications require expanded memory. The default is 0. You must manually edit SYSTEM.INI to change this setting.
SystemVMPriority = <Fore Number>,<Back Number>	Determines the foreground and background priorities of virtual machines. Windows automatically assigns the background virtual machine a value of one-half the foreground priority if you do not assign it a value. The default settings are 100, 50. The PIF settings automatically override these values. A high value gives that application a higher priority. A low value places that application at a lower priority. By setting these values carefully, you can greatly enhance system throughput. Never change these values manually; always select the 386 Enhanced icon of the Control Panel and specify a Scheduling value.
SysVMV86Locked = <0|1>	This value affects whether or not the system virtual machine is locked in memory. Because Windows handles this function automatically, there are no speed or memory benefits to gain by locking it. The default value is false (0). You must manually edit SYSTEM.INI to change this setting.
SysVMXMSLimit = <K>	This value determines the amount of XMS that Windows will allocate to a device driver or memory resident software. Setting the value to -1 allows Windows to give the application all the memory it requests. The default setting is 2048K. Setting this value to a lower amount might save some system memory. However, setting it too low might cause Windows to hang when a device driver or TSR fails due to lack of memory. You must manually edit SYSTEM.INI to change this setting.
SysVXMSRequired = <K>	Determines the amount of XMS memory required to start Windows. Leave this value at 0 if there are no XMS

users on the system virtual machine. The default setting is 0. You must manually edit SYSTEM.INI to change this setting.

TimerCriticalSection = <*ms*> Tells Windows to go into a critical section each time it receives a timer interrupt. A positive number ensures that each virtual machine will receive timer interrupts. Some networks and global TSRs will fail unless you specify a value for this entry. However, setting this entry also slows system performance. The default value is 0. You must manually edit SYSTEM.INI to change this setting.

TokenRingSearch = <*0|1*> Forces Windows to search for a token ring adapter on PC/AT machines. Set this entry to false if you are not using a token ring adapter and search interferes with another device. The default setting is true. You must manually edit SYSTEM.INI to change this setting.

TranslateScans = <*0|1*> Determines if Windows will translate scan codes from non-standard keyboards into standard IBM scan codes. The default setting is no (0). You must manually edit SYSTEM.INI to change this setting.

TrapTimerPorts = <*0|1*> (Windows 3.1) Set this entry to false (0) to allow all applications to read from and write to the system timer ports. This might allow some applications to change system timing and therefore interfere with Windows time keeping capability. Set this entry to true to prevent an application from changing the timer interval without letting Windows know first. This will slow any application that accesses the system timer. The default setting is false. You must manually edit SYSTEM.INI to change this setting.

UniqueDOSPSP = <*0|1*> Forces Windows to start each application at a new PSP address when set to true (1). This prevents a network from mistaking one application for another based on PSP address. The default setting is false (0) unless you use the Microsoft Network or LAN Manager. Setting this entry to true will waste memory, leaving less to start new non-Windows applications. You must manually edit SYSTEM.INI to change this setting.

UseableHighArea = <*Paragraph Range*>
(Windows 3.1) Determines what area of upper memory that Windows will scan for unused address areas regardless of what is located there. This setting takes precedence over ReserveHighArea if you specify ranges that overlap. You must specify a range between A000h and EFFFh. For example, if you wanted to scan the VGA ROM area of upper memory, then you would specify a range of C000-C7FF. You may specify more than one area by using multiple statements. The default setting is

Table 9-3 Continued

Entry	Description
	none. You must manually edit SYSTEM.INI to change this setting.
UseInstFile = <0|1>	Specifies if Windows should look in the INSTANCE.386 file for information it can use to determine which data structures within DOS are local. This entry provides compatibility with Windows/386 Version 2.x. The default setting is false. You must manually edit SYSTEM.INI to change this setting.
UseROMFont = <0|1>	(Windows 3.1) Allows Windows to use the soft font stored in video ROM to display messages when non-Windows applications are running in full-screen mode. If you see random characters or dots appear on your display, set this entry to false (0). The default setting is true (1). You must manually edit SYSTEM.INI to change this setting.
VCPIWarning = <0|1>	This entry tells Windows to display an error message when a program tries to access the Virtual Control Program interface (VCPI) when set to true (1). Because Windows does not support this interface, it interferes with normal Windows function. Set this entry to false (0) if the software you use runs under Windows even if VCPI is unavailable. The default setting is true. You must manually edit SYSTEM.INI to change this setting.
VGAMonoText = <0|1>	(Windows 3.1) Set this entry to false if you have a VGA display adapter installed, do not plan to use a monochrome display, and there are no other adapters installed in the area between B000h and B7FFh. This provides an additional 32K of upper memory for Windows use. You must manually edit SYSTEM.INI to change this setting.
VideoBackgroundMsg = <0|1>	(Windows 3.1) Setting this entry true (1) tells Windows to display a message each time a background application is suspended or it's video display cannot update due to low video memory. You can suspend the display by setting the entry to false (0). The default setting is true. You must manually edit SYSTEM.INI to change this setting.
VideoSuspendDisable = <0|1>	(Windows 3.1) When set to true (1), this entry tells Windows not to suspend applications when their video memory becomes corrupted. A setting of false (0) suspends the application and display an error message if VideoBackgroundMsg is set true. The default setting is false. You must manually edit SYSTEM.INI to change this setting.

VirtualHDIRQ = <*0|1*> Suspends interrupts from the hard drive when set on. Setting this entry off forces Windows to pass the hard drive interrupts to the BIOS, slowing system performance. Some hard drives might require BIOS handling of interrupts. The default setting is on. You must manually edit SYSTEM.INI to change this setting.

WindowKBRequired = <*K*> Specifies the amount of free conventional memory required to start Windows. The default value is 256K. You must manually edit SYSTEM.INI to change this setting.

WindowMemSize = <*Number*> | <*K*> Determines the amount of conventional memory that Windows may allocate for itself. Using the default value of -1 allows Windows to allocate as much memory as it wants. If Windows will not start in enhanced mode, try setting this value to a positive integer less that 640. You must manually edit SYSTEM.INI to change this setting.

WindowUpdateTime = <*ms*> Specifies the update time for a windowed non-Windows application. The default setting is 50 milliseconds. You must manually edit SYSTEM.INI to change this setting.

WinExclusive = <*0|1*> Setting this entry to yes (1)prevents any non-Windows application from executing in the background. The default setting of no (0), allows background execution of DOS applications. Never change this entry manually; always select the 386 Enhanced icon from the Control Panel.

WinTimeSlice = <*Number*> , <*Number*>
There are two numbers associated with this entry. The first number specifies the relative execution time slice of Windows foreground applications. The second number denotes the relative processing time of Windows background applications. The higher the number, the more processing time the application receives. The default setting is 100, 50. Never change this entry manually; always select the 386 Enhanced icon from the Control Panel.

WOAFont = <*Font Filename*> (Windows 3.1) This entry determines which font Windows loads into memory when running non-Windows applications. The default setting is DOSAPP.FON. You must manually edit SYSTEM.INI to change this setting.

XLatBufferSize = <*K*> (Windows 3.1) Determines the size of the buffer used to translate DOS calls from protected mode to Virtual 386 Enhanced mode. Increasing this value will improve the performance of most Windows applications at least slightly. The more disk intensive the program, the higher the performance gain. However, increasing this entry

Table 9-3   Continued

Entry	Description
	might reduce the memory available to DOS applications if you are not running 32-bit disk access. The default setting is 4. You must manually edit SYSTEM.INI to change this setting.
XMSUMBInitCalls = < 0	1 >	(Windows 3.1) Specifies if Windows should call extended memory drivers UMB management routines. In most cases Windows can call these drivers without any ill-effects. However, some memory managers do not work well with Windows. Setting the entry to false (0) can avoid conflicts. The default setting is true (1). You must manually edit SYSTEM.INI to change this setting.

Understanding PIFs

When dealing with Windows 3.0 and 3.1, you should know about two types of program information files (PIFs). (Even though version 3.0 supports real mode, we won't examine it here.)

The first type is the Standard mode PIF shown in Fig. 9-6. As we'll soon see, Standard mode requires much less configuration information to obtain optimum performance than an Enhanced mode PIF. Figure 9-7 shows a typical Enhanced mode PIF file. Notice the Advanced button on the bottom of the display. These advanced options set the Enhanced mode PIF apart from its Standard mode counterpart. Figure 9-8 shows the advanced options required to configure an application for Enhanced mode operation. As you can see, Enhanced mode is much more difficult to work with but produces far better results in many cases. Windows automatically selects the proper PIF format based on the current operating mode. If you want to create a PIF for a different mode, all you must do is click on the mode menu. A menu containing the available modes pops down. The following paragraphs provide detailed information on how to set up each type of PIF.

Common elements

Several pieces of information are common to both types of PIF. The first four entries describe the program itself. The Program Filename entry contains the executable filename. For example, if you wanted to create a special DOS prompt PIF, you would enter COMMAND.COM in this blank.

The Windows Title blank contains the descriptive name you want to appear as a title for your program. (This option does not appear to work properly in Windows 3.1. Use the File Properties option of Program Manager to name the window instead.) For example, using our DOS prompt PIF as an example, you might

```
┌─────────────────────────────────────────────────────────────┐
│ ═                                              ▼  ▲          │
├─────────────────────────────────────────────────────────────┤
│  File   Mode   Help                                          │
│                                                              │
│   Program Filename:    │                                   │ │
│                                                              │
│   Window Title:        │                                   │ │
│                                                              │
│   Optional Parameters: │                                   │ │
│                                                              │
│   Start-up Directory:  │                                   │ │
│                                                              │
│   Video Mode:          ◉ Text    ○ Graphics/Multiple Text   │
│                                                              │
│   Memory Requirements: KB Required │128│                    │
│                                                              │
│   XMS Memory:          KB Required │0│    KB Limit │0│       │
│                                                              │
│   Directly Modifies:   ☐ COM1    ☐ COM3    ☐ Keyboard       │
│                        ☐ COM2    ☐ COM4                      │
│                                                              │
│   ☐ No Screen Exchange          ☐ Prevent Program Switch    │
│   ☒ Close Window on Exit        ☐ No Save Screen            │
│   Reserve Shortcut Keys:  ☐ Alt+Tab   ☐ Alt+Esc  ☐ Ctrl+Esc│
│                           ☐ PrtSc     ☐ Alt+PrtSc           │
│                                                              │
├─────────────────────────────────────────────────────────────┤
│  Press F1 for Help on Program Filename.                      │
└─────────────────────────────────────────────────────────────┘
```

Fig. 9-6   Standard Mode PIF form.

want to enter DOS as the window title. Every time you double click on the DOS icon, a window appears with the window title you select if you didn't select a name for the program using the File Properties option of Program Manager. (We'll see how this works later.)

The Optional Parameters blank allows you to add any command line parameters that you normally add. For example, with the DOS parameter, you could add the /E : 1024 parameter to increase the environment space to 1024 bytes.

The final blank contains the startup directory. Windows changes to this directory prior to executing the program, which allows your program to find its data and help files quickly. As before, you can override this setting using the File Properties option of Program Manager. Once you get past these four entries, you'll notice that the two PIF formats are much different.

Configuring Standard mode PIFs

This section describes the parts of the Standard mode PIF that differ from the Enhanced mode PIF.

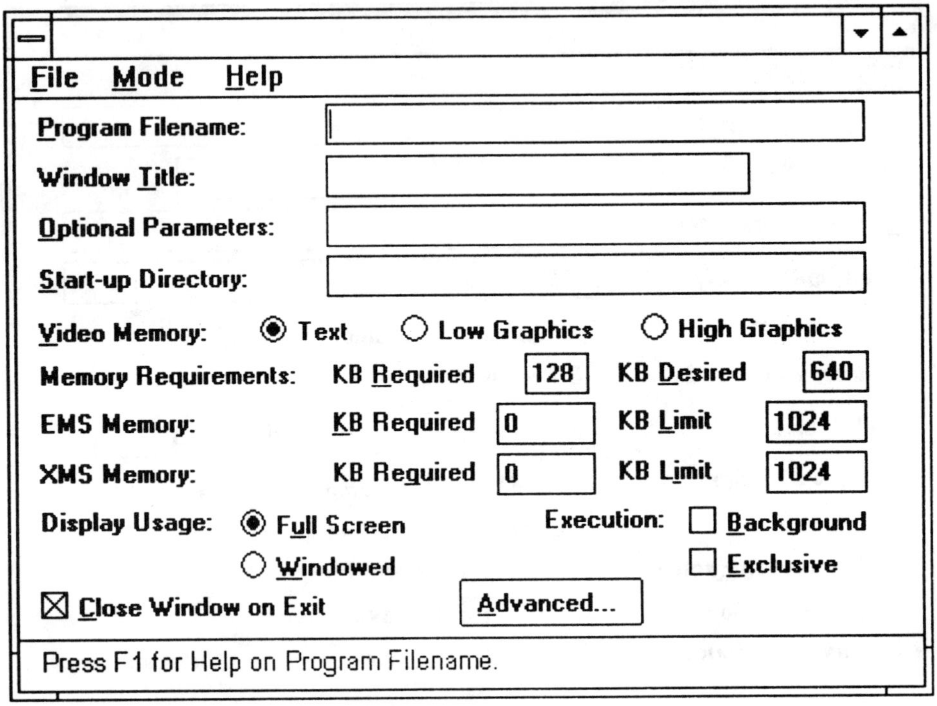

Fig. 9-7   Enhanced Mode PIF form.

Video Mode   You first need to decide which video mode to use—usually pretty simple to figure out. If your application runs in text mode, select the Text entry. If it runs in graphics mode, select the Graphics/Multiple Text entry. The difference between the two entries is the amount of video memory Windows allocates for the application.

Some text applications use more than one page of video memory to speed the display of text. While your display shows one screen, the program is busy writing to a different screen—one that's hidden. Video adaptors like the VGA display adaptor can provide 8 or more text pages for application programs to use. Programs that use ROM fonts to make a text display look like a graphics display also use more video memory. They store these fonts in the memory normally used for text display pages. In these cases, you need to use the larger memory allocation provided by the Graphics/Multiple Text entry. However, always try the text entry with text mode applications first. You may use as little as 4K of video memory instead of the 64K window normally reserved for graphics displays.

Memory Required   The next entry is Memory Required. Some people confuse this with the vendor recommended minimum memory configuration. What you actually want to put in this blank is the minimum amount of memory that provides adequate performance and enough room to store your data. This may require a little experimentation on your part since everyone's needs are different.

```
┌─┐
│─├──────────────────────────────────────────────────────────────┐
│  ┌─Multitasking Options ──────────────────────┐                │
│  │ Background Priority:  ▨5▨    Foreground Priority:  ┌───┐ │ ┌───────┐
│  │                                              │ 100 │ │ │  OK   │
│  │           ⊠ Detect Idle Time                 └───┘ │ └───────┘
│  └──────────────────────────────────────────────────┘ ┌───────┐
│  ┌─Memory Options ──────────────────────────────────┐  │Cancel │
│  │    □ EMS Memory Locked        □ XMS Memory Locked│  └───────┘
│  │    ⊠ Uses High Memory Area    □ Lock Application Memory
│  └──────────────────────────────────────────────────┘
```

Fig. 9-8   Enhanced Mode PIF Advanced Options form.

For example, many people write short documents with their word processor so they only require a little memory for their data. Someone who writes entire books may require a lot more memory for their data. If you notice that the program's performance is less than adequate, or that you can't load all the files you need to, then you may want to increase the Memory Required entry. The tradeoff of adding memory to one application is that you will most certainly take it away from another application.

XMS Memory   Many applications use XMS memory to enhance the features they provide. Windows provides DOS Protected Mode Interface (DPMI) compliant memory, not Virtual Control Program Interface (VCPI) memory. Some applications like Lotus 1-2-3 use VCPI memory. Windows cannot allocate XMS memory to these applications. Whenever possible, attempt to use the application without the benefit of XMS memory. If it still works, then you might want to place a VCPIWarning=False entry in SYSTEM.INI—this suppresses the warning message that Windows displays each time you start the application.

The applications that do use DPMI compliant memory will benefit from the XMS Memory Required/KB Limit entries. The first entry tells Windows how much memory you have to have in order to run the application. Put the vendor recommended minimum in the XMS Memory Required blank. Even if you can't load every data file you own, you can still perform useful work with the application if you get the minimum memory required. The XMS KB Limit entry provides a way for telling Windows how much memory you would like to have. Don't place a ridiculously high entry in this blank; doing so could reduce the memory available to other applications. Rather, enter a number that will allow you to run the application at high speed and load the largest data file you expect to use. If your application does not use extended memory, leave both blanks at 0.

Note   If necessary, you can set the XMS KB Limit to −1. This allows the application to request as much memory as it needs, up to the total memory available on your machine. However, using this setting may result in slow system performance and a lack of memory for other applications. In most cases, you should assign an actual value to the XMS KB Limit entry.

Directly Modifies   Five Directly Modifies check boxes are displayed on the Standard mode form. The first four deal with the communication ports. In most cases, you do not need to check a port if the application uses a serial mouse. Most applications can share this resource without difficulty; the same is true of printers connected to a serial port, only a little less so. Imagine what would happen if two DOS applications tried to print to a serial printer at once. Some applications check the port to see if it is busy before trying to print, while others do not. You might end up with parts of both documents mixed together as output. If this happens, then you must check the COM port that connects the serial printer for the offending application. Always check the COM port that connects to a MODEM used by a communications program; you do not want another program to interfere with communications. By checking the box, you maintain exclusive control over the resource. Unfortunately, whenever you check one of the Directly Modifies check boxes, you lose the ability to switch between applications until you exit the current application. Windows keeps any application that might cause conflicts in the foreground so the application receives higher priority processing.

Never check the Keyboard entry. Always try to configure your applications so they do not modify the keyboard or interfere with other applications. Some TSR and security programs directly modify the keyboard in ways that make it unusable for other applications. While a security program that prevents access to your computer presents little problem (they usually set the keyboard for normal operation once you enter a password), a TSR could have devastating results.

Other Configuration Options   The next four entries directly affect the program environment. The No Screen Exchange entry allows you to determine if the application will have access to Windows' clipboard. Checking the box saves the memory that Windows normally allocates for this function, but deactivates the Alt-Print Screen and Print Screen keys.

The Prevent Program Switch entry is a memory saver as well. Windows usually allocates a small amount of memory for each application for the task switcher. Checking this box saves the memory used by that function. Unfortunately, this also means that you must physically exit the application to return to Windows or switch to any other application.

Most generally you will want to keep the Close Window on Exit entry checked. All this does is make sure that Windows actually closes the application window when you exit the application. Sometimes, however, you will need to keep the Windows open. For example, if the application you use displays messages on screen after you exit, you will want to close the window manually; otherwise, you might not get to read the message before the application windows closes.

Windows normally retains an image of the application screen when you switch to another application. While this uses between 4K and 64K of RAM, it does ensure that your application screen will look the same when you return. You can save this memory if your application possesses an automatic redraw command. Instead of saving the screen image, Windows will simply tell the application to redraw its screen when you return to the application. The downside to this is that the application might take longer to redraw the display than Windows would have used to restore it. This is especially true of graphics intensive programs like AutoCAD or PFS:First Publisher where the memory savings are greatest. As a result, you might have to choose between saving memory or high-speed switching.

The final Standard mode PIF entries refer to keys normally reserved by Windows. Some applications might use these keys as well. If you check one of the boxes, then Windows turns control of that key over to the application. Instead performing its Windows function, the key will perform its original application function. Unfortunately, in doing this, you might lose specific capabilities provided by Windows.

Configuring Enhanced mode PIFs

The Enhanced mode PIF starts with the same four entries as the Standard mode PIF. However, these entries are simultaneously more complex and flexible than the options offered by the standard mode PIF.

Video Memory   Like the Standard mode PIF, the Enhanced mode PIF has a section for determining the amount of video memory to allocate to an application. However, the Video Memory section for Enhanced mode contains three entries. The Text selection is the same as Standard mode. Any text application uses about 4K of RAM. However, EGA and VGA displays have two other choices. (Because a CGA display does not offer high resolution graphics, both the graphics options are effectively the same.) The Low Graphics selection equates to CGA resolution graphics displays. Windows allocates about 16K for this mode. In most cases, this memory allocation also provides more than enough memory for text mode applications that use RAM fonts or more than one display page. The High Resolution selection provides the full 64K of RAM for graphics.

Memory Requirements   The Memory Requirements section provides two blanks. In most cases you want to place the vendor recommended minimum memory requirement in the first blank (unless this requirement never meets your application and data storage needs) and the maximum memory that your application requires in the second blank. Never simply assume that your maximum need is the full 640K limit of this section. Some applications can use far less memory and still get the job done. Always allocate only the memory you need, saving memory for other applications.

EMS and XMS Memory   The next two sections work together. Few, if any, applications use both EMS and XMS memory simultaneously. (The only exception to this might be a DOS window used to run various applications.) As a result, always set both entries in one of the sections to 0, which will prevent Windows from allocating memory that you will never use. As before, state the vendor required minimum requirements in the KB Required blank and the maximum memory required by your application and data storage needs in the KB Limit blank.

Display Usage   Once you configure the memory section, you must decide how you'll run the application. The Display Usage section tells Windows whether you want to run the application in Full Screen or Windowed mode. In Full Screen mode, the application uses far less memory but you cannot exchange information between it and other applications as easily. The Windowed mode offers ease of use but uses more memory. The main difference is that Windows must allocate more memory for text mode applications to run in a graphics environment than in a text environment. In most cases, you cannot run graphics applications in a Window.

Execution   Program execution is an area where you can really optimize an application. You must consider two different modes. First you must decide whether or not you want the application to have exclusive control when it is in the foreground. Giving an application exclusive control can greatly enhance the performance of that application but will prevent all of your background applications from running. You must consider whether the application really uses enough system resources to benefit from exclusive execution before you check this box.

Some applications require exclusive operation by virtue of the task they perform. For example, a backup program requires exclusive control of the system. Windowed applications can run in exclusive mode, but they never truly receive full control of the system. Windows reserves part of the system resources for itself. Therefore, if you want an application to have absolute control of the system environment, select Execution Exclusive and Display Usage Full Screen.

Background execution is another factor you must consider. First, will the application safely run in the background? For example, a word processor is probably not a good candidate for background execution because most of the work performed with a word processor is done in the foreground. On the other hand, a database management system will certainly perform useful work in the background. For example, you could reindex a database while performing some other task. The second factor you must consider is how background execution will affect the speed of other applications running on the system. If the program is a resource hog, then it might not be a good candidate for background execution.

For example, if you had a spreadsheet performing an intensive recalculation, then perhaps you shouldn't let it execute in the background if you must run another memory-intensive program. You could safely run a disk-intensive program like a database manager, though. Some programs that seem natural candidates for background execution do not perform well on all occasions. For example, if you try to perform a high-speed file transfer (9600 baud or above) with a communications program running in the background, the transfer will probably fail if you don't give the application a high enough priority. Unfortunately, if you increase its priority, then all the other applications running on your machine will suffer. Of course, performing a low speed transfer (2400 baud or less) in the background might work.

Close Window on Exit   The final entry on the first Enhanced mode display is Close Window on Exit. This entry works just like the one in the Standard mode PIF. In most cases, you want to close the Window as soon as the application exits. The only exception to this rule is when you run an application that displays information after you exit. In this case, you will want to close the window manually.

Configuring Enhanced mode PIF advanced options

Fully optimizing your application in the Enhanced mode environment requires that you spend a little time in the Advanced Options display. Simply click on the Advanced... button on the first display and the Advanced Option form appears.

Multitasking Options   The first section is Multitasking Options. It is composed of three parts. First, you must tell Windows the foreground priority of the application. Second, you must tell Windows the background priority of the application. Finally, the Detect Idle Time check box tells Windows to determine when the application is waiting for keyboard input. When Windows detects this condition, it gives the processing cycles normally used by the application to other applications running on the system.

Now that we've looked at the three options, exactly what is the foreground and background priority about? These two selections determine how much processing time an application gets when compared to all the other applications running on the system. For example, if you had three applications running and the first one had a foreground priority of 100, the second had a background priority of 50, and the third had a background priority of 150, then the first application would receive approximately 1/3 of the system resources, the second would receive 1/6 of the system resources, and the third would receive 1/2 the system resources. This isn't exactly what happens, but it gives you a good rule of thumb. The actual Windows environment is slightly more complex. The difference between foreground priority and background priority is fairly simple to understand. If you are using an application, it's in the foreground. If an application is running by itself, then it's in the background. There is only one foreground application; all the rest are in the background.

To use this feature to its best advantage, give high priority tasks a higher priority and low priority tasks a lower priority. For example, you may want to transfer data in the background, recalculate a spreadsheet, re-index a database, and work on your word processor. You know that the communications program requires a lot of processing cycles so you give it a background priority of 300. The spreadsheet will recalculate for a long time, but you don't want it to bog the system down, so you give it a priority of 25. The database is also a back-burner task, but it's a little more important than the spreadsheet, so you give it a background priority of 50. Your word processor gets the default foreground priority of 100. As you can see, each task receives the processing cycles based on a combination of its requirements and your work needs.

So what happens if a client calls and needs that spreadsheet right now? Simply click on the spreadsheet icon. If it's a DOS application, you'll get a dialog box with a Settings... entry. Click on the Settings... entry and you'll see another dialog box. Notice that you cannot only change the background and foreground priorities, but you can tell the application to run either windowed or full screen, in the background, or in exclusive mode. Changing the Settings... display temporarily overrides the PIF settings. The settings return to normal the next time you start the application.

Memory Options The Memory Options section holds four choices. The first two deal with the way Windows treats the memory used by the application. At the beginning of the chapter, we examined the benefits of 32-bit access. One of those benefits is that Windows can use virtual memory management techniques with DOS applications. In most cases, this is true. However, two cases require special attention. If you use either a memory resident program or DOS device driver that uses XMS or EMS memory, then you might need to make certain that the application resides in memory at all times. The reason is simple: these two classes of program often perform unexpected actions that would result in system deadlock. If you find that your TSR or device driver locks the system, then you might want to check the appropriate box (either EMS Memory Locked or XMS Memory Locked) to see if that restores your system.

Check the Uses High Memory Area box only if your application uses the HMA. In most cases you will want to leave this entry blank.

The Lock Application Memory check box tells Windows to keep the application in memory instead of swapping parts of it to disk. While this dramatically speeds the application, it does cause two problems. First, using this option will reduce the number of DOS applications you can run. Second, this option also slows all the other applications on the system. Windows cannot manage memory efficiently if you do not give it full access to your applications.

Display Options   The Display Options section contains five entries, with the first three entries (Text, Low Graphics, and High Graphics) being interrelated. What happens if you switch from one application to another, and the first application leaves the display adaptor in an uncertain state? Hopefully, the second application detects this and restores its display. In fact, this is what happens in the majority of cases. The Monitor Ports options help those applications that don't perform this monitoring. If your application doesn't seem to restore the screen properly, selecting the option matching the application's video mode will help. Of course, allowing Windows to perform this extra monitoring reduces application speed, so only check these boxes when absolutely necessary.

Some applications use the ROM BIOS routines for all displays. Switching back and forth between protected and virtual 86 mode slows the application down. Checking the Emulate Text Mode box can speed these applications by allowing Windows to perform all the BIOS calls using a virtual driver in protected memory. If you find that the display gets scrambled or the cursor appears in the wrong place, then clear this box. Otherwise, you can get a significant speed increase by checking it.

Many applications switch video modes while you run them. For example, Harvard Graphics for DOS switches between text mode and high graphics mode. Windows normally tries to recover memory when you switch to a less demanding video mode so that you can use it for other applications. When the application goes back to original mode, Windows allocates the memory it requires for video. But what happens if you don't have the memory required to display the information? Freeing memory by closing an application is one alternative; choosing the check the Retain Video Memory box is the other. When you check this box, Windows does not reallocate the video memory freed when an application switches modes.

Other Options Section   The other options section contains four main entries. The first entry, Allow Fast Paste, allows Windows to paste information using its quick method. If you don't check this box, Windows uses a slower method that places a time interval between each character. Some applications require this additional time or they lose characters. Try using Fast Paste first. If your application loses characters, clear the box.

The Allow Close When Active is perfect for applications that you want automatically closed when you exit Windows. For example, you might have a copy of DOS running on the machine at all times. Closing this application without actually ending it won't cause any damage in many circumstances. Never check this box if you are uncertain about the results of simply terminating the application.

The third section allows you to reserve shortcut keys for your application. As with the standard PIF, reserving keys combinations for your application restores the application's standard function but reduces your ability to interact with Windows.

The final section allows you to assign a shortcut key to your application, which means that you can switch from application to application without going back to Windows. Using this option greatly reduces the effort of switching between two DOS applications that you use together on a regular basis.

Conclusion

This chapter examined many of the more important aspects of optimizing Windows for optimum performance. The two most important features of the Windows environment are the WIN.INI and SYSTEM.INI files. Making certain these two files are optimized will provide the best overall system performance enhancements. Remember that you need to get DOS configured before you tackle Windows. Also remember that PIF files are the basis for every improvement you can expect from DOS applications running under Windows.

The next chapter will explore many of these same features under DESQView. You will discover that Windows and DESQView are worlds apart when it comes to optimal configuration, even though they share some of the same elements.

10
CHAPTER

Using DESQview

DESQview is an alternative multitasking solution to Microsoft Windows. It provides a transparent interface that allows a suite of DOS applications to run concurrently on all PC platforms.

DESQview increases its user options and flexibility as you upgrade the power of your PC.

DESQview's features can enhance productivity in running DOS or Windows-based applications.

Why use DESQview?

In the last chapter, you received an introduction to the world of Microsoft Windows. You may have observed that building proficiency in the Windows world is almost equivalent to leaving MS-DOS for a new operating system. Apple Macintosh users have been after PC users to do this for years, and they might finally succeed. It's true that Windows applications include powerful productivity features, but they also require the user to master a new set of "computer reflexes."

Quarterdeck's DESQview takes a simpler approach to the problem of multitasking programs (or switching between them). Quarterdeck's philosophy in DESQview is that you'd rather keep using the applications you already own. You've attained proficiency using a series of DOS programs and what you really want is more convenient access to them. DESQview allows you to multitask the programs you already know with minimal intrusion from the operating environment. After reading the last chapter you might be tempted to say, "Well, Windows does this, too!" And, indeed, both operating environments allow DOS multitasking on 80386 and above computing platforms, but DESQview has several advantages that might make it your multitasker of choice.

- DESQview task switches and multitasks successfully using hardware approximately half as powerful as what you need for Windows. Work that requires a 33 MHz 80386 using a suite of Windows applications might well be accomplished with DESQview and DOS programs on a 16 MHz 80386SX or even on an 80286! Windows applications are bringing unprecedented features and flexibility to PC computing. If you have the resources to invest in Windows, it might ultimately return your investment with increased computing power. But there's a price to pay along the way: switching abruptly to the Windows world with modest hardware resources can be frustrating. The idea of running Word for Windows 2.0 on your 1M 80286 turns out to be a lot more attractive in theory than in practice. DESQview's advantage is that it can provide a robust multitasking environment on an 80286 (or 16 MHz 80386) with only 2−3M of memory. Windows, in contrast, can't multitask DOS applications at all on any platform below 80386. To gain equivalent application performance under Windows, you need at least a 33 MHz 80386DX with 4−8M of installed memory.

  Your system's graphic resolution is another consideration. Day-to-day use of Windows requires VGA as a minimum standard. (Super VGA resolution of 800×600 or 1024×768 is preferred.) DESQview is comfortable with EGA graphics, and Hercules monochrome or EGA for text-based applications. (As with Windows, VGA is preferable if your work requires intensive use of graphics-based programs.)

- Besides requiring less sophisticated hardware and less onboard memory to multitask, DESQview will also offer more robust application performance on that hardware than Windows. If your chief concern is the speed of spreadsheet recalculations or data-retrieval searches, DESQview will allow you to do these things faster.

- Windows can't multitask DOS-extender programs that use Virtual Control Program Interface (VCPI) technology. As we learned in Chapter 4, many powerful applications now break the 640K barrier through the use of industry-standard VCPI. Because Windows replaced this standard with DPMI, users can't multitask the 80386 versions of AutoCAD, Paradox, Mathematica, Oracle SQL, etc. DESQview allows you to multitask these applications, and even run them in small-screen windows! (Some DOS extended applications now use the DOS Protected Mode Interface (DPMI) technology supported by Windows.)

- The process of installing the program and learning the operating interface is simpler with DESQview.

Of course, if you have the hardware to handle Windows' more stringent requirements, then you also have some sound reasons for choosing Windows instead of DESQview as a multitasking environment.

- Windows offers a standard command interface that applies to all Windows-based applications. This can ease the learning curve with new applications for users who don't already know how to use DOS programs.

- Additionally, with Windows you need only one set of fonts, video drivers, and print drivers for a suite of productivity applications. This simplifies installation of new programs.

- Windows also offers more complete inter-application connectivity through its clipboard. Text, bit-mapped art, and object graphics can all be cut and pasted between Windows programs. In Windows 3.1, the new object linking and dynamic data features make it possible to combine several applications into a unified productivity module. DESQview offers only text-based file management utilities and text-only cut and paste between programs.

To illustrate the differences between Windows and DESQview, let's look at some typical productivity scenarios.

The situation that comes to mind naturally for a computer book author is that you are a writer. For either fiction or non-fiction writing, writers might want to view several drafts of the same document on the screen simultaneously. While writing, they might also want to read other documents, access a database, or work on a chapter outline. As you work, you might find it necessary to perform file maintenance tasks: format a diskette, copy files, or organize a file directory. Ideally, you should be able to do all of these things without breaking the flow of concentration that goes into your writing. For instance, a writer in the middle of a chapter about landscaping and gardening may suddenly decide that a series of figures and tables should be placed in the same directory with the chapter. The writer might even want to call up a graphic figure and keep it handy on the screen while composing the chapter.

If you already own programs that accomplish these tasks separately, DESQview simply allows you to have all of the programs open at the same time. The DESQview interface remains unobtrusively in the background. You only have to know one keystroke to bring up the DESQ menu, open more programs, or switch between programs. DESQview can open both DOS text-based and graphics-based programs.

In our writer's scenario, you might have a chapter outline open in one screen window and load a duplicate copy of your word processor to work on the chapter text (which is especially useful if your word processor doesn't provide multi-document views). While you write, you might open another window to display figures in a graphic file-viewer or paint program. This trick becomes even more convenient if you add a second monitor to your system. One of the simplest and least known productivity boosters for multitasking is to add a Hercules card and monochrome monitor to a VGA system—possible by spending only $100 or less. You can use one monitor as a cut-and-paste work area while the other displays your foreground application. (We'll examine the technical logistics of this trick later on in the chapter.)

The difference between using DESQview and using Windows for this scenario is that Windows would need 4M of installed RAM instead of 2M, and you would probably want a 25 MHz 80386DX just to switch between DOS applications!

Note If you were using Windows for this project, you might want to acquire Microsoft's Word for Windows. Word for Windows includes an outline view, document display, and some rudimentary figure drawing capabilities in one package. Using both Windows and Windows applications will ultimately increase your user options, but you will need to learn new keystrokes, and new techniques to use them effectively. You could do the same project with DESQview and some stand-alone DOS programs like WordPerfect and PC Paintbrush.

Here are a few other multitasking scenarios:

- A secretary needs the computer to do double-duty as a database reference tool and a word processing station. The computer needs to switch rapidly between WordPerfect, dBASE/FoxPro, or 1-2-3.

- A real estate broker wants to download statistical information through a modem while preparing a report. The broker might run a package like DayMar concurrently with Ask Sam and a word processor.

- An MIS manager needs to simultaneously track EMAIL from several clients on a network. To do this, a network mail server must be configured to accept concurrent input from multiple nodes. Again, DESQview allows you to implement these configurations on less sophisticated hardware than Windows and it delivers more robust application performance. In the area of telecommunications, for example, DESQview allows a higher rate of background data transfer (up to 34,000 bps, compared to Windows 9600 bps).

On 80286 and above platforms, you can even run Windows in one DESQview program window. Why would you want to do this? Again, the answer is that DESQview permits smooth multitasking on less powerful hardware. If you need to use Word for Windows or Pagemaker on a low-end 80286/80386 machine, DESQview allows you to call these programs up and put them to sleep again faster than using Windows by itself. (Figure 10-1 shows Windows 3.1 in Standard mode running inside of DESQview along with several DOS applications. This trick is especially useful for 80286 users because it effectively allows them to run Windows and multitask DOS programs at the same time.)

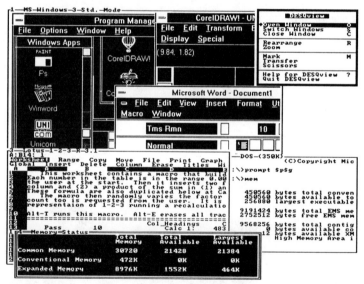

Fig. 10-1   Windows Standard mode running in a DESQView window.

If you're interested in how Windows and DESQview compare with respect to speed on various computer platforms, you may want to examine Table 10-1.

Hardware strategies for using DESQview

As your computing platform increases in power, DESQview takes advantage of increased hardware capabilities.

DESQview has a slight edge over Windows in foreground performance efficiency, but Windows apps outperform DOS apps in benchmarks.

Time to complete 250 spreadsheet recalculations is given in minutes:seconds.
Search and Replace efficiency for word processors is given in replace instances per minute.
Print efficiency in word processors is given in pages per minute.
Download efficiency in communications programs is given in characters per second.

Combinations tested:

123	Excel	WordPerfect	Word for Windows	PCPlus	XTalk/(Win)
WordPerfect	Wordperfect	123	123	123	123
PCPlus	PCPlus	PCPlus	PCPlus	WordPerfect	WordPerfect

Note Foreground apps rotate between "native DOS" and "native Windows" applications.
The background apps in all tests are always DOS apps.

	386DX 20MHz/4M		**286 16MHz/4M** **(w/ALL Chargecard)**
	WINDOWS **w/ Smartdrive 512K**	**DESQview** **w/ Smartdrive 512K**	**DESQview** **w/Smartdrive 512K**

SPREADSHEET
IN FOREGROUND

With WP Text Macro in background

123 Recalc	5:03	3:53	3:13
WP Text Macro	68 inst./min	76 inst./min	69 inst./min
PCPlus Download	219 cps	215 cps	212 cps
Excel Recalc	3:00	1:58	2:38
WP Text Macro	88 inst./min	57 inst./min	59 inst./min
PCPlus Download	205 cps	226 cps	156 cps

With Print job in background

123 Recalc	5:36	3:48	3:14
WP Print job	2 pp/min	1.6 pp/min	1.2 pp/min
PCPlus Download	219 cps	215 cps	222 cps
Excel Recalc	2:52	1:55	2:31
WP Print job	1 pp/min	1.6 pp/min	2 pp/min
PCPlus Download	220 cps	231 cps	183 cps

GRAPHICS TABLE

	386-20		**286-16**	
	Windows	**DESQview**	**Windows**	**DESQview**
Open DOS app at 1024x768 resolution	Yes	Yes	Yes	Yes
Restore screen display of 1024 x768 window	Yes	Partial	Won't Switch Out	Partial
Open DOS app at 800x600 resolution	Yes	Yes	Yes	Yes

Table 10-1   Continued

Restore screen display of 800x600 window	Yes	Yes (16 colors)	Won't Switch Out	Yes (16 colors)

COMPATIBILITY TABLE

	WINDOWS	DESQVIEW
AUTOCAD 386	Yes[1]	Yes[2]
IBM INTERLEAF PUBLISHER	Yes[1]	Yes[2]
Intel SATISFAXION BOARD	Yes	Yes (with DV Patch)
LANTASTIC, v.3/4	Partial[3]	Partial[3]
LOTUS, r 3.0	Yes[1]	Yes
LOTUS, r 3.1	Yes	Yes
MATHEMATICA	Yes[1]	Yes
ORACLE SQL	Yes[1]	Yes
PARADOX 386	Yes[1]	Yes
PCKWIK POWERPAK, v2.13	Yes	Partial
TOPS, v. 3.01	Partial (Real/Standard modes)[4]	Partial[4]
High Speed Telecommunication	Up to 9600 bps in foreground/ 2400 bps in the background (Higher transmission speeds are possible with special hardware & software)[5]	9600-38,400 bps in foreground and background

---

[1]These programs, which use VCPI DOS Extender technology, were incompatible with Windows 3.0 in Enhanced mode. Under Windows 3.1, they may be run in either Standard or Enhanced mode.

[2]Graphics based VCPI programs must run in full-screen windows.

[3]Artisoft recommends not running Windows in Enhanced Mode or DESQview on the server with version 3.0

[4]Network printing and client filesharing available. Not always stable and reliable.

[5]Windows may send and receive files at up to 19,200 bps in the foreground with the addition of an NS16550 UART chip to the serial port, and special software that can enable the chip's communications buffer. (Most communications programs don't provide that option, although TURBOCOM from xxxxx can send and receive at 38.400bps (38,400 in the foreground, 9600bps in the background in special cases.)

Hardware strategies for using DESQview   **319**

8088/8086 PCs

640K Only   DESQview task switches or multitasks applications with combined memory requirements approximately 450K or less. (For example, you might multitask a word processor like PC Write or WordPerfect 4.2 with a modest communications program like ProComm 2.43 or Commo.) You can task switch additional single applications that require up to about 450K in this configuration by allowing DESQview to swap dormant programs to the hard disk. Generally, swapping programs to disk is slow and unwieldy.

640K + 512K of EMS 3.2 Memory   The same program size limitations apply, except that DESQView can swap dormant programs to EMS 3.2 memory instead of to the hard disk. Doing this speeds task switching and makes it a more viable option.

640K + 512K of EEMS or EMS 4.0 Memory   DESQview will multitask applications where the first program uses approximately 450K and subsequent programs use up to the amount of conventional memory backfilled from the EMS card. If 384K of conventional memory is backfilled from the EMS card, then you can multitask additional programs of up to 384K. (See the section on configuring EMS cards in Chapter 5 for more details). Adding more EMS 4.0 memory increases the number of 384K programs that you can open in expanded memory.

TIP for Hercules/CGA Users   Included on our utilities diskette is a public domain program called EEMRAM. EEMRAM can add an additional 64K to 96K to the maximum DESQview program size on systems with EEMS/EMS 4.0 memory and CGA or Hercules graphics cards. If your system has an EGA or VGA graphics card, you may still take advantage of EEMRAM by configuring DESQview to use the CGA or Hercules video driver.

You can also obtain more memory on 8088 systems equipped with EEMS/EMS 4.0 memory by using Quarterdeck's QRAM utility to load programs into upper memory. (See the section on QRAM in Chapter 8.)

80286 PCs

640K + 384K Extended Memory Installed on Motherboard   Optimal configuration allows DESQview to task switch or multitask applications with combined memory requirements of approximately 550K. On 80286 systems that have 64K of extended memory, make sure to load Quarterdeck's QEXT.SYS in CONFIG.SYS. Users of MS-DOS 5 will obtain best results by deleting the DOS = H I GH statement in CONFIG.SYS and removing Microsoft's HIMEM .SYS driver. The QEXT.SYS driver replaces HIMEM.SYS and allows DESQview to make more efficient use of the HMA area. With QEXT installed, you can task switch additional applications totalling up to about 550K by letting DESQview swap dormant programs to the hard disk. But be aware that swapping programs to the hard disk might result in slow and unwieldy performance.

640K + 64K of Extended Memory + 512K of EMS 3.2 Memory Make sure Quarterdeck's QEXT.SYS driver is installed as previously described. The same program size limitations apply, except that DESQView can swap dormant programs to EMS 3.2 memory instead of to the hard disk. Doing this speeds up task switching and makes it a more viable option.

640K + 64K of Extended Memory + 512K of EEMS \ EMS 4.0 Memory Install Quarterdeck's QEXT.SYS driver as previously described. DESQview will multitask applications where the first program uses approximately 550K and subsequent programs use up to the amount of conventional memory backfilled from the EMS card. (If 384K of conventional memory is backfilled from the EMS card, you can multitask additional programs requiring up to 384K.)

Note As with 8088 \ 8086 systems, the EEMRAM program on our utilities diskette can add 64K to 96K to the size of DESQview windows if you run DESQview in CGA or Hercules graphics modes. Quarterdeck's QRAM utility can free up still more memory by loading programs and drivers above 640K. (See the section on QRAM in Chapter 8 for details).

640K + 384K (or more) of Extended Memory + Memory Management Unit (All ChargeCard or SOTA Pop) This configuration is the most desirable one for DESQview, short of upgrading to an 80386/80486 machine. Install Quarterdeck's QEXT.SYS driver in CONFIG.SYS, placing it before the device driver for the memory management unit. (See the section on configuring the ALL Chargecard in Chapter 8 for details.) DESQview will multitask multiple applications.(Each) The first application may use up to 570K of conventional memory on a VGA system. Extended memory will be converted transparently (converted) to EMS 4.0 as on 80386/80486 systems. You can multitask additional programs of 550K+ in expanded memory, up to the total of extended memory originally present on the system.

Note If DESQview is run in CGA or Hercules graphics modes, the software provided with the memory management unit can use the EGA/VGA video area to add 64K to 96K to the size of DESQview windows (allowing program sizes of over 640K!). See the section on configuring the ALL Chargecard software in Chapter 8 for details.

80386/80486 systems

640K + 384K of Extended Memory or Shadow RAM Without Quarterdeck's QEMM, DESQview multitasks applications whose combined memory total is 480K to 554K. Gaining that extra 64K is contingent upon getting DESQview to load some of its code in the HMA. If you don't use Quarterdeck's QEMM, and you have at least 64K of extended memory, then you want to load

DESQview's QEXT driver in CONFIG.SYS. As with 80286 machines, this allows DESQview to load code into the HMA. You may also remap all, part, or none of the system's dedicated shadow RAM as extended memory—depending upon your BIOS and the motherboard's design.

Tip Some systems allow you to remap dedicated Shadow RAM to extended memory through settings in the CMOS setup routine (see Chapter 2 for details). If your system's SETUP program allows you to remap only part of Shadow RAM, QEMM or 386MAX might recover more of it if you keep the Shadow RAM settings in the CMOS enabled. You might want to experiment by toggling Shadow RAM off and on, to see which configuration reclaims more RAM for use by QEMM or 386MAX.

MS-DOS 5 or one of the 80386 memory management packages examined in Chapter 8 can convert any remaining extended memory to EMS 4.0 for DESQview's use.

Note As on 80286 machines, MS-DOS 5 users will get more memory in DESQview windows if they remove the DOS = HIGH statement from CONFIG.SYS. Users of memory management packages with load high capabilities may place drivers and TSRs in upper memory. (DR DOS 6 users can also place the operating system in upper memory.) Loading programs into upper memory will certainly gain more conventional memory outside of DESQview. Whether this technique will gain more memory inside of DESQview windows is a variable factor: DESQview can load some of its code into the same UMB spaces staked out by load high utilities. If all the UMB space is occupied by drivers and TSRs, DESQview must place more of itself in conventional memory.

640K + More Than 384K of Extended Memory DESQview will multitask or task switch individual applications requiring up to 580K of conventional memory if you use QEMM (or QEXT.SYS plus another EMS 4.0 memory manager). The number of applications that you can multitask increases as more memory is added to the system. Quarterdeck's QEMM provides added enhancements for DESQview on an 80386 and is the preferred memory management package for serious DESQview users. With QEMM, DESQview occupies less conventional memory and also has the ability to virtualize text and graphics. Virtualized text and graphics allow ill-behaved text applications, and graphic-based programs to run in small-screen DESQview windows.

As on 8088 and 80286 machines, you can add 64-96K to the size of DESQview windows by running DESQview in Hercules or CGA graphics modes. The VIDRAM utility bundled with QEMM allows you to toggle use of added video memory on and off without rebooting the system. (See the section on using QEMM in Chapter 8.)

Configuring Memory for DESQview

8088 machines

On 8088 machines, your best strategy (short of upgrading to an 80386) is to place an expanded memory card in the system and backfill as much memory as possible from the card to the motherboard.

The following are typical configurations for the REMM.SYS expanded memory manager used with AST's RAMPAGE boards:

```
DEVICE = REMM . SYS  /P = 16  /C = 16  /L = A000 - B7FF
        /X = B800 BFFF
```

Lets you reclaim 96K of RAM if you have a Color Graphics Adaptor (CGA).

```
DEVICE = REMM . SYS  /P = 16  /C = 16  /L = A000 - AFFF
        /X = B000 BFFF
```

If you're using a Monochrome or Hercules Graphics Adapter, lets you gain 64K of additional memory by including A000-AFFF.

```
DEVICE = REMM . SYS /P = 16 /C = 16 /L = B000 - B7FF
```

Lets you include the unused monochrome areas available if you have an EGA or VGA adaptor attached to a COLOR monitor.

```
DEVICE = EMM . SYS PC C800 208
```

You can obtain best results with the Intel's Above Board+ by placing the expanded memory page frame as low as possible because Intel's EMM.SYS will not recognize upper memory above the page frame.

If you use Quarterdeck's QRAM to load programs into upper memory, you must load the QRAM.SYS device driver after the expanded memory manager. (See the section on QRAM in Chapter 8 for more details.)

80286 machines (ISA)

You must reserve at least 64K of extended memory on 80286 machines for Quarterdeck's QEXT.SYS device driver. You do this on AST and Intel memory cards by setting dip switches on the card. AST's BRAVO and PREMIUM 80286 machines include FASTRAM memory cards that have similar dip switch options. (See chapter 5 for an explanation of optimal configuration for an 80286 motherboard with 1M of onboard memory.)

You should load the QEXT driver before any expanded memory manager in CONFIG.SYS so DESQview can access the HMA. Users of MS-DOS 4 & 5 or Microsoft Windows should delete any occurrence of the HIMEM.SYS device driver because QEXT provides a superset of HIMEM's features. (You will also be able to run Microsoft Windows in Standard Mode, since QEXT functions as an XMS memory manager.)

If you are using Quarterdeck's QRAM to load programs into upper memory, place QRAM.SYS after the expanded memory manager. Examples:

```
DEVICE = QEXT.SYS
DEVICE = ALLEMM4.SYS RAM     (All ChargeCard—QRAM not
                              necessary)

DEVICE = QEXT.SYS
DEVICE = REMM.SYS /P = 16 /C = 16 /L = B000-B7FF /S = E000
DEVICE = C:\QRAM\QRAM.SYS     (AST 286 or Rampage card)

DEVICE = QEXT.SYS
DEVICE = EMM.SYS at C800 208
DEVICE = C:\QRAM\QRAM.SYS     (Intel Above Board)
```

80286 machines (IBM PS/2)

Quarterdeck's QEMM50/60 is a software device that allows you to convert extended memory on PS/2 Model 50/55/60 machines to expanded memory at the price of disabling the first megabyte of memory on the machine. Thus, if you have 4M on the machine, after running QEMM50/60 you will wind up with 640K conventional memory plus 2424K that you can use as either extended or expanded memory.

80386/80486 machines

MS-DOS 5 users who use QEMM should remove the DOS = HIGH and DOS = UMB statements from CONFIG.SYS. If you use QEMM, a tradeoff exists between the amount of upper memory available for loading high and the amount reserved for DESQview's use. If QEMM finds your machine compatible with its Stealth feature, insert the ST:M or ST:F parameter on the QEMM command line to create more mappable upper memory.

If you use a memory manager other than Quarterdeck's QEMM, you will want to load the QEXT.SYS driver included with DESQview before the line that loads the memory manager in CONFIG.SYS. Examples:

MS DOS 5
```
DEVICE = C:\QEXT.SYS
DEVICE = C:\DOS\EMM386.EXE RAM xxxx b = 1000
```

Note that QEXT takes the place of HIMEM.SYS. The b = 1000 parameter allows EMM386 to map the greatest possible conventional memory address space for DESQview windows, where xxxx is the total amount of memory to convert to EMS 4.0.

386MAX
```
DEVICE = C:\QEXT.SYS
```

```
DEVICE = C : \ 386MAX \ 386MAX . SYS pro
        = C : \ 386MAX \ 386MAX . PRO
```

Version 6.0 of 386MAX incompatible with QEXT. Consult their technical support department to obtain an upgrade that fixes this problem.

NETROOM CONFIG.SYS

```
DEVICE = C : \ NETROOM \ RM386 . SYS   NOXMS   NOHMA   EXT = 64
EMS = B000 - B7FF
EMS = C800 - DFFF

. . . .
```

When using Helix's NETROOM, load QEXT in AUTOEXEC.BAT using NETROOM's DEVLOAD command.

NETROOM AUTOEXEC.BAT

```
C : \ NETROOM \ DEVLOAD C : \ DV \ QEXT . SYS

. . . .
```

See the README.DV file in your NETROOM directory for more information.

Using QEMM As we mentioned in an earlier section, the easiest way to configure memory for DESQview on an 80386 or above platform is to use Quarterdeck's combined DESQview-80386 package. QEMM's default installation will guarantee good performance with DESQview. If all of your resident programs and TSRs successfully load into high memory without Stealth, then Quarterdeck doesn't install this feature. If you would like the maximum amount of memory inside of DESQview windows, try adding the Stealth parameter, anyway, and rerun OPTIMIZE. If Stealth is compatible with your system, it could increase DESQview window sizes by as much as 32-64K.

How DESQview works

DESQview searches your hard disk for common DOS productivity applications during installation. It installs any "found" programs automatically on the "Open A Program Menu." The user can start programs by typing a two-key abbreviation or by pointing and clicking with a mouse. You can also start a program by highlighting its name with the cursor keys and pressing Enter. Depending on their individual setup configuration, programs open into either full-screen or small-screen windows. The user can change the size and position of any small-screen window or zoom it up to full-screen. When you're working in a program, the program behaves just as it would if you had started it from the DOS command line.

The program you are working in (the one that has control of the keyboard) is called the "Foreground" application. Any other programs that you have running are called "Background" applications. DESQview lets you cycle between open programs by pressing the DESQ key followed by the number of the window. (If you don't know which window a program is in, you can get to it by invoking the DESQ key, placing the cursor on the "Switch Windows" option and pressing Enter. This brings up a numerical menu of open programs.) By default, the DESQ key is the Alt key (either one, if the keyboard has two of them). Pressing Alt or clicking with a mouse brings up the main DESQview menu. DESQ+1 (i.e., Alt-1) switches automatically to the first program you opened, DESQ+2 (i.e., Alt-2) to the second program, etc. up to the 9th open program. After that, DESQview numbers the windows alphabetically, and you must switch to them through the Switch Menus window, or by clicking with the mouse.

Some users have difficulty with DESQview's Alt hot key when they want to invoke an Alt-Keystroke option inside of an application. For instance, in WordPerfect, pressing Alt-F2 brings up WordPerfect's search and replace menu. If the second keystroke is not pressed rapidly, DESQview assumes that you want to bring up the DESQ menu when you press Alt. Although DESQview is written to wait and distinguish between a simple tap of the Alt key and an Alt-keystroke combination, some users still become confused and bring up the DESQ menu by mistake. To easily fix the problem, just remap the DESQ key to a different keystroke combination or assign it to only one of the Alt keys on the keyboard. The default for the DESQ key is changed by running DESQview's SETUP utility either from the DOS command line or within DESQview. Once in SETUP, press Enter and select "K" for keyboard. On the next menu, enter Y in the "Change system keys?" option; this brings up a menu that allows the Alt key to be remapped to a number of different combinations. (See Fig. 10-2 and Fig. 10-3.)

```
┌1═Advanced═Setup═══════════════════
│
│    Type the letter that corresponds
│    to the option you wish to change:
│
│         Auto Dialer          A
│         Colors               C
│         Keyboard             K
│         Logical Drives       L
│         Mouse                M
│         Network              N
│         Performance          P
│         Video Monitor        V
│         Window Positions     W
│
│         DONE                 ↵
│
└────────────────────────────────────
```

Fig. 10-2   DESQView Advanced
Setup menu.

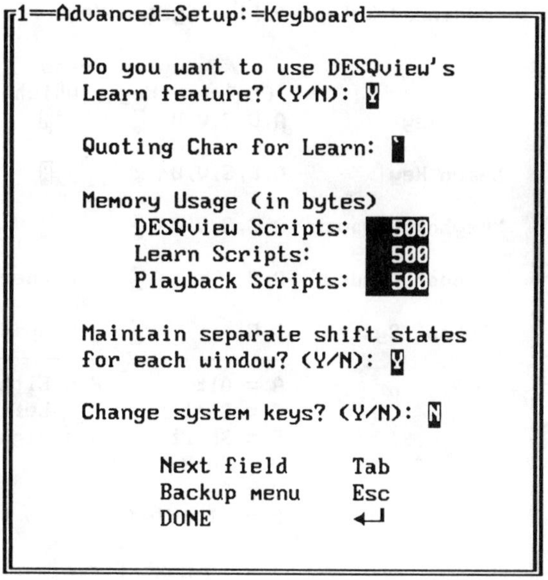

```
r1══Advanced═Setup:═Keyboard══════════════

              Do you want to use DESQview's
              Learn feature? (Y/N):  Y

              Quoting Char for Learn:  █

              Memory Usage (in bytes)
                 DESQview Scripts:    500
                 Learn Scripts:       500
                 Playback Scripts:    500

              Maintain separate shift states
              for each window? (Y/N):  Y

              Change system keys? (Y/N):  N

                    Next field       Tab
                    Backup menu      Esc
                    DONE             ↵
```

Fig. 10-3   LEARN DESQ Hot Key
Configuration Screen #1.

Setting up and configuring DESQview

After you copy DESQview's files to your hard disk using the INSTALL program, the DV SETUP program opens. Users have a choice between SIMPLE and ADVANCED setup options. The SIMPLE setup is accessed by pressing the space-bar and determines whether you have a COLOR monitor and the configuration of a MOUSE through a series of Yes/No questions. Default values are used for other DESQview settings.

The ADVANCED setup allows a complete customization of DESQview features. It is accessed by pressing the Enter key. Figure 10-4 shows the nine configuration categories presented in the ADVANCED setup menu.

Auto Dialer

If you have a modem installed, DESQview allows you to automatically dial a telephone number that appears anywhere in a text document by placing the cursor on it and selecting the Auto-Dial option from the "Mark" submenu. The Auto Dialer setup option tells DESQview which serial port your modem uses, the baud rate, and any access codes you want to insert before dialing the number.

Colors

DESQview allows each new window either to come up in a different color or to default to the colors used by the application. If you want DESQview to supply the

```
┌1═Advanced═Setup:═Define═System═Keys══════════════════════════════┐
│                                                                   │
│                     Key to Press        Key(s) to Hold Down       │
│                  Choices  Key   Which    Alt     Shift    Ctrl    │
│  DESQ Key        A,C,S,Q,0 Ⓐ     Ⓡ       Ⓓ       Ⓝ       Ⓝ       │
│                                                                   │
│  Learn Key       A,C,S,Q,0 Ⓐ     Ⓡ       Ⓓ       Ⓔ       Ⓝ       │
│                                                                   │
│  "Keyboard Mouse" A,C,S,Q,0 Ⓒ    Ⓔ       Ⓝ       Ⓝ       Ⓓ       │
│                                                                   │
│  "Reboot Window"  D,0      Ⓓ    Either    Ⓔ       Ⓓ       Ⓔ       │
│                                                                   │
│  "Reboot System"  D,0      Ⓓ    Keypad    Ⓝ       Ⓛ       Ⓔ       │
│                  ─────────────────────────────────────────────   │
│                  A = Alt      E = Either  N = Neither held down   │
│                  C = Ctrl     L = Left    E = Either held down    │
│                  S = Shift    R = Right   L = Left key held down  │
│                  Q = SysRq                R = Right key held down │
│                  D = Del                  B = Both keys held down │
│                  0 = Disabled             D = Don't care          │
│                                                                   │
│                     Next field    Tab                             │
│                     Backup menu   Esc                             │
│                     DONE          ←┘                              │
└───────────────────────────────────────────────────────────────────┘
```

Fig. 10-4   LEARN DESQ Hot Key Configuration Screen #2.

colors for each window, this option allows you to set defaults for foreground, background, and highlighted text.

Keyboard

DESQview includes a built-in keyboard macro recorder called LEARN. This option allows you to set defaults for LEARN and to tell DESQview whether to maintain separate keyboard states for individual programs. The CapsLock, NumLock, and Scroll Lock keys may be set to keep the same on/off status over all program windows, or maintain separate status for individual programs. Figure 10-3 and Fig. 10-4 show how this option also allows you to change the default for the {DESQ} hot key.

Logical drives

To avoid the necessity of typing in long path names for subdirectories, DESQview allows you to assign a logical drive letter to a specified path. For instance, if your WordStar documents reside in a directory called C: \ WORDSTAR \ REPORTS \ JANUARY, you may type this path in next to a logical drive letter shown on this menu. If you type the path in next to G:, then while you are in DESQview, you may access files in this directory by searching "Logical Drive G" instead of specifying C: \ WORDSTAR \ REPORTS \ JANUARY each time you want to retrieve a document.

This option also controls where DESQview swaps dormant programs for task switching. If no expanded memory is present, or if the allocated expanded memory has been exhausted, DESQview may swap dormant programs to files on disk. The SWAP: field allows the user to designate where DESQview's swap files are placed.

Mouse

This option tells DESQview about the type of mouse you use, both the manufacturer and the port location. Additionally, you may reverse the function of the two mouse buttons for DESQview by choosing "Left-handed mouse."

Network

This option is for users of IPX-based networks (Novell Netware) or NETBIOS-based networks (Microsoft Lan Manager, generic IBM). It substitutes DESQview's internal network driver to regulate network traffic inside of DESQview windows. If you have trouble running a program under DESQview while on the network, you can increase the number of network buffers allocated. (For example, this might be useful for IBM 3270 gateway access.)

Performance

Performance is the most important submenu for ADVANCED DESQview setup. Its first option allows you to set the CPU sharing ratios for foreground and background programs. The PC clock produces approximately 18 clock cycles per second. The default foreground/background ratio of 9:3 is designed for optimal performance on mid-range machines. If you have a 25 MHz 80386 or above, you might want to experiment by reducing the foreground/background ratio to 4:2 or 3:1. This can produce smoother multitasking on fast machines. The two boxes under "Memory Usage (in KB)" allow you to control the total of memory DESQview takes for internal housekeeping. "Common Memory" is used to keep track of the screen display for various programs. If you intend to run graphics applications, or open a large number of windows, increase this number from the default of 17K to 25-35K. "DOS Buffer for EMS" is a setting useful with 8088 and 80286 systems that use add-on EMS cards. For 80386/80486 systems using QEMM as the memory manager, this setting can remain at 0.

Note The memory allocated in these settings subtracts from the total of conventional memory available in DESQview windows, so you should use the smallest numbers commensurate with satisfactory program performance. (If the setting for "Common Memory" is too low, DESQview will complain with pop-up messages.)

Setting "Optimize communications" to Yes is useful if you have a high speed modem. In addition to a Y/N choice, you may also place a number in the box, representing the interrupt used by your communications port. (You can use one of the system inventory utilities discussed in Chapter 2 to find the interrupt used on your system.) For instance, a "3" in the "Optimize communications" box assigns priority to the port using IRQ 3.

You should generally set "Allow swapping of programs" to Yes, unless you have a specific reason for wanting to disable this feature (for instance, if you have limited expanded memory, and you don't want "swapped" programs to take up space on your hard disk). You can also enable or disable swapping for individual applications through DESQview's "Change A Program" menu. If you have more than one printer active on your system while using DESQview, set the "Manage printer contention" option to Yes. Otherwise, leave it at the default setting.

Video monitor

This setting tells DESQview what type of monitor your system uses. Normally, the Install program makes appropriate choice automatically. You can set this option to No if you prefer not to show text and graphics on the screen at the same time. On slower systems, this will speed up screen redraw. If your video card has an automatic mode-sensing feature, you might want to set "Synchronized access" to Yes. Some video cards automatically detect the graphics mode desired by a given program and switch the system to that mode when the program is opened. (If the video card allows you to disable the automatic mode sensing feature, this generally results in smoother performance within DESQview. If, for instance, you still need to switch from VGA to EGA or CGA for some programs, it's better to use software commands in a batch file run within that application's individual DESQview window.)

The last option in the Video Monitor submenu controls DESQview's screen saver. The screen will go blank if there is no keyboard activity for the number of minutes specified in the box. A 0 disables screen blanking.

Window positions

DESQview has a default screen placement for each of the first nine programs run in small screen windows. By varying the row and column coordinates, you can change the default positioning for each window.

Using DESQview's features

DESQview has a number of built-in features that can increase your productivity with individual applications.

Mark and Transfer

Mark and Transfer is DESQview's cut-and-paste tool. You can use it to block out text in one application, and then copy and store it to memory. You can then paste the text into an application running in a different window. For instance, database fields or spreadsheet cells can be transferred to a word processor. DESQView can also copy text from a word processor and send on-line through a communications program. Data received from a communications program can be captured and transferred to another window.

Learn

DESQview's built-in macro feature allows you to record any combination of keystrokes and assign them to a playback key within any window. Learn macros can be used within an individual program, or used globally between programs. You may use Learn to automatically open or close program windows and to switch between programs. Even if your word processor already has a macro feature, Learn can enhance it. For instance, you might devise a routine that invokes a program's "escape-to-DOS" shell, executes file maintenance functions, and returns to the program, all with a single keystroke.

Configuring an Automatic Start-Up Macro

1. Press the Learn key (Shift-Alt).
2. Press Start Script.
3. Select a key to call the macro manually.
4. When you type in the script name, make the first letter an exclamation point (!).
5. Record the macro.
6. Press the Learn key and select "Finish Script."

If you begin recording the script with the DESQ menu open, DESQview will execute it automatically on start-up. If you begin recording the script from within a program window, DESQview will execute the script when you launch the program. Script files for programs are stored in the DESQview directory in the form XX-SCRIP.DVS, where XX is the two-letter combination used to open the window. Global DESQview scripts are stored in a file called DESQVIEW.DVS. You can delete all macros in a program window by deleting the script file for that window.

To cancel a global DESQview start-up script, you can either rename or delete the DESQVIEW.DVS file in the \ DV directory. In fact, you can configure multiple start-up scripts, and subsequently rename each of them. Save the alternative scripts as START1.DVS, START2.DVS, etc. To choose a start-up scenario for DESQview, write a batch file like this one:

```
DV1.BAT
CD \DV
COPY DESQVIEW.DVS TEMP.DVS
COPY START1.DVS DESQVIEW.DVS
DV
COPY TEMP.DVS DESQVIEW.DVS
```

You can construct similar batch files for other start up scenarios. To run DESQview without a start-up script, write a batch file that simply renames DESQVIEW.DVS without replacing it.

DOS services

DOS Services is DESQview's built-in command shell. It allows you to run all common DOS commands from a pull-down menu. You may display a file list by date and/or file type, mark specific files, and copy them to a different subdirectory or delete them. DOS Services uses only a small amount of RAM, so it can run concurrently with other programs even on a 640K-only machine. You may invoke the DOS Backup command and create a backup set in the background while you continue to work in a different foreground application (as shown in Fig. 10-5).

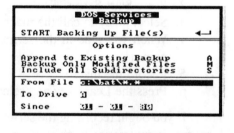

Fig. 10-5 Invoking DOS Backup as a background application.

Memory status

DESQview's Memory Status utility is your multitasking gas gauge. Selecting MS from the Open Window menu gives you a dynamic display of memory usage under DESQview. Once loaded, Memory Status monitors all multitasking operations, automatically updating its display to show how the RAM in your PC is allocated.

Memory Status is organized into three rows by three columns of information. Reading down, there are three categories. Reading across, the display shows the total amount on the system in each category, the total remaining for application use, and the largest total available for a single application.

Common memory is an internal DESQview buffer used for housekeeping and system video display. Conventional memory shows the total memory in the 0 to 640K DOS range available for programs. This total includes any "backfilled" RAM from an EMS board, or video memory annexed to DOS with Quarterdeck's VIDRAM. Expanded memory represents the total of RAM in your system controlled by an expanded memory device driver. The Memory Status display in Fig. 10-6 shows us that the total amount of conventional memory after loading DESQview is 552K. Of that memory, 152K is available for loading other programs, and 149K represents the maximum size for an individual program. Note that out of a total of 8960K of expanded memory, 3728K remains available for running programs and the largest amount available for a single program is 544K. You may wonder what this means—Is the largest available memory for a single program equal to 149K or 544K? Actually, if the next program you launch needs

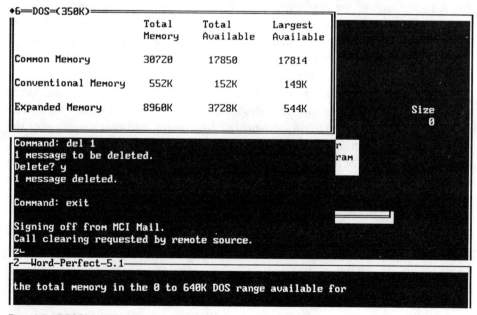

Fig. 10-6 DESQView Memory Status display.

149K or less, DESQview will take memory from the remaining conventional total. If the program requires 150K to 544K, DESQview will leave the conventional memory total undisturbed, and allocate memory from the expanded memory pool. (Recall that DESQview can map expanded memory into the 0-640K address space to allow multitasking. See Chapter 4 on expanded memory for a detailed explanation of how this works.)

The important lines to watch in the "gas gauge" are in the third, "Largest Available" column. If you notice that the Common Memory total falls below around 8K, you might want to use DESQview's SETUP program to increase the amount of available common memory. If DESQview runs out of common memory, applications may refuse to load or the system may even crash. (DESQview is more likely to simply complain with a "Not Enough Common Memory" message.

If the conventional and expanded memory totals in the "Largest Available" column are both insufficient to start an application, then DESQview will either swap a program to disk or display an "insufficient memory" message, depending on the way you configured it. The default SETUP option is to swap programs to disk files in the DESQview directory when memory is exhausted. You may also designate another drive as the swap area or suspend program swapping altogether. (See the paragraph on Logical Drives in the section above on DESQview setup.)

Change a Program

DESQview's Change A Program utility allows you to change the DESQview profile files for each of the applications listed in the Open Window menu. The settings entered in the two setup screens (Basic and Advanced) are stored in DESQview's equivalent of Windows' PIF files. The naming convention for DESQview profile files is XX-PIF.DVP, where XX is replaced by the two-letter menu code used to launch the program.

The first screen of Change A Program information is used to name and locate a program, allocate memory, and describe video and serial port usage. The Advanced Options screen allows for further fine tuning and customization of the way the program runs.

Basic Options (Screen 1). The top third of the screen contains the program name, as it will appear in the Window title, the two-letter shortcut to launch the program, and its conventional memory requirements. The middle third of the screen specifies the name of the executable file that starts the program, any command-line parameters and the start-up directory. If you wanted to bring up a word processor with a specific document, for example, you would enter the document name on the parameters line.

The bottom third of the screen contains the basic control options for displaying and working with your program once it is launched. To increase display speed, some programs bypass the standard BIOS and DOS routines that control screen display. If the program does this, it is said to "write directly to the screen." If a program writes directly to the screen at a hardware register level, DESQview runs it in a full-sized window. If the program is well-behaved and uses BIOS video calls, DESQview can run it in a small window. "Writes text directly to screen" should be set according to the program's behavior. (On 80386 and higher machines, DESQview can run ill-behaved applications in small-screen windows by "virtualizing" text and graphics—see next.)

DESQview also wants to be told whether an application is character-based or uses a pixel-based graphics mode. DESQview can launch an application in any graphics mode supported by your video card, but on 8088 and 80286 machines, graphics programs must run in full-sized windows. 80386 \ 80486 machines allow graphics applications and ill-behaved text applications to run in small windows. This is called *virtualizing* text or graphics. The "Virtualize text/graphics" option allows DESQview to virtualize a program in graphics mode, in text mode, only, or in neither mode. Lotus 1-2-3 release 3.1 is an example of an application that DESQview must virtualize in text mode, to run it in a small window.

Note EGA and VGA graphics applications run considerably slower when "Virtualize Text/Graphics" is set to Yes. You will generally get better performance for all applications by setting this parameter to No, and running graphics applications in full-sized windows.

"Use Serial Ports" lets DESQview reserve specific control of one or more serial ports requested by the application. If you set "Use Serial Ports" to "2," DESQview will hide COM1 from the application to avoid conflicts. Set to No, DESQview will hide all serial ports from the application. "Requires Floppy Diskette" is an option designed mainly for PCs with limited or no hard disk space. Normally, you should set this option to No. Setting this option to Yes makes DESQview display an "Insert diskette in floppy drive" prompt before starting an application. (You might also have to set this option if you run a copy-protected program that needs a "key diskette" inserted into drive A.)

Advanced Options (Screen 2). The Advanced Options screen for Change A Program allows you to fine tune application memory usage, control screen display, and set foreground/background multitasking defaults. The Advanced Screen is divided into four sections: the topmost controlling memory usage, the next controlling the DESQview window position, the third for customizing performance with DESQview "shared programs," and the bottom section for fine tuning multitasking defaults.

System Memory is set to 0 by default. If the application has unusual video requirements (such as loading alternate DOS screen fonts), you might want to increase its system memory allocation.

Maximum Program Memory Size sets the maximum amount of conventional memory you want DESQview to allocate to your application. In conjunction with the Memory Size parameter on the basic options screen, this option lets you set a sliding range of memory for a program to use. For instance, if you set "Memory Size" on the basic screen to 128K and "Maximum Program Memory Size" to 512K, this establishes a lower and upper bound for DESQview to assign memory. The application will be opened if as little as 128K of memory is present. DESQview will assign additional conventional memory (up to 512K) to the program if the memory is available. (See the description of DESQview's Memory Status utility next for more information on sizing up memory requirements and limitations.)

Note If you want an application to use as much conventional memory as possible, enter a large number like 800 in the Maximum Program Memory Size box. DESQview won't really give the program 800K, but it will get the maximum conventional memory available to the system.

Script buffer size sets the amount of memory (in bytes) available for DESQview's LEARN macro feature. Usually 500 to 1000 bytes is sufficient.

Maximum Expanded Memory Size sets an upper limit on the amount of expanded memory an application can request. If the field is left blank, an EMS-using application will get all of the expanded memory it demands. A zero in the field allocates no expanded memory for the application. Some programs like WordPerfect or Xerox Ventura Publisher will attempt to grab all of the expanded memory on the system when you open them. If you do not specify an upper bound for EMS usage, then DESQview gives all available memory on the system to one of these applications. Consequently, as soon as you open an EMS-hog, no memory remains to run other programs. Establishing an upper EMS limit of 256 – 1024K for a program avoids this problem.

Text Pages and Graphics Pages affect the amount of video memory DESQview reserves to display your application. For most simple text-based applications, one text page and 0 graphics pages are sufficient. For text applications that display more than one screen, or call up sub-windows, set Text Pages to 2. For CGA and Hercules graphics-based application, one graphics page should be sufficient. For EGA and VGA applications using no more than 16 colors or 640×480 pixel resolution, 2 graphics pages should suffice. For Super-EGA or Super-VGA applications at resolutions of 800×600 pixels or higher, allocate 4 graphics pages.

Initial Mode is left blank by default. If your application starts up in a nonstandard mode (for instance, Hercules graphics on a Multisync monitor), you may specify the start-up screen mode by placing a numerical entry from 1 to 25 in this box. Another example: If you have a dual monitor system and use the VGA as your principal display, you may automatically open windows on the monochrome monitor by setting the start-up video mode to 7. (See the documentation that comes with your video card and the DESQview manual for more details.)

The Interrupts field allows you to exclude application use of individual DOS interrupts. Normally, this setting is left at the default. Window Position allows you to specify the on screen position for the program window by row and column coordinates. DESQview includes nine automatically configured windows positions, so you might not need to use this feature. The main thing about the Window Position settings you may need to know is that you need to change the Maximum Height setting to 43 or 50 to view applications that use extended VGA text modes. (For instance, you may view 80 columns by 50 rows in WordPerfect 5.1 by entering a maximum height of 50 and then choosing the 80x50 display option in Word-Perfect's Shift-F1 configuration menu.)

The Shared Program parameters are reserved for special DESQview-aware utilities used in common by a group of applications. If you use an electronic mail program custom-written for DESQview, you would enter it here. Only one shared program is included with DESQview. NOFF.SHP is a utility that corrects screen display problems with programs that seek to comply with IBM's old TOPview interface. NOFF.SHP screens out video calls to the FF function of Interrupt 10. Older versions of WordPerfect, particularly, benefit from NOFF.SHP being entered in the Shared Program/Pathname field.

The bottom fourth of the Advanced Options screen contains some of the most interesting fine-tuning parameters. The DESQview manual provides complete details. The following parameters are the ones that you should become familiar with because they're closely tied to application efficiency.

Runs in Background

A yes in this box lets a program continue working when another application is in the foreground. "No" in the box suspends the program when you switch away. If you leave the field blank, DESQview decides whether the program should run in the background. Applications like word processors, drawing programs, and file managers generally waste CPU time if you run them in the background. By setting "Runs in Background" to No for these programs, you can save shared CPU time for telecommunication, spreadsheet recalculations, database searches, and other tasks that continue usefully while you work in another window. Of course, if you want an application to print in the background, then set this parameter to Yes.

A good strategy for faster performance on low-powered hardware is to set "Runs in Background"to No for any application that doesn't need background time. For printing from a word processor or drawing program, you may actually alter the application's background status on-the-fly from DESQview's "Tune Performance" menu. (Select [R] earrange from the main menu, followed by [T] une Performance. You may enter a "Y" or "N" for "Runs in Background" to temporarily change the program's default settings.)

Share EGA when foreground zoomed

EGA and VGA graphics applications running in the foreground will cause other programs to stop if this option is set to No (whether the graphics applications run in full-screen or virtualized windows). Setting the option to Yes allows background operation of other programs.

Close on Exit

With this option set to Yes, DESQview closes a program's window when you quit the program. Set to No, the window remains open at the DOS command prompt after you quit the program. A blank in the box lets DESQview decide internally what to do.

Tip If an application hangs the system when you close it, try setting "Close on Exit" to No. This may allow you to exit the program gracefully.

Allow Close Window command

With this parameter set to Yes, the "Close Window" command on the main DESQview menu allows you to terminate a program abruptly. With this parameter set to no, DESQview makes you use the application's own "exit" command to close the window. Setting this option to no prevents you from carelessly closing a program window while it contains open data files.

Note Even with this option set to No, DESQview allows you to close the window on a hung program by pressing Ctrl-Alt-Del. When DESQview is running, Ctrl-Alt-Del reboots only the foreground program window, not the entire system. (Pressing Shift-Ctrl-Alt-Del allows a complete system reboot.)

Uses Math coprocessor

Set this option to Yes if the application can make use of an 80287/387 80486DX or Weitek coprocessor for numerical calculations. (If you aren't sure whether your application supports a math coprocessor, consult its documentation. CAD design programs and spreadsheets are applications that can typically make use of this feature.)

Share CPU when in foreground

Setting this parameter to Yes allows appropriately configured applications to continue running in the background. A no in this box causes background programs to be suspended with this application in the foreground, regardless of the default settings of the background programs. This setting may be overridden on the fly from DESQview's Tune Performance menu.

Can Be Swapped Out

With this parameter set to Yes, DESQview can swap the program to disk or EMS memory, to make room for a subsequently launched application. Setting this parameter to no, forbids DESQview to swap the program out of active memory. "Can Be Swapped Out" should be set to No for telecommunications programs or any other application that might malfunction when swapped to disk and subsequently returned to memory.

DESQview Companions & other add-ons

To enhance the DESQview operating environment, Quarterdeck markets several productivity utilities separately. The DESQview API (application program interface) also published by Quarterdeck, allows other third-party vendors and shareware authors to write DESQview aware applications and utilities. Quarterdeck's own "DESQview Companions" consist of the following applications.

Notepad

The Notepad is a small word processor with a WordStar-like interface. It's chief selling point is that it allows you to edit DESQview's LEARN scripts directly, without converting back and forth to ASCII text.

Calculator

The Calculator is a small pop-up calculator containing standard mathematical functions. It includes a simulated paper tape roll that scrolls as you enter new calculations.

Link

Link is a simplified telecommunications program including a host-mode and scripting language. Quarterdeck includes nine prewritten scripts with the package. The prewritten scripts allow you to log on automatically to the DESQview support BBS or commercial services like CompuServe. Link's upload and download capabilities are limited to XMODEM, and ASCII files. The host-mode feature allows other people to call your computer and leave files or messages without interrupting your work in another foreground application.

Datebook

Datebook is a pop-up clock/calendar and appointment scheduler. You can use it to view appointments by day, week, month and year. The alarm feature pops up to remind you of appointments. You can shrink Datebook down to a one-line clock/calendar and position at the top of the screen. The alarm can be configured to go off as much as 90 minutes early.

The four utilities just described are bundled together by Quarterdeck in one package. A good number of shareware enhancements for DESQview are also available on public bulletin board systems. DV Commander, included on our utilities diskette, is a useful Swiss-Army knife utility that allows you to open multiple nested program menus that complement DESQview's Open Window. Figure 10-7 shows why this might be useful. Rather than making you sort through the large number of programs on the main menu, DV Commander's nested submenus let you find applications quickly. Here we launched PC Write from the Publishing Applications submenu.

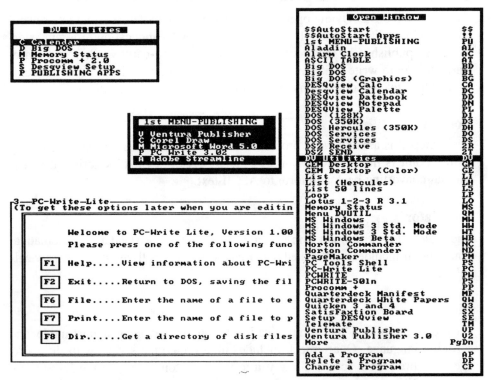

Fig. 10-7   DV Commander.

DV Commander also lets you execute any DESQview menu command or combination of commands from the DOS command line. Program windows can be opened, re-arranged, and sent to the foreground from batch files. This feature can be used for setting up timed functions. DV Commander even lets you shut down DESQview, entirely, thus allowing you to arrange for timed backups or disk maintenance with software that is not compatible with DESQview's multitasking environment.

Application productivity tips

Dual monitor configuration

DESQview allows you to run programs on two monitors attached to the same computer. One monitor must be monochrome (Hercules or IBM MDA), while the other monitor is color (CGA/EGA/VGA). To accomplish this, you must add a second graphic adaptor card to your system. If you already own a VGA system, you can probably purchase a second Hercules-compatible card and TTL monitor for less than $100. When you install the second card in your system, both graphics adaptors must reside in 8-bit slots on the bus. (If your VGA adaptor formerly occupied a 16-bit slot, you might have to move it to an 8-bit slot or configure it for 8-bit operation. Running the VGA adaptor as an 8-bit card instead of a 16-bit card might cause some slowdown in certain video screen functions, but you probably won't notice this on 80386 and 80486 systems.)

Once both monitors are installed, you can bring DESQview up on the color monitor and open specific programs on the Hercules monitor. To force a program to open on the Hercules monitor, open its program information profile in Change A Program: on the first options screen, set "Writes text directly to screen" to Yes. On the advanced options screen, enter 07 in the "Initial Mode" box; this will cause the application to open on the monochrome monitor when called from the menu.

With a dual monitor configuration, you may still use DESQview's Mark and Transfer utility to transfer text from a program on the VGA screen to a program on the monochrome screen. Mark the text on the VGA screen by selecting Mark from the main DESQview window: place the cursor where you want the block to begin and press B. Block out the text and press E to end. Then switch to the monochrome application and select Transfer from the main DESQview menu. You can even copy blocks of marked text directly to disk files from the DOS command prompt within a window. To do this, mark the desired text as described above, then switch to a DOS command-line window. At the command prompt, type COPY CON F I LENAME . EXT and press Enter. Then TRANSFER the marked text to the window. Press Ctrl-Z or F6 to save the copied file to disk.

DESQview and MS-DOS 5

The following paragraphs contain key points you should know about running DESQview under Microsoft's MS-DOS 5.

DESQview versions 2.34 and above are specifically written to work with DOS 5. DESQview versions previous to 2.34 are generally compatible, but users might have difficulty with DOS utilities like SETVER.EXE, DOSKEY, and the DOS Task Swapper. DESQview 2.34 or above is required if you want to run Windows 3.x applications under DESQview in Standard Mode.

Use of DOS=HIGH Statement If you plan to make DESQview your main operating environment, you will get more memory in program windows by removing the DOS=HIGH statement from CONFIG.SYS. Let DOS load low—DESQview can use more of the 64K HMA for itself than DOS can. (For DESQview to use the HMA, you must load either Quarterdeck's QEXT.SYS or QEMM386.SYS in CONFIG.SYS. See Chapter 8 and the earlier part of this chapter for more details.)

If you use QEMM386 with the Stealth parameter, you might want to experiment with DOS=HIGH and DOS=LOW statements in CONFIG.SYS. In some cases, you may gain more program memory for DESQview with DOS=HIGH because Stealth permits large chunks of DESQview to load in upper memory. The size of DESQview program windows will vary with the number of TSR utilities and device drivers loaded in upper memory. A tradeoff exists between using upper memory as high RAM for TSRs and allowing DESQview to claim the address space as mapped memory pages.

Tip To see how much HMA and upper memory DESQview uses in a specific system configuration, start DESQview with the /L parameter. If you type DV /L or XDV /L, DESQview displays a memory map of the regions it will use and the amount of code to be placed in each region. The "Area" column shows the starting address for the region, the "Size" column shows the total contiguous address space available for the region, and the "Used" column shows how much of that space will be filled with DESQview.

Figure 10-8 shows that DESQview will use the HMA (actually starting at address FFFE) and place 0FF2h or 63.8K of code there. 06EFh bytes (24.2K) will be loaded at upper memory address C000h. 0010h (16 bytes) will load at address E8EDh, and 0C51h (48K) will load at address E999. In this configuration, DESQview places approximately 136K of itself above 640K. Should the user load additional device drivers or TSRs high, the address space at E8ED or E999 available for DESQview diminishes.

```
c:\dv>xdv /l


Area   Size   Used

FFFE   1000   0FF2
C000   0C00   06EF
E8ED   0010   0010
E999   1760   0C51
1AB0   8550   0000


Press any key to continue...
```

Fig. 10-8   DESQview Memory Usage display.

Use of DOS 5's HIMEM.SYS Use either QEXT.SYS (included with all versions of DESQview), or QEMM (included in the DESQview-386 package) to replace HIMEM.SYS. The Quarterdeck drivers provide a superset of Microsoft's XMS memory management. They are completely compatible with any program that normally needs Microsoft's HIMEM.SYS. (There is no need to use both QEMM and QEXT, QEXT and HIMEM, or QEMM and HIMEM.SYS. Only one XMS manager needs to be present in CONFIG.SYS. Remove any extraneous XMS managers.)

Use of DOS 5's EMM386 While Microsoft's EMM386 can convert extended memory for DESQview to use on 80386/80486 machines, it also limits DESQview's efficiency. Running under EMM386, DESQview will probably provide smaller program windows and a diminished ability to run programs in the background. DESQview under EMM386 will also lack the ability to "virtualize" ill-behaved DOS programs in small windows. If you run DESQview on an 80386 or above platform, you'll be happier in the long run with QEMM as your memory manager. You can buy DESQview combined with QEMM in Quarterdeck's DESQview-386 package.

If you must use EMM386 as the memory manager, it will provide more memory for DESQview if you add the following parameter to its line in CONFIG.SYS:

```
Device = EMM386.EXE RAM b = 1000
```

(See the reference section on EMM386 in Chapter 8 for more details.)

Use of DOS=UMB As previously mentioned, there's a tradeoff between using upper memory as high RAM and as mappable EMS. If you use EMM386 as your expanded memory manager, you might want to experiment with the DOS = UMB switch in CONFIG.SYS to see if DESQview yields more program memory with or without DEVICEHIGH and LOADHIGH statements in the start-up files. If you use Quarterdeck's QEMM (or QRAM on 8088/80286 machines), you should remove the DOS = UMB statement from CONFIG.SYS and use the Quarterdeck loadhigh utilities.

Use of DOSKEY You must load the DOS 5 DOSKEY utility inside each DESQview window where you intend to use it. For instance, you might load DOSKEY into a "Big DOS" window by starting "Big DOS" with the batch file DOS.BAT:

```
PROMPT $P$G
DOSKEY
```

To make "Big DOS" run the batch file automatically on start-up, select "Change A Program" from DESQview's main menu, type in the two-letter abbreviation for "Big DOS" and enter DOS.BAT next to "Program..." on the first "Change A Program" screen.

Use of DOSSHELL   If you run DOSSHELL inside of a DESQview window, you should disable the DOSSHELL Task Swapper. Use DESQview instead, to launch additional applications.

Use of UNDELETE   You can run DOS 5's Undelete utility inside a DESQview window, but use it carefully. If a program systematically writes and deletes files in one window, you might not want to confuse it by undeleting the files in another window.

DESQview and Microsoft Windows

Microsoft Windows 3.0 and/or Windows applications can run in Real or Standard Mode under DESQview on both 80286 and 80386 platforms. Windows 3.1 may run in Standard Mode only. DESQview does not allow Windows to run in 80386-Enhanced mode. (Because you can use DESQview to multitask DOS applications, though, this drawback shouldn't be serious.)

80286 considerations

To run Windows under DESQview in Standard Mode on an 80286, you must make sure that at least 256K of extended memory is reserved for Windows' use. (See Chapters 8 and 9 on configuring memory for Windows.) You must start DESQview with either the /W3 or /XB:50 command-line switch (the two are equivalent). If you omit the start-up switch and try to launch Windows in Standard Mode, an error message will warn you to quit and restart DESQview with the /XB:50 switch. You must also install "MS Windows 3 Std. Mode" from the DESQview "Add A Program" Menu. You can't simply type WIN /S from a DOS window because DESQview needs a special program loader to switch the system into protected mode.

Once you've installed Windows on DESQview's program menu, you can modify the program profile to launch specific Windows applications. For instance, to start Word for Windows, select "Change A Program" and open the Standard Mode Windows profile. Add WINWORD.EXE after WIN.COM /S in the parameters box of the first "Change A Program" screen, as shown in Fig. 10-9. (You must also include the directory for the Windows application in your initial Path statement before starting DESQview, or you'll need to write a batch file to modify the path for Windows.) The setup in Fig. 10-9 assumes that the drive and directory for WINWORD.EXE are included in your initial path statement in AUTOEXEC.BAT.

If WINWORD.EXE is not in the default Path statement, then you can copy the information in the "Change A Program" screen into a batch file. The listing in the "Program..." box would be replaced by W.BAT, where W.BAT consists of the following:

PATH=[D:]\WINDOWS;[D:]\WINWORD....   *(other directories)*

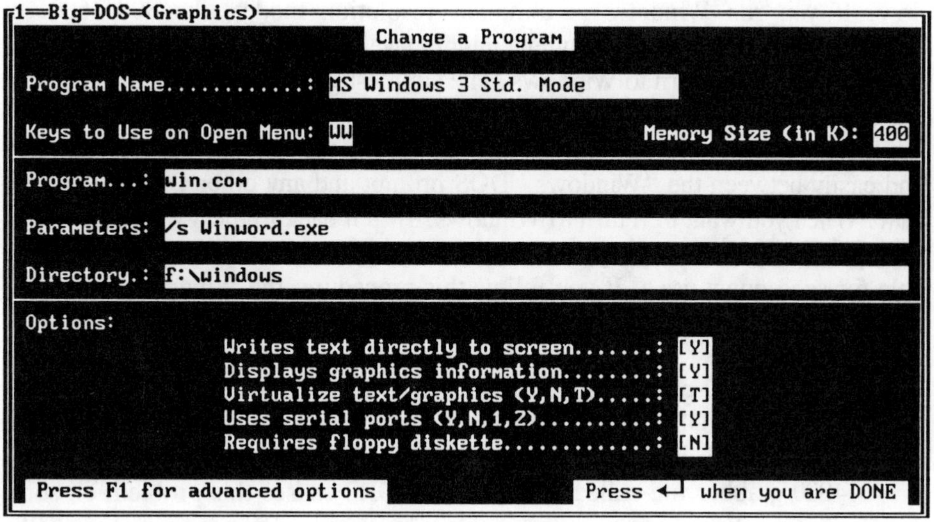

```
┌1═Big═DOS═(Graphics)═══════════════════════════════════════
│                         Change a Program
│
│   Program Name............: MS Windows 3 Std. Mode
│
│   Keys to Use on Open Menu: WW         Memory Size (in K): 400
│───────────────────────────────────────────────────────────
│   Program...: win.com
│
│   Parameters: /s Winword.exe
│
│   Directory.: f:\windows
│───────────────────────────────────────────────────────────
│   Options:
│               Writes text directly to screen.......: [Y]
│               Displays graphics information........: [Y]
│               Virtualize text/graphics (Y,N,T).....: [T]
│               Uses serial ports (Y,N,1,2)..........: [Y]
│               Requires floppy diskette.............: [N]
│───────────────────────────────────────────────────────────
│  Press F1 for advanced options    Press ↵ when you are DONE
└───────────────────────────────────────────────────────────
```

Fig. 10-9   Adding Windows to DESQView.

[D:] *(Log onto the drive where windows resides)*
CD \WINDOWS
[D:]\DV\W3-LOAD.COM WIN.COM /S WINWORD.EXE

80386 considerations

On 80386 machines, Windows 3.0/3.1 can run without using special DESQview loader files or setup parameters. (You may use the special Windows program profiles, if you want to.) By default, Standard Mode Windows is allocated 1024K in addition to its conventional memory overhead. If you want Windows to use more memory, open the program profile in "Change A Program" and press F1 for the Advanced Options screen. Increase the number in the "Maximum Expanded Memory Size" box from 1024 to the desired amount. (You may also decrease the amount of memory available to Windows, but this could adversely affect Windows' performance inside of DESQview.)

You may also launch Windows 3.0 applications in Windows' Real Mode inside of DESQview. Install "MS Windows 3—Real Mode" from "Change A Program." To launch a specific Windows application, follow the procedure outlined above for Standard Mode Windows. Type in the application's name in the "Parameters..." box on the "Change A Program" Screen, or construct your own start-up batch file.

Switching between Windows and DOS programs under DESQview

If you run Windows in its ordinary 640×480×16 color mode on a VGA system, you can simply bring up the DESQ menu to switch to another DESQview window. If you run Windows in a higher resolution mode, like 800×600, or $640 \times 480 \times 256$ colors, DESQview might have difficulty restoring the screen when you want to return to Windows. The simplest way to avoid this is to click on the DOS icon while inside Windows; Windows will then swap itself out and load the DOS command prompt in its own program window. You may switch quickly and easily between the "Windows" DOS prompt and any other DESQview window. When you want to return to Windows, switch back to the "Windows" DOS prompt and type EXIT (or press Alt-Tab to keep the "command prompt" available for subsequent use.). If you follow this procedure, the Windows screen will restore itself correctly.

Note   Certain third-party Super VGA driver packs might cause Windows to lock up inside of DESQview if you click on a DOS icon inside of Windows and try to switch back to the Program Manager with Alt-Tab. The TSENG 4000 grabber file called VGACOLRX.GR2 causes this problem on some systems. You can correct the problem by restoring Windows' native 80286 grabber in SYSTEM.INI. Open Windows' SYSTEM.INI file in a text editor and make the following substitution in the section headed [boot]:

286grabber = VGACOLOR.GR2   *(or VGACOLOR.2GR for v. 3.1)*

Miscellaneous tips

To run Windows in DESQview under MS-DOS 5, you need DESQview version 2.34 or higher.

Make sure that CONFIG.SYS includes a FILES = statement with at least 20 files. If you set Files equal to less than 20, Windows won't run (even if you load more files later with Quarterdeck's FILES.COM utility.)

Running communications programs under DESQview

Quarterdeck's Manifest can help you determine whether the expanded memory on your system is fast enough for high speed telecommunications (9600 baud or more). Open Manifest, and select Expanded Memory (third row), Benchmarks (last column). A score of 400 or less on the "Real Alternate Map Set" test indicates that a 9600 baud modem can accurately exchange data in the background. If the result of this test is higher than 400, you may improve performance by increasing the number of alternate map registers allocated by your expanded memory manager.

Another strategy for solving telecommunications problems is to replace the slower UART chips in a serial card with an NS16550 chip. Many I/O cards contain a chip numbered 8450 or 16440 in a socket. This chip can be pulled and replaced with a more efficient communication chip called the NS16550. The

NS16550 chip provides a hardware buffer for data coming into the serial port. Many telecommunication packages automatically recognize the NS16550's enhanced capacity.

Running WordPerfect 5.0/5.1

To increase the efficiency of WordPerfect 5.0 and 5.1, increase the memory available to these programs to 450K or more. When WordPerfect is short on memory, it swaps files out to disk. More available memory means faster disk access. WordPerfect 5.1 automatically recognizes and uses expanded memory. You may want to set a limit of 256-500K for WordPerfect's expanded memory quota in the "Maximum Expanded Memory" box on the advanced "Change A Program" screen, or else it might eat up all of your remaining expanded memory.

If you have trouble with WordPerfect's screen display on an EGA/VGA system, you can try several different things. One, make sure that any auto-sensing mode switch on an EGA/VGA card is disabled. Two, go into the WordPerfect text display setup (Shift-F1-2-3) and try "auto select." If this doesn't work, try "IBM VGA 80x25 16 colors" or "IBM EGA 80x25 16 colors." Finally, you may try starting WordPerfect with the /n f parameter.

DESQview problems with Hercules displays

Programs that allow the user to do "graphic page previews" on a Hercules system shift back and forth between text and graphics modes. DESQview configured for a Hercules card can't always follow these shifts accurately. After you see a graphic preview, the screen might get scrambled when you shift back to text mode. Quarterdeck has a fix for this called DVHERC.COM, which you can run from the \ DV directory before starting DESQview or inside of a DESQview window. DVHERC.COM allows you to force the Hercules card to return to text mode. When DVHERC is resident, you can restore the text screen at any time by pressing Ctrl-Alt-1.

DESQview and GEM version of Ventura Publisher 2.0/3.0

Xerox Ventura Publisher hogs memory. The Base Version 2.0 requires at least 550K without EMS, or 525K with EMS installed. An 80286 system with a VGA or EGA card installed might have difficulty configuring a DESQview window that large. Ventura Professional Extension 2.0 and Ventura Publisher 3.0 can both use more expanded memory, reducing the necessary conventional overhead. If you're within 5-10K of enough memory, you might gain more memory by decreasing the amount of common system memory allocated to DESQview (see the section on DESQview setup). You can also disable DESQview's Learn macro feature.

If you run Ventura Publisher in a high-resolution Super VGA mode, increase the number of graphic pages allotted in "Change A Program" to 4. (See also, the general hints in Chapter 6 on reducing Ventura Publisher's memory overhead with the /A= switch.)

DESQview and Lotus 1-2-3

1-2-3, release 3.1, requires a total of 700K of conventional and extended memory combined in order to load. On 80386 systems, QEMM allocates extended memory for 1-2-3 automatically. On 80286 systems, you will need to reserve an amount of extended memory for 1-2-3 that complements the available DOS memory. If CHKDSK shows that you have 550K of available conventional memory, make sure that at least 150K of extended memory is reserved for Lotus when you set up your expanded memory hardware/software.

DESQview and the Intel SATISFAXION board

To send and receive faxes successfully inside of a DESQview window with a SATISFAXION board, you must run a utility called HOOKINT.COM prior to loading the CASMGR and FAX modules. HOOKINT is included on our utilities diskette. Copy HOOKINT.COM to your DESQview directory. To start the SATISFAXION software inside of a DESQview window with the default FAX configuration, construct a batch file (called possibly FAX.BAT) similar to the following in your FAX directory:

```
[D:][\DV]HOOKINT 72 2f (the numbers may vary, see HOOKINT.DOC)
CASMGR CASMGR.CFG
FAXPOP
FAX
```

See the documentation included with HOOKINT.COM for more details.

About DESQview-X

DESQview-X is a new product from Quarterdeck due to be released as we go to press. It will let 16-bit PCs tap the power of 32-bit 80386 and 80486 machines. DESQview-X links DOS and UNIX machines, allowing both DOS applications and UNIX X-Windows applications to appear side by side on a local computer. One or more of the applications can actually run from a remote workstation over a network. DESQview-X retains all of the standard features of DESQview, transferring them to an X-Windows graphic interface running under MS DOS.

X-Windows is a UNIX standard that has traditionally permitted multiple applications on UNIX-based machines to run in a mouse-driven, multi-windowed environment. An X-Window system is a hardware- and operating system-independent graphic interface that operates over a network or on a stand-alone machine.

An X-Server is an X-Window System program that controls the computer's display screen. An X-Server handles the screen drawing for multiple applications concurrently. Each application may appear on the screen in an individual window.

An X-Client is an application (word processor, spreadsheet, drawing program) that communicates with a computer through an X-Server.

DESQview-X running under MS-DOS makes text-based DOS or Microsoft Windows applications appear to the local system as X-Windows clients. In addition, DESQview-X acts as a true X-Windows server for X-Client applications running on UNIX machines over a network.

What this means is that a user may set up DESQview-X on a low-powered 80286 machine and connect through a TPC/IP-based or NETBIOS-based network to other PCs running MS-DOS (including high-powered 80386/80486 machines) or any other computer running a UNIX X-Windows interface. Users may multi-task local applications on their own machine as they would under the traditional version of DESQview. Additionally, users may access and run X-Client applications originating on the UNIX machine, or MS-DOS and Microsoft Windows applications originating on a networked MS-DOS machine. (See Fig. 10-10.)

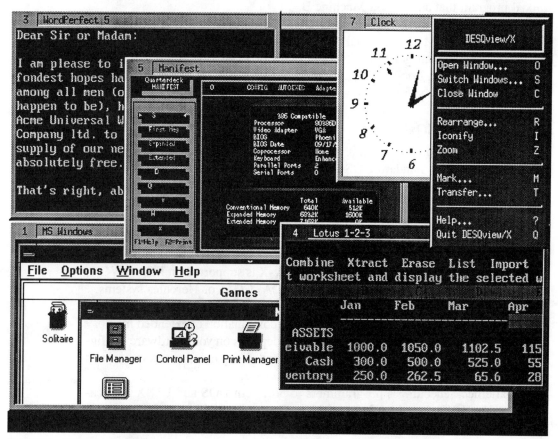

Fig. 10-10   DESQview-X display.

Users on Sun Workstations or Macintoshes running AU/X may log into a PC running DESQview-X and run Lotus 1-2-3 or Microsoft Windows remotely, seeing the display through their own X-Windows server.

Effectively, network users may establish a multi-platform application-base. PCs, IBM 3270s, VAXes, and Sun Workstations may be integrated into a single computing environment.

To get an idea of the usefulness of DESQview-X, imagine a series of PCs all running Microsoft Windows, linked through a Novell network. This setup also provides a graphic-based multitasking platform, but all the user can do is run other DOS and Windows applications from remote workstations. Your local copy of Windows or other network shell might have to handle each remote program as a procedure-oriented system. You could enter input into each program only at specific times and at specific prompts. An X-Windows server is an event-driven system—that is to say, it defers response to user input to allow another program to use the processor. If three computers are linked on a network, an X-Client running on machine A can appear on machine C, while machine C devotes processor time to a local program that appears on Machine B.

DESQview-X includes system level DOS extenders and a system-level version of Adobe Type Manager to make fonts available to X-Clients. It allows users to select a window manager from several prominent X-Window interfaces including OSF/Motif, Open Look, and Quarterdeck's own DWM interface. (If you own Geoworks Ensemble, you may already be familiar with Motif.)

Limitations of DESQview-X

True X-Clients may be run through the DESQview-X interface in either small or full-screen windows. Standard DOS graphics applications emulate X-Clients, but run in full-screen windows only. Remote users on UNIX machines are limited to running DOS text-based applications or Microsoft Windows applications originating on the PC. Remote users on MS-DOS based machines can run DOS graphics applications in full-screen windows. DOS text applications and Microsoft Windows applications can run in small windows through DESQview-X to any other compatible X-Window environment. DESQview-X is supported on EGA \ VGA, 8514, and DGIS graphic display, but not on MDA, CGA, or Hercules systems.

A minimum requirement of an 80286 processor and 2M of memory is recommended to run DESQview-X. On an 80286, the combination of extended memory vs. expanded memory applications you can run depends on your hardware configuration. For 80386 and above systems, the extended/expanded memory issue is transparent with good memory management software.

Quarterdeck encourages programmers to port both DOS and UNIX applications to the X-Window interface, making them accessible to DESQview-X. Developers will be able to create Real mode, 16-bit, and 32-bit DOS extended X-Clients with the developer version of DESQview-X.

Undocumented DESQview command switches

Over the years that Quarterdeck has supported DESQview, their in-house programmers have developed a number of fine-tuning command switches that are not documented in the manual. Quarterdeck's philosophy in this is basically "Don't fix it if it isn't broke." As a service to advanced DESQview users, information on the use of these command switches is provided here. Quarterdeck emphasizes that in most cases these switch parameters are not necessary and might increase incompatibility problems rather than fixing them. (In some cases, they might also cause a hard disk crash!) Not all switches are present in all versions of DESQview. If you are having any problems with DESQview, the first thing you should do is remove any command- line parameters and see if the situation improves. Still, some of these parameters are useful and might solve problems that occur in specific configurations.

ALWAYSSAVEMAP (/AS = y or n)

This parameter could be useful for owners of AST RAMPAGE cards. It saves the EMS map if the previous program uses EMS. The default setting is to check for a previously loaded program's claim on the pageframe. Set to Yes; the EMS map will always be saved, a slower but safer choice. A No setting might produce faster performance but isn't as safe.

CODEVIEW (/CV)

This parameter facilitates the use of Microsoft's Codeview debugger.

COMMLOAD (/CL = F, H or L)

By default, DV loads part of itself into high memory unless high memory is twice as slow as conventional. This switch might force DESQview to load certain parts of itself low or high. The switch takes one of three characters to indicate where parts of DESQview should load. The EMM.DVR driver, the stack DV uses for hardware interrupts, and the code for hardware interrupts with behavior = B (see HW switch) are loaded according to the setting of the COMMLOAD switch. The three valid settings are

F   Load into high memory if available unless high memory is more than twice as slow as low memory (this is the current default).
H   Load into high memory regardless of how slow it is.
L   Load into low memory even if high memory is available and reasonably fast.

DELAYMSMOUSE (/DM = y/n)

This parameter delays a program's asynchronous Microsoft mouse handler. Set to Yes, it might solve problems with mouse menu programs like Mouse-Perfect and allow Prodigy to run in a DESQview window. It will also cause sluggish mouse response, especially on slower machines.

DONTPATCHDOS4 (/DP4)

This parameter restores default DOS 4 (non-EMS 4.0 compatible) calls. If this switch is invoked, DESQview does not resolve conflicts with the /X option for BUFFERS, FASTOPEN or VDISK. The user must explicitly exclude upper memory regions with the /X parameter, instead of letting DESQview handle this automatically. This switch takes effect only with MS DOS 4.01 or PC DOS 4.01, and should probably not be used.

DOS TERMINATE (/DT)

This parameter allows DOS to terminate a file in a window instead of closing the file with DESQview routines. (This parameter might be of benefit to Novell client workstations and could resolve incompatibilities when the DOS Share utility is loaded.)

EXCLUDE (/X = mmmm-nnnn)

This parameter excludes the designated upper memory region from use by DESQview. A special application, /X = fffe, prevents DESQview from loading itself in the HMA.

EXCLUDE BANK (XB:vv)

DESQview normally uses two banks of eight interrupts for its internal functions. (You may determine which interrupts DESQview will use by starting DV.COM or XDV..COM with the /FIRSTBANK and /SECONDBANK switches.) If a program wants one of these interrupts for its internal use, you may use the /XB switch to exclude use of that interrupt by DESQview. (DESQview's Windows 3.0 loader makes uses interrupt 50, hence the instruction to start DESQview with the /XB:50 switch on an 80286 machine.)

EXTERNALNOTIFY = ## (/EN = ##)

This switch takes a number (in hex) that tells DV what AH register value to use for its interrupt 2Fh external device programming interface (XDI). (This parameter is of use to API programmers in making DV status check calls.)

FILE = (F = Filename)

This switch causes DESQview's XDV.COM to load a copy of DESQview named something other than DV.EXE (or a copy of DV.EXE located in a different directory.)

FIRSTBANK (/FB)

This switch causes DESQview to display the address location of the first bank of interrupts it will use for standard hardware functions.

GENERICEEM (/EE)

You can use /EE to force DESQview to make EEMS calls instead of EMS 4.0 calls with older versions of AST's REMM.SYS (REMM3.xx)

HWINT /HW : vv = bb

vv is the number of a traditional software interrupt paired with a hardware interrupt (IRQ) and bb is a behavior code instruction from the list appended below.

IRQs 0-7 correspond to software interrupts 08h through 0fh, while IRQs 8-15 correspond to software interrupts 70h through 77h. (For example, IRQ 13 corresponds to software interrupt 75h.)

This is a potentially dangerous switch that directs DESQview to assign an interrupt based on certain program "behavior" characters. By default, the first bank of hardware IRQs uses software Interrupts 08h through Int 0Fh. The second bank is assigned to Interrupts 70h to 77h. Programs routinely use these interrupts in the course of execution. DESQview wants prior control of the interrupts before passing them on to applications. DESQview reprograms the 8259 controller chip to substitute its own handlers for the sixteen hardware-related interrupts.

There are three sets of behavior characters. The first set tells DV how to determine which program should get the interrupt. The second set tells DV whether other interrupts should be masked out while processing the interrupt. (This maximizes performance by making sure the interrupt handler is not interrupted). The third set of behavior characters tells DESQview whether the interrupt handler writes to the screen.

You can choose one behavior from each of the following sets when using the /HWINT command line switch. Behaviors that affect who gets the interrupt are as follows:

O   Means that DV should not manage the interrupt at all and should instead pass it directly to the handler that was in place before DV was started. Thus, no program running in a DV window can grab the interrupt.

L   Means that DV should give the interrupt to the last program that has hooked it. This is the default for communications interrupts.

D   Means that DV should give the interrupt to the program that is currently using DOS. This is the default for disk interrupts.

F   Means that DV should give the interrupt to the foreground program. This is the default for the mouse interrupt handler.

B   Means that DV should give the interrupt to the handler in place before DV started, but should switch stacks and set up the interrupt 15h vector (and BASIC DS) prior to calling that handler.

C Means that DV should give the interrupt to the currently running program. This is the default for the coprocessor interrupt handler (interrupt 75h).

9 A behavior only meaningful for hardware interrupt 71h. It means that when an interrupt 71h occurs, DV should only check for a program grabbing that interrupt and should not give the interrupt to a program that has grabbed interrupt 0Ah (IRQ 2).

2 A behavior only meaningful for hardware interrupt 71h. It means that when an interrupt 71h occurs, DV should check for a program grabbing that interrupt, and then check for a program that has grabbed interrupt 0Ah (IRQ 2). This is the default behavior if the interrupt 71h vector is pointing to a handler inside of the F000h ROM when DV starts up.

Behaviors that affect other interrupts being masked:

M Means that all interrupts that might write to the screen (i.e. the timer, keyboard and mouse by default) should be masked out during this interrupt handler. This maximizes performance of the handler, but if the handler relies on getting one of those interrupts, then it won't work to mask them out. This is the default for the comm 1 and comm 2 handlers (interrupts 0C and 0B, respectively) except if the mouse is connected to the port.

U Means that no interrupts should be masked out during this interrupt handler. This is the default for all handlers other than interrupts 0B and 0C.

Behaviors that affect the screen state for the handler:

V Means that the interrupt handler writes to the screen, and that therefore DV should set up the correct interrupt 10h vector and DV 386 should set up the correct "virtualizing" state for the interrupt handler to use. This is the default for the mouse interrupt.

X Means that the interrupt handler doesn't need its interrupt 10h vector and "virtualizing" state set up. This is the default for all interrupts except for the mouse interrupt.

As a quick summary of HWINT, three kinds of behavior are controlled: who gets the interrupt, screen display behavior associated with an interrupt, and whether other interrupts are masked out. (Examples of who would normally get an interrupt are: the foreground program (keyboard interrupt), the current app (timer interrupt) and the last window that grabbed the interrupt (communications interrupt).

The HWINT switch lets you match any of the sixteen software interrupts associated with the system hardware interrupts to any of the "behavior strategies" just listed.

Quarterdeck's technical support department suggests the following uses for this switch:

If you are having trouble with a mouse inside of DESQview, you can try matching the "F" and "V" behaviors with the IRQ used by the mouse. If the mouse uses IRQ2, start DESQview with the following parameter.

XDV /HW:0A:FV

For a mouse using IRQ3, the switch setting would be /HW:0B:FV. If a tape drive unit refuses to work inside of DESQview, run it from DOS, and pop Manifest up inside of it to determine the application's interrupt usage. (See Chapter 8 for details on using Manifest). If the tape drive uses Int76h, you might try the following use of the HWINT switch:

XDV /HW:0E:L or (HW:76:L)

DESQview normally reassigns an interrupt before passing it to a requesting program. For example, a math coprocessor may use IRQ 13 (Software Interrupt 75). If you append the parameter /HW:75:0 when DESQview starts, then by the table examined above, this instructs DESQview to make no attempt to control IRQ 13/Int 75h. Instead this interrupt will be passed directly to the requesting program. The setting /HW:75:L might be helpful with programs that use a math coprocessor inside of DESQview, if you are getting coprocessor error messages. (/HW:75:L forces DESQview to assign Interrupt 75h to the last requesting program.)

DESQview masks communications interrupts to improve serial port efficiency, which can cause problems with networks that expect other high priority interrupts to occur while they perform. Unmasking interrupt 3 for BANYAN might improve performance: the setting /HW:0b:U would unmask software interrupt 0bh (associated with IRQ 3). Unmasking interrupts for IRQ 3 or 4 might improve network performance.

DESQview's normal mode of operation is to check the address pointed to by Interrupt 71. If Int 71 points at the ROM BIOS (Address F000), then requests are passed to IRQ 2 (Interrupt 0Ah). If Interrupt 71 does not point at F000 by default, DESQview assumes another program has grabbed it. This has the potential to cause problems with QEMM's new Stealth feature with respect to mice and other serial port functions. (up to dv 2.42.) If you see "mouse droppings" on the screen, have difficulty with an IBM 3270 emulation, or are on a network that uses IRQ2, the following use of HW: may improve the situation:

XDV /HW:71:2

The HWINT switch can be potentially very dangerous to your system's integrity. Use it carefully!

MACHINETYPE = ## (/MT = ##)

This parameter changes DESQview's switches for machine-specific interrupts. The specified number tells DESQview what settings to use for certain machine-specific data. The number is a combination of 8-bits, one for each behavior, as follows:

80h Reserved

40h On if there are two interrupt chips in the machine

20h On if the keyboard interrupt goes through interrupt 69h (default for HP Vectras)

10h On if the machine has a new-style keyboard (default for all AT class machines)

08h On if the machine has a keyboard controller that has the auxilliary device go through the keyboard controller (default for PS/2 models 50 and above and Compaq 80386s).

04 On if the machine has a timer chip that must be dismissed (default for micro channel machines).

02 On if the first bank of interrupts must be diverted in a way compatible with the HP Vectra (default for HP Vectra).

01 On if the interrupt chips are programmed to be level-sensitive (default for micro channel machines).

At present, there is no clear-cut method for determining which of these values is used by your specific machine. All you can do is read the listed descriptions and guess. You must check characteristics bit by bit over whole byte to arrive at the machine type. For instance, if you guess the bits for your default machine type sum to 80h, and you think bit 01 is on, you can turn bit 01 off by subtracting 01 from 80 and entering MT = 7F.

MINSHAREDMEMORY (/MS = nn)

This parameter sets the minimum size for the shared conventional memory DESQview uses to launch a program. The default is 0, which satisfies most programs. However, the default setting causes some programs to swap prematurely instead of loading concurrently. Setting /MS = 1 or /MS = 2 will cure this "premature swapping," and allow multiple programs to coexist.

NOSETUP (/NS)

This parameter disables configuration options stored in the DVSETUP.DV file. /NS forces DESQview to use the basic default settings, except that "Optimize Communications" is set to Off.

NOTOKENRING (/NT)

This parameter disables DESQview's detection of token ring port for other cards that have a conflict when they use the port addresses reserved for IBM Token Ring adaptors.

OLDKEYBOARD (/O KB)

This switch tells DESQview to make old-style calls to get keystrokes. It is useful for a BIOS that claims to support new 101-key keyboards but really doesn't. It's also necessary for compatibility with keyboard enhancers and keyboard monitors that don't support the newer keyboard functions (Interrupt 16, function 10h, 11h). Cures a problem with Sidekick on systems running DOS 4.

PARTIALMAPPINGOK (/PM = y/n/3)

This switch tells DESQview whether to save and restore the EMS pageframe when the timer interrupt invoked. The default, y, uses EMS 4.0 function 16. /PM = n causes DESQview to remain in the pageframe, instead of slipping in and out to accommodate other programs. This may resolve problems with DESQview and a poorly written memory manager. /PM = 3 causes DESQview to make EMS 3.2 memory calls to restore the EMS pageframe. This parameter can affect mouse performance and screen display. Try experimenting with it if you see "mouse droppings" inside of a DESQview window.

PROTECT OPEN (/PO)

This is a safety feature that might be of interest to system administrators. It disables the Add Program, Change Program, and Delete Program options on the DESQview menu.

RAMPAGE (/RP)

This switch is for users of AST RAMPAGE EMS boards. It forces the expanded memory driver to talk directly to the hardware ports of a RAMPAGE. This can speed up performance with the REMM.SYS 4.xx memory managers, allowing high-speed telecommunication.

ROUNDROBIN (/RR)

This parameter slows keyboard and mouse performance by telling DESQview not to return immediately to the foreground window on keyboard and mouse events.

SECONDBANK (/SB)

This parameter causes DESQview to display the address location of the second bank of interrupts it will use for standard hardware functions.

SWAPUSINGEMM4 (/U4)

The default is to use EMS 3.2 switch. EMS function 24 not supported in LIM 3.2 but might cure EMS swapping problem with EMS 4.0.

UNPROTECTEXTENDED (/UX)

If programs running inside of DESQview require oldstyle extended memory (Pre-XMS), this parameter allows more than one app to extended memory inside of DESQview.

WINDOWS3 (/W3)

This parameter allows Windows 3.x to load in Standard mode on an 80286 machine. (This switch is equivalent to /XB : 50.)

11
CHAPTER

Multitasking with OS/2

How does the OS/2 Presentation Manager differ from environments that rely on DOS as a starting point? An environment that integrates with the host operating system can provide specific advantages.

What are the best techniques for running DOS and Windows programs under OS/2? There are advantages to using some of the utilities provided with OS/2 to prepare your applications prior to use under this environment. There are also ways of running programs to minimize memory usage or conflicts with OS/2.

When is it better to use the dual boot installation option instead of using separate partitions for each operating system? What are the disadvantages to using this method? There are three different ways to install OS/2 on your computer. Each method provides advantages in either speed, memory usage, or optimal hard disk configuration.

How do you monitor the OS/2 environment? Just like DOS, OS/2 provides some methods to monitor your environment—most notable being memory and resource usage.

Introduction

OS/2 is the operating system that's supposed to replace DOS in the long run according to some analysts. The reasons are simple. OS/2 is a full-fledged preemptive multitasking operating system designed to take advantage of the full capabilities of the 80386 and above processors in ways that DOS simply can't. (Previous versions of OS/2 also worked with the 80286, but the current version requires an 80386.) Before you can fully understand OS/2, though, you must understand how it addresses some of the failings of current operating systems and operating system environments for the PC.

Windows is a non-preemptive operating environment. Because it is non-preemptive, it cannot ensure that each application running under it receives its fair share of processing time. One application might grab almost all the processing cycles, while others languish in the background. In most cases, this is not very apparent to the user. You might notice that the application runs a little jerky at times, starting and stopping at odd times, but that's about it. However, once you run OS/2, the difference becomes very apparent. OS/2 runs more applications at an overall greater throughput using the same equipment as a similar Windows environment. (OS/2 does not do as well on individual applications, but some fine-tuning measures to help you get past this hurdle are described later.)

DESQView does multitask more efficiently than Windows, but it doesn't provide the ease of use that you'll get from OS/2. The Workplace Shell provided in this version of OS/2 makes using the PC no harder than using a Macintosh. In fact, in some ways OS/2 might even provide greater ease of use. Instead of searching through directories of information for the files you need, you simply open a folder and double click on the document you need to edit. You don't need to know where to find the document, simply knowing that it exists is sufficient.

OS/2 provides more than efficient multitasking and an easy to use interface, though. The high performance file system (HPFS) provided by OS/2 is a major advance in making your machine faster. The HPFS is a more efficient method of formatting and maintaining your disk. For example, every time DOS wants to get information from your drive it moves back and forth between the FAT and the location of your data. Because the data might appear at one end of the drive and the FAT at the other, you could waste a significant amount of time simply moving the drive head back and forth. OS/2 places its version of the FAT in the middle of the drive, effectively reducing worst case head movement time by half. Informal disk testing by the authors shows that using OS/2 with the HPFS is about twice as fast as using it with the FAT system used by DOS.

One feature that Windows and DESQView have in common with OS/2 is a protected environment for your applications. If one application tries to use the data area used by another application or simply locks up, the operating system/environment will help you recover. However, there is a big difference between OS/2 and DOS-based environments. OS/2 always stays in protected mode; therefore it always protects your applications. Windows and DESQView must switch to real mode each time an application requests a DOS service. During these switches to real mode, your application environment is unprotected; one application can crash the entire system.

Of course, you must pay some penalties when using OS/2. You must have at least an 80386 with 6M RAM to even run OS/2. (The authors recommend a 33 MHz 80486 with 8M RAM as a minimum.) OS/2 takes a lot more hard disk space when compared to other operating systems. To efficiently run OS/2, you must have at least 30M with a minimum configuration. The reason is simple: You need at least 15M for the operating system files and room for the swap file and directories created as you use the operating system. Of course, this means that you have to have at least a 100M drive to do any useful work with OS/2. Many applications require 15M or more hard disk space just for program files. That old monochrome display won't do you much good either. You need a Super VGA display capable of producing 800×600 resolution as minimum. Otherwise you'll never have enough screen real estate to manage your desktop. One application could conceivably grab the entire display. As you can see, the hardware requirements for OS/2 are rather steep.

OS/2 also has a few quirks. For example, instead of using the left button to drag items around this display, you use the right button. There is no central repository for configuring your environment. Each object provides its own set of controls. While these concepts are not difficult to grasp, they are different from those that many users have experienced in the past, increasing the OS/2 learning curve.

Installation methods

You can install OS/2 in three different ways; each technique has advantages and disadvantages over the other two. Unlike DOS, the installation method you choose under OS/2 depends on which features you need and which you don't. The following paragraphs provide you with insights into the differences between each method of installation. More importantly, they tell you how to weigh the relative advantages and disadvantages of each installation.

Full OS/2 installation

Use the full installation method if you never plan to boot another operating system in place of OS/2. This approach has several advantages. First, your hard drive remains unfragmented. You can access the entire disk as one logical drive, which reduces the complexity of installing programs and the amount of drive space wasted in unusable fragments. Second, your entire drive uses the high performance file system (HPFS). Using this file system in place of the file allocation table (FAT) system used by DOS increases the efficiency of OS/2, which means that it takes less time to swap data and programs stored in memory to disk and that programs load quicker. Finally, the HPFS allows you to use longer, more descriptive filenames than the FAT system. You can create very descriptive names using 254 characters, while the 8 characters offered by DOS provide little room for creativity.

Of course, this method has a few disadvantages as well. First, some programs will not run from the DOS emulation window or from a system booted from drive A. Most of these programs include older copy-protected applications like dBASE III 1.0, game programs that directly access the hardware to gain a speed advantage like F19 Stealth Fighter, most protected mode software like Windows 3.1 and Lotus 1-2-3 3.0, and many pieces of software that use the undocumented features of DOS like CPBackup (the backup program provided with PC Tools Deluxe). Second, you might find it difficult, if not impossible, to retain your data should you decide to remove OS/2 from your system, basically due to the long filenames permitted by OS/2 and differences in the HPFS and FAT system. Using either the dual boot or multiple partition options allows you to maintain your data on a FAT compatible disk; then, even if you decide to remove OS/2, your data is still safe.

Dual Boot option

Of the three options, the dual boot option is most convenient for people who want to install OS/2 on a disk that currently contains DOS. You don't have to reformat or repartition the drive, a major undertaking on some systems. More importantly, although you lose time backing your system up, you don't lose any restoring your files. On some systems, this can save 30 minutes or more per installation. (The OS/2 installation already takes about an hour.)

There are other reasons to use the dual boot option. Some programs simply refuse to run under OS/2, no matter how you configure and run them. In these cases, you need a copy of DOS that has total control over your machine. For example, you cannot run Windows 3.1 while OS/2 is running; you'll get an error message stating that the extended memory managers conflict. With the dual boot option installed, all you must do to change operating systems is double click the dual boot icon in the OS/2 desktop, or enter BOOT /OS2 at the DOS prompt (in the OS2 subdirectory). This is probably the best option for people who need a single version of DOS and OS/2 on their system, but no other operating system.

Like the full installation, the dual boot option also allows you to keep your drive in one piece. You don't have to create the minimum of four partitions required for the multiple partition option (one for the boot manager, one for OS/2, one for DOS, and one for your data). Of course, this means that you won't waste hard drive space. You have access to all the available space no matter which operating system you use.

Using the dual boot option means that there is less chance for program conflicts and that you won't need to reconfigure them. Some programs depend on the FAT system; placing them on a HPFS drive could render them unusable. Backup programs are an example of this class. Unless you want to purchase and OS/2 specific backup program (or use the one IBM supplies), you need to maintain a FAT system partition for your data at least. Also, you must specifically configure some programs for a drive. Wordstar is an example of such a program. If you decide to use the multiple partition method, you might end up reconfiguring a lot of programs so they can find their overlay and data files.

You also use less memory with the dual boot option. Because OS/2 doesn't need to load the HPFS manager, you save both RAM and hard drive space (you don't have to install the HPFS files if you don't want to). By not loading the HPFS, you save at least 0.4M hard disk space and about 200K of RAM.

A few problem areas appear when using this scheme. The most noticeable is the reduced disk efficiency that OS/2 sessions will experience. Because OS/2 spends a lot of time swapping files to disk, you will notice the loss of disk efficiency as a loss of program execution and swap speed. In addition, programs load slower from a FAT system disk. In addition, while you won't lose the memory required by the HPFS, you won't gain any of the benefits either. For example, the maximum number of characters for a filename remains at eight. Other subtle differences include reduced hard disk life. Because the HPFS is designed to reduce head movement, your hard disk will actually last longer using OS/2 than the FAT system. (This assumes that your drive head mechanism wears out, not the bearings supporting the drive spindle.)

Multiple partition option

The multiple partition option provides the most flexibility of the three installation methods. You can have up to four operating systems on your machine at once using this option (assuming that you will place OS/2 2.0 in the extended partition.)

Other advantages include the ability to use a HPFS partition for OS/2 and FAT partitions for both DOS and your data. Using this technique, you simply reboot your computer to DOS and use your favorite backup program to back up your data. Of course, you still have to use the OS/2 backup program to back up the HPFS partition, which also means that you get some of the advantages of the HPFS without many of the problems. You will experience the gain in program execution and swap speed because OS/2 places its swap file in the HPFS partition. Application programs still take the same amount of time to load as the dual boot option because they're located on the FAT partition. However, the small amount of time you'll waste waiting for the application to load is insignificant compared to the savings you'll encounter using the HPFS partition for the swap file. Of course, you can only use 254-character filenames on the HPFS partition.

The biggest disadvantage of using this method is the inefficient use of hard disk space you'll encounter. What happens if you run out of space in your data partition while the OS/2 partition still has plenty of room? Will you want to repartition the drive to distribute the space evenly? Questions like these plague anyone who uses multiple incompatible partitions on their hard drive. It is no longer a matter of simply moving data from one partition to another but instead becomes a matter of repartitioning the drive. You can't move the excess data to the DOS partition because then it's not accessible when using OS/2. The same is true in the reverse situation. The only way to ensure that your data is available to both operating systems is to place it in the data partition. As you can see, making an error in judgment could result in a lot of lost time.

Monitoring the OS/2 environment

It is very important to monitor your environment, especially if you're using a multitasking operating system. Running out of memory or hard disk space becomes easy when you have more than one application to consider. Unlike Windows and DOS, the number of monitoring options available to you under OS/2 are limited and inconclusive. You never know exactly how much memory and other resources you have left, but you can get a ball park estimate. The following paragraphs describe some of the methods available to you for monitoring the state of your OS/2 resources.

Using the Pulse program

Figure 11-1 shows the Pulse program provided with OS/2. As you can see, it displays system activity as a graph. More precisely, it displays the amount of proces-

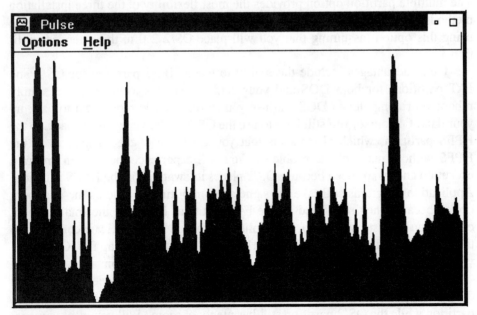

Fig. 11-1   OS/2 Pulse program. IBM's OS/2 2.0©1992 by International Business Machines Corporation.

sor power any active applications are using. The higher the peaks on the graph, the higher your system utilization. This is the only OS/2 utility that monitors the entire system.

While your system might occasionally peak at 100% utilization, especially during program loading or file saving, sustained levels indicate that you are making heavy demands of your system. Usually this results in reduced performance levels and an increased chance of fatal errors. When you begin to notice this situation, close one or more non-essential applications to free system resources. You should notice a speed increase in your active applications.

The problem with Pulse is that there are no graticule lines. You never know exactly what you're at. Needless to say, this program only provides a limited amount of information. However, it does provide you with enough information that you can tell when you need to close non-essential applications.

Monitoring DOS with the MEM command

Unlike MEM under DOS, MEM under OS/2 only measures the amount of RAM available to the current DOS session. You could have more than one DOS session active and each session could have its own memory configuration. However, unless you specify otherwise (by booting from an image file or a floppy drive), OS/2 starts each DOS session with the parameters in the OS/2 CONFIG.SYS and AUTOEXEC.BAT files.

The OS/2 version of the MEM command operates exactly like the MEM command for DOS 5.0. See Chapter 7 for further details on using the MEM command to improve the performance of your DOS sessions. The only caveat is that you must modify the OS/2 CONFIG.SYS and AUTOEXEC.BAT files instead of the ones used for DOS when using the dual boot option. These are the files present in the root directory when you're running OS/2. (They get swapped with the DOS CONFIG.SYS and AUTOEXEC.BAT when you reboot the DOS operating system.) The OS/2 files are more complex than their DOS counterparts. Make certain that you do not inadvertently change an OS/2 command when you really meant to change a DOS command. Use the section on "Understanding the OS/2 CONFIG.SYS File" found in this chapter as a point of reference.

Note   OS/2 normally configures DOS to load low and does not provide any UMB. The OS/2 CONFIG.SYS file contains the same DOS = entry as the DOS CONFIG.SYS file. Simply change it to read DOS = HIGH, UMB instead of the default DOS = LOW, NOUMB to turn on the loadhigh capabilities of the DOS session. Using this option does increase the memory usage of each DOS session that you start.

Using the Windows' About box

Just as you can use the MEM command to monitor the resources available to your DOS sessions, you can use the Windows' About box to monitor the resources of any Windows sessions. As with the OS/2 DOS session, the About box will only tell you about the resources available to the current Windows session, not the OS/2 system as a whole. You must use the Pulse program described previously to monitor system usage from within the OS/2 desktop.

Figure 11-2 shows the About dialog box.

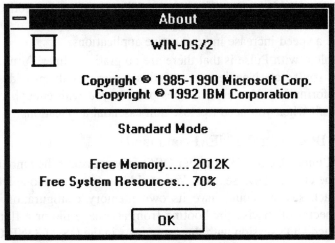

Fig. 11-2   OS/2 Windows Emulation About dialog box.
IBM's OS/2 2.0©1992 by International Business Machines Corporation.

You should notice three items. First, you can only use Windows in Standard mode under OS/2. While this doesn't prohibit you from using most Windows applications, it might stop you from using some. The real difference is that you will not receive the same level of performance from an OS/2 Windows session as you do under DOS. The reason is simple: You can't run Windows in Enhanced mode to take advantage of the power provided by the 80386 environment. Some programs like Mathematica require the 32-bit access provided by Windows Enhanced mode. (See Chapter 9 for a full explanation of the differences between Standard and Enhanced modes of operation.) Second, the About Box tells you that this is an OS/2 Windows session, not a standard version of Windows. Some applications that normally run under Windows might not run under the OS/2 version. None of the DOS applications that you normally run from Windows will work; you must run them from the OS/2 desktop. Finally, an OS/2 Windows session normally provides less resources than one run under DOS. Both the amount of available memory and the local memory space are less. For example, under DOS, the About Box registers about 3M of available RAM. The OS/2 About Box shows only about 2M on the same machine.

Note   You can use the SYSTEM.INI and WIN.INI documentation in Chapter 9 to modify the files for your OS/2 session. In many cases you can realize a significant performance gain by doing so because OS/2 installs default values for the entries in these files.

In addition, you can use many of the same drivers for OS/2 Windows as you do for Windows 3.0. For example, you can use a screen driver to bring the increase the resolution and number of available colors. Unfortunately, using some of these drivers might cause problems when switching between OS/2 and Windows. For example, a high resolution screen driver might cause the OS/2 screen to roll.

Understanding the OS/2 CONFIG.SYS file

Configuring OS/2 doesn't stop when you get it installed. Like DOS and other operating systems, OS/2 requires configuration. Of course, the OS/2 configuration is much more complex than the standard DOS configuration. Figure 11-3 shows a typical CONFIG.SYS immediately after OS/2 completes its installation. As you can see, the file contains a lot more entries than a similar DOS CON FIG.SYS. The following paragraphs explain these entries in detail and provide suggestions on how you can change them to enhance your OS/2 configuration.

```
IFS=C:\OS2\HPFS.IFS   /CACHE:64 /CRECL:4

PROTSHELL=C:\OS2\PMSHELL.EXE

SET USER_INI=C:\OS2\OS2.INI

SET SYSTEM_INI=C:\OS2\OS2SYS.INI

SET OS2_SHELL=C:\OS2\CMD.EXE

SET AUTOSTART=PROGRAMS,TASKLIST,FOLDERS

SET RUNWORKPLACE=C:\OS2\PMSHELL.EXE

SET COMSPEC=C:\OS2\CMD.EXE

LIBPATH=.;C:\OS2\DLL;C:\OS2\MDOS;C:\;C:\OS2\APPS\DLL;

SET
PATH=C:\OS2;C:\OS2\SYSTEM;C:\OS2\MDOS\WINOS2;C:\OS2\INSTALL;C:\;C:\OS2
\MDOS;C:\OS2\APPS;

SET
DPATH=C:\OS2;C:\OS2\SYSTEM;C:\OS2\MDOS\WINOS2;C:\OS2\INSTALL;C:\;C:\OS
2\BITMAP;C:\OS2\MDOS;C:\OS2\APPS;

SET PROMPT=$i[$p]

SET HELP=C:\OS2\HELP;C:\OS2\HELP\TUTORIAL;

SET GLOSSARY=C:\OS2\HELP\GLOSS;
```

Fig. 11-3   Typical OS/2 CONFIG.SYS file.

```
PRIORITY_DISK_IO=YES

FILES=20

DEVICE=C:\OS2\TESTCFG.SYS

DEVICE=C:\OS2\DOS.SYS

DEVICE=C:\OS2\PMDD.SYS

BUFFERS=30

IOPL=YES

DISKCACHE=384,LW

MAXWAIT=3

MEMMAN=SWAP,PROTECT

SWAPPATH=C:\OS2\SYSTEM  2048

BREAK=OFF

THREADS=256

PRINTMONBUFSIZE=134,134,134

COUNTRY=001,C:\OS2\SYSTEM\COUNTRY.SYS

SET KEYS=ON

REM SET DELDIR=C:\DELETE,512;

BASEDEV=PRINT01.SYS

BASEDEV=IBM1FLPY.ADD

BASEDEV=IBM1S506.ADD

BASEDEV=OS2DASD.DMD

SET BOOKSHELF=C:\OS2\BOOK;

PROTECTONLY=NO

SHELL=C:\OS2\MDOS\COMMAND.COM C:\OS2\MDOS /P

FCBS=16,8

RMSIZE=640

DEVICE=C:\OS2\MDOS\VEMM.SYS

DEVICE=C:\OS2\MDOS\VMOUSE.SYS

DOS=LOW, NOUMB

DEVICE=C:\OS2\MDOS\VDPX.SYS

DEVICE=C:\OS2\MDOS\VXMS.SYS /UMB

DEVICE=C:\OS2\MDOS\VDPMI.SYS
```
Fig. 11-3 Continued

```
DEVICE=C:\OS2\MDOS\VWIN.SYS

DEVICE=C:\OS2\MDOS\VCDROM.SYS

DEVINFO=SCR,VGA,C:\OS2\VIOTBL.DCP

SET VIDEO_DEVICES=VIO_VGA

SET VIO_VGA=DEVICE(BVHVGA,BVHSVGA)

DEVICE=C:\OS2\MDOS\VSVGA.SYS

DEVICE=C:\OS2\POINTDD.SYS

DEVICE=C:\OS2\PCLOGIC.SYS SERIAL=COM1

DEVICE=C:\OS2\MOUSE.SYS TYPE=PCLOGIC$

DEVICE=C:\OS2\COM.SYS

DEVICE=C:\OS2\MDOS\VCOM.SYS

CODEPAGE=437,850

DEVINFO=KBD,US,C:\OS2\KEYBOARD.DCP
```

DETACH < Command >

Use the Detach command to run OS/2 applications in the background without taking memory for the command processor. For example, if you ran DETACH DIR, the directory command would run in less memory than if you ran it at the command line. In order to use this command, the application must run without using either the keyboard or display. However, you can redirect the input and output of the file to make this possible. For example, the directory command usually uses the display for output, but you could redirect it to a file as follows: DETACH DIR > SOMEDIR.TXT. When the directory command completes, the file SOME-DIR.TXT would contain the results. Running applications in the background with the Detach command saves both system memory and reduces the number of processor cycles required. Because the application no longer goes through the command processor, the cycles used for that processing are eliminated.

DISKCACHE < Size > [, LW] [, < Threshold >] [, AC: < Drive >]

The DiskCache command allows you to allocate part of system memory as a disk cache. As with other commands that use RAM, you must weigh the advantages of the disk cache with the loss of RAM for application use. Preliminary testing shows that a disk cache less that 512K is relatively poor at speeding system performance. OS/2 is both multitasking and multithreading, meaning that there are a lot more demands for data from the hard drive. A cache that would be sufficient on a non-multithreaded system might not work under OS/2. A good rule of thumb to follow is to always maintain 6M of RAM as a minimum on your system. So, if rearranges the applications in memory so there is one large piece of free RAM, you had 8M RAM on your system, you may want to allocate a 1M disk cache, leaving 7M for the rest of OS/2. Of course, you would need to subtract the memory used by other speed enhancers like RAM disks and print spoolers as well.

Four parameters are associated with DiskCache, but only the first parameter is required. Size specifies the size of the disk cache in kilobytes. You may specify any size between 64K and 14,400K. The larger your disk cache, the better its performance. The LW parameter tells DiskCache to use lazy writes, which means that DiskCache holds a write until it detects system idle periods. DiskCache never holds the write more than 5 seconds. If you do not specify this parameter, then DiskCache writes all data to the disk immediately. The Threshold parameter specifies the number of sectors you want placed in the cache at one time. You may specify any value between 4 and 128 sectors (4 is the default). There are many ways to determine the size of this parameter. If you normally use database management systems, you might want to set this value higher because there's a good chance that your data is stored sequentially on the disk. However, if you use applications with a lot of small files, then reading a small number of sectors into the cache allows DiskCache to hold the data longer. The AC parameter tells Disk-Cache that you want it to automatically check the disk for damage each time you start the system. You cannot specify drives A or B—only drives C through Z. Using this parameter is equivalent to running CHKDSK each time you start your system.

Using DiskCache is fairly easy. For example, if you wanted to create a 1M cache that read 17 sectors at a time, used lazy writes, and automatically checked drives C and F, then you would use the following command: DISKCACHE 1024, LW, 17, AC:CF. Always use this command within CONFIG.SYS, not on the OS/2 command line.

DOS = < Low | High >, < UMB | NoUMB >

Use the DOS command within CONFIG.SYS to determine where DOS loads and whether or not it provides UMB. This command works much like the DOS 5.0 command discussed previously. The Low/High options determines where DOS is placed in memory. Loading DOS high is usually the most efficient means of using the UMB unless you have a driver that can use it more completely.

The UMB/NoUMB parameter tells DOS whether or not you want it to allocate UMBs. Under OS/2 this parameter works slightly different than its DOS 5.0 counterpart. If you choose the UMB parameter, then DOS may load applications in the UMB, but they cannot allocate any of the UMB for themselves. This means that some exploding applications might not load high under OS/2, even though they did load high under DOS 5.0. If you choose the NoUMB parameter, DOS cannot load applications in the UMB area. Applications may, however, allocate some of that memory for their own needs.

You should set these parameters to the ones that you will use most often under OS/2. Because each DOS session starts as a separate object, you can change these settings. The configuration in CONFIG.SYS represents the default session settings if you do not specify an other.

IOPL = < Yes | No | List >

The Input/Output Privilege Level (IOPL) setting is one of the most crucial settings for system integrity. A standard application runs at privilege level 3. At this level, OS/2 can monitor the application and successfully avoid most if not all system integrity violations, which means that even if the application does freeze, the rest of the system won't. However, some applications need to write directly to the hardware ports (something not allowed at level 3). The IOPL setting allows you to run these applications at privilege level 2, where direct port access by an application is allowed. Many people simply set IOPL to Yes, granting every application the right to run at level 2. Clearly this hurts system integrity. However, running every application at level 3 (by setting IOPL to no) may not work either. The best situation is to create a list of the applications that required level 2 access as follows: IOPL = SOMEPROG, OTHRPROG. This allows you to maintain firm control of system integrity without reducing the ability of your software to function.

MAXWAIT = < Seconds >

MaxWait is a system timing parameter. Each time OS/2 receives a request for service, it prioritizes the request according to the requestor's priority level. If a lot of high priority tasks request operating system time at the same time that a low priority task does, the low priority task could wait forever. To prevent this, OS/2 temporarily raises the priority level of the task after it waits a specified amount of time for service. MaxWait is the system parameter assigned to set this value. You may specify a time interval from 1 to 255 seconds between priority changes for an application. Lowering the number increases overall system performance by reducing the time background and low priority applications spend waiting for service. Raising the number increases foreground and high priority task performance. However, your background applications might take a long time to execute if you raise the number too high.

MEMMAN = [< Swap|NoSwap >] [,< Move|NoMove >] [,< Protect >]

The MEMMAN parameter determine how OS/2 allocates and manages storage. As you run new applications within OS/2 and close old ones, your system memory becomes fragmented, much like your hard drive does after a period of inactivity. In addition, system memory may contain pieces of applications that are not needed, they simply take space that an active application could use. There are several ways of circumventing these problems. First, OS/2 can compact memory. It rather than a lot of small pieces. Second, it can create a swap file on disk to store unused data and executable code, which frees RAM for other applications and allows those applications to overcommit memory. For example, even if you only have 4M of physical RAM on your machine, you could create a DOS session that provides 16M of EMS or XMS.

Five parameters are used with MEMMAN. The Swap/NoSwap parameters allow you to determine if OS/2 can swap data from RAM to a swap file on disk. It also tells OS/2 whether or not to perform storage compaction. The Swap parameter allows OS/2 to do both operations, while NoSwap does not.

The Move/NoMove parameters operate differently if you start OS/2 from a floppy rather than the hard drive. If you select Move, the OS/2 will perform both storage compaction and disk swapping on a hard drive. On a floppy drive, OS/2 performs storage compaction only. Select NoMove disables both storage compaction and disk swapping on either a hard or floppy drive.

The Protect parameter determines if some APIs can use protected memory. This is operating system memory that only high level applications can use. If an application experiences a failure while it uses protected memory, then the entire system may freeze. You do not normally use this parameter unless an application requires access to protected memory. Using this setting greatly reduces system integrity and opens your machine to lockups from failed applications.

PRINTMONBUFFSIZE = < LPT1: >, < LPT2: >, < LPT3: >

Use this device driver to create a print buffer for each parallel port. Each port uses it's own buffer. The minimum memory you can provide to a port is 134 bytes, the maximum is 2048 bytes. Increasing the size of the buffer increases print performance. However it negatively impacts system performance because less RAM is left for applications. OS/2 must swap more application data to disk.

PRIORITY = < Absolute | Dynamic >

You can use two different methods to assign a priority level to an application. You can either allow OS/2 to assign a priority dynamically based on current system status, or statically based on how the application starts. OS/2 assigns each application to one of 32 priority levels. Using the Absolute Priority setting disables OS/2's ability to reassign this priority. Thus, you might not obtain optimal system performance, but performance is very predictable. If you run time critical applications in concert with background applications, the Absolute setting is the best way to ensure your time critical application performs as expected.

The Dynamic setting allows OS/2 to reassign priorities based on current system usage and the perceived needs of the application. Because OS/2 cannot determine what is a critical application to you, you might not receive the performance you expect from a single application, but overall system performance will improve. In most cases, you will want to use the default setting of Dynamic to receive the best overall system performance possible.

PRIORITY_DISK_IO = < Yes | No >

Use the PRIORITY_DISK_IO setting to determine if foreground applications receive priority disk service from OS/2. Setting the parameter to On increases the performance level of foreground applications. OS/2 fulfills their needs before any background application requirements. Setting PRIORITY_DISK_IO off improves overall system performance. Many of your background tasks will execute in about the same time as they would in the foreground.

PROTECTONLY = < Yes | No >

The PROTECTONLY setting determines if you can run DOS applications. Setting this parameter to No (the default) increases system overhead and reduces overall system performance. However, this setting also allows you to run DOS applications. If you only intend to run OS/2 applications, you can change this setting to yes. Reducing system overhead is one way to improve overall performance.

RMSIZE = < Number >

Use the RMSIZE setting to change the DOS environment size. This is not the environment used to store DOS parameters (set with the COMMAND.COM /E parameter) but the actual size of the DOS session. You specify a size in kilobytes, from 0−640K. The default setting is either 640K or 512K depending on the amount of low memory installed on your machine. You may specify 640K even if your system only has 512K installed in the low memory area. Reducing this number saves system memory. Using the UMB to load your device drivers, TSRs, and DOS makes a 512K DOS session feasible. Using the 512K size will reduce system memory requirements for the session, leaving more for other applications.

SWAPPATH = < Drive > [< Path >] [< Minimum >] [< Initial >]

SWAPPATH determines the size and location of the OS/2 swap file. The drive and path parameters determine the location of the swap file. The only required parameter is the drive. If you do not specify a path, OS/2 assumes that you want to place the swap file in the root directory of the drive. The Minimum setting allows you to determine the minimum amount of disk space that OS/2 leaves for application data. You may specify any value between 512K and 32,767K. The Initial setting allows you to specify the starting size of the swap file. You may specify any value up to the limit imposed by the Minimum setting.

THREADS = < Number >

Use the Threads parameter to limit the number of simultaneous actions that OS/2 can perform. Every OS/2 application provides for one or more paths of execution, effectively running multiple background applications. Increasing this number allows OS/2 to do more things at once, allowing you to place more applications in the background. However, the overhead imposed by this method of execution does reduce overall system performance. Reducing the number of threads reduces the overhead and increases overall performance. However, if you set the number of threads too low, some operations may have to execute sequentially, rather than concurrently, reducing single application performance levels.

TIMESLICE = < Minimum > [, < Maximum >]

The TimeSlice setting changes the amount of time that OS/2 devotes to each task. The minimum setting determines the minimum time that OS/2 spends with an particular task, while the maximum setting determines the maximum amount of time. Low priority tasks typically use the minimum setting, while high priority tasks use the maximum setting. You must set the minimum value to at least 32 milliseconds. The maximum setting must be greater than the minimum setting, but no more than 65,536 milliseconds.

Using small settings makes overall system performance smoother. Each application receives enough time to make it appear that all applications are running in tandem. Using large settings increases overall system performance because OS/2 does not spend as much time switching between tasks. However, using large settings can make the each session perform in a jerky and unusable manner. Base your setting on the type machine you use and the number of tasks you plan to run. If you have a slower machine or a large number of tasks, you may want to use smaller settings to get smoother performance.

Understanding the OS/2 AUTOEXEC.BAT file

Unlike CONFIG.SYS, the OS/2 AUTOEXEC.BAT file looks much like the one you use with DOS. Figure 11-4 shows a typical OS/2 AUTOEXEC.BAT file. One thing you should notice is that during installation, OS/2 REMs out any TSRs or device drivers it thinks might conflict with the OS/2 environment. In general, you can remove the REM statements one at a time and test your installation. Most well-behaved TSRs work well under OS/2. Never use a TSR that directly manipulates the hardware. For example, you don't want to use your copy of Central Point's PC Shell within an OS/2 session.

Optimizing the OS/2 environment

The OS/2 environment provides an almost infinite number of configuration possibilities, any of which might improve your system performance. However, there

```
@ECHO OFF

ECHO.

PROMPT $P$G

REM SET DELDIR=C:\DELETE,512;

PATH
C:\OS2;C:\OS2\MDOS;C:\OS2\MDOS\WINOS2;C:\;C:\WIN;C:\WIN\SYSTEM;C:\WIN\
WINWORD;C:\WIN\CORELDRW;C:\DOS;C:\PKZIP;C:\PCTOOLS;

LOADHIGH APPEND C:\OS2;C:\OS2\SYSTEM;C:\DOS;

REM LOADHIGH DOSKEY FINDFILE=DIR /A /S /B $*

REM SET DIRCMD=/A
```

Fig. 11-4   Typical OS/2 AUTOEXEC.BAT file.

are some ways to improve performance for a wide variety of machines. Besides the installation method you choose (discussed in a previous section of this chapter), you can use three other techniques to optimize OS/2: organization, environment configuration, and application configuration.

Organizing your environment

Organization consists of the techniques you use to organize your entire system. For example, you can modify the path commands in CONFIG.SYS and AUTOEXEC.BAT to place the most commonly used paths at the beginning and the least recently used at the end. This is the same technique used by both DOS and Windows to reduce the time required to find a particular program.

Placing like files in the same folder (directory) can reduce the time required to find not only program files but data files as well. It is important that you don't layer these folders too deeply, however. Doing so increases the length of the path to each application you run, which in turn increases the time required to find a file or application.

Make certain that you associate data files with the application used to create them. OS/2 can use the association to find and load applications more quickly. It also makes it easier for you to use the OS/2 environment. Why use a graphical user interface (GUI) when you don't benefit from it?

Configuring your environment

Environment configuration is the next way to optimize your OS/2 environment. You begin by removing any device drivers not required by the system. Excess device drivers use system resources that could run another DOS, Windows, or OS/2 session. The following paragraphs provide a list of common OS/2 device drivers and their purpose. If you find these drivers in CONFIG.SYS or

AUTOEXEC.BAT and you don't need them, then eliminating them might free some memory for other purposes.

DEVICE=ANSI.SYS [< On|Off >]

This device driver acts much like ANSI.SYS for DOS. It provides extended keyboard and display handling services. Unlike the DOS version, you can type ANSI at the OS/2 prompt. If you type ANSI without any parameters OS/2 displays the current status of the driver. Adding either off or on sets the extended support off or on.

DEVICE=COM.SYS

This device driver installs support for the serial ports in your machine. If you don't install this driver, then you won't be able to use your serial ports. You must install any special drivers that your machine might require to use the serial ports prior to installing this device driver in CONFIG.SYS.

DEVICE=EGA.SYS

This device driver provides support for the EGA register set in DOS sessions. You never need to load this driver unless you have an EGA display adapter and applications that write directly to the display. (Game programs fall into this category.)

DEVICE=EXTDSKDD.SYS [/D: < Drive >] [/T: < Tracks/Side >] [/S: < Sectors/Track >] [/H: < Heads >] [/F: < Form Factor >]

Use this device driver to install extended disk support for your machine. For example, if you have one of the newer 2.88M 3.5″ drives, you can use this driver to assign it a drive letter under OS/2. The /D : parameter assigns the drive a letter. 0 is the first physical drive (A:) in the system. The /T : parameter determines the number of tracks per side. A standard 3.5″ and a high density 5.25-inch drive use 80. A low density 5.25″ drive uses 40. The default value is 80 tracks per side. The /S : parameter tells how many sectors per track the disk provides. Both a low density 5.25″ and a low density 3.5″ drive have 9 sectors/track. A high density 3.5″ drive uses 18 sectors/track, while a high density 5.25″ drive uses 15. The default value is 9. The /H : parameter determines the number heads for the drive. In most cases, this is 2 (the default value). The form factor parameter /F : determines what type of drive is installed. In many cases, this also indicates the formatted capacity of the drive. See the OS/2 on-line help for an exact description of available drive types.

Note   Always place any VDISK entries after the EXTDSKDD entries. Otherwise, a virtual disk drive letter might conflict with a physical disk installed in your computer.

IFS = < Drive > : < Path > < Filename > < Arguments >

The Installable File System provides the means for installing support for a particular file system. In this case, the only file system driver provided with OS/2 is the HPFS. If you are not using the HPFS, then you do not need this driver installed. You never need the HPFS using the dual boot installation option. In most cases you will use the HPFS with both the multiple partition and the full OS/2 installation methods.

The HPFS driver does provide some interesting parameters. The /C: <Cache Size> parameter specifies the amount of RAM in kilobytes that you want to use for the disk cache. OS/2 uses a default value of 64K, which is too small for most purposes. Always specify a cache size of at least 1M. The largest cache that you can use is 2M. The /AUTOCHECK: <Drive Letters> parameter forces OS/2 to run CHECKDISK on the specified drives prior to starting OS/ 2. This way you can fix any drives left in an unstable condition (due to power outages or other unforeseen circumstances that may have damaged the disk) before you start your OS/2 session. Finally, the /CRECL: <Record Size> parameter determines the size of each cache entry. This entry is always a multiple of 2K. The default value is 4K and the range is from 2−64K. You can use this entry to optimize disk access by retrieving one track at a time. For example, if your drive holds the standard 17 sectors per track and each sector is 512 bytes, then a maximum record size of 10K would hold one full track and part of another. The actual value you use depends on the applications you run. Database managers will probably benefit from a smaller record size, while word processors will benefit from a larger record size.

Note   Always make your cache size an even multiple of the maximum record size for better cache efficiency. For example, if your maximum record size is 10K, than using a 1020K cache is more efficient than using a 1024K cache.

DEVICE=LOG.SYS [/E: < Error Buffer >] [/A: < Alert Buffer >] [/Off] and RUN=LOGDAEM.EXE [/E: < Filename >] [/W: < File Size >]

Use the LOG.SYS and LOGDAEM.EXE device drivers to load error tracking for OS/2 on your system. The /E: parameter of LOG.SYS specifies the size of the error buffer. This is where the actual error message data appears until it gets written to disk. The default buffer size is 8K. The size can range between 4K and 64K. The /A: parameter determines the size of the alert buffer for LOG.SYS. There is no default size for this parameter, you may specific any value between 4K and 64K. The /Off parameter allows you turn error logging off from the OS/2 command line. You normally turn error logging off from the SYSLOG utility menu.

There are two parameters for LOGDAEM.EXE. The first parameter, /E:, determines the filename of the log file. If you do not specify a filename, then LOGDAEM uses a default setting of LOG0001.DAT. The /W: parameter determines the size of the log file. The default setting is 64K, while the minimum size you can specify is 4K.

Figure 11-5 shows the SYSLOG display. Each time OS/2 detects an error, it logs into the error log. Third-party vendors and IBM can use this information to determine where problems exist in your system. Each error condition creates one record in the system log. The records contain two types of information. The first part contains system related information (e.g., the time and date), while the second part contains variable data depending on the offending piece of hardware of software. In most cases, this will appear as hexadecimal numbers. The important use for this utility is to determine where errors occur in your system, If you aren't experiencing any errors, then you don't need to add these device drivers to CONFIG.SYS.

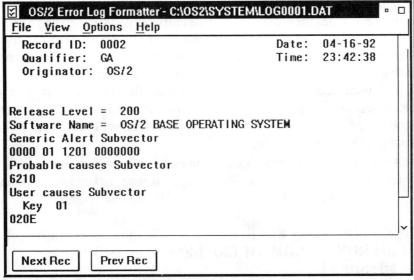

Fig. 11-5   OS/2 SYSLOG display. IBM's OS/2 2.0©1992 by International Business Machines Corporation.

DEVICE=MOUSE.SYS QSIZE=<Size> TYPE=<Name>; DEVICE=POINTDD.SYS; DEVICE=<Driver> SERIAL=<Port>

There are theoretically three drivers required for mouse support under OS/2. The first driver, POINTDD.SYS, provides mouse support in text mode. The second driver, DEVICE=<Driver> SERIAL=<Port>, provides the hardware specific driver. This is the part of OS/2 that directly interfaces with the mouse. The SERIAL parameter tells the driver where to look for the mouse. The third driver, MOUSE.SYS, provides the interface between the mouse driver and OS/2.

It is the device independent part of the driver. There are two parameters for this device driver. TYPE tells the driver what type of mouse you have installed. This isn't a specific brand name, but refers to the protocol used by the mouse. The second parameter, QSIZE, determines the number of mouse events that the device driver will store. Because OS/2 is a multitasking environment, there are occasions where it cannot service a mouse request immediately. The queue provided by the mouse driver ensures that none of the requests are lost. You always place these four lines before any serial driver support (the COM.SYS driver). The following lines show a typical configuration:

```
DEVICE=C:\OS2\POINTDD.SYS
DEVICE=C:\OS2\PCLOGIC.SYS SERIAL=COM1
DEVICE=C:\OS2\MOUSE.SYS TYPE=PCLOGIC$
DEVICE=C:\OS2\COM.SYS
```

There is one device driver that you can safely eliminate in some cases. The POINTDD.SYS driver is only needed by some text mode applications. Try eliminating this driver from CONFIG.SYS to see if your applications still work. If not, you can always add the driver back in.

DEVICE=PMDD.SYS

This device driver provides pointer draw support for OS/2. Removing it from CONFIG.SYS will result in a system failure. OS/2 will not restart. If this does happen, restore your old CONFIG.SYS using the procedure you'll find in the OS/2 manual.

DEVICE=TOUCH.SYS QSIZE=< Size > TYPE=< Name >; DEVICE=POINTDD.SYS; DEVICE=< Driver > CODE=< Parameter > INIT=< Parameter >

OS/2 loads this set of device drivers whenever it detects a touch device attached to your computer. As with the mouse, you need to load a series of device drivers to provide full support for the touch device. The first device driver is the device specific file. This is the driver that interacts directly with the device. You must include two parameters. The CODE parameter provides the name of a file containing microcode that the device driver sends to the device. In most cases, the device requires this code to start. The second parameter, INIT, provides the name of a file containing initialization parameters for the device driver.

The second driver is TOUCH.SYS. It provides the interface between the touch device driver and OS/2. It is the device independent part of the driver. There are two parameters for this device driver. TYPE tells the driver what type of touch device you have installed. This isn't a specific brand name, but refers to the protocol used by the device. The second parameter, QSIZE, determine the number of device events that the device driver will store. Because OS/2 is a multitasking environment, there are occasions where it cannot service the touch device request immediately. The queue provided by the driver ensures that none of the requests are lost.

The third device driver calibrates the touch device. Unlike a mouse, most touch devices require calibration, much like the calibration you perform when using a joystick. Without calibration, OS/2 and the device do not share common points of reference.

Surprisingly, the fourth device driver is the MOUSE.SYS driver. The parameters for this driver appear in the previous paragraphs. You always place these four lines before any serial driver support (the COM.SYS driver). The following lines show a typical configuration:

```
DEVICE=C:\OS2\POINTDD.SYS
DEVICE=C:\OS2\PDITOU0x.SYS CODE=C:\OS2TOUCO21.BIN
INIT=C:TOUCH.INI
DEVICE=C:\OS2\TOUCH.SYS TYPE=PDITOU$
RUN=C:\OS2\CALIBRATE.EXE-C C:\OS2CALIBRAT.DAT
DEVICE=C:\OS2\MOUSE.SYS TYPE=PDIMOU$
DEVICE=C:\OS2\COM.SYS
```

As with the mouse driver, you can experiment with the touch device to see if you can eliminate the POINTDD.SYS file from CONFIG.SYS. In many cases you can, depending on what applications you intend to run.

DEVICE=VDISK.SYS [<Bytes> [, <Sectors> [, <Directories>]]]

The VDISK device driver creates a RAM disk. Using a RAM disk can greatly improve the loading and execution speed of some applications. This is especially true of applications that use overlay files or DLLs. However, you must balance the speed increase you receive from one application using a RAM disk against the speed reduction for the system as a whole. The RAM used to create the RAM disk could provide a speed boost for the entire system. Instead of swapping data to and from disk, OS/2 could use the much faster RAM for data storage. While RAM disks are practical in a less demanding environment, they are impractical under OS/2 unless your system possesses more RAM than your applications can use.

There are three parameters used with VDISK.SYS. The first parameter specifies the size of the RAM disk in KB. The default value for this parameter is 64K, but you can specify any value in the range of 16−4096K. The second parameter determines the sector size. Use a small sector size if you have a lot of small files to load. Each file you load onto the RAM disk consumes a minimum of one sector. Therefore, if a file were only 1 byte, then the rest of the space in that sector is wasted. Using large sectors if you have a few large files reduces overhead and the amount of space used to track the files on the RAM disk. The default setting for this parameter is 128 bytes. However, you may also choose values of 256, 512, and 1024 bytes. The third parameter determines the number of directory entries that the RAM disk will support. Use the least number of entries that you need to hold your files. Each entry consumes memory that you could use for data storage or other needs. The default setting is 64 entries. You may specify any value in the range from 2−1024 entries.

DEVICE=VEMM.SYS [<Size>]

VEMM.SYS specifies the amount of EMS memory provided for each DOS session. The only parameter you need to provide is the amount of memory you want to allocate within the range of 0−32M. OS/2 uses a default value of 4M. Specifying a size of 0 disables EMS for all DOS sessions. You may override the default setting by changing the DOS setting for an individual object.

DEVICE=VMOUSE.SYS

This is an undocumented driver. It controls whether or not DOS and Windows applications will see the mouse. However, it does not appear to affect OS/2 application use of the mouse. Removing the VMOUSE.SYS will save some RAM if you do not intend to run DOS or Windows applications. Otherwise, you must keep it in CONFIG.SYS.

DEVICE=VXMS.SYS [XMMLIMIT=<Total>, <Session>] [HMAMIN=<Number>] [NUMHANDLES=<Number>] [NOUMB] |UMB]

This device driver provides the management tools required to create XMS memory. The XMMLIMIT parameter determines the maximum XMS memory allocated for the entire system and per session in kilobytes. You may specify any value in the range of 0−65535K. Specifying a value of 0 disables XMS memory for all sessions unless specifically overridden in that session's settings. The HMAMIN parameter determines the minimum amount of XMS (in K) that an application can request before the request is successful. Setting this value above zero keeps applications with minimal requirements from fragmenting the UMB. The default setting is 0. You may specify a number in the range of 0−63K. The NUMHANDLES parameter determines the number of XMS handles allocated to each session. The session must have a handle available before an application can request XMS. The default setting is 8 handles, which is usually enough for any application. However, you may request any number of handles between 0 and 128. The UMB parameter tells the XMS driver to create upper memory blocks. The NOUMB parameter (default) inhibits the use of the upper memory area. The XMS driver does not create any memory blocks.

Note This driver emulates XMS memory. Some application programs require true XMS memory. For example, Windows 3.1 will not start in either Standard or Enhanced mode due to conflicts with the memory manager. If you have an application that does not appear to work under the emulated session, try to use it by booting off a disk in drive A. If this doesn't work, you will need to use a full version of DOS where OS/2 is not running in the background.

Configuring your applications

Once you get your system organized and your environment configured, you can begin to concentrate on optimizing individual applications. The reason you wait to perform this step last is that any changes you make in CONFIG.SYS, AUTO EXEC.BAT, and the environment will affect all your applications. So, any changes you make prior to optimizing your environment may actually reduce, not enhance application efficiency.

You normally add an application to the OS/2 desktop using the Migration facility in the System Setup folder of the OS/2 folder. The Migration facility creates an object containing the default parameters for the application you've migrated. To change the setting on an application, simply click on the object once using the right mouse button. Select Open, then Settings from the menus that appear. You should see a Program Setup dialog box similar to the one shown in Fig. 11-6.

As you can see, there are five tabs along the side of the book. Clicking on a tab brings up that page of the book. The Program page provides information on where the program is located, what its working directory is and any command line parameters. The Association page shows how the object is associated with other objects. In the case of a program, you select either a data file type or a specific filename. OS/2 allows you to use wildcard characters within the name. For example, if you wanted to associate your word processor with every data file containing a .DOC extension, then you would type *.DOC in the blank. The Window page tells OS/2 how you want the object handled. When you minimize the object, OS/2 can place hide it, minimize it to the viewer, or minimize it to the desktop. When you maximize the object, OS/2 can use the existing screen or create a new one. The General page allows you to add a title and icon to the object. You can use the default icon or edit to meet your specifications. Checking the Template box allows you to use the object as a template for creating other objects.

The Session page is the page that you use to customize the application. There are three basic scenarios. You can make the object a full-screen or windowed OS/2 session, a full-screen or windowed DOS session, or a full-screen or windowed Windows session. Each session type offers you further choices for configuration as explained in the following paragraphs.

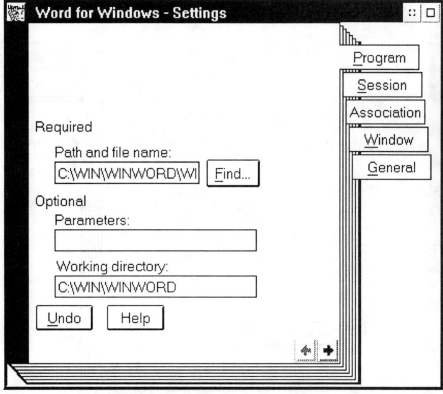

Fig. 11-6   Program Object Settings display. IBM's OS/2 2.0©1992 by International Business Machines Corporation.

Configuring an OS/2 session

Of the three session configuration types, configuring an OS/2 session is the easiest. Figure 11-7 shows the four options available for configuring an OS/2 session.

You may choose to run an OS/2 session either full screen or in a Window. Running an application full screen does provide you with more viewing area. In addition, the program runs a little faster than in windowed mode. The windowed mode provides advantages in allowing you to move from session to session quickly. It also seems a little easier to exchange data with other sessions. The Start Minimized option allows you to start the program as an icon. This is really useful if you start the application when you start OS/2. By running the application minimized, you don't immediately clutter your display. The Close Window on Exit option tells OS/2 to automatically close the window once the application completes. This is very useful with most presentation manager programs. However, you may want to avoid it on character mode OS/2 applications like CHKDSK. Because the window closes immediately, you don't get to view the data CHKDSK provides before it disappears.

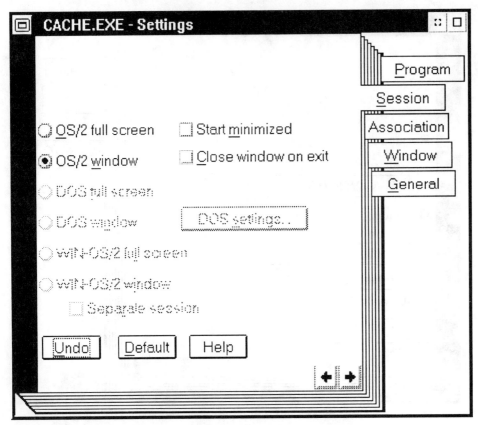

Fig. 11-7   OS/2 session settings. IBM's OS/2 2.0©1992 by International Business Machines Corporation.

Configuring a DOS session

The DOS session is quite a bit harder to configure than the OS/2 session. Figure 11-8 shows a typical DOS session page. Notice that both the DOS full screen and DOS Windowed options are highlighted. These perform the same function as the OS/2 equivalents. There is no real difference in performance between running DOS sessions windowed or full screen. The Start Minimized radio button offers the same functionality as before. The new command button is DOS Settings. Pressing this button displays the new screen shown in Fig. 11-9.

The DOS Settings dialog box allows you to perform an in-depth configuration of your DOS session. There are four areas to the dialog box. The Setting area contains a listing of items you can set. This is much like setting up a CONFIG.SYS file except all the parameters are already in place for you. All you need do is ascertain what value you want to assign them. The Value area provides a listing of appropriate values for the setting. It also provides a text box for those occasions when a setting could have more than one value. For example, when you want to load some device drivers prior to starting the application. The third area is

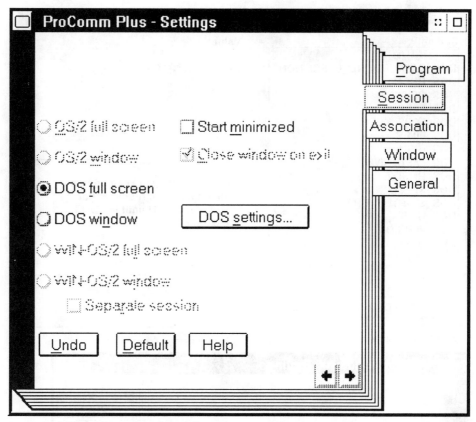

Fig. 11-8 DOS session settings Screen #1. IBM's OS/2 2.0©1992 by International Business Machines Corporation.

Description. This area gives you a brief overview of what function the setting performs. If you need additional information, you can always select the Help button at the bottom of the dialog box.

Three other controls appear at the bottom of the dialog box. The Save button saves the configuration you've created for the object. The Default button sets all the parameters for the object to match the default settings in CONFIG.SYS. The Cancel button allows you to leave the Settings dialog box without changing any of the settings.

Configuring a Windows session

Configuring a WIN-OS/2 session is only a little more complex than configuring a DOS session. Figure 11-10 shows the typical WIN-OS/2 Session page. As before, you can select between full screen or windowed operation. Unlike the other two sessions, Windows programs actually perform better when running in an OS/2 window than a full screen session. You can also get a performance boost by selecting the Separate Session check box. Checking this option tells OS/2 to run the

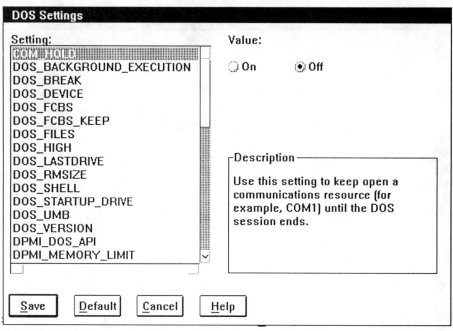

Fig. 11-9   DOS session settings Screen #2. IBM's OS/2 2.0©1992 by International Business Machines Corporation.

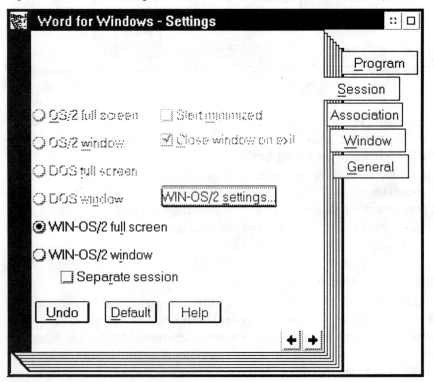

Fig. 11-10   Windows session settings Screen #1. IBM's OS/2 2.0©1992 by International Business Machines Corporation.

application in its own Windows session. This means that you can fully optimize the Windows session for that application, without regard for how it might affect any other application.

The WIN-OS/2 Session page also provides the WIN-OS/2 Settings button. When you select this option a dialog box like the one in Fig. 11-11 appears. As you can see, this dialog box looks much like the Settings dialog box provided for the DOS session. It uses the same four areas to provide a complete configuration environment. Many of the settings are different, however. For example, one of the settings allows you to determine which mode Windows will start in.

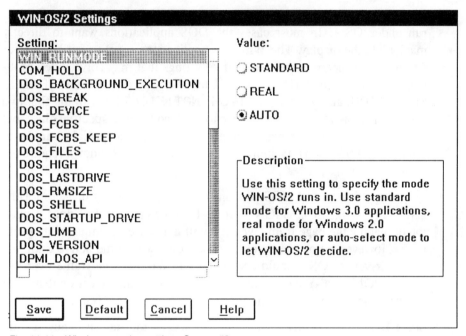

Fig. 11-11   Windows session settings Screen #2. IBM's OS/2 2.0©1992 by International Business Machines Corporation.

Reducing conflicts

Even with the best configuration technique, you will occasionally find a program that conflicts with OS/2 or a DOS/Windows session. The following paragraphs provide a list of things that you can try to eliminate, or at least reduce the conflict.

Checking the program settings

While there isn't much you can do about OS/2 application conflicts, you can clear up a wide variety of DOS and Windows conflicts by customizing the settings for that particular object. The Configuring Your Applications section of this chapter provides you with the information you need to use the Session page of the object settings.

Remember that the Session settings, especially the options in the Settings dialog box, are like CONFIG.SYS entries on a computer using DOS. Most of the same rules apply for finding problems. For example, in a DOS session you can choose to have XMS, EMS, or DPMI memory available for program use. The following checklist should give you an idea of what setting to look at:

- Check the included and excluded areas of memory (MEM_EXCLUDE _REGIONS and MEM_INCLUDE_REGIONS) to make certain that you are not overwriting a ROM chip or device driver. DOS and Windows session use these areas for both EMS and XMS emulation.

- Video problems seem to plague many DOS and Windows programs that run under OS/2. In most cases the DOS applications want to directly manipulate the display. The Windows applications seem to fail because of device driver incompatibilities. Three settings that may solve video problems for you are VIDEO_ROM_EMULATION, VIDEO_RETRACE_ EMULATION, and VIDEO_SWITCH_NOTIFICATION. In the first two cases, an application might expect to find code in a specific place but doesn't. In the third instance the application requires a special reminder to redraw itself. (Some DOS applications running under Windows require the same notification.)

- Both the Windows and DOS sessions use a default setting of Auto for the EMS_FRAME_LOCATION setting. In most cases, OS/2 does a good job of placing the page frame where it will not cause incompatibility problems. However, some pieces of hardware do not become active until you load a driver, so OS/2 could accidentally locate the page frame over this board's ROM area. You can manually set the page frame location to an area you know is free of ROMs and device drivers using this setting.

- Some DOS applications are easily confused by the mouse. They require exclusive access to the mouse. Indications of mouse problems include a mouse pointer that won't move, or worse yet, two or three mouse pointers on a single display. Use the MOUSE_EXCLUSIVE_ACCESS setting to get rid of this problem.

As you can see, there are a wealth of settings you can use to reduce conflicts between OS/2 and your application programs. By coupling these settings with appropriate CONFIG.SYS entries, you can eliminate or at least reduce the majority of the conflicts that you'll see.

Booting from the A drive

Unfortunately, you might find that even with all the settings provided by OS/2 that you cannot get an application to work correctly. Another alternative to running the

DOS emulation provided by OS/2 is to run the real thing. OS/2 is still active, so you may still run into problems with an application that normally runs fine under DOS. This other alternative consists of creating a DOS system disk (while booted under the DOS operating system), loading a special file system driver into CON-FIG.SYS, and performing some other slight modifications to your standard DOS environment. (The on-line help provides excellent instructions on how to create the disk.) Once created, all you need to do to activate the disk is click on the "DOS from Drive A" icon in the Command Prompts folder of the OS/2 System folder. You'll get a copy of DOS running over the top of OS/2.

Booting from an Image file

You might find that you have quite a few programs that require a real version of DOS to run. It's a little inconvenient keeping a copy of DOS on a disk in your A drive, so IBM furnishes a utility designed to create an image file of the disk. You place the image file on your C drive and boot from it instead of the floppy. When DOS appears on the display, you will still get an A prompt. As before, the on-line help provides complete instructions for using the VMDISK utility to create this disk image.

Using the Dual Boot and Boot Manager options

After you've exhausted every other option, you might still find a few applications that won't run with a copy of OS/2 loaded in memory. Examples of such programs include Lotus 1-2-3 3.0 (the 3.1 version does work under OS/2), Windows 3.1, and other applications that either require full access to the machine or need pro-tected mode memory. In these cases, you have no other choice but to run a full copy of DOS without OS/2 loaded in memory. Both the Dual Boot and the Multi-ple Partition installation techniques afford you the opportunity to load a full copy of DOS without losing access to your data.

Conclusion

This chapter provides you with the tools you need to use OS/2 efficiently. The first section describes the installation options at your disposal. Remember, there is no best method for installation; choose the method that is best for *you*. Any method has advantages and disadvantages, and this section points these out for you.

The second section shows you how to monitor your environment once you get OS/2 installed. This is an important concept to understand. Running out of resources could produce unpredictable results. Understanding how to manage those resources is paramount to understanding how to use OS/2. Remember that the MEM command only monitors DOS resources and the Windows About box only monitors Windows resources. You must use the OS/2 Pulse program to mon-itor system resources as a whole.

The third section tells you how to interpret the OS/2 CONFIG.SYS and AUTOEXEC.BAT files. While the CONFIG.SYS is much more complicated than its DOS counterpart, the AUTOEXEC.BAT file looks about the same. You should always change these files prior to optimizing the OS/2 environment. Changes in this area affect not only the OS/2 session, but the DOS and Windows sessions as well. Always add TSRs and device drivers one at a time. Otherwise, you might find it difficult to isolate problem programs that won't migrate to the OS/2 environment.

The fourth section provides you with the information you need to optimize your environment. You can do this under OS/2 in three ways: organize your system, optimize your environment by removing unnecessary drivers and reconfiguring others, and optimize your applications using the system settings. Performing all three steps will provide you with the best environment possible.

The final section showed you how to reduce conflicts between various applications and OS/2. Even though OS/2 purports to be a direct replacement for DOS and Windows, sometimes you'll need to spend some time configuring the session before you can accomplish this goal. Of course, some DOS and Windows applications will never operate correctly under the OS/2 environment. Make certain you check the requirements of the application you want to migrate to ensure that OS/2 can support its requirements.

A

APPENDIX

Quarterdeck
technical notes

The following tips on using QEMM-386 were written by the Quarterdeck technical support department. All material in this chapter is reprinted with the permission of Quarterdeck Office Systems, (c) 1991.

Exception #12, #13 and QEMM
What is an "Exception #12"? What is an "Exception #13"?
What can be done to prevent Exception #12's and #13's?

Exceptions are unusual or invalid conditions associated with the execution of a particular instruction by the 80386 processor (or higher processors). The 80386 recognizes several different classes of exceptions and assigns a different vector number to each class. The DESQview386 memory manager, QEMM-386, has been designed to capture these 80386 exception vectors and display them directly to the user.

Exception #13 is the "General Protection Fault" error. Any privileged instruction or any instruction that references memory can trigger an Exception #13. It is the most commonly encountered 80386 fault.

The two circumstances that can cause an Exception #13 require very different troubleshooting approaches. In the first case—privileged instructions—the Exception #13 could indicate that a program has violated the protected mode of the 80386 by executing a privileged instruction or I/O reference. Thus, when the prompt "Terminate, Reboot or Continue?" is issued, the "Continue" option puts the system back into Real mode, and the program should continue to execute.

(After choosing the "Continue" option, one should not necessarily assume that the system is stable. You'd probably be wise to reboot at the earliest convenient time.

The second case—instructions that reference memory—however, is far more common to DESQview 386 (and QEMM-386) users. Here the exception might indicate that an application has a bug or that adverse circumstances have sent it out of control. It has overwritten its memory partition and might in fact be running wild, executing meaningless code. This situation can occur with some programs that were written for use on the 8088 processor and might not be usable in the 80386's virtual 8086 mode.

A few other programs might not be compatible with QEMM-386. In some cases the problem occurs even without QEMM present (in which case it manifests itself as a crash instead of an error message). What this usually adds up to is that when "Terminate, Reboot, or Continue?" is displayed, the user can usually only "Terminate."

On a technical level, this overwriting of the memory partition generally means that a word or a double word value has been fetched from or written to the last byte of a segment. The problem or "bug" in the application program or in the system shows up as an attempt to wrap the value to the next segment of memory.

What can the user do to prevent Exception #13's? Because a great many problems can result in Exception #13's, it is sometimes necessary to resort to general troubleshooting techniques. The DESQview 386 user should start with two simple steps: first, run Change a Program and try to allocate more memory to the application. Second, the user can try to increase the protection level of the afflicted window to 3, which will not remove the source of the Exception #13 but might pass more descriptive error messages through to the user.

When Exception #13's are obtained outside of DESQview, they are either caused by applications written for the 80386 protected mode or they are not. If the faulting application is written for the protected mode of the 80386, it is likely that this program has no VCPI (Virtual Control Program Interface) support. Because QEMM-386 is a protected mode program, such faulting applications cannot be run under QEMM without VCPI. The user has no choice but to reboot without QEMM and contact the developer of the faulting application to request VCPI support.

If the faulting application was not written for the protected mode of the 80386, it's very likely that the QEMM user has installed QEMM with the RAM parameter (which is necessary to LOADHI drivers and TSR's). In this case, the faulting program might be running in an area of high RAM that contains a memory conflict. To correct this problem, the user might opt to RAM only specific areas of memory, as described on page 6 of the QEMM-386 manual, rather than to RAM all mappable areas. Of course, an area of conflict that is not RAMmed is still an area of conflict and might cause problems if another application tries to map expanded memory into that region. A better solution to such memory conflicts might be to use the EXCLUDE parameter (described on page 5 of the QEMM manual) on the area in conflict.

When in doubt about which areas to exclude, the user might want to pay special attention to areas that are marked "RAMmable" on the QEMM.COM Type screen, or to High RAM areas in the F000FFFF area. "RAMmable" areas are usually adjacent to ROM areas, and the possibility exists that the ROM is slightly bigger than QEMM could detect and is spilling over into the "RAMmable" area. High RAM areas in the F000FFFF region are mapped over pieces of the system ROM that either QEMM or the user have judged not to be in use. Obviously, this judgment should be questioned when Exception #13 messages occur. The F000FFFF area should be scrutinized especially carefully when floppy disk access generates the exception error.

The QEMM.COM Accessed screen (also available as the Manifest QEMM-386 \ Accessed screen) can give the user valuable hints about what areas of memory are in use. To use the Accessed screen, replace the RAM parameter on the QEMM line in the CONFIG.SYS file with the ON parameter and reboot the machine. Any area that the Accessed screen then shows as having been touched, but that the Type screen shows as Mappable or Rammable, is a good candidate for exclusion. If the Exception #13 error only occurs with the RAM parameter present, you can now safely perform the action that usually generates the error, and then consult the Accessed screen to see what areas of memory have been newly touched.

Some pieces of hardware can come into conflict with QEMM or DESQview and generate Exception #13 errors. The most frequent offenders are busmastering devices (hard disk controllers, network cards, CDROM controllers, etc.) and autoswitching video cards. Busmastering hard disk controllers often cause Exception #13 errors upon any use of the LOADHI programs, for instance. For approaches to this problem, see the Quarterdeck Technical Note titled "Busmastering Devices and QEMM-386." Not all autoswitching video cards come into conflict with QEMM or other pieces of software. When a conflict occurs, however, it does not always take the form of a video problem and sometimes results in the Exception #13 message. Disabling autoswitching is the only solution to such a problem.

General troubleshooting methods, like temporarily removing all TSR's, device drivers and questionable QEMM parameters, often provide valuable information about the exception error. It sometimes happens that a circumstance that generates an Exception #13 with QEMM present simply causes the machine to crash without any message when QEMM is removed. In such a case, QEMM is simply the bearer of bad news.

Exception #12 is the "Stack Segment" fault. The stack segment fault occurs when the processor detects certain problems with the segment addressed by the SS segment register. This exception too can be the result either of a bug in a program or of some system malfunction that eventually results in a stack error. All of the above methods of troubleshooting Exception #13 messages should also be used when trying to track down the cause of an Exception #12. The one difference that should be kept in mind is that Exception #12 messages are not generated by an application simply going into protected mode, executing privileged instructions, or accessing privileged registers. Therefore you need not consider the possibility that the application needs to incorporate VCPI support to run with QEMM.

Troubleshooting Stealth

This document discusses how to diagnose and cure problems occasioned by the use of the Stealth feature of QEMM-386, version 6. All users should review the read.me file that comes with QEMM-386, version 6 for additional information.

Step #1 The first step is to ascertain whether Stealth is involved with the problem. Remove the Stealth parameter (ST : M or ST : F) from the QEMM-386 line of the CONFIG.SYS. Reboot the computer and try to duplicate the problem. If the problem still happens then Stealth is not causing the problem and you must address the problem by the means explained in the troubleshooting section of the QEMM-386 manual.

Section 1

Step #2 If Stealth is involved in the problem restore the Stealth parameter (ST : M) and add XST = F000. Reboot the computer. If this works, go to Step #3; if this does not work, go to Section 2. On this step, the QEMM-386 line of the CONFIG.SYS should look something like this:

DEVICE = C : \ QEMM \ QEMM - 386 . SYS RAM ST : M XST = F000

Step #3 If XST = F000 solves your problem, replace it with X = F000 FFFF, reboot and try again. The QEMM-386 line of the CONFIG.SYS should look something like this:

DEVICE = C : \ QEMM \ QEMM - 386 . SYS RAM ST : M X = F000 - FFFF

If this works, add the parameter FSTC to the QEMM line, like this:

DEVICE = C : \ QEMM \ QEMM - 386 . SYS RAM ST : M
            X = F000 - FFFF FSTC

Then reboot. If this works, continue; if this does not work (and FSTC might not work in all circumstances), then remove the FSTC parameter and reboot with the previous QEMM-386 line. See the section about FSTC later for an explanation of FSTC. In either case, enter Manifest and look at the QEMM-386/Analysis screen. Examine the last line; it should look something like this:

Fn00 IIII IIII IIII IIOO

The portions of the address space with the O in them are being accessed directly. Some program or piece of hardware is trying to read the contents of the ROM here directly, not merely access them through interrupts. This portion of the address space must be allowed to be accessed directly. This is done by excluding QEMM-386 from mapping this area. In this case, the target region is FE00FFFF. The appropriate Exclude is X = FE00-FEFF. The correct QEMM-386.SYS line of the CONFIG.SYS is the following:

DEVICE = C : \ QEMM \ QEMM - 386 . SYS RAM ST : M X = FE00 - FFFF

This Exclude allows Stealth to do its job and costs you only 8K of high address space.

Step #4   If XST = F000 solves your problem while X = F000-FFFF does not, then you should try using ST : F instead of ST : M. You might get more high RAM with ST : F than with ST : M XST = F000.

Section 2

This section is only for users with video ROM. Hercules-compatible monochrome and CGA systems do not have video ROM and thus this section does not apply. Some machines have their video ROM elsewhere, usually E000−E7FF. Such users should use E000 (or wherever their video ROM begins) instead of C000.

Step #5   If XST = F000 does not solve your problem, then try XST = C000. The QEMM-386 line of the CONFIG.SYS should look like this:

DEVICE = C : \ QEMM \ QEMM - 386 . SYS RAM ST : M XST = C000

If XST = C000 does not work, go to Section 3. If XST = C000 does work, go to the next step.

Step #6   If XST = C000 solves the problem, then try placing the page frame at C000. Do this only if the entire C segment is available to put the page frame in. The QEMM-386 line of the CONFIG.SYS should look like this:

DEVICE = C : \ QEMM \ QEMM - 386 . SYS RAM ST : M FR = C000

If this works, then this might be an acceptable solution. All the address space in which high RAM can be created is being used in this configuration. If this step does not work or if you cannot put the page frame at C000, go to Step #7.

Step #7   If XST = C000 solves the problem but you do not want to (or cannot) put the page frame at C000, then try the parameter FAST INT10 : N, where N tells QEMM-386 to allow the video ROM's own code to be used. By default, QEMM-386 replaces some of the video ROM's code with its own video code. This parameter tells QEMM to use the ROM's code. The QEMM-386 line of CONFIG.SYS should look like this:

DEVICE = C : \ QEMM \ QEMM - 386 . SYS RAM ST : M FAST INT10 : n

If this works, then all ROMs are being Stealthed. You may choose to try Step #8 as an alternative, though. If this does not work, go ahead to the next step. There is a further discussion of FAST INT10 later.

Step #8 If XST = C000 solves the problem but FR = C000 or FAST INT10 : N does not (or you cannot put the page frame at C000 or do not want to use FAST INT10 : N) then replace XST = C000 with X = C000 - C7FF. The QEMM-386 line of the CONFIG.SYS should look like this:

DEVICE = C : \ QEMM \ QEMM - 386 . SYS RAM ST : M X = C000 - C7FF

If this works, add the parameter FSTC to the QEMM-386 line like this:

DEVICE = C : \ QEMM \ QEMM - 386 . SYS RAM ST : M
        X = C000 - C7FF FSTC

Then reboot. If this works, continue; if this does not work (and FSTC might not work in all circumstances), then remove the FSTC parameter and reboot with the previous QEMM-386 line. See the section about FSTC later for an explanation. In either case, enter Manifest, go to the QEMM-386/Analysis screen, and look at the Cn00 line. It should look something like this:

Cn00 0 I I I I I I I 0000 0000

This indicates that the first 4K region of the C segment, in the video ROM, is being accessed directly. This portion of the address space must be Excluded when QEMM-386 is Stealthing. The appropriate QEMM-386 line in the CONFIG.SYS is the following:

DEVICE = C : \ QEMM \ QEMM - 386 . SYS RAM ST : M X = C000 - C0FF

Section 3

Step #9 On some machines are other ROMs that can be Stealthed; often these are disk ROMs. Follow the same procedure: try XST = ??00, then replace it with the appropriate Exclude of the old kind (X = ??00 - !!FF) to see if the problem is related to Stealthing or just don't have some portion of the ROM's address space directly accessible. You can also use the trick of making the page frame begin at the beginning of the disk ROM. If XST = ??00 solves your problem, try replacing it with FR = ??00, presuming that there is a 64K portion of the address space free beginning at ??00 and that ?? is a multiple of 16. If some portion of the address space must be Excluded for Stealth to work, you should check Analysis with the FSTC and X = ??00 - !!FF parameters on the QEMM line. Because of the way the ROMs are written for the IBM PS/2 machines, and, perhaps, other Microchannel machines, you must load HOOKROM.SYS before QEMM-386.SYS in the CONFIG.SYS for XST = E000 to work. For example:

```
DEVICE = C : \ QEMM \ HOOKROM . SYS
DEVICE = C : \ QEMM \ QEMM - 386 . SYS RAM ST : M XST = E000
```

Step #10   Use XST = F000, XST = C000, XST = ??00, and simultaneously for all ROMs being Stealthed. Then replace the XSTs one by one with the appropriate regular Exclude (X = F000-FFFF, X = C000-C7FF, X = ??00-!!FF...), look at the QEMM- 386/Analysis screen of Manifest and discover what portions of the address space need to be directly available.

Step #11   If ST : M does not work, try ST : F instead. If ST : F does not work, you should try ST : F XST = C000 (and XST = ??00) for other Stealthed ROMs other than the one(s) overlain by the page frame.

Step #12   If none of these steps solve the problem, please pin down exactly what program is failing (and at what point) and file a report with Quarterdeck.

Interesting questions

What should I do if QEMM reports "Cannot find ROM handler for interrupt XX"?

Load "HOOKROM.SYS" at the beginning of the CONFIG.SYS. Use a line like DEVICE = C : \ QEMM \ HOOKROM . SYS. If this does not work, then you might need to tell QEMM-386 to stop Stealthing this interrupt. The parameter that does this is XSTI = XX, where XX is the number of the interrupt reported by the error message. When you do this you must do an Analysis with an Exclude (of the old kind) of the address space being occupied by all Stealthed ROMs. Here is a typical QEMM-386 line to do an Analysis:

```
DEVICE = C : \ QEMM \ QEMM - 386 . SYS RAM ST : M XSTI = 70 FSTC
          x = C000 - CFFF X = F000 - FFFF
```

Reboot with this QEMM-386 line, look at the QEMM ANALYSIS MAP in Manifest. It may look something like this:

```
n = 0123 4567 89AB CDEF
0n00 0000 0000 0000 0000
1n00 0000 0000 0000 0000
2n00 0000 0000 0000 0000
3n00 0000 0000 0000 0000
4n00 0000 0000 0000 0000
5n00 0000 0000 0000 0000
6n00 0000 0000 0000 0000
7n00 0000 0000 0000 0000
8n00 0000 0000 0000 0000
9n00 0000 0000 0000 0000
An00 0000 0000 0000 0000
Bn00 0000 0000 0000 0000
```

```
Cn00 1111 1111 0000 0000
Dn00 0000 0000 0000 0000
En00 0000 0000 0000 0000
Fn00 0000 1111 1111 1110
```

This indicates that the first 16K of the F segment is being accessed by the INT 70 handler and must remain Excluded. The final QEMM line for this case is the following:

```
DEVICE=C:\QEMM\QEMM-386.SYS RAM ST:M XSTI=70
          X=F000-F3FF
```

We at Quarterdeck would very much like to know about the machine that is reporting this error. The only cause that we've seen is the case of some users on XT machines with Inboards. XTs do not have a second bank of hardware interrupts (which use interrupts 70−77), but some ROMs on XTs mistakenly report that they do and QEMM-386 looks for the interrupt handler of some interrupts that do not have handlers. For such machines, no Exclude is necessary because no ROM code handles the interrupt. In particular, we'd like to know where this interrupt is pointing when Stealth is not being used. This can be discovered in Manifest on the First Meg Interrupts screen.

Inboard-PC users Inboard-PC users might need xsti=70 xsti=74 xsti=75 xsti=76. The device line is as follows:

```
DEVICE=C:\QEMM\QEMM-386.SYS RAM ST:M XSTI=70
          XSTI=74 XSTI=75 XSTI=76
```

What is FASTINT10:N?

QEMM-386, when Stealthing a video ROM, replaces some of the video ROM's code with replacement code written by Quarterdeck. This replacement code is suitable for most video cards. The FASTINT10:N (which might be abbreviated F10:N) parameter tells QEMM-386 not to use its own replacement code but the literal code of the video ROM. This in no way limits the amount of high, RAM Stealth creates and might be an acceptable solution for those users who need it. It should only be necessary on unusual video cards. If placing the page frame at the beginning of the video card's ROM works or if a small regular Exclude also solves the problem, you may choose to use this solution instead.

What is FSTC?

The purpose of the FSTC parameter is to make the Analysis procedure accurate. Some system and video ROMs might not function properly with the FSTC parameter. If this is the case on your system, you will have to perform the Analysis procedure without the FSTC parameter. However, you should be aware in this case that some of the Exclude statements that Analysis prompts you to use might not be necessary.

You can try reducing these Excludes on a trial-and-error basis if you want. When QEMM-386 Stealths a ROM, certain tables might need to be stored by QEMM-386 in its own data area, which uses a few kilobytes of high RAM. When a ROM is being Stealthed but the address in which the ROM resides is Excluded (as with X = C000-C7FF), then QEMM-386 cleverly figures out that it doesn't need to make copies of these tables in its own data area, so it saves this memory by not making copies of the tables. Thus, when you do Exclude the portion(s) of the ROM where these tables are stored, the ROM will be accessed directly (although it would not be if it were not Excluded). This will cause Analysis to report that a portion of the address space is OK when Excluded even though it would not be accessed directly were it not Excluded.

FSTC (FORCESTEALTHTABLECOPY) forces QEMM-386 to make copies of these tables so that inappropriate Excludes are not recommended for the above reason. FSTC should only be used when you are testing a portion of a ROMs address space for direct access by Excluding the whole ROM. It is not an appropriate parameter for a final configuration.

What are advanced disk features?

The BIOS has a set of function calls intended for use by multitasking programs: Int 15, functions 90 and 91. The system ROM or disk ROM may issue the Int 15, Fn 90 call while it is waiting for the disk controller to read or write a sector, allowing other programs to execute during this wait. When the sector is ready, the disk interrupt handler issues an Int 15, Fn 91, signaling the multitasking program that the disk information is ready to be processed by the system or disk ROM.

Some disk caches hook this call to allow your system to go ahead and execute your current program while the system or disk ROM is waiting for its requested sector. Whereas these caches preserve the stack and register state for the BIOS and the application when doing this pseudo-multitasking, they do not preserve the mapping of the page frame. Thus, if the BIOS uses the page frame itself (as does Stealth), this could generate conflicts and system failures.

Because no known disk cache does the proper page frame preservation, QEMM automatically suppresses Int 15, function 90 calls from the BIOS, effectively disabling advanced disk features. Caches that save and restore the page frame when using advanced disk features can use a programming interface to QEMM-386 to re-enable advanced disk features. You can negate QEMM-386's defeating of this feature with the VIRTUALHDIRQ:N (VH I : N) parameter on the QEMM-386 line of CONFIG.SYS. If your cache has these "Advanced Features" and does not save and restore the page frame, you will crash or corrupt data on the cached drive(s).

Why does XST=E000 only work on PS/2 machines if I use HOOKROM.SYS?

The code in the E000−EFFF portion of the ROM on PS/2 and, perhaps other Microchannel machines, is not directly pointed to by the interrupt table. The interrupt table points to addresses in F000−FFFF, which then point to the appropriate code in the E000−EFFF segment. You can see this in the FirstMeg/Interrupts section of Manifest. When you load HOOKROM.SYS, it traces down the redirection of the interrupts to the place where the executing code begins, so that interrupts serviced by code in the E000−EFFF segment actually point to addresses in the E000−EFFF segment. How to use HOOKROM.SYS for this purpose is examined in the last paragraph of the previous Step #9.

Why does my system setup no longer come up with ST:M?

On machines with a built-in system setup program in the BIOS, ROM that can be popped up at any time Stealth might make this feature inaccessible after you have booted. This happens because the setup program accesses the ROM directly. In order for it to work after QEMM-386 has been loaded, you must Exclude the portion of the address space where it is stored. On most machines, this is in F000−F7FF or thereabouts.

You might decide that it is better to use the system setup only on boot and be able to use this portion of the address space for high RAM when you are running. Many systems are this way today, and you must reboot to implement the changes anyway, so you might consider this a fair trade. Machines with a setup program that loads as a regular program might not present this problem.

What is going on?

With ST : M, Stealth is moving out of the address space all ROMs accessed by means of interrupts (you can see what interrupts are being handled by what ROMs in the First Meg/Interrupts screen of Manifest when you are not Stealthing.) When these interrupts are asserted, QEMM-386 puts the ROM code that services the interrupt into the page frame. With ST : F, Stealth is allowing the page frame to share the address space used by the ROM, making the underlying ROM code available in the page frame when an interrupt pointing into the ROM is asserted.

How can it fail?

The Stealth technology relies on the practice of using the code in ROMs only by means of interrupts. With the exceptions listed next, when the code in a ROM is accessed directly, the program or hardware using this code (or information) will find high RAM there instead with ST : M and will malfunction. Although this is uncommon, it does happen.

Sometimes programs look for identification information. For video cards, this usually happens in the bottom 4K; for system BIOS, this usually happens in FE00−FEFF. Most users for whom Stealth fails can recover almost all the high RAM Stealth can create with small Excludes of this kind.

Exceptions are as follows:

- QEMM-386 does not map high RAM into the last 64 bytes of the system BIOS ROM because they are commonly accessed directly. Accesses here do not cause Stealth a problem.

- When a ROM accesses itself directly, then it should work IF the page frame begins at this ROM's beginning address. Some video cards and disk controllers fail because the video ROM (disk ROM) does not tolerate relocation. The ready cure for this symptom is to put the page frame at C000 (or whatever is the beginning of the appropriate video or disk ROM) so that when an interrupt that points into the video ROM (disk ROM) is asserted, and QEMM restores the contents of the video ROM (disk ROM) into the page frame, then the ROM code can access itself where it expects to find itself. The previous Step #6 addresses this.

- Direct accesses of one ROM to another work with ST:F.

Disk caches that write directly to and read directly from the page frame cause Stealth to fail unless DISKBUFFRAME=?? (DBF=??) is used.

Stealth relies on interrupts pointing into a ROM in order to make it a target for Stealthing. If there is a ROM in the address space that QEMM-386 cannot detect as being used, then it will not be Stealthed. This might happen for some disk ROMs and for devices that use the ROM only upon initialization. If there is a ROM without an interrupt pointing into it, it could be unused. You should use the Analysis feature of QEMM-386 to discover if this ROM is being used at all; if it isn't, then the address space it occupies can be reclaimed with an INCLUDE.

Summary

The Stealth technology has been exhaustively tested but the wide variety of software and hardware in the PC world has surprises in it for every program. The actual Stealthing of interrupts is very successful. The most common failure is due to programs (or other ROMs) trying to access a portion of the ROM directly, rather than by means of interrupt.

For this to work, the target region of this access must be in the address space at the time of access. This can be achieved by an appropriate Exclude of the old kind, usually at a cost of only 4−8K of the additional high RAM Stealth is creating; see Steps #3-11 for a procedure to figure these Excludes out.

If the video ROM or adaptor ROM is the target ROM of a problem, then placing the page frame over the video ROM or adaptor ROM might work; see Step #6. The "Advanced Disk Features" that some disk caches use are incompatible with

Stealth. QEMM-386 disables these by default whenever possible if Stealth is used. Some disk caches write directly to the page frame. Such caches should be told to use extended memory or the DISKBUFFRAME = ?? (DBF = ??) should be used with QEMM-386; see Step #2. If you have a problem intractable by any of these means, Quarterdeck would like to hear about it.

Microchannel adapters, MCA .ADL, QEMM-386, QEMM 50/60, and QRAM

I get the message "Unrecognized Microchannel Adapter" whenever I boot my machine when QEMM-386 (QEMM 50/60, QRAM) is loading. Why?

The reason you get this message is that you have a Microchannel adapter that is not in the file MCA.ADL.

What is MCA.ADL?

MCA.ADL is a file that comes with QEMM-386, QEMM 50/60 and QRAM. It contains the configuration information about Microchannel cards so that QEMM-386 (QEMM 50/60, QRAM) can read the configuration of the cards installed in your computer. Many add-in boards such as network cards, memory cards, and fax boards occupy memory between 640K and 1M. The entries in the MCA.ADL file tell QEMM-386, QEMM 50/60 and QRAM what portions of the address space those cards are using and keep QEMM-386 (QEMM 50/60, QRAM) from mapping high RAM into the portions of the address space being occupied by these cards.

Why isn't my card in the MCA.ADL?

New cards are being made constantly but your MCA.ADL file was written when your QEMM-386 (QEMM 50/60, QRAM) was released. Here at Quarterdeck, we are updating our MCA.ADL whenever we receive the configuration file of a new Microchannel adapter.

How can I get a new copy of the MCA.ADL?

A current copy is available on the Quarterdeck BBS (310-314-3227). You might find one on a more current QEMM-386 (QEMM 50/60, QRAM) purchaser's disk. The file is the same for all Quarterdeck products.

Is there another way to get the entry for my card?

If you do not want to download the latest MCA.ADL from the BBS, then you can contact Quarterdeck Technical Support and have the entry for your card FAXed or mailed to you.

What do I do with the entry for my card?

The MCA.ADL is a plain text file. Any word processor that can save a non-formatted file (WordStar in non-document mode, Microsoft Word as "unformatted," WordPerfect as "DOS Text," for example) can be used to edit the MCA.ADL. Although the entry can be inserted anywhere in the file, good form would suggest that you enter it in numerical order. The Microchannel ID numbers are hexadecimal numbers.

What if my device is not on the latest MCA.ADL?

Then you should send a copy of the file "@XXXX.ADF" (where "XXXX" is the number of the unrecognized Microchannel adapter) by mail or FAX to Quarterdeck Technical Support so that we can make an appropriate entry for the master MCA.ADL (which, coincidentally, is why it changes so often) and have a copy of the proper entry sent to you by return mail or FAX. The file @XXXX.ADF resides on the reference disk that comes with the adapter card. It should also be on the reference diskette of the computer.

What if I am not having a problem?

QEMM-386 (QEMM 50/60, QRAM) use the Microchannel configuration only for the purpose of making sure that they do not map high RAM (or the page frame for QEMM-386 and QEMM 50/60) into portions of the address space occupied by the adapter cards. Many other factors are involved in the Microchannel configuration, but they have no direct bearing upon Quarterdeck products.

In addition to using this Microchannel-specific method of detecting address conflicts, QEMM-386, QEMM 50/60, and QRAM also use more conventional methods to detect high address space usage, methods that are used both on Microchannel and non-Microchannel machines. When they detect such usage of memory, high RAM will not be mapped into the address space being occupied by the adapter card even if there is no entry for the card in the MCA.ADL. If the card does not use any high address space (and many do not), then the entry in the MCA.ADL is for informational purposes only and is not necessary for QEMM-386 (QEMM 50/60, QRAM) to configure itself to work on the system.

An unrecognized Microchannel Adapter message is still reported but can be safely ignored for these kind of adapters, so you might be able to work without an entry for the unrecognized adapter. When there is an unrecognized Microchannel adapter installed, QEMM-386 (QEMM 50/60, QRAM) will report an error and give you the option of not loading itself. If you are having no problem, you can press any key to continue at this point and QEMM-386 (QEMM 50/60, QRAM) will load. If you want to suppress this error message, you may put the NO PAUSEONERROR (NOPE, for short) parameter on QEMM-386 (QEMM 50/60,

QRAM). This is not advisable, as QEMM-386 (QEMM 50/60, QRAM) will not report any error. A better temporary solution is to make a temporary entry in the MCA.ADL for the target card. This entry will look like this:

```
XXXX Waiting for a correct MCA.ADL entry from Quarter-
deck
```

where XXXX is the number of the unrecognized Microchannel adapter.

Example

You are getting the message "Unrecognized Microchannel Adapter @5600." Your MCA.ADL looks like this in this area:

```
5500 COREtape Controller
5502 CORE CNT-MCF Tape Controller
5606 Cabletron Ethernet Board E3010
X X000XXXX /ARAM = C000-C3FF
X X001XXXX /ARAM = C400-C7FF
X X010XXXX /ARAM = C800-CBFF
X X011XXXX /ARAM = CC00-CFFF
X X100XXXX /ARAM = D000-D3FF
X X101XXXX /ARAM = D400-D7FF
X X110XXXX /ARAM = D800-DBFF
X X111XXXX /ARAM = DC00-DFFF
```

5600 is absent. The correct entry for 5600 is as follows:

```
5600 Cabletron Ethernet Board E3020
X X000XXXX /ARAM = C000-C3FF
X X001XXXX /ARAM = C400-C7FF
X X010XXXX /ARAM = C800-CBFF
X X011XXXX /ARAM = CC00-CFFF
X X100XXXX /ARAM = D000-D3FF
X X101XXXX /ARAM = D400-D7FF
X X110XXXX /ARAM = D800-DBFF
X X111XXXX /ARAM = DC00-DFFF
```

You must obtain this entry from Quarterdeck Technical Support as mentioned earlier. Insert the entry in the MCA.ADL file between the entries for 5502 and 5606. The final result will look like this:

```
5500 COREtape Controller
5502 CORE CNT-MCF Tape Controller
5600 Cabletron Ethernet Board E3020
X X000XXXX /ARAM = C000-C3FF
```

```
X X001XXXX /ARAM = C400 - C7FF
X X010XXXX /ARAM = C800 - CBFF
X X011XXXX /ARAM = CC00 - CFFF
X X100XXXX /ARAM = D000 - D3FF
X X101XXXX /ARAM = D400 - D7FF
X X110XXXX /ARAM = D800 - DBFF
X X111XXXX /ARAM = DC00 - DFFF
5606 Cabletron Ethernet Board E3010
X X000XXXX /ARAM = C000 - C3FF
X X001XXXX /ARAM = C400 - C7FF
X X010XXXX /ARAM = C800 - CBFF
X X011XXXX /ARAM = CC00 - CFFF
X X100XXXX /ARAM = D000 - D3FF
X X101XXXX /ARAM = D400 - D7FF
X X110XXXX /ARAM = D800 - DBFF
X X111XXXX /ARAM = DC00 - DFFF
```

Banyan Vines network setup

Are Quarterdeck products compatible with Banyan network drivers?

Yes. In fact, Banyan has published Application Notes certifying QEMM and DESQview with Vines.

Can I load the network drivers "High" (in the memory area between 640K and 1024K)?

Yes. If you have EMS 4.0 or EEMS memory using QRAM or an 80386 with QEMM-386, you may load Files, Buffers, FCBs, and small TSR programs as well as Banyan's drivers into the unused areas in high memory, provided you have either one 112K or two 64K "High RAM" regions available.

How do I LOADHI Banyan's network drivers?

You can LOADHI the drivers by modifying your network batch file as this example for Ethernet shows:

```
BAN /NC
LOADHI ETHERBAN
LOADHI EPCBFS
```

Are there any special considerations with QEMM and network cards?

Yes. If your network card (such as Token Ring) has a RAM buffer, you should exclude it from QEMM so that other memory is not mapped over the RAM buffer address. For more information on this subject, obtain TOKEN.TEC from Quarterdeck's Technical Support Department.

Do I have to do anything special to run DESQview with Vines or Grapevines?

Some PC compatibles require a parameter when starting DESQview. The symptom is that when a 25th line message is received, the system will hang. If this happens to you, first determine what IRQ your network card is set at. The example given is for an Ethernet card set on IRQ 3.

    DV /HW : 0B = U

The /HW stands for hardware IRQ, the :0B5 represents IRQ3. 0C would stand for IRQ 4, 0D would stand for IRQ 5. Note that the 0 is a *zero*, not an O. The = U stands for unmask.

B
APPENDIX

Network considerations with Helix's NETROOM

Novell networks

You can load the Novell drivers into memory in several ways. With MS-DOS 3 & 4, NETROOM automatically places a Novell NETXX.COM shell into the HMA with its NETHMA utility. With MS-DOS 5, the default loads DOS into the HMA. You can manually place the NETXX shell into the HMA with MS-DOS 5 by making the following change in your CONFIG.SYS:

```
DEVICE = RM386.SYS [Parameter 1] [Parameter 2..] NOHMA
```

Also, add the following statement as the last line of the CONFIG.SYS:

```
INSTALL = [d:] \ NETROOM \ XLOAD.EXE [d:] \ NETROOM
            \ DOSUMB.COM
```

You must also change your AUTOEXEC.BAT file like this,

```
NETHMA NET XX.EXE
```

where NETXX is the name of the network shell for your particular Novell network.

This configuration will load the DOS operating system into upper memory and the Novell shell into the HMA. The IPX driver will load in upper memory (if there is room) or in conventional memory.

An alternative approach is to place the IPX driver in the HMA with the HMALOAD utility. This will work with versions of IPX up to 3.01. HMALOAD uses 7K more of the HMA for the driver than Novell's native XMSNET utility.

A third approach is to load IPX and/or Novell's EMSNET shell into upper memory with NETROOM's XLOAD utility. This approach might not be compatible with all versions of IPX.COM. You may experiment with loading IPX.COM "high" and determine whether this causes incompatibilities on your individual system. EMSNET is a version of the Novell shell designed to swap itself in and out of expanded memory. It may be loaded either high or low on any system that has sufficient EMS 4.0 memory available.

Using NETROOM's NETSWAP utilities with networks

NETROOM's NETSWAP and NETSWAP4 utilities allows you to swap 64K to 576K, respectively of network drivers to an expanded memory virtual machine. For a Novell network, you may load the three drivers discussed in the previous section and Novell's NETBIOS.EXE emulator all into EMS 4.0 by creating a Novell batch file as follows:

```
NETSWAP4 -ANOVELL.ALK NOVELL.BAT
```

where NOVELL.BAT is

```
IPX.COM
NETXX.EXE
NETBIOS.EXE
```

NOVELL.ALK is a text file found in the NETROOM directory. It contains a list of NOVELL commands that will force the network drivers back into conventional memory while each command is being executed. NETROOM also supplies ALK (AutoLock) files for BANYAN and IBMLAN. Some LANs might become confused while executing specific commands if their drivers are loaded into expanded memory. These drivers in EMS allow read/write access to network drives but report errors when the user attempts commands like LOGIN, LOGOUT, ATTACH, etc. The -A AutoLock parameter avoids these problems by temporarily returning the drivers to conventional memory for the duration of any network commands listed in the .ALK file.

The following are some NETSWAP configurations for other popular PC networks:

DCA 10NET

CONFIG.SYS

```
FILES=40
BUFFERS=20
DEVICE=RM386.SYS FRAME=E000 AUTO
```

AUTOEXEC.BAT

```
PATH=C:\;C:\DOS;C:\NETROOM
PROMPT $P$G
CD \10NET
NETSWAP4 -A10NET.ALK 10 NET.BAT
10Net.alk
10NET.EXE
```

10NET.BAT

```
SYSSVC.COM
MAC586.COM /i=7
XPMGR.COM
10NB4.COM
10NET.EXE SUPER.PRO
```

3COM 3+ OPEN

CONFIG.SYS

```
DEVICE=\RM386.SYS FRAME=E000 AUTO
SHELL=\COMMAND.COM /E:256 /P
DEVICE=\MOUSE.SYS
FILES=35
BUFFERS=25
LASTDRIVE=Z
```

AUTOEXEC.BAT

```
PATH=\3OPEN\DOSWKSTA\LANMAN;\3OPEN\DOSWKSTA\
LANMAN\DRIVERS;
C:\NETROOM;C:\;D:\;E:\
PROMPT $P$G
NETSWAP4 -A3COMOPEN.ALK 3COMOPEN.BAT
LOGIN
3F LINK D:\\S1\APPS /NP
```

3COMOPEN.BAT

```
\NETROOM\DEVLOAD.COM\ORITNAB,DIS /I:\
\NETROOM\DEVLOAD.COM\ELNKMC.DOS
\NETROOM\DEVLOAD\.COM\XNSTP.DOS
XNSTP.EXE
RNDISETH.EXE /MCASTS:4 /STACKS:5
RNDISETH /U
```

```
NETBIND.EXE
NETBIOS.EXE
MINSES12.EXE
NET START WORKSTATION
SETNAME $$3COM$$ /e
\SPRTSC
\RECVMSG
```

3COMOPEN.ALK

```
NET.EXE
3F.EXE
LOGIN.EXE
```

Microsoft Lan Manager

CONFIG.SYS

```
SHELL=C:\COMMAND.COM /P /E:1000
FILES=20
BUFFERS=25
STACKS=0,0
DEVICE=C:\NETROOM\RM386.SYS AUTO
```

AUTOEXEC.BAT

```
PATH=C:\LANMAN\DRIVERS\PROTMAN;C:\;C:\DOS;C:\
NETROOM
NETSWAP4 -ALANMAN.ALK LANMAN.BAT
```

LANMAN.BAT

```
DEVLOAD.COM  D:\LANMAN\DRIVERS\PROTMAN\PROTMAN.DOS
/I:D:\LANMAN
DEVLOAD D:\LANMAN\DRIVERS\TOKENRNG
\IBMTOK\IBMTOK.DOS
DEVLOAD D:\LANMAN\DRIVERS\PROTOCOL
\NETBEUI\NETBEUI.DOS
D:\LANMAN\DRIVERS\PROTMAN\NETBIND.EXE
D:\COMMSRV\DEV\COMNDIS.COM 2
D:\LANMAN\NETPROG\NET.EXE START WORKSTATION
D:\LANMAN\NETPROG\NET.EXE LOGON
```

LANMAN.ALK

```
NET.EXE
NETUSER.EXE
CHKNET.EXE
```

```
SETNAME . EXE
NETMOVE . EXE
NETCOPY . EXE
USE . EXE
WINPOPUP . EXE
PMSPL . EXE
```

C
APPENDIX

The shareware utilities disk

The utilities diskette included with this book contains both free/public domain programs and shareware programs. Free programs have no technical support and no upgrade policy. They might be copyrighted—which gives their authors the right to control their distribution—or they might be "public domain," which means there are no restrictions on their use.

Shareware programs are not free or public-domain programs. They are copyrighted, commercial programs that might include technical support, bound manuals, and/or free upgrades to advanced versions for registered users.

The free programs on this diskette are as follows:

ASQ	COLDBOOT	EEMRAM	DNANSI
HDTEST	IRQS	MSLOOKUP	PMAP
QTEST	SSTAT	WARMBOOT	

The shareware programs on this diskette are as follows:

BIGDESK	BOOT.SYS	DMP
DV Commander	Hyperdisk	Nifty James Ramdisk
The TSR Utilities		

The following license agreement for shareware programs follows the guidelines set out by the Association of Shareware Professionals, where Program is the specific shareware program, and Company is the program's author or publisher:

Each of the shareware programs on the diskette has its own license agreement and terms. These are included with the program on the disk.

The Program is supplied as is. The author disclaims all warranties, expressed or implied, including, without limitation, the warranties of merchantability and of fitness for any purpose. The author assumes no liability for damages, direct or consequential, that might result from the use of the Program.

The Program is a "shareware program" and is provided at no charge to the user for evaluation. Feel free to share it with your friends for noncommercial use, but do not give it away altered or as part of another system. The essence of "user-supported" software is to provide personal computer users with quality software without high prices, and yet to provide incentives for programmers to continue to develop new products. If you find this program useful, and find that you continue to use the Program after a reasonable trial period, you must make a registration payment to the Company. The registration fee will license one copy for one use on any one computer at any one time. You must treat this software just like a copyrighted book. An example is that this software may be used by any number of people and may be freely moved from one computer location to another, as long as there is no possibility of it being used at one location while it's being used at another—just as a book cannot be read by two different persons at the same time.

Commercial users of the Program must register and pay for their copies of the Program within 30 days of first use or their license is withdrawn. Site-license arrangements may be made by contacting the Company.

Anyone distributing the Program for any kind of remuneration must first contact the Company at the address provided for authorization. This authorization will be automatically granted to distributors recognized by the Association of Shareware Professionals as adhering to its guidelines for shareware distributors, and such distributors may begin offering the Program immediately. (However, the Company must still be advised so that the distributor can be kept up-to-date with the latest version of the Program.)

You are encouraged to pass a copy of the Program along to your friends for evaluation. Please encourage them to register their copy, if they find they can use it. All registered users will receive a copy of the latest version of the Program.

Each of the programs and documentation thereto are published and distributed with this book with the written permission of the authors of each. The programs herein are supplied as is. Lenny Bailes, John Mueller, and TAB Books individually and together disclaim all warranties, expressed or implied, including, without limitation, the warranties of merchantability and of fitness for any particular purpose, and assume no liability for damages, direct or consequential, that might result from the use of the programs or reliance on the documentation.

How to use our utilities diskette

You can install these utility program in one of two ways, depending on your penchant for difficulty. If you want to do things the easy way, simply use the Install program included on your disk. To run this program, simply load your disk, change to drive A: (or whatever drive letter refers to your floppy disk), and type

    INSTALL

at the prompt. Now simply follow the instructions on the menu that will appear. The program will do all the messy copying and unpacking for you.

Alternately, if you'd prefer to install things manually so that you can be sure of exactly what's going on, just copy the self-extracting .EXE file to a subdirectory on your hard disk. Typing the filename will unpack the program. For instance,

    COPY A: \ HYDK431 . EXE C: \ UTIL

Log onto drive C: and type HYDK431 from the C: \ UTIL directory. The Hyperdisk files will be uncompressed into the directory, and you may then delete HYDK431.EXE from your hard disk.

The following are descriptions of the diskette files:

UTILS
: A collection of free and public domain utilities that can display system memory statistics, hard disk statistics, system interrupt information, automatically reboot the system, speed up the screen display, or retune your hard disk.

EEMRAM20
: Chris Dunford's utility that allows 8088 and 80286 machines with true EEMS/EMS4.0 memory to annex 64−96K to conventional memory, producing a total of 704K or 736K.

PMAP210
: Chris Dunford's memory display utility

IRQS
: Small program that shows which hardware interrupts (IRQs) on the system are used and which are available. (Requires that the ANSI driver be loaded for proper display)

DNANSI
: A replacement for DOS's ANSI.SYS driver. Creates a remarkable speed up in text display, especially inside of DESQview and Microsoft Windows. (Supports only basic ANSI screen calls)

MSINT
: An online reference for DOS interrupt usage. Allows you to type in keywords and determine how to program basic DOS interrupt functions.

SSTAT104
: A utility that displays system memory usage, hard drive information, and complete map of used and free disk space.

HDTEST
: A hard disk diagnostic, benchmark and low-level formatting utility.

The UTILS.EXE compressed file also contains QTEST.COM and QTEST .TEC. QTEST is a free inventory utility from Quarterdeck Office Systems that checks your system for compatibility with Quarterdeck memory management products.

ASQ130   Online memory tutorial and system inventory utility from Qualitas, Inc., the manufacturers of 386MAX.

BOOT.SYS A shareware system utility that allows you to select different start-up configurations for your computer without rebooting and using different AUTOEXEC.BAT and CONFIG.SYS files.

DMP205   A shareware printspool utility that can store print data in extended memory, expanded memory, or hard disk space.

DSK233   BIGDESK. A shareware utility that creates a larger (virtual) screen display for MS Windows, v. 3.x. The package includes a resident application launcher. (Useful for multitasking a series of Windows and DOS applications under Windows.)

DVC18   DESQview Commander. A shareware enhancement for Quarter-deck's DESQview that allows users to construct program launch submenus, or invoke DESQview features from batch files.

HYDK431   Hyperdisk. A powerful shareware state-of-the-art disk cache that supports all Intel processor types, and all memory configurations. In actuality, this executable contains the version of Hyperdisk 4.3.2.

NJRAM14   Nifty James Ramdisk. A shareware EMS/XMS RAMdisk utility that lacks the 4M size limitation of MS-DOS 5's RAMdisk.

TSRCOM33 The TSR Utilities. A shareware package that allows you to install and remove terminate-and-stay resident utilities without rebooting the computer.

D
APPENDIX

Public bulletin board systems

The following list names public BBS systems that contain files and/or conference information about Quarterdeck products. (Most probably have Windows 3 related areas as well.)

USA and Canada

Phone Number	BBS Name	Location	Net
201-568-7293	THE BOSS	Tenafly, NJ USA	SmartNet
201-729-2602	Chuck's Attempt BBS	Sparta, NJ USA	SmartNet
201-927-0329	The Odyssey BBS	Flanders, NJ USA	SmartNet
201-984-5555	Atrium Way	Morris Plains, NJ USA	DVNet
203-564-8579	Plainfield News	Plainfield, CT USA	DVNet
203-791-8532	Treasure Island	Danbury, CT USA	DVNet
203-934-9852	Ascii Neighborhood	W Haven, CT USA	DVNet
204-837-9704	Polar Bear Heaven	Winnipeg, MB USA	DVNet
206-244-8860	Seattle/Everett Hub	Seattle, WA USA	DVNet
206-253-9770	Pacifier BBS	Vancouver, WA USA	DVNet
206-367-2596	Poverty Rock	Seattle, WA USA	SmartNet
206-566-8854	Puget Sound Gtwy.	Puyallup, WA USA	DVNet
206-850-0809	The Wee Hoose	Kent, WA USA	SmartNet
207-439-9367	SeaCoast Opus	Kittery Pt, ME USA	DVNet
207-766-2467	The Northern Lights	Peaks Is., ME USA	U'NI-net
209-298-9461	Stingray!	Clovis, CA USA	DVNet
209-823-0093	Bertha Board	Mantica, CA USA	DVNet
212-431-1194	The Invention Factory	New York, NY USA	SmartNet
213-387-5901	Little Angels PCBoard	Los Angeles, CA USA	SmartNet
310-399-3802	QOS Support (QOS USA)	Santa Monica, CA	SmartNet
310-459-6053	DPS	Pacific Palisades, CA USA	SmartNet
310-474-8309	Topology System Serv	West Los Angles, CA USA	SmartNet

Phone Number	BBS Name	Location	Net
310-540-0337	The ACTION BBS	Redondo Beach, CA USA	SmartNet
310-838-9229	West Los Angeles BBS	West Los Angles, CA USA	U'NI-Net
214-358-1205	Dallas Email	Dallas, TX USA	DVNet
214-458-2620	Inns of Court	Dallas, TX USA	DVNet
214-556-2982	Southern Crossroads	Dallas, TX USA	DVNet
215-364-3324	SataLink	Huntingdon Valley, PA USA	SmartNet
215-641-0270	U.S.S. Intrepid	Spring House, PA USA	DVNet
215-725-9134	Walsh Microsys	Philadelphia, PA USA	DVNet
215-797-7409	Optical Illusion	Allentown, PA USA	DVNet
216-545-2318	Steel Valley BBS	Girard, OH USA	DVNet
216-928-8565	NHampton Data	Cuyahoga Falls, OH USA	DVNet
217-398-2800	Wolfram Research	Champaign, IL USA	DVNet
219-824-5628	The Jokerman BBS	Bluffton, IN USA	DVNet
301-252-0717	AviTechnic	Lutherville, MD USA	DVNet
301-428-8998	Addict's Attic	Germantown, MD USA	DVNet
303-320-4822	World Peace BBS	Denver, CO USA	DVNet
303-651-0225	Twin Peaks BBS	Longmont, CO USA	SmartNet
305-220-8752	Southern Cross BBS	Miami, FL USA	DVNet
307-472-3615	Oregon Trail XRoads	Casper, WY USA	DVNet
313-435-5766	Son of Royal Joke	Royal Oak, MI USA	DVNet
313-435-7566	The Royal Joke	Royal Oak, MI USA	DVNet
314-973-4073	TRAVEL ONLINE	St. Louis, MO, USA	SmartNet
315-458-8602	Rivendell * TAP/1	Syracuse, NY USA	DVNet
316-687-0719	Information Link	Wichita, KS USA	SmartNet
317-353-9981	Someplace BBS	Indianapolis, IN USA	DVNet
318-537-3620	Ft Polk Info	Fort Polk, LA USA	DVNet
319-337-9878	Icarus	Iowa City, IA USA	DVNet
403-483-1896	Information Corner	Edmonton, AB CAN	DVNet
404-261-1312	System Support BBS (SS	Atlanta, GA USA	SmartNet
404-998-2804	Atlanta Data Base User	Atlanta, GA USA	Smartnet
405-360-4261	Ascension	Norman, OK USA	DVNet
407-676-2998	E.I.L.C.	Palm Bay, FL USA	DVNet
408-248-0198	Carl's Corner	San Jose, CA USA	DVNet
408-248-9704	Carl's Corner	San Jose, CA USA	DVNet
408-270-4085	PDS-SIG	San Jose, CA USA	U'NI-Net
408-737-9447	Higher Powered BBS	Sunnyvale, CA USA	SmartNet
409-762-2761	DragonNet	Galveston, TX USA	DVNet
412-373-8612	Ecclesia Place	Monroeville, PA USA	DVNet
413-256-1037	Pioneer Valley PCUG1	Amherst, MA USA	DVNet
414-476-8468	County Line BBS	W Allis, WI USA	DVNet
415-337-5416	The PC GFX Exchange	San Francisco, CA USA	SmartNet
415-344-4348	SeaHunt BBS	Burlingame, CA USA	DVNet
415-474-4523	The Network 2000	San Francisco, CA USA	SmartNet
415-595-2427	Toad Hall BBS	San Carlos, CA USA	SmartNet
415-621-2609	SF PCUG BBS	San Francisco, CA USA	DVNet
415-829-6027	Easy Access	San Ramon, CA USA	SmartNet
416-387-5507	Tobacco Road	Hamilton, ON USA	DVNet
416-733-2285	Rose Media	Willowdale, ON CAN	U'NI-net
416-629-7000	Canada Remote Systems	Mississauga, ON CAN	SmartNet
416-937-3685	I.T.T. (QOS Canada)	Welland, ON CAN	DVNet
503-245-9730	Atarian BBS	Portland, OR USA	DVNet
503-297-9043	Bink of an Aye	Portland, OR USA	DVNet
503-297-9078	P C Support	Portland, OR USA	DVNet
503-620-5910	NW Computer Support	Portland, OR USA	SmartNet
503-771-4773	Busker's Boneyard	Portland, OR USA	DVNet
503-775-7926	Busker's Boneyard	Portland, OR USA	DVNet
504-888-6515	Silver Streak RBBS	NewOrleans, LA USA	DVNet
506-635-1964	Atlantic Access	St John W, NB CAN	DVNet
508-433-8452	IBM Tech Fido	Pepperell, MA USA	DVNet
508-481-7147	Waystar BBS	Marlborough, MA USA	DVNet
508-682-5329	The Business Card	Lawrence, MA USA	DVNet
509-545-1789	SunDial BBS	Pasco, WA USA	DVNet
509-735-9399	TRI-CATS BBS	Kennewick, WA USA	SmartNet
512-822-7519	Last Chance TBBS	San Antonio, TX USA	DVNet

Phone Number	BBS Name	Location	Net
512-835-4848	Middle Earth	San Antonio, TX USA	DVNet
513-921-5568	The Mountain Top	Cincinnati, OH USA	DVNet
514-687-9586	Arcane BBS	Laval, PQ CAN	DVNet
516-536-1546	Big Apple BBS	Rockville Ctr, NY USA	SmartNet
516-737-8217	LogyLink	Ronkonkoma, NY USA	DVNet
517-655-3347	Programmers' Attic	Will., MI USA	DVNet
603-886-5722	The Toy Room BBS	Hudson, NH USA	DVNet
604-242-3398	KB'S BBS	Tumbler Ridge, BC CAN	SmartNet
604-727-7374	Big Blue & Cousins	Victoria, BC CAN	U'NI-Net
604-962-5971	The Exchange	Prince George, BC	DVNet
609-386-1989	Capital City	Burlington, NJ USA	DVNet
609-482-8604	Maple Shade Opus	Maple Shade, NJ USA	DVNet
609-692-3260	Harred On-Line	Vineland, NJ USA	SmartNet
612-571-7774	ExchangeNet	Fridley, MN USA	DVNet
613-236-1232	Bytown BBS	Ottawa, ON CAN	SmartNet
613-236-1730	Bytown BBS	Ottawa, ON CAN	SmartNet
613-523-8965	Ned's Opus HST	Ottawa, ON CAN	DVNet
613-731-7168	Ned's Opus	Ottawa, ON CAN	DVNet
613-731-8132	Ned's Opus	Ottawa, ON CAN	DVNet
613-829-0282	AFI Comm	Nepean, ON CAN	DVNet
614-861-8377	Corvette BBS	Pickerington, OH USA	DVNet
615-353-3476	EET BBS	Nashville, TN USA	DVNet
615-966-3574	Data World BBS	Concord, TN USA	SmartNet
617-354-8873	Channel 1 (tm)	Cambridge, MA USA	Smartnet
617-551-0495	Rainbow's Edge	Westwood, MA USA	DVNet
619-466-9505	Gandalf's	El Cajon, CA USA	DVNet
702-647-4427	$in City Bit Pit	Las Vegas, NV USA	DVNet
703-532-7143	The Arlington Sof Exch	Arlington, VA USA	SmartNet
703-719-9648	Data Bit NETWork	Alexandria, VA USA	SmartNet
707-778-8944	VOR BBS	Petaluma, CA USA	SmartNet
713-520-1569	Ye Olde Bailey	Houston, TX USA	SmartNet
713-667-7213	Conch Opus	Houston, TX USA	DVNet
713-681-1920	TEJAS	Houston, TX USA	SmartNet
713-771-2802	The Abend BBS	Houston, TX USA	SmartNet
717-657-2223	The Other BBS	Harrisburg, PA USA	DVNet
801-586-3589	BBS-Buena Park	Cedar City, UT USA	SmartNet
802-879-4753	The Ozone Layer	Williston, VT USA	DVNet
804-393-2199	Suffolk News BBS	Suffolk, VA USA	DVNet
804-723-7280	The Night Shift	Hampton, VA USA	DVNet
804-744-2583	OMICRON BBS	Richmond, VA USA	SmartNet
804-793-6094	Just For Fun	Danville, VA USA	DVNet
808-293-9547	Open Window	Laie, HI CAN	DVNet
809-783-9542	Island Sun	Caparra Heights, PR USA	DVNet
813-755-0575	Jos' Lounge	Bradenton, FL USA	DVNet
816-761-4039	Rampart General	Kansas City, MO USA	DVNet
817-265-8938	The Gas Company	Arlington, TX USA	DVNet
817-540-3527	Spare Parts	Bedford, TX USA	DVNet
817-799-1570	TSTI INFO NET	Waco, TX USA	DVNet
818-330-0580	Medi-Call	La Puente, CA USA	SharkNet
818-352-3620	The Ledge PCBoard	Tujunga, CA USA	U'NI-net
818-564-9475	The Hotline	Pasadena, CA USA	SmartNet
819-561-5268	Synapse BBS	Gatineau, PQ CAN	U'NI-Net
904-668-1092	Other World	Tallahassee, FL USA	DVNet
907-452-1460	65'North	Fairbanks, AK USA	DVNet
912-432-2440	Software Designer	Albany, GA USA	DVNet
912-432-2440	Software Designer	Albany, GA USA	DVNet
914-353-2157	PC-Rockland BBS	Nyack, NY USA	SmartNet
916-961-1042	The HIDEAWAY BBS	Sacramento, CA USA	SmartNet
916-961-1042	The HIDEAWAY BBS	Sacramento, CA USA	SmartNet
916-753-6321	Opus 386	Davis, CA USA	DVNet
919-286-7738	Psychotronic BBS	Durham, NC USA	DVNet
919-447-3321	Dungeon Quest II	Havelock, NC USA	DVNet

Countries other than USA and Canada

Phone Number	BBS Name	Location	Net
32-11-568620	BBS_D.C.V.V.	Maaseik, Belgium	DVNet
32-11-581344	QBBS_H.S.P.	Miskom, Belgium	DVNet
34-3-219-3452	Replicants Factory	Barcelona, Spain	DVNet
39-10-3770080	Genova 2000	Genova, Italy	DVNet
31-3483-4072	The HEKOM Board	Netherlands	DVNet
31-40-122083	The Mailbox	Eindhoven, Netherlands	DVNet
41-41-538607	MICS Lucerne BBS	Lucerne, Switzerland	DVNet
43-222-6040844	Blumenkistl	Vienna, Austria	DVNet
44-61-483-4105	Road Runner	Manchester, UK	DVNet
44-858-466594	Aureal Srchlght	Market Harborough, UK	DVNet
44-905-775191	TUG II Droitwich	Worcester, UK	DVNet
44-905-795002	Enigma Variations	Worcester, UK	DVNet
46-8-7411244	Capital City BBS	Haninge, Sweden	DVNet
49-201-483735	M.U.G. Info Board	Essen, Germany	DVNet
49-202-305803	The 49er's	Wuppertal, Germany	DVNet
49-203-408799	Radio Kaos M-O	Duisburg, Germany	DVNet
49-211-5961291	Blues Project	Dusseldorf, Germany	DVNet
49-2129-4891	Andi's BBS	Haan, Germany	DVNet
49-2159-2717	MIDI-Mailbox	Meerbusch, Germany	DVNet
49-2166-24468	Data City	Moenchengladbach, Germany	DVNet
49-30-735148	Median	Berlin, Germany	DVNet
49-521-208152	BitMaster BBS	Bielefeld, Germany	DVNet
49-69-6311235	E.I.S.2	Frankfurt, Germany	DVNet
49-911-5705983	AVALON BBS	Roethenbach, Germany	DVNet
61-2-418-6682	Sentry's Shadow	Lane Cove, NSW Australia	DVNet
61-2-428-4687	Sentry	Lane Cove, NSW Australia	DVNet
61-3-725-1621	Southern Mail	CBCS, Victoria Australia	DVNet
61-3-874-8927	Central Source	ICBS, Victoria Australia	DVNet
61-7-371-5864	Marwick's MadHouse	Brisbane, Australia	DVNet
61-8-3805505	Phone Box	Inglewood, S Australia	DVNet
61-9-451-7288	COMPUlink	Perth, WA Australia	DVNet
65-294-3597	Billboard BBS	Singapore	U'NI-net
65-298-0497	Billboard BBS	Singapore	U'NI-net
85-2-789-1267	TAIC Maximus	Kowloon, Hong Kong	DVNet

E
APPENDIX

Vendor address list

AddStor, Inc.
3905 Bohannon Dr.
Menlo Park, CA 94025

Adlersparre & Associates, Inc.
1803 Douglas St., Ste. 501
Victoria, B.C. Canada
V8T 5C3

ALL Computers, Inc.
1220 Yonge St., 2nd Floor
Toronto, Ontario
Canada, M4T 1W1
(416) 960-0111

William E. Allen
P.O. Box 834
Howell, MI 48843

AMI (American Megatrends, Inc.)
6145-F North Belt Pkwy.
Norcross, GA 30093
(800) U BUY AMI

Artisoft, Inc.
575 East River Rd.
Tucson, AZ 85704

AST Research, Inc.
16215 Alton Pkwy.
Irvine, CA 92714

ATI Technologies
3761 Victoria Park Ave.
Scarsborough, Ontario
Canada, M1W3S2

Award Software
130 Knowles Dr.
Los Gatos, CA 95030
(408) 370-7979

Banyan Systems, Inc.
120 Flanders Rd.
Westboro, MA 01581
(508) 898-1000

Boca Research, Inc.
6401 Congress Ave.
Boca Raton, FL 33487
(407) 997-6227

Borland, International
P.O. Box 660001
Scotts Valley, CA 95066
(408) 438-8400
(800) 331-0877

Central Point Software
15220 N.W. Greebrier Parkway, #200
Beaverton, OR 97006
(503) 690-8090

Chips & Technologies, Ltd.
3050 Zanker Rd.
San Jose, CA 95134
(408) 434-0600

Cove Software Group
P.O. Box 1072
Columbia, MD 21044
(301) 992-9371

COMPAQ Corporation
20555 SH 249
Houston, TX 77070
(713) 374-4583

Cumulus
23500 Mercantile Rd.
Cleveland, OH 44122
(216) 464-2211

Dariana Corporation
5241 Lincoln Ave., Ste. B-5
Buena Park, CA 90620
(714) 994-7400

DataStorm Technologies, Inc.
P.O. Box 1471
Columbia, MO 65205
(314) 474-8461

DiagSoft, Inc.
5615 Scotts Valley Dr., #140
Scotts Valley, CA 95066

Digital Research, Inc.
Box DRI 70 Garden Ct.
Monterey, CA 93940
(408) 649-3896

DMP Software
204 East 2nd Ave., Ste. 610
San Mateo, CA 94401

Everex Systems, Inc.
48431 Milmone Dr.
Fremont, CA 94538
(510) 498-1111

Executive Systems, Inc.
4330 Santa Fe Rd.
San Luis Obispo, CA 93401
(805) 541-0604

GeoWorks
2150 Shattuck Ave.
Berkeley, CA 04704
(415) 644-0883

Hans Salvisberg
Bellevuestr. 18,
CH-3095
Berne, Switzerland
(800) 242-4775

hDC Computer Corporation
6742 185th Ave, NE
Redmond, WA 98052
(800) 321-4606

Helix Software Co.
47-09 30th St.
Long Island City, N.Y. 11011
(718) 392-3100

Hewlett-Packard Company
19310 Pruneridge Ave.
Cupertino, CA 95014
(800) 387-3867

Hyperware
RR #1, Box 91
Pall Mall, TN 38577
(615) 864-6870

IBM
Entry Systems Division
1000 N.W. 51st St.
Boca Raton, FL 33432
(800) 426-3333

IBM Corporation
Old Orchard Rd.
Armonk, N.Y. 10605
(800) IBM-2468

Intel PCEO
5200 N.E. Elam Young Pkwy.
Hillsboro, OR 97124
(503) 681-8080

JDR Microdevices
2233 Branham Ln.
San Jose, CA 95125
(800) 538-5000

LaserTools Corporation
5900 Hollis St., Suite G
Emeryville, CA 94608
(800) 346-1353

Lotus Development Corporation
55 Cambridge Pkwy.
Cambridge, MA 02142
(617) 577-8500

Micron Technology, Inc.
2805 E. Columbia Rd.
Boise, ID 83706
(208) 368-3800

Microsoft Corporation
One Microsoft Way
Redmond, WA 98052-6399
(206) 882-8080

Mike Blaszczak
112 Verlinden Dr.
Monroeville, PA 15146

Multisoft Corporation
15100 S.W. Koll Pkwy, Ste. L
Beaverton, OR 97006
(800) 888-5945

NEC Electronics
401 Ellis St.
Mountain View, CA 94039
(415) 960-6000

Newer Technology
1117 South Rock Road, Ste. 4
Wichita, KS 62707
(800) 678-3726

Novell Corporation
122 E. 1700 South
Provo, UT 84601
(800) 526-5463

Orchid Technology
45365 Northport Loop W
Fremont, CA 94538
(415) 683-0348

Phar Lap Software, Inc.
60 Aberdeen Ave.
Cambridge, MA 02138
(617) 661-1510

Quadtel
3190-J Airport Loop
Costa Mesa, CA 92626
(714) 754-4422

Quadram
One Quad Way
Norcross, GA 30093
(404) 564-5522

Qualitas, Inc.
7101 Wisconsin Ave.,
Ste. 1386
Bethesda, MD 20814
(301) 907-6700

Quarterdeck Office Systems
150 Pico Blvd.
Santa Monica, CA 90405
(213) 392-9851

RYBS Electronics, Inc.
2590 Central Ave.
Boulder, CO 80301
(303) 444-6073

SoftLogic Solutions
One Perimeter Rd.
Manchester, N.H. 03103
(603) 627-9900

SoftNet Communications, Inc.
15 Hillcrest Dr.
Great Neck, N.Y. 11021

SOTA Technology
551 Weddell Dr.
Sunnyvale, CA 94089
(800) 933-7682

SP Services
P.O. Box 456
Southampton, United Kingdom

Spirit of Performance
73 Westcott Rd.
Harvard, MA 01451
(508) 456-3889

Symantec Corporation
10201 Torre Ave.
Cupertino, CA 95014
(408) 252-4694

Teletek Enterprises, Inc.
4600 Pell Drive
Sacramento, CA 95838
(916) 920-4600

The Periscope Co.
1197 Peachtree St.
Atlanta, GA 30361
(800) 722-7006

Touchstone Software Corporation
2130 Main Street, Ste. 250
Huntington Beach, CA 92648
(714) 960-1886

TurboPower Software
P.O. Box 49009
Colorado Springs, CO 80949

V-Communications, Inc.
4320 Stevens Creek Blvd., Ste. 275-PCS
San Jose, CA 95129
(408) 296-4224

Western Digital Corporation
800 E. Middlefield
Mt. View, CA 94043
(415) 960-3360

WordPerfect Corporation
1555 N. Technology Way
Orem, UT 84057
(801) 225-5000

WordStar International
201 Alameda Del Prado
Novato, CA 94948
(415) 382-8000

Index

Other Bestsellers of Related Interest

MICROSOFT® MONEY MANAGEMENT
—Jean E. Gutmann

Written especially for first-time Windows users, *Microsoft® Money Management* is a complete guide to effective financial record-keeping with Microsoft Money—the new money management software for Windows that's perfect for individuals and small businesses that don't need a full-fledged, double-entry accounting package. With this user-friendly guide, you'll become a pro in no time as you take advantage of the expert hints and proven techniques not found in software manuals. 272 pages, 132 illustrations. Book No. 4172, $17.95 paperback only

BATCH FILES TO GO: A Programmer's Library
—Ronny Richardson

Ronny Richardson, respected research analyst and programmer, has assembled this collection of ready-to-use batch files featuring over 80 exclusive keystroke-saving programs. These fully developed programs—all available on disk for instant access—can be used as they are, or altered to handle virtually any file management task. 352 pages, 100 illustrations. Book No. 4165, $34.95 paperback only

VISUAL BASIC POWER PROGRAMMING
—Namir C. Shammas

With this resource, you'll have a programmer's toolbox complete with routines for file management, text and graphics manipulation, calculations, scientific plotting, and much more. Shammas's book goes beyond introductory books by telling you how to "put the program to work" and taking a modular approach in which each chapter can stand alone. The code contained in the book is provided on disk for easy use. 392 pages, 160 illustrations. Book No. 4149, $29.95 paperback, $39.95 hardcover

EASY PC MAINTENANCE AND REPAIR
—Phil Laplante

This easy-to-understand volume provides all the guidelines you need to maintain and repair your computer in your home or office. Repair or replace your monitor or keyboard . . . upgrade your microprocessor . . . add or replace memory . . . no technical experience is necessary to benefit from Laplante's authoritative, diagnostic advice. He provides simple maintenance, repair, and upgrade strategies for whatever IBM PC-XT, 286, 386, or 486 compatible computer you use. Book No. 4143, $14.95 paperback, $22.95 hardcover

NORTON UTILITIES® 6.0: An Illustrated Tutorial—Richard Evans

Richard Evans shows you how to painlessly perform the most dazzling Norton functions using the all-new features of Norton Utilities 6.0. He also reviews the best from previous releases, providing clear, easy-to-follow instructions and screen illustrations reflecting Norton's new developments. You'll also learn about NDOS, a new configuration and shell program that replaces COMMAND.COM. 464 pages, 277 illustrations. Book No. 4132, $19.95 paperback, $29.95 hardcover

THE INFORMATION BROKER'S HANDBOOK
—Sue Rugge and Alfred Glossbrenner

This one-of-a-kind volume is the definitive guide to starting and running a profitable information brokerage. You'll examine all of the search and retrieval options today's successful information brokers use, everything from conventional library research to online databases, special interest groups, CD-ROMs, and bulletin board systems. No successful information broker should be without this valuable reference tool for his or her office. 408 pages, 100 illustrations. Book No. 4104, $29.95 paperback, $39.95 hardcover

BUILD YOUR OWN 386/386SX COMPATIBLE AND SAVE A BUNDLE—2nd Edition
—Aubrey Pilgrim

Assemble an 80386 microcomputer at home using mail-order parts that cost a lot less today than they did several years ago. Absolutely no special technical know-how is required—only a pair of pliers, a couple of screwdrivers, and this detailed, easy-to-follow guide. 248 pages, 79 illustrations. Book No. 4089, $18.95 paperback, $29.95 hardcover

WRITING AND MARKETING SHAREWARE: Revised and Expanded—2nd Edition—Steve Hudgik

Profit from the lucrative shareware market with the expert tips and techniques found in this guide. If you have new software ideas, but are not sure they'll be competitive in today's dynamic PC market, this reference will show you how to evaluate and sell them through shareware distribution. Plus, you get a 5.25" disk—featuring a shareware mailing list management program and a database with over 200 shareware distributors—through a special coupon offer. 336 pages, 41 illustrations. Book No. 3961, $18.95 paperback only

ONLINE INFORMATION HUNTING
—Nahum Goldmann

You can cut down dramatically on your time and money spent online, and increase your online productivity with *Online Information Hunting*. This helpful book will give you systematic instruction on developing productive, cost-effective research techniques for large-scale information networks. You'll also get detailed coverage of the latest online services, new hardware and software, and recent advances that have affected online research. 256 pages, 125 illustrations. Book No. 3943, $19.95 paperback, $29.95 hardcover

THE ENTREPRENEURIAL PC
—Bernard J. David

Put that expensive home PC to work for you. You will learn about the profit-making potential of computers in typing, word processing, desktop publishing, database programming, hardware installation, electronic mail, and much more. David uses detailed, real-life examples to describe some of the more popular avenues of entrepreneurship for the home PC owner. 336 pages, 50 illustrations. Book No. 3823, $19.95 paperback, $29.95 hardcover

BUSINESS APPLICATIONS SHAREWARE
—PC-SIG, Inc.

Shareware allows you to evaluate hundreds of dollars worth of software before buying it. Once you decide, you simply register the shareware you want at a fraction of the cost of buying commercially marketed packages. *Business Applications Shareware* shows you a wide variety of these programs including: PC Payroll, Bill Power Plus, Painless Accounting, Graphtime, PC Inventory Plus, Formgen, and more. 312 pages, 81 illustrations. Book No. 3920, $29.95 paperback only

COMBATING COMPUTER CRIME: Prevention, Detection, Investigation
—Chantico Publishing Company, Inc.

This timely handbook outlines practical solutions for identifying, preventing, and detecting computer crimes, and represents the experiences of over 2,000 participating organizations from industry, commerce, and government. Step by step, the authors show you how to establish a computer crime policy and provide a management plan of action for implementing that policy. Detailed checklists and worksheets are included. 350 pages, 100 illustrations. Book No. 3664, $39.95 hardcover only

THE STEPHEN COBB COMPLETE BOOK OF PC AND LAN SECURITY—Stephen Cobb

Discover how to protect your valuable hardware through alarm and security systems, product registration and insurance, fault tolerance, and more. Cobb covers software protection, encryption systems, passwords, add-ons, alternative power supplies, and backup strategies. A final section focuses on securing a network against unwanted intruders, including a chapter on virus prevention. 576 pages, 206 illustrations. Book No. 3280, $24.95 paperback, $36.95 hardcover

THE ILLUSTRATED VETERINARY GUIDE FOR DOGS, CATS, BIRDS, AND EXOTIC PETS
—Chris C. Pinney, DVM

You'll keep your menagerie wagging, purring, chirping, hopping, or swimming with this guide. It's by far the most detailed do-it-yourself pet care manual available for dogs, cats, birds, rabbits, hamsters, and fish. You'll find sections on caring for older pets, diseases people can catch from animals, treating cancer in pets, and the difficult euthanasia decision. 704 pages, 364 illustrations. Book No. 3667, $29.95 hardcover only

HOME VCR REPAIR ILLUSTRATED
—Richard C. Wilkins and Cheryl A. Hubbard

This guide can save you hundreds of dollars in repair bills by showing you how to correct many of the most common VCR malfunctions right in your own home—no expensive tools or test equipment are required. It guides you through every step of the repair, from getting inside the VCR to examining the remote control. You'll repair problems with picture and sound quality, fast forward and rewind, DC motors, tension and roller guides, undercarriages, take-up spindles, audio heads, and more. 400 pages, 459 illustrations. Book No. 3711, $19.95 paperback, $29.95 hardcover

Prices Subject to Change Without Notice.

Look for These and Other TAB Books at Your Local Bookstore

To Order Call Toll Free 1-800-822-8158
(in PA, AK, and Canada call 717-794-2191)

or write to TAB Books, Blue Ridge Summit, PA 17294-0840.

Title	Product No.	Quantity	Price

☐ Check or money order made payable to TAB Books

Charge my ☐ VISA ☐ MasterCard ☐ American Express

Acct. No. _____ Exp. _____

Signature: _____

Name: _____

Address: _____

City: _____

State: _____ Zip: _____

Subtotal $ _____

Postage and Handling
($3.00 in U.S., $5.00 outside U.S.) $ _____

Add applicable state and local
sales tax $ _____

TOTAL $ _____

TAB Books catalog free with purchase; otherwise send $1.00 in check or money order and receive $1.00 credit on your next purchase.

Orders outside U.S. must pay with international money in U.S. dollars

TAB Guarantee: If for any reason you are not satisfied with the book(s) you order, simply return it (them) within 15 days and receive a full refund. **BC**